Forms of Krishna

EXPLORATIONS IN INDIC TRADITIONS: THEOLOGICAL, ETHICAL, AND PHILOSOPHICAL

Series Editor
Jeffery D. Long, Elizabethtown College

Advisory Board
Purushottama Bilimoria, Christopher Key Chapple, Jonathan Gold, Pankaj Jain, Nathan Katz, Kusumita Pedersen, and Rita D. Sherma

The region historically known as the Indian subcontinent (and more recently as South Asia) is rich with ancient and sophisticated traditions of intellectual and contemplative investigation. This includes both indigenous traditions (Hindu, Buddhist, Jain, and Sikh) and traditions that have found a home in this region (Islamic, Christian, Jewish, and Zoroastrian). This series is devoted to studies rooted in critical and constructive methodologies (such as ethics, philosophy, and theology) that show how these traditions can illuminate universal human questions: questions about the meaning of life, the nature of knowledge, good and evil, and the broader metaphysical context of human existence. A particular focus of this series is the relevance of these traditions to urgent issues that face humanity today—such as the ecological crisis, gender relations, poverty and social inequality, and religiously motivated violence—on the assumption that these traditions, far from being of merely historical interest, have the potential to enrich contemporary conversations and advance human understanding.

Recent Titles in Series

Forms of Krishna: Collected Essays on Vaishnava Murtis by Steven Rosen
The Politics and Promise of Yoga: Contemporary Relevance of an Ancient Practice, by Anjali H. Kanojia
The Hindu Self and its Muslim Neighbors Borders of Belonging in Bengal, by Ankur Barua
The Philosophy of Sri Chinmoy: Love and Transformation, by Kusumita Pedersen
Gandhi and Rajchandra: The Making of the Mahatma, by Uma Majmudar
Swami Vivekananda: His Life, Legacy, and Liberative Ethics, edited by Rita D. Sherma
Beacons of Dharma, edited by Jeffery D. Long, Michael Reading, Christopher Miller

Thinking with the Yogasutra of Patanjali: Translation and Interpretation, edited by Christopher Key Chapple and Ana Funes Maderey

The Metaphysics of Paradox: Jainism, Absolute Relativity, and Religious Pluralism, by Wm. Andrew Schwartz

Forms of Krishna

Collected Essays on Vaishnava Murtis

Steven J. Rosen
Foreword by Kenneth Valpey

LEXINGTON BOOKS
Lanham • Boulder • New York • London

Cover photo by Sadasiva Pandit Das, copyright, 2022. Used with permission.

The Author thanks Back to Godhead Magazine for permission to reproduce portions of three articles of the author published by Back to Godhead - "Ropes of Rapture: The Transcendental Pastimes of Sri Sri Radha-Damodara," "Lord Jagannatha: God Transformed by Ecstasy," and "The Majestic Glory of Sri Sri Rukmini-Dvarakadi." Back to Godhead Inc. reserves all Copyrights in those articles, except as licensed.

Permission to reprint "*Dashavatara*: The Ten Incarnations of Vishnu" granted by MOSA-Museum of Sacred Art.

Published by Lexington Books

An imprint of The Rowman & Littlefield Publishing Group, Inc.

4501 Forbes Boulevard, Suite 200, Lanham, Maryland 20706

www.rowman.com

86-90 Paul Street, London EC2A 4NE

British Library Cataloguing in Publication Information Available

Library of Congress Cataloging-in-Publication Data

ISBN 9781666930269 (cloth : alk. paper) ISBN 9781666930276 (electronic)

∞™ The paper used in this publication meets the minimum requirements of American National Standard for Information Sciences—Permanence of Paper for Printed Library Materials, ANSI/NISO Z39.48-1992.

समर्‌पण: सर्‌वोत्‌तमप्‌रतिमां प्‌रति

samarpaṇaḥ sarvottamapratimāṃ prati

To Prati,

The best Pratimā of all

Contents

Foreword

Kenneth Valpey, Research Fellow,
Oxford Centre for Hindu Studies

Reginald Heber, Anglican Bishop of Calcutta, might be forgiven for writing the now infamous lines, "The heathen in his blindness/bows down to wood and stone." After all, the year of his hymnotic writing was 1819, a time of considerable religious missionary zeal amid rising British imperial hopes. Influenced by iconoclastic passions rooted in early biblical texts, Heber could not exercise the necessary reflexivity to recognize his own blindness to the richness and theological depth of India's worship practices.

We have good reason to hope and expect that today an increasing open-mindedness among Westerners in particular and late-modern folks in general enable us to examine and appreciate the complex and profound theology and aesthetics of image worship exemplified in Steven Rosen's study of a particularly prominent tradition, that of the Vaiṣṇavas—worshippers of the supreme Lord as Vishnu and more specifically as Krishna. Indeed, the beauty of this work is in its focus on several of the physical images in Krishna-dedicated temples, whereby specific "Deities" (three-dimensional physical images) of Vishnu or, again, more specifically Krishna, serve as dynamic devotional lenses through which to view specific aspects of Vaiṣṇava theology and history. The end result is a large tapestry (to venture a two-dimensional visual analogy) of the broad and globally expanding vision of Krishna devotion as a living tradition rooted in ancient and medieval Sanskrit and Bengali texts and thriving as new writings on the subject such as this one appear.

As I have explained elsewhere, specific sacred texts serve as "garments" that "clothe" the Krishna Deities in ways that serve to make their already attractive forms all the more attractive by telling the narratives of Krishna's pastimes (*līlā*), by describing details about his multiple forms and qualities, and prescribing the specific methods by which his votaries can please him. Perhaps most widely known among these texts is the Bhagavad-gītā, containing Krishna's essential instructions to his friend Arjuna on the meaning, purpose, and practices of yoga by which a person can attain a state beyond the cycle of death and rebirth to participate in ever-fresh devotional relationality with Krishna and his wondrous associates.

This present book adds significantly to and makes more accessible this garment of texts, for readers with little, moderate, or considerable familiarity with the tradition. Readers making initial entrance into the world of Indic culture and religion will be rewarded by Rosen's sensitive and judiciously clear explanations of Vaiṣṇava essentials of thought and practice. Thus, for example, his explanation of the intricacies of *avatāra* theology serve well to prepare the reader for the later chapters focusing on specific Krishna Deities. Also, those readers relatively familiar with the multi-contoured landscape of Indic—especially "Hindu"—devotional temple practices will find Rosen's descriptions and explanations of each Krishna Deity a progressively engaging entrance into the subtleties of Vaiṣṇava theology and practice. Finally, readers—like me—who are largely familiar with the Gauḍīya Vaiṣṇava tradition in particular and who may have even visited one or several of the temples where the specific Deities presented in these pages reside will be sure to learn much, not least numerous fascinating historical details and variations on certain legends regarding specific Deities' histories (be sure to read the endnotes along with the main text!).

It was some five decades ago that I first visited a Krishna temple in—of all places—Hamburg, Germany. "Temple" is a grand word for what was, by outward appearance, a small converted warehouse. My ignorance of what—or rather who—I was viewing was eased somewhat by my curiosity to know and understand what this was all about. But had there been Steven Rosen's book available at that time, it would have been infinitely easier for me to enter into the wonder-world of Krishna-bhakti. It would have been so much easier to understand how this world is populated with Krishna's wonderful forms, each welcoming his servants—us wayward souls—into his eternal service by the sublime practices of bhakti-yoga. It would have been so much easier to understand how these practices of bhakti-yoga have been taught by the tradition's line of teachers (*ācāryas*) stretching all the way back from the present to the time of Krishna's personal presence in our world just prior to our present era, said to be the dark age of Kali that began some five thousand years ago.

This book will aid in seeing where the light of Lord Krishna's smile continues to get in to illuminate our world with the sort of powerful hope that can be given only from beyond this world, from the atemporal world of pure spiritual love. It may be too much to ask that the likes of Reginald Heber would be moved to retract his idea that the worship of Krishna in his Deity form is a consequence of "blindness," or that what is being worshipped is mere "wood and stone." Be that as it may, this book challenges us to shed our own blindness to see the bright and at times mischievous face—and full form—of the All-Attractive One and to celebrate this vision of hope that he gives us all.

Acknowledgments

Though many pundits, professors, and *pūjārīs* helped with this work, family and friends were no less involved, allowing me to complete the manuscript with minimal distraction. Special mention must be made of Bob Golden, who was my initial inspiration in terms of writing about Krishna Deities and who helped with individual chapters in ways too numerous to mention. I would also like to thank the BBT international and Nagarāja Dāsa of *Back to Godhead* for their insights and support and for their punctuality in terms of getting me the necessary permissions for previously published material. Jeffrey Long, Trevor Crowell, and Megan White of Lexington Books are to be thanked as well—Jeff for encouraging me with this project from the beginning and Trevor for acquiescing in terms of the book's focus and extending patience toward me throughout the initial process. Special thanks to Megan for seeing the project through to completion. Finally, I would like to thank Dr. Kenneth Valpey, research fellow at the Oxford Centre for Hindu Studies, for his decorous and thoughtful foreword, without which I would have considered the volume incomplete.

Introduction

The nature of beauty has been a primary and enduring theme in both Eastern and Western philosophy. When seen as deeper than mere external appearances, it has been counted among the ultimate virtues worth living for, along with goodness, truth, and justice. "Many have conjectured," writes Swāmī B. V. Tripurāri, "that truth is beauty. If this is so, can one relish beauty without form or image? . . . The canvas and the brush, the words and their order, make accessible the beauty of art and literature. Beauty itself is abstract, yet it requires form for its expression. From within the Hindu pantheon and beyond it, if we are to search all cultures and their myths, it would be hard to find a better candidate for the form of ultimate beauty than Krishna [Kṛṣṇa]."[1] Indeed, Indic wisdom texts refer to Krishna not only as Bhagavān, or God, but more importantly as Akhila-rasāmṛta-mūrti—"the nectarean form of unbounded spiritual relationships," the very embodiment of aesthetic Vedānta.[2]

And yet, even in India, we find those who underappreciate Krishna's form. For example, it is not uncommon to find various *yogīs* and philosophers—and even common folk—who seem to prefer an impersonal absolute, devoid of all form and character. Such people are sometimes referred to as impersonalists and Māyāvādīs, for they have a penchant for depersonalizing divinity and, in terms of describing his "descents," or *avatāras*, often mischaracterize them as material, or products of *māyā*, the illusion of material existence. "The impersonalists hanker to merge into the effulgence of the Supreme," Krishnaite scholar Ravīndra Svarūpa Dāsa tells us. "But when they hear about the form beyond that effulgence, the transcendental form of Krishna, the embodiment of all beauty, they think of it as material, as *māyā*. This is because their own mentality is so rigidly materialistic. They are unable to accept the notion of 'transcendental form' because as far as they are concerned, all form is material. . . . But why should we impose our material ideas of name, form, qualities, and actions on God? Who says that all form has to be material form?"[3]

For Vaishnavas, Krishna is the epitome of beauty, and his form is 100 percent spiritual.[4] Indeed, Vaishnava teachings opine that Krishna lies far beyond the impersonal Brahman—that he is in fact the ultimate basis upon which

Brahman rests.[5] It is difficult to overestimate the high regard with which Vaishnavas hold Krishna's form, along with its attendant beauty.

To give some idea: Imagine, if you will, witnessing someone or something so beautiful, so indispensable, so singularly riveting, that you could neither breathe nor move nor speak, for the experience of that vision forces you into a state of momentary ecstatic paralysis. Now multiply that moment's sensation a million times over—this would provide a mere hint of how Vaishnavas view Krishna's beauty. Self-realized devotees throughout history, as we shall see, attest to that beauty repeatedly, telling us, for example, that even the sound of Krishna's flute, enthroned on his lotus lips, drives one to utter madness, changing the listener's very concept of reality forevermore—what to speak of actually beholding his form, the vision of which has the power to stop one from ever returning home, i.e., reverting to normal. Indeed, Rūpa Gosvāmī (circa 1489–1564), Gauḍīya Vaishnava patriarch par excellence, offers a now famous verse that points in this very direction: "My dear friend, if you are attached to your worldly friends and intimates, do not look at the smiling face of Lord Govinda [Krishna] as he stands on the bank of the Yamunā at Keśīghāṭa. Casting alluring glances, he holds his flute to his transcendental lips, which seem like newly blossomed twigs. His spiritual body, in threefold bending posture, appears very bright in the full beams of the night's moon."[6]

Having once seen the form of Krishna, it is impossible to forget him, and sometimes there is even a sense of "remembering" him from previous lifetimes. According to the Vaishnava tradition, there is a reason for this that goes beyond his haunting beauty and our innate desire to be connected to him: Devotees claim that Krishna is part of our own soul, or, rather, that we are part of his. And so, seeing him, whether in the form of a painting, an icon, or in some intuitive, internal reverie, something is rekindled, a memory from long past, before the dawn of time—a connection we have all but forgotten. Thus, for those who are extraordinarily intuitive, say the Vaishnavas, Krishna's visage will look pleasingly familiar. This is because he is embedded in the subconscious—somehow, deep down, we know that form, and through grace we begin to remember it yet again: "Krishna, who is known as Govinda, is the supreme form of divinity, with a spiritual embodiment that is eternal, fully cognizant, and blissful. He is the origin of all and the initial cause of all causes." (*Brahma-saṁhitā* 5.1)[7] According to the Vaishnava tradition, these words come from Brahmā, the first created being, expressed while in a trance of self-realization. At that time, it is said, he saw Lord Krishna standing before him, face-to-face. Brahmā fully described his profound vision:

> "I worship Govinda, the primeval Lord, the original ancestor, who is always tending his magical cows in a rural environment. When not roaming the fields, he can be found in innumerable opulent dwellings composed of spiritual gems,

> surrounded by millions of wish-fulfilling trees, where he is served with great reverence and affection by hundreds of thousands of goddesses. (*Brahma-saṁhitā* 5.29)
>
> "I worship Govinda, the primeval Lord, whose neck is decorated by a swinging garland of jeweled flowers and ornaments, including a beautifully precious moon-locket. His two lotus-like hands are always engaging his melodious flute while he revels in pastimes of love. His darkish, incomparable threefold bending form is eternal. (*Brahma-saṁhitā* 5.31)
>
> "I worship Govinda, the primeval Lord, who cannot be accessed through mere study of the Vedas, but who is obtainable by pure, unalloyed devotional service. He is distinct from all other living beings, and is never subject to decay—he is without beginning, and has an infinite, indescribable form. Indeed, he is himself the beginning of all, the original soul of the universe. Yet he is a person possessing the beauty of youth in full bloom. (*Brahma-saṁhitā* 5.33)
>
> "I worship Govinda, the primeval Lord, who is adept at playing on his flute, whose gorgeous eyes are like lotus petals, whose head is bedecked with a peacock feather, who is known as Śyāmasundara, "dark and beautiful," the hue of looming rainclouds, and who has innumerable, inconceivable attributes—the pure devotees see him deep within their hearts with the eye of devotion tinged with the salve of love." (*Brahma-saṁhitā* 5.38)

Brahmā goes on at some length, and throughout history his insights and revelations have been affirmed, reaffirmed, and enhanced by great saints and sages of the tradition. Thus, Krishna's form has become established for Vaishnavas in their literature and culture, integral to the tradition and accessed through a process of self-realization called Bhakti-yoga, or the yoga of devotion. This intricate and highly sophisticated spiritual technique arose as a result of the massive intellectual efforts of Krishna aficionados throughout history, who gave us a plethora of philosophical tomes, poetry, art, and so on. The fruits of their work created a facility that would reveal Krishna's form to all earnest practitioners, enabling sincere souls to see him, as Brahmā did, and then to develop love for him, for Krishna's image never truly evokes any other response. Indeed, say the Vaishnavas, everyone is ultimately attracted to Krishna, but to be reminded of this, they must first see him in their heart of hearts.

Ravīndra Svarūpa Dāsa, in eloquently descriptive language, further portrays Krishna's beautiful, captivating form, particularly in relation to his incomparable surroundings, Vrindavan, which include the forest's flora and fauna and his playful and loving cowherd associates:

> The forest of Vrindavan is lush with tropical fecundity; an exuberant nature has spilled out life in more abundance and variety than bush, treetop, glade, and stream could seem to hold. Myriads of varicolored birds, their bright plumes flashing in the foliage, fill the air with their musical calls, to which the monkeys tumbling in the treetops add a chattering counterpoint. The vagrant breezes gather scents from a multitude of flowers, stirring them together into a heady perfume that enchants the deer and leaves the leopards languorous and tame.
>
> Then the forest creatures smell a far richer fragrance—a delectable, ambrosial musk that diffuses through the thickets. Breathing deeply, they shiver with joy. The enthralled animals begin to move into the wind, helplessly following the irresistible lure. As the intoxicating aroma intensifies, the creatures glimpse its source moving among the dense flower-burdened shrubs. It is Krishna, the ultimate object of all vision, wandering through the Vrindavan forest. The animals all follow, completely captivated by the unparalleled beauty of His exquisitely formed body with its bluish-black luster. Ecstatic love fills their hearts, overflows, and pours out of their throats in sounds of delight. Surrounded by their songs, Krishna moves through a chorus of creaturely praise that extends from the bass lowing of the cows to the soprano trilling of the birds. And then Krishna answers, calling back to each kind in its own language.[8]

Apropos of all this, the very word *krishna* is Sanskrit for "all-attractive." But before exploring how this is so, let it be said that the word more commonly refers to a color, i.e., black or blue-black, which, of course, most practitioners will take as an allusion to Krishna's beautiful dark complexion. But in terms of its original Sanskrit root, *kṛṣ* means "to plow," or "to pull in," or "to draw to oneself," the latter of these definitions obviously pointing to "attraction."[9]

"Krishna" in terms of meaning "all-attractive," as most practitioners would have it, requires poetic extrapolation as much as recourse to Sanskrit grammar. In fact, the tradition has long held that the root *kṛṣ* means "attractive." Thus, Krish-na would mean, "one who attracts." That is to say, Krishna is in fact a nominal form of the root that is created with the suffix *-ṇa*.[10] This derivation is often found in traditional commentaries on both the *Bhāgavata Purāṇa* (i.e, *Śrīmad Bhāgavatam*) and the *Mahābhārata*, particularly when explicating the *Viṣṇu-sahasranāma* ("the Thousand Names of Vishnu"). As for the *Bhāgavatam*, we need look no further than Jīva Gosvāmī (circa 1513–1596), lauded as one of the greatest philosophers, linguists, and commentators in the history of Sanskrit literature. In his commentary on *Śrīmad Bhāgavatam* 10.8.13, for example, we find an eloquent if succinct instance of equating Krishna with the principle of attraction: "Because he attracts (Krishna = *ākarṣaka*) everyone, the name 'Krishna' is most suitable for him."[11] Regarding the *Viṣṇu-sahasranāma*, if we look under "*Kṛṣṇaḥ*," numerous traditional commentaries include statements such as this: "He attracts people by his graceful beauty (*saundaryam*) and by his other exceptional qualities (*kalyāṇa guṇa*). He irresistibly attracts his devotees, and for this reason he is known as Krishna." (*saundarya sāratayā sarvalokakarṣaṇāt kṛṣṇaḥ/niyamanādinā karṣaṇācca kṛṣṇaḥ//*)[12]

To be sure, this same reading can be found in many Sanskrit and Bengali dictionaries, along with other definitions. To cite but one example, the *Śabdakalpadruma*, a famous encyclopedic lexicon compiled by Raja Rādhā-kāntadeva (1784–1867), offers this: "[He is called Krishna because] he draws to himself, attracts, with pure joy, fulfilling the hearts of his devotees" (*karṣati, ātmasāt karoti ānandatvena parinamayatīti mano bhaktānām*).[13] Additionally, in Jīva Gosvāmī's famous Sanskrit grammar, the *Hari-nāmāmṛta-vyākaraṇam,* we find further support that Krishna's name is understood in terms of "attraction."[14]

In fact, because "Krishna" is so intertwined with the principle of "attraction," the etymology of the word shows connection to the Sanskrit word for "magnet." Indeed, although "Krishna" comes from the adjective, *ākarṣaka*, which means "attractive," as a noun, it quite literally refers to a "magnet," as per Monier Williams's *A Sanskrit-English Dictionary*.[15]

In summary, then, "attraction" is cognate with the Latin root "tract," which means "drag" or "pull," as in tractor or traction. It is thus related to the Sanskrit root *Kṛṣ*, "to pull" or "to possess traction." All this considered, Krishna indicates that supreme entity who pulls to himself (attracts) our mind and senses either directly, through his grace, or indirectly, through his illusory energy—just like a magnet. That is to say, Krishna is he who possesses "traction" with everyone and everything in every way.

Once one knows this basic truth, one sees that the entire tradition revels in Krishna's all-attractive (*sarvākarṣaka*) nature. In the *Caitanya-caritāmṛta* (Madhya 24.38), for example, we read, "Lord Krishna is exalted due to his being more attractive than anything or anyone else. He is the most sublime abode of bliss. By the strength of his own beauty, he causes one to forget all other ecstasies" (*sarvākarṣaka, sarvāhlādaka, mahā-rasāyana āpanāra bale kare sarva-vismāraṇa*). Or consider Jīva Gosvāmī's words, as stated in *Krishna-sandarbha* (Anuccheda 92): "Due to being himself dark complexioned, and due to being all-attractive, his name is Krishna" (*svayaṁ kṛṣṇatvāt sarvākarṣakatvāc ca kṛṣṇa iti*). Verses such as the above indicate that the form of Krishna is not ordinary—it is transcendental (*divyam*) and all attractive (*sarvākarṣaka*)—and that there is obviously more to that form than meets the eye.

Krishna's all-attractive form manifests variously, not only in his original cowherd depiction but as any number of expansions, incarnations, and manifestations. The Śrīvaishnava tradition generally acknowledges five overarching categories, and with slight variations, this list would abide in other lineages as well:

1. The supreme (*parā*) form. This refers to the eternal, unchanging Krishna (in Goloka) or Vishnu (in Vaikuṇṭha), i.e., in the spiritual world.
2. The emanations (*vyūha*). There are four primary emanations called Vāsudeva, Saṅkarṣaṇa, Pradyumna, and Aniruddha, who expand from the original personality of Godhead.
3. Manifestations who appear in the world at particular times (*avatāra*), some of whom we will meet in this book.
4. The Inner Controller (*antaryāmin* or *Paramātmā*). This is an all-pervasive yet localized form of the Lord that resides within the hearts of all living beings and in every atom as well.
5. Finally, there is the *ārcāvatāra*, or the Deity form of the Lord. While ostensibly made of material elements, this form is considered an actual manifestation of God, composed of spiritual substance. Much of this book will be about such Deities.[16]

At first, the iconic form of the Lord can be provocative, particularly for a Westerner: "Is it 'a graven image,' the kind that is condemned in the Bible?" "How can God be a material object?" "A statue might *represent* him, but it could never *be* him." Such questions are logical enough, and they are answered in the world's religious scriptures both East and West. Indeed, all sacred texts tell us not to worship concocted images, or idols, in place of God. Plain and simple.

And yet believers of one religion are quick to view those of another as idolaters. Are Vaishnavas really worshipping idols? Are they approaching God, as such, in the Deities, or is their attention turned to someone or something else, other than God? That, and only that, is the sin of idolatry. Worshipping God—in any form—is never wrong. The question is whether the Deity of Krishna is actually God or not. Ask the worshipper. Clearly, those who actually see and worship the Deity find the beauty of his form, the elegance of his dress, and the enthusiasm with which he is worshipped to be fundamentally pleasing, and they *know* they are worshipping God. When witnessing Krishna and his worship, it is hard not to smile. Are we smiling at the worship of idols?

Not everyone views the Deity in the same way. Some see divine images as merely a means to an end, a visible symbol leading to the "real" divinity, who is unmanifest. Usually, those with an impersonalistic understanding, as mentioned earlier, hold this point of view, downplaying the importance of Deity worship.[17] The vast majority of Hindus, however—and properly trained Vaishnavas, in particular—do not see Krishna Deities in this way. They tend to see the visible form in the temple as an alternate and especially accessible manifestation of God, with no qualifying caveat.

Though there have been foreign invaders who were iconoclastic, both literally and figuratively, this naturally came from outside the Hindu tradition, viewing Deities as one might expect outsiders to view them. Such naysayers included Islamic and British (i.e., Christian) conquerors/critics, whose preconceived notions were birthed from within their own religious traditions, as we will see in upcoming chapters of this book. Indeed, only outsiders would see Deity worship as idol worship. "No people," writes Harvard scholar Diana L. Eck, Professor of Comparative Religion and Indian Studies, "would identify themselves as 'idolaters,' by faith. Thus, idolatry can be only an outsider's term for the symbols and visual images of some other culture. Theodore Roszak, writing in *Where the Wasteland Ends*, locates the 'sin of idolatry' precisely where it belongs: in the eye of the beholder."[18]

In English, "idolatry" is a pejorative term, used primarily by those condemning or at least misunderstanding such practices. Nonetheless, perhaps because the English language was imbibed through the occupying British, many Indians, to this day, use the word "idols" to describe their Deities, and even "mythology" to describe their sophisticated religious traditions, without realizing the often negative implications of these words. Actually, the best words for the Indic notion of Deities are what might be called "non-translatables," that is to say, the concept of Krishna's incarnation in material elements is best left to well-established Sanskrit words.[19] For example, words like *mūrti, pratimā, vigrāha, arcā, svarūpa*, and so on, when understood in the context of their long history in the religious traditions of India, are much more suitable as synonyms for the Deity, or the icon, in Krishna temples, even if, in common parlance, these words, too, can be translated as "shape, form, likeness, personification," etc., not unlike the word "idol." The reason they are better is that they do not come with the same baggage as idol, especially when understood in terms of the sacred texts and cultural traditions from which they are derived.

Again, the objections so frequently voiced in the Abrahamic traditions loom large. "But in the end—isn't this still idol worship? Just what does Deity worship mean? In what sense can this visible form be God? Why would rational people worship a material object in this way?" It is beyond the scope of this book to look into the minutiae of idol worship, particularly in terms of how the Deity tends to be misunderstood in the Biblical tradition. I have explored this elsewhere.[20] For now, let us again consider the words of Diana Eck, herself a Christian who has gone to great lengths to understand this somewhat exotic practice of worshipping Krishna Deities: "The image, which may be seen, bathed, adorned, touched, and honored does not stand between the worshipper and the Lord, somehow receiving the honor properly due to the Supreme Lord. Rather, because the image is a form of the Supreme Lord, it is precisely the image that facilitates and enhances the close relationship of the worshipper and God and makes possible the deepest outpouring of emotions in worship.[21]

"[Vaishnava] worship," Eck continues, "is certainly not an occasion for yogic withdrawing of the senses . . . but it is rather an occasion for awakening the senses and directing them toward the divine. Entering the temple, a worshipper clangs a big overhead bell. The energy of the senses is harnessed to the apprehension of God. Thus, it is not only vision that is refined by *darśana* [seeing the Deity], but the other senses as well are focused, ever more sharply, on God."[22] The tradition itself supports her view. In the words of Pillai Lokacharya, a great teacher in the Śrīvaishnava tradition: "This is the greatest grace of the Lord, that being free He becomes bound, being independent He becomes dependent for all His service on the devotee. . . . In other forms, man belonged to God. But behold the supreme sacrifice of Ishvara [Krishna] in the form of the *mūrti,* for here the almighty becomes the property of the devotee. . . . He carries the Lord about, fans Him, feeds Him, plays with Him—yea, the Infinite has become finite, that the child soul may grasp, understand, and love Him."[23]

After all, those of us who live in the world of conditioning cannot see the divinity as he appears in the spiritual world, but we *can* see the Deity, and through this vision, along with the rich spiritual assets it affords us, we can get ever closer to him in his original form, just as self-realized sages do in relation to God in the spiritual world. In this way, through "matter" we can approach "spirit." This is the purpose of the Deity for an aspiring spiritualist. Indic studies expert Kenneth Valpey explains this as follows:

> Although *bhagavān* [God] makes himself visible to all as *avatāra*, it is [only] the spiritually adept sage (*ṛṣi*) or pure devotee (*śuddha-bhakta*) who can receive the form of the Lord as vision (*darśaṇa*), seeing him as he is, and can then communicate that vision for others to hear, repeat, meditate upon, and then sculpt. The sculpted form [the Deity], if faithful to the specifications of revealed scripture (*āgama-śāstra*, or *śilpa-śāstra*, understood to be the faithful recordings of such visionaries' descriptions), can then be worshiped by prescribed procedures which, if properly practiced, enable the practitioner to gain the same vision of the Lord as the sages or devotees who see him "directly."[24]

Julius Lipner, Professor of Hinduism and the Comparative Study of Religion at the University of Cambridge, understands this point well: "Since the Kali age is *dharmically* a perverse age," Lipner tells us, "the natural capacities of humans are inferior to those of the earlier eras, and this sets up new barriers between the deities and humans. However, there is a good side to this state of affairs, for through the eyes of faith the deity remains permanently visible and proximate to the believer in the consecrated image, and worship becomes both easy and congenial for all."[25] Lipner elaborates,

> The fundamental point is this: image-worship is *necessary* for humans to worship the Supreme Being, which per se possesses a transcendent (invisible) essence to earthly eyes. As an actualized, phenomenal reality, the image is of a piece with the actualized, phenomenal reality of both the human worshipper and the everyday world. The existential correspondence between these three *relata* makes image-worship a conducive way of worshipping a personal Godhead. Being *in* the world and present to the worshipper as an image, the deity can benefit the worshipper and the world in a fitting manner.[26]

Finally, to understand something more about the Deity and how worshipping him allows us to actually inch closer to God, Śrīla A. C. Bhaktivedanta Swami Prabhupāda (1896–1977) explains the Deity in analogical terms:

> A crude example may be given here. We may find some mailboxes on the street, and if we post our letters in those boxes, they will naturally go to their destination without difficulty. But any old box, or an imitation that we may find somewhere but that is not authorized by the post office, will not do the work. Similarly, God has an authorized representation in the Deity form, which is called *archa-vigraha*. This *archa-vigraha* is an incarnation of the Supreme Lord. God will accept service through that form. The Lord is omnipotent, all-powerful; therefore, by His incarnation as *archa-vigraha* He can accept the service of the devotee, just to make it convenient for the man in conditioned life.[27]

Prabhupāda elaborates further:

> The Lord in His *archa-murti*, or form made of material elements, is not material, for those elements, although separated from the Lord, are also a part of the Lord's energy, as stated in the *Bhagavad-gita*. Because the elements are the Lord's own energy and because there is no difference between the energy and the energetic, the Lord can appear through any element. Just as the sun can act through the sunshine and thus distribute its heat and light, so Krishna, by His inconceivable power, can appear in His original spiritual form in any material element, including stone, wood, paint, gold, silver, and jewels.[28]

My introduction to the form of Krishna came through my involvement with the Hare Krishna movement, more technically known as the International Society for Krishna Consciousness (ISKCON), which I first encountered some fifty years ago. Being an initiated disciple of Śrīla Prabhupāda, the movement's founder and spiritual preceptor, mentioned above, no doubt influenced my understanding and perspective on three-dimensional Deity forms as depicted in this volume, and the form of Krishna in general. That said, as my interest in the Krishna tradition grew, I expanded my studies, attempting to unearth truths about these venerable forms of Krishna in their own right, beyond ISKCON, especially where they have pan-Indian significance. To this end, I have studied both the ancient textual tradition, particularly from Sanskrit and Bengali sources, with Western academics, as per my editorial involvement with the *Journal of Vaishnava Studies*, and conducted interviews with indigenous devotees who care for these Deities and worship them today on a regular basis. The Deities you read about in this book will be both traditional Deities in India and ISKCON-founded Deities throughout the world. Although Deities of Krishna number in the thousands, the smattering addressed in these pages will serve as a sampling of all the rest. My project here is to elucidate Vaishnava philosophy through prominent Deities, using their form and narrative history to uncover theological truths in relation to their worship.

To be sure, I acknowledge ISKCON in the lives of these Deities wherever its existence is pertinent. For example, in the text before you, I will analyze Lord Jagannāth from Purī, arguably one of the most important Krishna Deities in the history of the subcontinent. Even if this larger-than-life *mūrti* has little connection to the modern-day Hare Krishna movement, it was Prabhupāda who in fact brought this Deity to the West, and his disciples continue to glorify and venerate the Deity in Western countries throughout the world. Accordingly, while the basis and history of Jagannāth worship will herein be explicated according to the ancient tradition and contemporary devotees in Purī who have nothing to do with ISKCON, presented along with the research of scholars in the field, I will also mention ISKCON's involvement in bringing Jagannāth to the West, for that is an unavoidable part of the Deity's history.

Additionally, some of the Deities covered in this book are specifically ISKCON Deities, such as Rukmiṇī-Dvārakādhīśa, and these are included to make certain distinct philosophical points—that is, worship of Krishna is always uplifting and transcendental, and while this is obvious when it focuses on simplicity and intimacy, as in the worship of Rādhā-Govinda Deities, it is equally the case with Rukmiṇī-Dvārakādhīśa, which evoke more of an awe and reverence mood.

Over the years, I have written literally dozens of essays about various Vaishnava Deities, some of which appear in print here as chapters for the first time—never before published in any form. On the other hand, several of these chapters have been available in other venues, but they are here refurbished and developed anew for inclusion in this volume. If there is any redundancy, it is specifically because these chapters were written separately for various purposes. It should also be mentioned that I have omitted two very important Deities because of space limitations, but I include others to compensate for them.[29]

Seekers and scholars of religion will find in these chapters informative introductions to Indic philosophy and Vaishnava history in general, particularly in terms of Krishna's form and the underlying theological and scriptural background for Deity worship. For devotees, many details of Krishna and his form are unveiled for the first time (at least in the English language), and this is especially so for the much beloved icons explored in these pages, whose full story may be hard to find, even in Sanskrit and Bengali literature.

Just as Krishna's form and its many variants are central to Vaishnava thought, the entire philosophy of the Gauḍīya tradition can be understood through these forms in both direct and indirect ways. For example, in our opening chapter on Yuga Avatāras, we learn not only about the various world ages and the Deities associated with each of them—we also learn about the differences among God's many forms and manifestations, like how they are essentially non-different, and yet how they have distinguishing qualities as well, making their differences as important as their sameness. Additionally, through the various *avatāras*, we become privy to the tradition's articulated stance on prescribed means, that is, we learn about the process of self-realization recommended for each world age.

The second chapter in this volume introduces us to the ten most popular forms of Krishna (Daśāvatāra), again indicating a certain equality between the *avatāras* even if they embody certain qualitative distinctions as well. Indeed, here we see why and how Krishna is known as the source of all incarnations, at least from a Gauḍīya perspective; we are introduced to summarized details of the *avatāras*' activities on Earth (known as *līlā*, or "divine play"); and we even become privy to how this ancient system of divine incarnation relates to contemporary evolutionary theory! With these two opening chapters, we have set the table for the main course, which is a series of popular Vaishnava Deities both in India and the West. In other words, while the first two essays explain Krishna's form and its many manifestations *conceptually*, the following chapter and the ones that come after it will look more at how these forms are worshipped in space and time—in terms of tangible, three-dimensional Deities that have loved and been loved by devotees through the centuries.

We begin with Śrī Śrī Rādhā-Dāmodara. In this chapter we are introduced to the various kinds of relationship (*rasa, sambandha*) that one might have with Krishna—and here we particularly learn about Mother Yaśodā's adoring and "nurturing" (*vātsalya*) mood toward the Supreme, as well as the love of Rādhā, who embodies the characteristic of conjugal love (*mādhurya*) that is unequalled in the history of devotion. In this chapter, too, we learn of faith and works, and how each of these teachings have virtues that bring us closer to God. To understand this topic more intimately, we look at both the ancient Śrīvaishnava tradition as well as Christianity, for both traditions have branches that emphasize one or the other.

Radha Raman (Rādhāramaṇa), the next specific Deity analyzed here, teaches us that there is more to the Deity than meets the eye—especially in this particular form. This famous Krishna icon is said to be three in one: Rādhā, Krishna, and Śrī Chaitanya. These three are fully present in Radha Raman, and Śrī Rādhā, in particular, is seen here as the greatest of all Deities, as elucidated in this chapter. Krishna is hopelessly in love with her, and bows down to her in eternal subservience—making her Krishna's Deity, if such a thing is even imaginable. Indeed, Gauḍīyas see themselves primarily as devotees of Rādhā. Going further, the ultimate Gauḍīya Deity is *premā*, the love of Rādhā and Krishna, rising beyond any individual aspect of the divine. All of this is seen in the Deity of Radha Raman.

Additionally, this chapter will outline the importance of seeing God in terms of his personal form, which is particularly enhanced by the process of Deity worship—one of the greatest and most enduring features of the Radha Raman tradition. Our Radha Raman chapter will thus outline the methods, dynamics, and techniques of such worship from various points of view, ranging from the most fundamental to the most esoteric, from Vaidhī-bhakti to Rāgānuga-bhakti. Finally, we look at Radha Raman in terms of how his form and worship represents the practitioner's relationship with the Deity (*sambandha*), the path leading to the unfolding of the relationship (*abhideya*), and the realizations that accrue in the culmination of that relationship (*prayojana*).

This leads us to the subject of Jagannāth, "Lord of the Universe," the Deity of Krishna who is known for his sense of mercy and universalism. In this chapter, his narrative is detailed as well as the philosophy behind his form: Unlike Krishna, he does not evoke the pleasing image of a youthful cowherd, but rather his features are stark, unrecognizable without the eyes of knowledge, and, more importantly, the vision of love. Apropos of Jagannāth's universalism, we discuss various religious traditions and denominations that have embraced him through the centuries, claiming him as their own. This includes Jains, Buddhists, and numerous others. An elaborate description of the temple and altar Deities—with esoteric detail—are a special feature of this chapter. Included too is a full explanation of the Ratha-yātrā festival, central to the worship of Lord Jagannāth. In explaining Ratha-yātrā, the Gauḍīya notions of *vipralambha* and *sambhoga*—in which are found the heartbreaking intensity of separation (*vipralambha*) and the enthusiastic joy of union (*sambhoga*)—come to light.

From here we move to an important form of Krishna now worshipped in the Appalachian hills of West Virginia, in a town Prabhupāda called "New Vrindaban." This was a highly controversial ISKCON community—one of

ISKCON's first—with Deities that were very important to Prabhupāda. There were deviations and illicit and illegal activity committed on this property by leading members, staining ISKCON's reputation in the eyes of many. But the perpetrators were expelled from the institution, brought to trial, convicted, and New Vrindaban as a whole was eventually reinstated as a respectable part of the larger institution. Through it all, the Rādhā-Krishna Deities (Rādhā-Vrindaban Chandra) at the heart of this community played a major role in the hearts of numerous devotees, not least that of Śrīla Prabhupāda, as we will see from this chapter.

Additionally, through Rādhā-Vrindaban Chandra we learn of Krishna's country charm, as opposed to his more urban dimension, and this highlights the Gauḍīya teaching of *aiśvarya* versus *mādhurya*, or power as opposed to sweetness, with the latter considered a higher and more sophisticated realization. This is a central teaching for Gauḍīyas, revisited in several of our chapters. It is a teaching that explains why the tradition underlines Krishna in contradistinction to Vishnu, though both are but various faces on the same divinity—Krishna represents sweetness and intimacy, whereas Vishnu represents power and opulence. This chapter also outlines the naming of various forests in New Vrindaban, correlating them with divine forests in the spiritual world (and with their corollaries in Uttar Pradesh, India) for meditative purposes.

If Rādhā-Vrindaban Chandra represent the rural, *mādhurya* atmosphere for ISKCON, the opulent Deities and community in Los Angeles represent its counterpoint: A lavish and kingly mode of worship for Rukmiṇī-Dvārakādhīśa, the manifestations of Rādhā and Krishna who are given to Vishnu-style worship, showing that the Lord has various dimensions, both intimate and grandiose. In this chapter, we explore the "difference and sameness" of these various forms of Krishna, and, while doing so, elucidate the history of ISKCON, particularly on America's West Coast—its world headquarters—and its penchant for Deity worship.

Next, the Deity of Śrīnāthjī is an "intra-sampradāya" *mūrti*. That is to say, like Śrī Raṅganātha Swami in Śrī Raṅgam—who we addressed in our chapter on Radha Raman—all *sampradāyas* (lineages) have the highest regard for this form of Krishna, particularly those in the Vallabha Sampradāya, as we will see in this chapter. This is important, for it shows that although there are numerous Vaishnava lineages, with significant nuances of difference, they all intersect where it counts most, acknowledging distinct harmony when it comes to core points. More importantly in our current context, this particular Deity is intimately connected with Mādhavendra Purī, a highly regarded predecessor to Chaitanya Mahāprabhu. The origins of this Deity, in relation to Mādhavendra Purī, virtually gave birth to the Gauḍīya Sampradāya, with its most confidential insights. Indeed, by studying the story of this Deity closely, we gain greater knowledge of *vipralambha-bhāva*, love in separation, mentioned earlier, which Gauḍīyas consider indispensable when reaching for the higher echelon of love in union. On a pragmatic level, we see how this important manifestation of Krishna made his way into ISKCON, where he is worshipped worldwide to this day.

In the chapter after this, we look at the manifestation of the Pañca Tattva in Hawaii. Unlike most Krishna Deities, this group of five shows God as he appears in his form of Śri Chaitanya along with his four comrades—Śri Nityānanda, Śri Advaita, Śri Gadādhara, and Śri Śrivāsa Thākura. This is Krishna in all his fullness, for Krishna is never alone. By definition, the very concept "Krishna" must include his expansion (Nityānanda), his incarnation (Advaita), his energy or *śakti* (Gadādhara), and his devotee (Śrivāsa).

Still, at first glance, the Gauḍīya Vaishnava idea of God in five features may seem peculiar. By definition, God is one, the unequaled source of everything. He is the Supreme Being, from whom all other beings originate. If another shared his preeminent position, he could not be considered God. And yet the Pañca Tattva expresses the notion of this one God in five forms, not unlike the Christian Trinity, which describes one God in three forms.[30]

Just as in the Christian conception God's love is passed to the world through the Son and the Holy Spirit, the Vaishnava tradition tells us that the Pañca Tattva danced together, again and again, and thus made it easier to drink the nectarean love of the spiritual realm.[31] They danced, laughed, cried and chanted like madmen, and in this way they distributed love of God, which became contagious in their presence. In this way, God sometimes manifests in multiple forms to share his own overflowing love, relishing it among his many expansions and incarnations and no less with all his many parts and parcels—the living beings of this world. In establishing Pañca Tattva Deities in Hawaii and in other parts of the world, Prabhupāda sought to spread Krishna's love, as expressed through Chaitanya and his associates, to one and all.

Finally, returning to India, we look at the recondite Deities of Rādhā-Gopīnāth, who represent Vaishnava esoterica at its most intense. But we begin the chapter by going back to the beginning, to the basics, just so readers can get a refresher course on what Deities in general mean to the tradition, and what place they play in day-to-day Vaishnava life.

We open by describing how God is understood in one of three ways: as an impersonal abstraction, the oversoul of the universe (Brahman); as an all-pervading supreme entity who interpenetrates every aspect of reality, from the hearts of all living beings to the very fabric of existence (Paramātmā); and finally as the supreme personality of godhead, who manifests variously, but knows his greatest and most intimate manifestation in Krishna (Bhagavān).

These confidential forms of Bhagavān are revealed nowhere as thoroughly as in Vaishnava literature, and while these texts offer a wide range of emanations, incarnations, and expansions, we reach a sort of culmination in the form of Rādhā-Gopīnāth.

Additionally, in this chapter, along with the esoterica of this specific Deity, which is considerable, we again underline the notion that various Deities represent different stages on the path of devotion—Deities that serve to introduce one to the world of Krishna (*sambhanda*), those that help one develop expertise on the path (*abhideya*), and Deities that bring one to perfection (*prayojana*) so that one may know and love Krishna in truth. Rādhā-Gopīnāth is the embodiment of all three.

Again, while the Deities represented in this book are just a sampling of Krishna icons worshipped throughout the world, they are a special sampling, in that through them one can understand the whole of Indian philosophy and spirituality. We ask our readers to approach these forms with an open mind, hearing about their history and exploits and the devotees who loved them with heart and soul. If you do, you, too, might find their allure inescapable, and you might just find yourself thinking about Krishna when you least expect it.

NOTES

1. See Tripurari Swami, *Form of Beauty: The Krishna Art of B. G. Sharma* (Eugene, OR: Mandala Publishing Group, 1998), vii.

2. *Bhaktirasāmṛtasindhu* 1.1.1. See Rūpa Gosvāmin, *Bhaktirasāmṛtasindhu*, translated with introduction and notes by David L. Haberman (New Delhi: Indira Gandhi National Centre for the Arts and Motilal Banarsidass Publishers, 2003).

3. See Ravindra Svarūpa Dāsa, "Yoga Mush and the Jerk Divine," in *Encounter with the Lord of the Universe: Collected Essays 1978–1983* (Washington, DC: The Gita Nagari Press, 1984), 37–38.

4. Vaishnavism (Vaiṣṇavism) is the largest of all Hindu denominations, focusing on the worship of God as Vishnu or Krishna, or any of his many incarnations or manifestations. It is a monotheistic tradition, though it partakes of the Indic notion that one God has many forms, a principle that is sometimes called polymorphic monotheism. Amongst God's many forms, Krishna, at least in the Gauḍīya Vaishnava tradition, is considered supreme. The Gauḍīya tradition originates with the saint known as Śrī Chaitanya (1486–1533), who is viewed by his followers as a combined manifestation of Rādhā and Krishna, the dual female-male godhead (making the tradition a form of polymorphic *bi*-monotheism), and partakes of the much older tradition stemming from the Brahmā-Madhva Sampradāya. It is one of several Vaishnava lineages and the one with which I am most familiar, thus informing a large part of this book. For more on the divinity of Krishna, Vaishnava monotheism, and the Chaitanya tradition, see Neal Delmonico, "The History of Indic Monotheism and Modern Chaitanya

Vaishnavism," in Edwin Bryant and Maria Ekstrand, eds., *The Hare Krishna Movement: The Postcharismatic Fate of a Religious Transplant* (New York: Columbia University Press, 2004), 31–34. Also see Graham M. Schweig, "Krishna, the Intimate Divinity," in Edwin F. Bryant and Maria L. Ekstrand, eds., ibid., 18–19.

5. "I am the basis of the impersonal Brahman (*brahmaṇo hi pratiṣṭhāham*)," Krishna says directly, "which is the constitutional position of ultimate happiness, and which is immortal, imperishable and eternal." (See *Bhagavad-gītā* 14.27)

6. *Bhakti-rasāmṛta-sindhu* 1.2.239. See Rūpa Gosvāmin, *Bhaktirasāmṛtasindhu*, op. cit.

7. The *Brahma-saṁhitā* is an ancient Sanskrit text focusing on a series of prayers offered by the demigod Brahmā. According to the Vaishnava tradition, the prayers were first articulated at the dawn of creation. See Bhaktisiddhānta Sarasvatī, Gosvāmī, (trans.), *Śrī Brahma-saṁhitā*, with commentary by Śrīla Jīva Gosvāmī, Sri Gaudiya Math 1932 (Los Angeles: Bhaktivedanta Book Trust, 1985, reprint). I have adapted the translations for clarity.

8. See Ravīndra Svarūpa Dāsa, "With Kṛṣṇa in the Peaceable Kingdom" in *Back to Godhead 17, no. 8 (August 1982): 29.*

9. For the more common meaning of Krishna as "black" (*kārṣṇa*), see the online Sanskrit Dictionary (https://sanskritdictionary.com/kṛṣṇa/696/6). For *kṛṣ* as traceable to "plowing" or "drawing into oneself, to pull," see *Monier-Williams Sanskrit-English Dictionary*, 1899. (https://www.sanskrit-lexicon.uni-koeln.de/scans/MWScan/2020/web/index.php)]

10. For an explanation of how this principle works in Sanskrit, see Robert P. Goldman and Sally Sutherland, *Devavāṇīpraveśikā: An Introduction to the Sanskrit Language*, 4th Edition (Berkeley: Institute for South Asia Studies, 2019), 184; also see A. M. Ruppel, *The Cambridge Introduction to Sanskrit* (New York: Cambridge University Press, 2017), 84.

11. See *Śrīmad Bhāgavatam: A Symphony of Commentaries on the Tenth Canto Volume Two Chapters 4–11*, trans., Charles A. Filion (Vindavan, UP: Rasbihari Lal & Sons, 2018), 391.

12. See the *Viṣṇu-sahasranāma* ("the Thousand Names of Vishnu"), Name 554: *Kṛṣṇaḥ* (https://www.sadagopan.org/pdfuploads/Vishnu%20Sahasranama%20v2.pdf), 233.

13. Originally written in the 1800s, the *Śabdakalpadruma* is an encyclopedic dictionary of Sanskrit words arranged in alphabetical order, often providing etymological origins. See Raja Rādhā-kāntadeva, *Śabdakalpadruma,* 5 volumes (Delhi: Nag Publishers, reprint 1988). The article about "Kṛṣṇa" is in Vol. 2, p. 180ff. I thank André Couture for bringing this reference to my attention.

14. See *Hari-nāmāmṛta-vyākaraṇam of Jīva Gosvāmī: The Grammar with the Nectar of Hari's Names*, Volumes One and Two, trans., Matsya Avatāra Dāsa (Vrindavan, UP: Rasbihari Lal & Sons, 2016). Numerous examples are found on pp. 22, 23, 426, 449, 452, 454, 735, and 833.

15. See *A Sanskrit-English Dictionary* (1872) by Monier-Williams (https://www.upasanayoga.org/AKAruna/docs/MWā-au.htm): *ākarṣa ā-karṣa*, among other meanings . . . magnetic attraction; a magnet, a loadstone; *ākarṣaka ā-karṣaka* . . . a magnet

or loadstone; *ākarṣaṇa ā-karṣaṇa* . . . any instrument for pulling; and *ākarṣika ā-karṣika* . . . magnetic, attractive.

16. For more on these five aspects of the Supreme from a Śrīvaishnava perspective, see Vasudha Narayanan, "The Distinctive Features of the Śrīvaiṣṇava Sampradāya" in *Journal of Vaishnava Studies 29, no. 2 (Spring 2021): 123. See also Vasudha Narayanan, "Śrīvaishnavism," in Brill's Encyclopedia of Hinduism*, edited by Knut A. Jacobsen, Vol. III (Leiden: Brill, 2011), 558. For more on deities of Krishna specifically, see Peter Bennett "Krishna's Own Form: Image Worship and Puṣṭi Mārga." *Journal of Vaiṣṇava Studies 1, no. 4 (Summer 1993): 109*–34; William H. Deadwyler (Ravīndra-svarūpa dāsa), "The Devotee and the Deity: Living a Personalistic Theology" In *Gods of Flesh, Gods of Stone: The Embodiment of Divinity in India*, edited by Joanne Punzo Waghorne and Norman Cutler (New York: Columbia University Press, 1996), 69–88; Diana L. Eck, *Darśan: Seeing the Divine Image in India* (Chambersburg, PA: Anima Books, 1985); Vasudha Narayanan, "Arcāvatāra: On Earth as He Is in Heaven." In *Gods of Flesh, Gods of Stone*, op. cit., 35–68; Kenneth R. Valpey, "Kṛṣṇa-sevā: Theology of Image Worship in Gauḍīya-Vaiṣṇavism," MA dissertation, Graduate Theological Union, Berkeley, 1998; Kenneth R. Valpey, *Attending Krishna's Image: Caitanya Vaishnava Mūrti-sevā as Devotional Truth* (London: Routledge, 2006).

17. Historically, there have indeed been movements that disparage Deity worship. The Bengali reformer, Ram Mohan Roy (1772?–1833), himself influenced by impersonalistic thought, immediately comes to mind, as does Dayananda Sarasvati (1824–1883). See Noel A. Salmond, *Hindu Iconoclasts: Rammohun Roy, Dayananda Sarasvati, and Nineteenth-Century Polemics against Idolatry* (Waterloo, ON: Wilfrid Laurier University Press, 2004).

18. Diana L. Eck, *Darśan*: *Seeing the Divine Image in India*, op. cit., 21. For Roszak's original quote, see Theodore Roszak, *Where the Wasteland Ends* (Garden City, NY: Doubleday & Co., 1972), chapter 4, "The Sin of Idolatry."

19. See Rajiv Malhotra and Satyanarayana Dasa Babaji, *Sanskrit Non-Translatables: The Importance of Sanskritizing English* (New Delhi: Amaryllis, 2020).

20. See Steven J. Rosen, *Essential Hinduism* (Westport, CT: Greenwood Press, 2006), Chapter 11, "Idols, Deities, Worship, and Temples."

21. Diana L. Eck, *Darśan: Seeing the Divine Image in India*, op. cit., 46.

22. Ibid., 49.

23. Bharatan Kumarappa, *The Hindu Conception of the Deity as Culminating in Ramanuja* (London: Luzac & Co., 1934), 316–17.

24. Kenneth R. Valpey, "Krishna-Seva: Traditional Ritual in the Practice of Bhakti Yoga," M.A. thesis, op. cit., 95–96. Indeed, the *Viṣṇudharmottara Purāṇa* (3.93.18–20) tells us that "In the Satya, Tretā and Dvāpara ages . . . the Deities appear as a visible manifestation (*āgacchanti saśarīrāḥ*) in this human world. Even so, they never present themselves in this way in the Kali age. In this age, they come only when summoned by Brahmins, who install them as Deities (*pratiṣṭhāsu*). In this way, the wise take great care to worship the Lord in his Deity form."

25. See Julius J. Lipner, *Hindu Images and Their Worship with Special Reference to Vaiṣṇavism: A Philosophical-Theological Inquiry* (London: Routledge, 2017), 206.

26. Ibid., 211.

27. See *Bhagavad-gītā As It Is* (1972), chapter 12.5, purport (https://vedabase.io/en/library/bg/12/5/).

28. See *Caitanya-caritāmṛta*, Madhya 5.97, purport (https://vedabase.io/en/library/cc/madhya/5/97/).

29. The two important Deities not covered in this volume but published elsewhere are Madan Mohan and Rādhā-Govinda: Satyarāja Dāsa, "Madan Mohan: Mesmerizer of Mesmerizers" in *Back to Godhead* 56, no. 4 (July/August 2022): 20–25; and "Kṛṣṇa's Long Journey from Braj to Brooklyn" in *Back to Godhead* 52, no. 5 (September/October 2018): 13–18. The reason these two are particularly significant is as follows: According to the *Caitanya-caritāmṛta* (Ādi 1.19), there are three sets of Deities that are considered special for Gauḍīya Vaishnavas, representing everything that Krishna is, not only in terms of his iconic form, but spiritually as well—these Deities are Madan Mohan, Rādhā-Govinda, and Rādhā-Gopīnāth. While the other two were published elsewhere, as above, the final Deity in this divine triumvirate will be elaborated upon in this volume for the first time.

30. For an extensive comparison between the Pañca Tattva and the Christian Trinity, see Steven J. Rosen, *Śrī Pañca Tattva: The Five Features of God* (New York: Folk Books, 1994).

31. See *Caitanya-caritāmṛta* Ādi 7.22.

Chapter One

Yuga Avatāras

God(s) of a Different Color

Krishna exists in an infinity of forms. When he descends into our world of three dimensions, he is referred to as an *avatāra*. Indeed, the wisdom texts of India tell us much about *avatāras*, a word that comes from the Sanskrit *ava√ tṛ*, "to cross down," "to descend." It refers to the Supreme Lord's "descent" to Earth, commonly called an "Incarnation of God."[1] All aspects of divinity, when appearing in this world, can be viewed as a type of *avatāra*, or a manifestation of the Lord, whether it is sacred literature (*grantha-avatāra*), the holy name (*nāmāvatāra*), sacred place (*dhāmāvatāra*), or iconic image (*arcāvatāra*), and so on. This volume is largely about the *arcāvatāra*.

Although the word *avatāra* does not appear in the *Bhagavad-gītā* as such, verses 4.7–8 tell us why the Lord does indeed repeatedly descend into the world of matter:

> *yadā yadā hi dharmasya glānir bhavati bhārata / adhyutthānam adharmasya tadātmānaṃ sṛjāmyaham // paritrāṇāya sādhūnāṃ vināśāya ca duṣkṛtām / dharmasaṃsthāpanārthāya sambhavāmi yuge yuge //*

> Whenever and wherever there is a decline in religious practice, O descendant of Bharata, and a predominant rise of irreligion—at that time I descend Myself. In order to deliver the pious and to annihilate the miscreants, as well as to reestablish the principles of religion, I advent Myself millennium after millennium (*yuge yuge*).

The Vaishnava exposition of God's various manifestations and aspects can get quite technical, but Gauḍīya texts summarize it into three basic categories: *svayaṁ-rūpa, tad-ekātma-rūpa*, and *āveśa*. These three are detailed in the *Caitanya-caritāmṛta* (Cc) Madhya-līlā 20, echoing Śrīla Rūpa Gosvāmī in his *Laghu-bhāgavatāmṛta,* a text that focuses on the subject of God's various manifestations.

Briefly, Śrī Rūpa reveals (in Pūrva-khaṇḍa, verse 12) that the original form of God (*svayaṁ-rūpa*) is independent and supreme, meaning, in this form, he is never subservient to other forms of the divine and is unique in his character and inherent nature—he is also distinct in that he alone is the fountainhead, the original source of all other sources. This highest manifestation, or, more correctly, this ultimate *manifestor*, is, according to the *Śrīmad Bhāgavatam* (1.3.28), Lord Śrī Krishna himself (*kṛṣṇas tu bhagavān svayam*).

Next, in Pūrva-khaṇḍa, verse 14, Śrī Rūpa describes the *tad-ekātma-rūpa* forms of the Lord: "They exist simultaneously with the *svayaṁ-rūpa* form and are non-different from him. Nonetheless, their bodily features and specific activities manifest differently." It might be added that the *tad-ekātma-rūpa* is further divided into two categories: *svāṁśa* (personal expansions) and *vilāsa* (activity expansions).

The *āveśa* forms of the Lord are also addressed in Śrī Rūpa's *Laghu-bhāgavatāmṛta* (Pūrva 18): "A living being who is specifically empowered by God with knowledge or strength or some other opulence is referred to as *āveśa-rūpa.*"

In general, all manifestations of the divine will fit into one of these three categories, and they descend to our earth in the form of *avatāras.*

Overall, the *Caitanya-caritāmṛta* (Madhya 20.245–46) sums up the various *avatāra* manifestations in yet another way: "There are six types of Krishna *avatāras*: Incarnations of Viṣṇu (*puruṣa-avatāras*); pastime incarnations (*līlā-avatāras*); incarnations that control various facets of nature (*guṇa-avatāras*); progenitor incarnations (*manvantara-avatāras*); incarnations that have a special function in a particular time cycle (*yuga-avatāras*); and those regular souls who are directly empowered by God (*śaktyāveśa-avatāras*). This chapter deals specifically with Yuga Avatāras.

YUGAS AND YUGA AVATĀRAS

First of all, what is a yuga? Basically, in this context, it is an epoch or era within a time cycle of ages. The duration of the material universe is limited, manifesting through cycles of kalpas. A kalpa is a day of Brahmā, the first created being, who lives for an inordinate amount of time. One day of Brahmā consists of a thousand cycles of four yugas or ages: Satya, Tretā, Dvāpara, and Kali.

The cycle of Satya is characterized by virtue, wisdom and religion, there being practically no ignorance and vice, and the yuga lasts 1,728,000 years.

In the Tretā-yuga, vice makes its appearance for the first time, and this yuga lasts 1,296,000 years. In the Dvāpara-yuga, there is an even greater decline in virtue and religion, vice increasing, and this yuga lasts 864,000 years. Finally, Kali-yuga (the yuga in which we now find ourselves) knows an abundance of strife, ignorance, irreligion and vice, true virtue being practically nonexistent. This yuga lasts 432,000 years, of which 5,000 have elapsed.

Turning to the Yuga Avatāras, Rūpa Gosvāmī's delineation, based on scriptural statements from the *Śrīmad Bhāgavatam* (11.5.21–42), identifies the particular bodily characteristic (*ākāra*), color (*varṇa*), and name (*nāman*) that Krishna assumes in each of the four ages. These source *Bhāgavatam* texts also proclaim the specific practices (*sādhana*) through which adherents might approach God in each of the yugas (Bhāg. 10.8.13; 12.3.52), as we will see. A few of the pertinent verses should be quoted:

Śrīmad Bhāgavatam 11.5.21–23:

In Satya-yuga the Lord is white and four-armed, has matted locks and wears a garment of tree bark. He carries a black deerskin, a sacred thread, prayer beads and the rod and waterpot of a brahmacārī. Here, the Lord is glorified by the names Haṁsa, Suparṇa, Vaikuṇṭha, Dharma, Yogeśvara, Amala, Īśvara, Puruṣa, Avyakta and Paramātmā.

Śrīmad Bhāgavatam 11.5.24–26:

In Tretā-yuga the Lord appears with a red complexion. He has four arms, golden hair, and wears a triple belt representing initiation into each of the three Vedas. Embodying the knowledge of worship by sacrificial performance, which is contained in the Ṛg, Sāma and Yajur Vedas, His symbols are the ladle, spoon, and other implements of sacrifice. In Tretā-yuga the Lord is glorified by the names Viṣṇu, Yajña, Pṛśnigarbha, Sarvadeva, Urukrama, Vṛṣākapi, Jayanta and Urugāya.

Śrīmad Bhāgavatam 11.5.27:

In Dvāpara-yuga the Supreme Personality of Godhead appears with a dark blue complexion, wearing yellow garments. The Lord's transcendental body is marked in this incarnation with Śrīvatsa and other distinctive ornaments, and he manifests his personal weapons.

Śrīmad Bhāgavatam 11.5.32:

In the age of Kali, intelligent persons perform congregational chanting to worship the incarnation of Godhead who constantly sings the names of Krishna.

> Although his complexion is not blackish, he is Krishna himself. He is accompanied by his associates, servants, weapons and confidential companions.

Rūpa Gosvāmī's exact verse, following the *Bhāgavatam*, runs as follows: "In Satya-yuga, Hari is Śukla, white; in Tretā Yuga, he is Rakta, red; in Dvāpara Yuga he is Śyāma, blue-black; and in Kali Yuga he is Kṛṣṇa, which means blackish" (*Laghu-bhāgavatāmṛta* 1.4.25).

In this way, according to Śrī Rūpa, the yuga avatāras are white, red, blue-black, and black, respectively, and this is the color sequence found in most Purāṇas. That being said, the *Bhāgavatam* (11.5.32, as seen above) leaves the wording of this list somewhat tentative, particularly in relation to the yuga avatāra for the current age of Kali, but not without a distinct purpose: It is so the great *ācāryas*, or the self-realized masters in disciplic succession, can pinpoint the secret avatāra of the age, Śrī Chaitanya Mahāprabhu, through sophisticated scriptural hermeneutics. And this is exactly what the tradition does.

Indeed, Kṛṣṇadāsa Kavirāja Gosvāmī, when elaborating on the yuga avatāra for the Kali Age (see *Caitanya-caritāmṛta,* Ādi-līlā, chapter 3), develops Śrī Rūpa's description by analyzing the inner implications of the *Bhāgavatam* verse in question. He says that the *avatāra* for the Age of Kali is "black in color (*kṛṣṇa-varṇa*) though not black (*akṛṣṇa*) in terms of his outer bodily luster": he is both black and not black. This enables the tradition to identify this *avatāra* more specifically with Śrī Chaitanya, who was well known for his golden (*gaura*) complexion.

The commentators offer an alternate explanation as well: The Kali-yuga *avatāra* is in the "category" of Krishna (*kṛṣṇa-varṇa*) but he is not blackish (*akṛṣṇa*) in an external sense. And yet another: *kṛṣṇa-varṇa* means that the syllables (*varṇa*) "*kṛṣ-ṇa*" are in his mouth—he is always chanting (*varṇayati*) Lord Krishna's name. We will return to this later.

Rūpa Gosvāmī sums up in the second verse of his *Caitanyāṣṭaka*: "In the age of Kali the wise directly worship him who is dark (*kṛṣṇa*) but whose limbs are not dark (*akṛṣṇa*) due to his immense luster, with sacrifices that consist of singing [his names]." The *ācāryas* elaborate: The *avatāra* of the Age is different in appearance, not blackish. This is because he has taken the mood (*bhāva*) and lustre (*kānti*) of Śrīmatī Rādhārāṇī. This is what makes him golden. In reality, however, he is black (*kṛṣṇa*), and therefore the traditional color of the yuga *avatāra* abides in him.

Regarding the four yuga *avatāras* in general, Śrī Rūpa says that they are *prābhava* forms of the Lord, meaning, among other things, that they manifest before our vision for a relatively short period of time (*Laghu-bhāgavatāmṛta* 1.4.46 and *Caitanya-caritamrta* Madhya 20.244, purport).

This too will be pertinent to our discussion. It is, in fact, for the above reason that we have very little information concerning the first two manifestations of divinity—the white *avatāra* and the red one. Our knowledge of them is scanty.

But the second two Yuga *Avatāras*, we shall soon see, are not ordinary *avatāras* at all but rather the original personality of Godhead (*avatāri*), Śrī Krishna and Śrī Chaitanya, respectively, and there is a deluge of scriptural information about them. Indeed, numerous Indian wisdom texts sing their glories.

It is especially meaningful, however, that Śrī Rūpa depicts the Kali-yuga *avatāra* as black. Again, this is in accordance with standard Purāṇic accounts and confirmed in the *Harivaṃśa*. It is Rūpa's way of paying homage to predecessor Vaishnava texts and asserting the usual state of affairs regarding Yuga *Avatāras*. But, let it be known: Once in a day of Brahmā, or every 4.3 billion years, the Supreme Lord comes in his original form, which is a special feature of the current Yuga *Avatāra* (Cc. Ādi 3.6). In this particular Kali-yuga, Śrī Krishna appears as Śrī Chaitanya, and although he accepts the name of Krishna (his name is "Śrī Krishna Chaitanya")—and devotes his incarnation to chanting the name of Krishna—he appears in golden hue, not a blackish one.

Rūpa acknowledges this elsewhere in his *Laghu-bhāgavatāmṛta*. In the text's second invocation verse, for example, he cites the *Bhāgavatam* verse already mentioned (11.5.32), stating that the Kali-yuga *avatāra* is not blackish but fair and glistening, alluding to Mahāprabhu's special manifestation as the golden yuga *avatāra*. Throughout Śrī Rūpa's writing, he makes it even clearer still, drawing on the *Bhāgavatam* and other proof-texts.

Śrī Rūpa's illustrious nephew, Jīva Gosvāmin, opens his *Tattva Sandarbha*, too, with *Bhāgavatam* 11.5.32, highlighting the importance of Śrī Chaitanya, whom he extols as the *avatāra* of Kali-yuga: "black (*kṛṣṇa*) inside and golden (*gaura*) outside." (See *Tattva Sandarbha* 1–2, with Jīva's auto-commentary in *Sarva-Saṃvādinī* 1) Thus, the golden *avatāra* is important to the Gauḍīya Sampradāya.

An oft-quoted verse in this connection is found in the story of Krishna's birth, during his name-giving ceremony (Bhāg. 10.8.13). The family priest Garga Muni said:

āsan varṇās trayo hy asya

gṛhṇato 'nuyugaṁ tanūḥ

śuklo raktas tathā pīta

idānīṁ kṛṣṇatāṁ gataḥ

> "Your son Kṛṣṇa appears as an incarnation in every millennium. In the past, He assumed three different colors—white, red and yellow (or golden)—and now He has appeared in a blackish color."

That Krishna appears in every millennium is significant. In other words, he has appeared in all of these colors before and he will do so again and again. Nonetheless, we see here a veiled reference to Śrī Chaitanya. Since Garga tells Krishna's father that the Lord appears in white, red and "now" blackish colors, there is only one yuga in the current millennium left to consider—Kali. Thus, by the process of elimination, the great teachers of the past conclude that the merciful golden or yellow incarnation appears in our current age of quarrel and hypocrisy. This is explained by the scholarly devotee, Gopīparāṇadhana Dāsa (1950–2011), who also points out that this is a little-known form, disguised for esoteric purposes:

> The appearance of Chaitanya Mahāprabhu occurs during the Kali age of the twenty-eighth *mahā-yuga* of the reign of Vaivasvata Manu in the day of Brahmā called the Śveta-varāha-kalpa [which is our current era]. . . . [Various] authorities have made such statements as . . . "the Supreme Lord Hari does not allow Himself to be seen in Kali-yuga." (*Vishnu-dharma Purāṇa* 104). . . . This being the case, the intelligent worshippers of Śrī Chaitanya Mahāprabhu understand the confidential significance of Prahlād Mahārāja's declaration that . . . "You appear as a disguised incarnation in Kali-yuga" (Bhāgavatam 7.9.38). . . . Prahlād's exact words were *channaḥ kalau yad abhavaḥ*. Here *channaḥ* ("covered") indicates that Lord Chaitanya is Krishna Himself covered by the [golden] complexion of His beloved Śrīmatī Rādhārāṇī. Krishna states in the Bṛhan-nāradīya Purāṇa, "O Brāhmaṇa, in the age of Kali I always disguise Myself as a devotee of the Supreme Lord ." The Upaniṣads also allude to Lord Chaitanya's descent: "Sometimes the Supreme Lord, the all-encompassing origin of creation, appears in a golden-complexioned form." (*Muṇḍaka Upaniṣad* 3.1.3)[2]

SATYA AND TRETĀ: WHITE AND RED

Briefly, the *Caitanya-caritāmṛta*, culling all available material on yuga *avatāras* in India's ancient wisdom texts, which is negligible, gives us a nutshell look at the white and red Incarnations: "In Satya-yuga the Lord appeared in a body colored white, with four arms and matted hair. He wore tree bark and bore a black antelope skin. He wore a sacred thread and a garland of *rudrākṣa* beads. He carried a rod and a waterpot, and he was a *brahmacārī*" (Cc Madhya 20.332). "In Tretā-yuga, the Lord appeared in a body that had a reddish hue and four arms. There were three distinctive lines on his abdomen, and his hair was golden. His form manifested the Vedic knowledge, and he bore the symbols of a sacrificial spoon, ladle and so on" (Cc Madhya 20.333). Thus, the *Caitanya-caritāmṛta* reiterates the information found in the *Śrīmad Bhāgavatam.*

While multiple names are supplied for these two Incarnations—for the white Incarnation, Śukla, Haṁsa, Suparṇa, Vaikuṇṭha, and so on, and for the red, Rakta, Viṣṇu, Yajña, Pṛśnigarbha, etc., as mentioned above—we find little about who they are in terms of known Puranic *avatāras*. Śrīla Prabhupāda offers several options.

For example, "Yugāvatāra means just like there are four *yugas*: Satya, Tretā, Dvāpara, Kali. The ages of each *yuga* we have mentioned already. Now in the Satya-yuga, when the *yugāvatāra* comes, He is white. He is Hayagrīva in the Satya-yuga. . . . Yes. He is white. And *rakta. Śukla-rakta-kṛṣṇa-pīta-krame cāri varṇa*. In the Satya-yuga when the incarnation of *yugāvatāra* comes, His complexion is white. And in the next *yuga*, Tretā-yuga, the complexion is red. And the next *yuga*, Dvāpara-yuga, the complexion is black, Krishna. And the next, Kali-yuga, the complexion is yellow. Lord Chaitanya is yellow."[3]

It seems, then, that Hayagrīva is the white Avatāra of Satya-yuga. But all is not so easy. According to *Śrīmad Bhāgavatam* (2.7.11) his body is also sometimes described as having a golden color (*tapanīya varṇaḥ*), which would disqualify him from being the yuga *avatāra*.

Additionally, Prabhupāda says elsewhere: "As the white incarnation, the Lord taught religion and meditation. He offered benedictions to Kardama Muni, and in this way He showed His causeless mercy" (Cc Madhya 20.334). Prabhupāda further writes in his purport to this verse: "Kardama Muni was one of the *prajāpatis*. He married Devahūti, the daughter of Manu, and their son was Kapiladeva. The Supreme Lord was very pleased with Kardama Muni's austerities, and He appeared before Kardama Muni in a whitish body. This happened in the Satya-yuga millennium, when people were accustomed to practicing meditation."

Thus, it is sometimes mistakenly said that Kapiladeva is the white Incarnation of Satya-yuga. But a close look finds resolution: In the *Śrīmad Bhāgavatam*'s Third Canto it is stated that the Lord appeared before Kardama Muni twice—first as Śukla (Yuga Avatāra) and then as his son Kapila. (Kapila is not an alternate name for Śukla.) The relevant verses are 3.21.16 (*śuklānimiṣāya tubhyam*), 3.22.19 (*śukla-proktān*), 3.23.23 (*śukla-kṛtaṁ tīrtham*), and 3.24.1 (*śuklābhivyāhṛtaṁ*).

Similarly, Lord Varāha, the Boar Incarnation, is sometimes referred to as being both the white and red *Avatāras* of their respective yugas. That is to say, there are two distinct Varāha *Avatāras* engaged in saving Mother Earth, as described in the Purāṇas. These Avatāras are Śveta (white) Varāha and Rakta (red) Varāha.

Nonetheless, Yuga Avatāras are known through the scriptures and must adhere to both *svarūpa-lakṣaṇa*, which refers to innate characteristics, and *taṭastha-lakṣaṇa*, or marginal characteristics. In context, *svarūpa-lakṣaṇa* refers to the given *avatāra*'s color or name, as revealed in the *Bhāgavatam*, while the *taṭastha* or relational characteristic would be the teaching of yuga-dharma.

In conclusion, if the Varāha Avatāras did not teach the prescribed practices of Satya- and Tretā-yugas when they descended to earth—and there is no evidence that they did—they cannot be counted as Yuga *Avatāras*, regardless of their having the proper color and manifesting at the appropriate time.

Interestingly, the White Varāha appears in the Svāyambhuva Manvantara and the Red Varāha in the Cākṣuṣa Manvantara, which are alternate time cycles (*Laghu-bhāgavatāmṛta*,1.3.10–11). This indeed is said to resolve the dilemma as to why the white and red incarnations in general are understood variously—different forms of these *avatāras* appear in different kalpas, as per the Lord's design—and since they are *prābhava* manifestations, little is known about them and we can only take recourse in the few verses afforded us by the Vedic literature, which, again, are minimal.

DVĀPARA AND KALI: BLACK AND GOLDEN

"In Dvāpara-yuga," the *Bhāgavatam* (11.5.27) tells us, "the Supreme Personality of Godhead appears with a dark blue complexion, wearing yellow garments. The Lord's transcendental body is marked in this incarnation with Śrīvatsa and other distinctive ornaments, and He manifests His personal weapons." The *avatāra* for the age was thus none other than the source of all *avatāras*, Lord Śrī Krishna, who is clearly described in this verse and others. "As the sunrise takes place once in twenty-four hours," writes Śrīla Prabhupāda, "similarly the pastimes of Lord Krishna take place in a universe once in a daytime of Brahmā, the account of which is given in the *Bhagavad-gītā* as 4,300,000,000 solar years. But wherever the Lord is present, all His different pastimes as described in the revealed scriptures take place at regular intervals" (SB 3.2.7, Purport).

This occurred some 5,000 years ago. From the beginning of Brahmā's day of 4,320,000,000 years, six Manus appear and disappear before Lord Krishna appears in His original form. Thus, 1,975,320,000 years of the day of Brahmā elapse before the appearance of Lord Krishna. This is an astronomical calculation according to solar years.

Living beings in our current millennium are, then, particularly blessed, for the original Personality of Godhead has recently walked the earth, purifying the atmosphere in an incomparably consummate manner.

And yet it gets better. If Lord Krishna appears once in each day of Brahmā, or once in fourteen Manvantaras, each of seventy-one Divya-yugas in duration—and that time is now—so too does Śrī Chaitanya, the golden *avatāra*, who is Krishna himself in his most intimate form as Rādhā and Krishna combined. And this occurred only five hundred years ago. The rapture of transcendence, according to the Gauḍīya tradition, is practically in our backyard.

Śrīla Jīva Gosvāmī commences his masterwork *Ṣaṭ-sandarbha with an original verse meant to capture the enthusiasm with which we should appreciate Śrī Chaitanya's glory, while also confirming him as the golden avatāra of Kali-yuga:*

antaḥ kṛṣṇaṁ bahir gauraṁ

darśitāṅgādi-vaibhavam

kalau saṅkīrtanādyaiḥ sma

kṛṣṇa-caitanyam āśritāḥ

"I take shelter of Lord Śrī Kṛṣṇa Chaitanya, who is outwardly of a golden complexion but is inwardly Kṛṣṇa Himself. In this Age of Kali He displays His expansions [His associates and intimate devotees] while performing congregational chanting of the holy name of the Lord."

Heartfelt chanting is all that Śrī Chaitanya requires. In other incarnations, Lord Krishna would ask the devotee to first surrender to him, and only then might one attain the fruits of spiritual practice: "Abandon all varieties of religion," says Krishna, "and just surrender unto me. I shall deliver you from all sinful reaction. Do not fear" (*Bhagavad-gītā* 18.66). But in his incarnation as Śrī Chaitanya, he traverses the world, far and wide—either directly or through his name and his followers—freely distributing Krishna-premā, or the highest form of love of God. This is the unique blessing of the age of Kali. Despite it being the most debilitating and unfortunate of all yugas, the process of self-realization is the simplest and most accessible, open to all living beings.

A COLORFUL PROCESS OF GOD-REALIZATION

Means of realization vary from age to age. According to the varying degrees of qualification exhibited by different populations, at different times, in different places, and which modulate accordingly from yuga to yuga, the scriptures prescribe particular practices specifically suited for the time period in which they thrive. The *Bhāgavatam* (12.3.52) proclaims,

> *kṛte yad dhyāyato viṣṇuṁ*
>
> *tretāyāṁ yajato makhaiḥ*
>
> *dvāpare paricaryāyāṁ*
>
> *kalau tad dhari-kīrtanāt*

> "Whatever result was obtained in Satya-yuga by meditating on Viṣṇu [or Krishna], in Tretā-yuga by performing sacrifices, and in Dvāpara-yuga by serving the Lord's lotus feet, can be obtained in Kali-yuga simply by chanting the name of Hari [Krishna]."

The same truth is expressed in the *Vishnu Purāṇa* (6.2.17), the *Padma Purāṇa* (72.25), the *Bṛhan-nāradiya Purāṇa* (38.97), and elsewhere.

"In Satya-yuga," we learn from the *Caitanya-caritāmṛta*, "people were generally advanced in spiritual knowledge and could meditate upon Krishna very easily. The people's occupational duty in Tretā-yuga was to perform great sacrifices. This was induced by the Personality of Godhead in His reddish incarnation" (Cc Madhya 20.335).

"In Dvāpara-yuga," continues the text, "people's occupational duty was to worship the lotus feet of Krishna directly [This usually occurred in the temple.] Therefore Lord Krishna, appearing in a blackish body, personally induced people to worship Him" (Cc Madhya 20.336).

Finally, the process for our current age is enunciated: "In Kali-yuga the occupational duty of the people is to congregationally chant the holy name of Krishna" (Cc Madhya 20.339).

Overall, the great masters in disciplic succession have summarized the process for each age as follows, in consecutive order: deep meditation (*dhyāyan*), elaborate Vedic sacrifices (*yajñais*), temple worship (*arcanā*), and congregational chanting of the holy name (*dhari-kīrtanāt*). Prabhupāda clarifies:

> Now, different ages, different methods are prescribed. So for this age, it is prescribed that *kalau tad dhari-kīrtanāt*. Whatever was possible to perform in the Satya-yuga by meditation, and in the Tretā-yuga by offering of great, I mean to

> say, costly sacrifices, and in the Dvāpara-yuga by offering prayers or *arcanā* in the temple, that can be made possible easily by Hari-kīrtana, by chanting the holy name of God. That is the prescription.[4]

One final point. It can be argued that Krishna, as the source of all *avatāras*, does not necessarily emphasize/bring the yuga-dharma for Dvāpara-yuga, at least not in the same way that "ordinary" Yuga *Avatāras* do. There may be some truth to this. We learn from scripture that Deity worship began in Tretā-yuga, the age prior to Dvāpara: "My dear King, when great sages and saintly persons saw mutually disrespectful dealings at the beginning of Tretā-yuga, Deity worship in the temple was introduced with all paraphernalia" (SB 7.14.39). As Prabhupāda confirms in his purport, "they introduced worship of the Deity in the temple. This began in Tretā-yuga and was especially prominent in Dvāpara-yuga (*dvāpare paricaryāyāṁ*)."

Nonetheless, as the *Avatāra* of the new age, Krishna lauds Deity worship in an unprecedented way. One sees this clearly in the *Bhāgavatam* (11.27), where he speaks of the practice as foremost of religious duties, "repeatedly declared by all the great sages as bringing the greatest benefit possible to human life." Uddhava, Krishna's great devotee, to whom he is speaking in this section (often known as the *Uddhava Gītā*), extolls its efficacy as well. He says it brings ultimate salvation to virtually anyone who engages in it.

Clearly, Krishna's very existence, in terms of his manifested pastimes, enhanced the yuga-dharma even further. Locana dāsa Ṭhākura offers elaboration in his *Caitanya-maṅgala* (Ādi 3):

> In Dvāpara-yuga Lord Krishna comes Himself as the Yuga Avatāra. But by what activities did He establish the *yuga-dharma*? Scriptures say that temple worship is the religious process for Dvāpara-yuga. But when and where did Lord Krishna establish temple worship? Listen closely and I will clarify this matter. . . . The Lord Himself, the completely independent Supreme Being, decides whether He'll establish the *yuga-dharma* or simply enjoy pleasure pastimes (*līlā*). The wonderful thing is that He did both at once.

In other words, by enacting his blissful *līlā,* Krishna allured devotees into savoring his divine form and incomparable pastimes, which led to their carving Deities of him and worshipping him in the temple. Accordingly, he both displayed his independently Supreme nature while solidifying the yuga-dharma.

Thus, a blossoming of *sādhana* (methods of devotional practice) developed through the successive progression of yugas, culminating in the singing of Krishna's holy names. The process for the first age, Satya-yuga was very internal, engaging practitioners in deep meditation, as could only be performed by highly evolved beings. Then, the next yuga brought this outward, and the processes of inner meditation evolved into *yajña*, where elaborate Vedic rituals and fire sacrifices were enacted externally. Even so, the *yajñas* were still confidential and esoteric, confined to meticulously constructed and circumscribed firepits, and were to be performed solely by highly qualified *brāhmaṇas*.

Consequently, in the next age, Dvāpara-yuga, Krishna minimized the importance of *yajña* (for instance by his exploits in Govardhana-līlā), and by dint of his sheer beauty, both through his form and his divine pastimes (*līlā*), forced the entire process still further outward. Thus, in remembrance of Krishna's unparalleled beauty, the impetus for creating iconic forms was born, and temple worship became the norm. This will be the emphasis of the book you now hold in your hands.

But in the final age, Kali-yuga, Mahāprabhu took it to its ultimate limit, crashing out of the temples altogether, taking it to the streets by establishing Nāgara-saṅkīrtana—congregational chanting—as the yuga-dharma for the modern age. This process is considered the topmost expression of the soul and is easily available to us in the current epoch of world history.

CONCLUSION

The multicolored incarnations who manifest as the yuga *avatāras* can be seen in various ways, invoking various layers of meaning. Indeed, early in the *Bhāgavatam*'s Tenth Canto (10.3.20), we see an allusion to the yuga *avatāras* with a reference, instead, to the three modes of material nature, goodness, passion, and ignorance: "My Lord, Your form is transcendental to the three material modes, yet for the maintenance of the three worlds, You assume the white color of Vishnu in goodness; for creation, which is surrounded by the quality of passion, You appear reddish; and at the end, when there is a need for annihilation, which is surrounded by ignorance, You appear blackish." Prabhupāda elaborates, following the Vaishnava commentator, Viśvanātha Chakravartī:

> Vasudeva prayed to the Lord, "You are called *śuklam*. *Śuklam*, or 'whiteness,' is the symbolic representation of the Absolute Truth because it is unaffected by the material qualities. Lord Brahmā is called *rakta*, or red, because Brahmā represents the qualities of passion for creation. Darkness is entrusted to Lord Śiva because he annihilates the cosmos. The creation, annihilation and maintenance of this cosmic manifestation are conducted by Your potencies, yet You are always unaffected by those qualities." As confirmed in the Vedas, *harir hi nirguṇaḥ sākṣāt*: the Supreme Personality of Godhead is always free from all material qualities. It is also said that the qualities of passion and ignorance are

> nonexistent in the person of the Supreme Lord. . . . In this verse, the three colors mentioned—*śukla, rakta* and *Krishna*—are not to be understood literally, in terms of what we experience with our senses, but rather as representatives of Sattva-guṇa [goodness], Rajo-guṇa [passion] and Tamo-guṇa [ignorance].[5]

In other words, the colors usually associated with the yuga *avatāras* are here used symbolically, as representing not only the three modes of material nature but also the Guṇa-avatāras, Brahmā, Vishnu, and Śiva.

Nonetheless, the yuga *avatāras* constitute one tattva, or truth. They may exist in many colors, but they are all manifestations of one supreme godhead. This can be understood more clearly by thinking in terms of race and bodily color as presented in the material world, which, perhaps coincidentally—and perhaps not, since the Lord is the source of all that is—also manifest as white, red, black, and yellow. This division by color, calling ourselves the white race, black race, red race, and yellow race is superficial. Science has now proven we are not four races but one. Our single race transcends ethnicity, culture, geographical origin, and, yes, skin color: we all partake of a single phenotype, even to the point of having similar observable anatomical features and behavior.

There is a similar truth in terms of the yuga *avatāra*. Though he exhibits variation in color, form, and purpose, Krishna is always Krishna, God is always God, even if he manifests variously. This is part of his inconceivable nature. His hundreds of millions of forms are, paradoxically, one and yet different. As he says in the *Bhagavad-gītā* (11.5): "My dear Arjuna, O son of Pṛtha, behold now My opulences, hundreds of thousands of varied divine forms, multi-colored (*nānā-varṇākṛtīni*) like the sea." Indeed, the many colors of the yuga *avatāras* only serve to highlight the ultimate truth of unity in diversity, as propounded by Śrī Chaitanya Mahāprabhu.

NOTES

1. "Incarnation" comes from the Latin *incarnationem* (nominative, *incarnatio*), which is literally the "act of being made flesh." The true *avatāra*, however, specifically descends in his spiritual body, not taking on a fleshy tabernacle at all.

2. See *Śrī Laghu Bhāgavatāmṛta of Śrīla Rūpa Gosvami,* trans and comm., Gopīparāṇadhana Dāsa (Mathura, UP: Giriraja Publishing, 2016), 11–12.

3. Prabhupada, lecture on the *Caitanya-caritamrta* Madhya-lila 20.330–35, New York, December 23, 1966.

4. Prabhupada, lecture on *Bhagavad-gita* 3.16–17, New York, May 25, 1966.

5. See *Srimad-Bhagavatam* 10.1 to 10.13, translations and purports (https://vaniquotes.org/wiki/Vasudeva_prayed_to_the_Lord_-_You_are_called_suklam._Suklam,_or_%27whiteness,%27_is_the_symbolic_representation_of_the_Absolute_Truth_because_it_is_unaffected_by_the_material_qualities).

Chapter Two

Ten From Infinity

The Daśāvatāra Story

Ten From Infinity, by author Paul W. Fairman, is the name of a sci-fi classic from the mid-1960s. It is the story of ten identical androids from outer space who come to earth on a reconnaissance mission. Their ultimate goal: to take over our planet.[1] The narrative is engaging enough, but the inclusion of the word "infinity" in the title always disturbed me. Outer space is vast, to be sure, but infinite? Well, perhaps.

As I began to study the literature and philosophy of India, I came upon another "Ten From Infinity," but this time the name seemed more appropriate. It refers to ten manifestations of God, and as such, by definition, refers to something truly infinite. Although there are unlimited manifestations of the divine, as will be explained below, the ancient Vaishnava tradition of India singles out ten as representative of the rest, and they have been given the Sanskrit title Daśāvatāra.

The prefix *daśa* means "ten," and *avatāra* means "descent," from the Sanskrit *ava* ("down") and *tarati* ("[he] crosses over"). This idea of God's descent into our realm should be properly understood. There is a pervasive notion that He "incarnates," but this is inaccurate. The word "incarnation," which, in relation to God, might be used for convenience, comes from the Latin *incarnationem*—it is the "act of being made flesh." The *avatāra*, however, is never embodied in the material sense. Rather, the tradition teaches that he descends in a totally spiritual form—visible, yes, but never made of matter. His body is composed of eternity, knowledge, and bliss (*sat-cit-ānanda*), and while it appears as if his various forms can be measured in terms of three dimensions, they are in fact infinite.

What inspires God to come down from his kingdom and to appear in our world in this particular way? The *Bhagavad-gītā* (4.7) tells us that, "Whenever and wherever there is a decline in religious practice, O descendant of Bharata, and a predominant rise of irreligion—at that time I descend

Myself."[2] Thus, throughout history, God has interacted with the world of matter, sometimes by coming as his *avatāra* and other times through the manifestation of his pure representative, or the spiritual teacher—even if he is *always* in our world, at least in a metaphysical sense. Indeed, the *Bhāgavata Purāṇa* (1.3.26), which contains the essence of ancient India's wisdom tradition, tells us that, "the incarnations of the Lord are innumerable, like rivulets flowing from inexhaustible sources of water."[3]

WHO ARE THEY?

Though there exist various versions of exactly which incarnations will appear on a given Daśāvatāra list, usually reflecting the particular lineage with which the list's compiler is aligned (see below), the following is a summary of the more prominent incarnations usually included in the Daśāvatāra schema. It should be noted that the *Purāṇas* offer detailed narratives for each of these *avatāras*, but below we find only the gist of their pastimes on earth. In general, these *avatāras* serve a function in the material world: restoring stability, doing away with demoniac elements, and pleasing the devotees. While their narratives include otherworldly beings and supernatural elements, challenging the nonbeliever to stretch the boundaries of possibility, it should be remembered that the stories depict divine entities and as such need not conform to ordinary standards of reality.

The initial four on any given Daśāvatāra list are always the same, and they appear in Satya-yuga, the first of the four cosmic age cycles. Thus, their appearance in our world occurred millions of years ago. In consecutive order, they are: Matsya, the fish, who rescued both Vaivasvata Manu (King Satyabrata, one of Brahmā's sons, the progenitors of mankind), and the *Vedas* from a devastating deluge; Kūrma, the tortoise, whose shell served as a pivot for Mandarachala Hill, which was being used as a churning rod by both theists and atheists throughout the universe so that they might attain a special nectar giving them immortality; Varāha, the boar, lifted the earth from the darkest regions of the netherworld on His tusks, thus correcting the misdeed of powerful demons, such as Hiraṇyākṣa, who hid it there; and Nṛsiṁhadeva, half-man and half-lion, used his ambiguous form, which was neither fully human nor fully beast, to defeat Hiraṇyakaśipu, the demonic brother of Hiraṇyākṣa, and to bring pleasure to His great devotee, Prahlāda.

The next three of the ten incarnations appeared in Treta Yuga, which follows immediately after Satya, millennia ago: Vāmana, the dwarf, retrieved the earth, which had been taken over by the misguided King Bali. Appearing before the king as a diminutive Brahmin, Vāmana asked him for only as much land as could be contained in three strides. Bali acquiesced, but then witnessed Vāmana assume an incalculably large cosmic form as Vishnu, thus engulfing the entire universe and Bali himself within the three allotted steps. Next is Paraśurāma, the bearer of the axe, who purged the earth of demoniac kings for twenty-one generations. And then there is Rāma, the prince of Ayodhyā. He defeated the evil Rāvaṇa, who had kidnapped Rāma's wife Sītā, and established Rāma-rājya, a reign of virtue and piety. These three are also on all major Daśāvatāra lists.

The eighth incarnation, Krishna, is arguably most beloved of all, particularly for Gauḍīyas, and is unique among the Daśāvatāras as the only one to have appeared in the Dvāpara-yuga. (However, Balarāma, His brother and immediate expansion, sometimes replaces Him in Daśāvatāra lists, and he, too, appeared in Dvāpara-yuga.)

Briefly, Krishna's appearance on earth involved playful childhood pastimes in the village of Braj, including stealing butter from the milkmaids, dancing with the cowherd women (*gopīs*), and battling with oppressive demons; he also governed a magnificent city in Dvārakā, from which he ventured off to assist the Pāṇḍava brothers in the battle of Kurukṣetra. It was while on that battlefield that he spoke the famous *Bhagavad-gītā*.

Sometimes, the Buddha is listed as the ninth incarnation.[4] The *Bhāgavata Purāṇa* (1.3.24), first compiled in antiquity, predicts: "Then, in the district of Bihar during the early part of Kali-yuga, the Lord will incarnate as Buddha, the son of Añjana, with the purpose of creating an illusion for the enemies of the faithful." What illusion will He create? The prediction continues: He will decry the Vedas, for, at that point in history (which came to pass some 2,500 years ago), unscrupulous Brahmins will misinterpret Vedic texts, using them to justify the slaughter of animals. Buddha will serve to redirect them away from the texts, creating the illusion that the Vedas and their teachings are antiquated. As Jayadeva indicates in his famous *Daśāvatāra Stotram*, long after the Buddha appeared in our world: The concealed mission of the Buddha was to save people from ignorantly killing animals in the name of Vedic sacrifices, and to this end he was to be counted among the *avatāras* of Vishnu.

The tenth avatar, Kalki, is scheduled to arrive on earth in 427,000 years, as Kali-yuga comes to a close. It is said that he will ride a white horse and carry a flaming sword meant to destroy the wicked. The entire world, at this time, will have debilitated into evil, and his task will be to restart a new creation, to restore the purity of a once righteous civilization. In the end, he will begin a new cycle—the end of Kali and the start of a renewed Satya-yuga.

Thus, most versions of Daśāvatāra agree on the first seven *avatāras* in the list of ten: Matsya, Kūrma, Varāha, Nṛsiṁha, Vāmana, Paraśurāma, and Rāma. They also generally agree that the tenth incarnation is Kalki. But the eighth and ninth *avatāras* will vary, as we will see below.

VARIATIONS ON A THEME

In terms of literature attributable to specific authors (as opposed to scriptures), the Tamil poet Periyāḻvār (c. eighth–ninth century CE) composed what is perhaps the earliest Daśāvatāra list.[5] Next comes Kṣemendra (c.990–c.1070 CE), a Kashmirian poet who is also counted among the first formulators of the Daśāvatāra theme. Kṣemendra composed his *Daśāvatāra Carita* in 1066 CE, and, unlike Periyāḻvār, he includes Buddha in his list.

In fact, when we start to compare early lists of the ten incarnations, we find that there are several significant variants. That being said, these can be narrowed down to three:

> Jayadeva's version (circa 1200 CE), which is accepted as authoritative by Gauḍīyas and other North Indian lineages, is as follows: Matsya, Kūrma, Varāha, Nṛsiṁha, Vāmana, Paraśurāma, Dāśarathi Rāma, Balarāma, Buddha, Kalki.[6]
>
> The *Daśāvatāra Stotram* of Vedānta Deśika (1269–1370), who is aligned with the Śrī Sampradāya, comes only slightly later: Matsya, Kūrma, Varāha, Nṛsiṁha, Vāmana, Paraśurāma, Dāśarathi Rāma, Balarāma, Krishna, and Kalki.
>
> Finally, Vadirāja Tīrtha (1480–1600) of the Mādhva Sampradāya offers this variant in his comparatively late *Daśāvatāra Stuti*: Matsya, Kūrma, Varāha, Nṛsiṁha, Vāmana, Paraśurāma, Dāśarathi Rāma, Krishna, Buddha, Kalki.

What do the variations in these lists tell us? First of all, the Śrī Sampradāya and the Mādhva Sampradāya tend to include Krishna in their lists, for they view Him as (merely) an *avatāra*, albeit a particularly complete one (*purṇāvatāra*), on a par with Vishnu,[7] and they see Nārāyaṇa (Vishnu) as the source of all incarnations—the Supreme Being who does not descend to our realm as an *avatāra* but instead stays in His supernal Vaikuṇṭha, the kingdom of God.

Conversely, Jayadeva, basing his version on the all-important *Bhāgavata Purāṇa* (1.3.28), sees Krishna as the source, and thus doesn't include him among the ten incarnations (for he is not merely an incarnation). In fact, Jayadeva suggests this truth at the end of his *Daśāvatāra Stotram* with a verse that parallels the one in the *Bhāgavata*: he tells us that Krishna is the source of the divinities just enumerated—that he is the original personality of Godhead, and that it is he who has assumed the ten divine forms.[8]

Additionally, in the Twelfth Canto of the *Gīta Govinda* (the larger work of which Jayadeva's *Daśāvatāra Stotram* is one small part), just before the Divine Couple's most erotic and humanlike pastimes of love, Jayadeva uses the name "Nārāyaṇa" in the refrain, indicating once again that Krishna is none other than God Himself, commonly known as Nārāyaṇa or Vishnu (12.2–9). It is with this as a backdrop that one can enter into the mysteries of the *Gīta Govinda*—and that of the *Daśāvatāra Stotram* as well.[9]

Other well-known variations include those found in Maharashtra and just a little further south, in Goa. There, the local manifestation of Krishna, known variously as Panduranga, Vitthala or Vithoba, occupies Buddha's place as the ninth incarnation in Daśāvatāra literature, visual representations, and temple recitations; and, in Orissa, where Krishna is worshipped in the form of Jagannāth, we find that the latter is in the ninth position.

As an addendum—and as an indication of just how diverse the Daśāvatāra lists can become—mention should be made of the Ismaili Khojas of East Africa, an Islamic community with Hindu ancestry. The Khojas cling to various teachings and customs of their forefathers, the most pertinent of which is a custom involving the recitation of a thirteenth-century text called *Das-Avatar*, written by Pir Sadardin (or, according to some, Pir Shams-al-Din). His Daśāvatāra list runs as follows:

1. Matsya
2. Kūrma
3. Varāha
4. Nṛsiṁha
5. Vāmana
6. Paraśurāma
7. Rāma
8. Krishna
9. Buddha
10. Ali

Interestingly, Kalki is replaced by the cousin and son-in-law of the Islamic prophet Muhammad, who ruled over the Muslim Caliphate from 656 to 661. According to some believers in this tradition, Ali was in fact Kalki Himself.[10]

ORIGINS OF DAŚĀVATĀRA

Despite God's limitless number of manifestations, a legitimate question arises in relation to Daśāvatāra: Just when, historically, did the ten major incarnations start to be classified together as a group? The answer is not so simple, though there are some noteworthy facts, and many scholars opine that it happened some time from the sixth to the eighth century. In *Vishnu: Hinduism's Dark-Skinned Savior*, Joan Cummins writes,

> The *Vishnu Purana*, of about the sixth to eighth century, offers a standard list of ten: Matsya the fish, Kurma the tortoise, Varaha the boar, Narasimha the man-lion, Vamana the dwarf, Parashurama the Brahmin, Rama the prince, Krishna the cowherd prince, the Buddha, and Kalki the avatar of the future. In other texts, the list varies because Krishna is often left off (being treated as Supreme God, more than an *avatar*) and is replaced by his brother Balarama, or Balarama replaces the Buddha. The *Bhagavata Purana* lists twenty-two *avatars*, all of them envisioned as manifestations of Krishna.[11]

Indeed, there is a certain fluidity in terms of the number of *avatāras* listed in India's sacred literature, with various texts calling upon particular incarnations for specific purposes. Still, the list of ten is hard to trace, and is quoted in scriptures such as the *Garuḍa Purāṇa* (1.86.10–11), the *Vishnu Purāṇa* (1.4.7), the *Mahābhārata* (*Śanti-parvan* 339, 103ff., Bombay Edition),[12] and the *Harivaṁśa* (Chapter 41), texts which, according to scholars, can be dated to the first centuries of the Common Era, or perhaps later.[13]

There is also early evidence for the Daśāvatāra theme in caves, temples, sculptures, and inscriptions throughout the subcontinent, some dating back to the fifth or sixth century. The Daśāvatāra Temple in Deogarh (Lalitpur District, Uttar Pradesh), for example, beautifully displays classic sixth-century Gupta architecture and stands as one of the world's most famous monuments to the ten incarnations. When Captain Charles Strahan first discovered the structure, it was simply known as "the Vishnu temple," but after some time renowned archaeologist Alexander Cunningham renamed it the "Dashavatara Mandir."[14] This was because of its most prominent sculptural theme: the ten incarnations of Vishnu.

In Mahabalipuram, South India, too, there is a Pallava inscription dated to about the late seventh century CE that enumerates the Daśāvatāra, and such indications of early Daśāvatāra representations exist throughout the length and breadth of India. "Among epigraphic artifacts illustrating the Daśāvatāra," writes researcher Ayush Goyal, "a prominent example is a stone inscription in Ajmer (Rajasthan) commissioned by the Chauhan king Vigraharaja between the 12th-13th century."[15]

In Maharashtra, we find the Daśāvatāra Cave of Ellora. Originally a Buddhist monastery, it was converted into a Hindu ashram in the eighth century. The open court includes a two-storied hall that is covered with reliefs depicting Vaishnava themes, including elements of the Daśāvatāra. Many other temples, sculptures, carvings and inscriptions could be mentioned as well, but Ayush Goyal has thoroughly documented these in his excellent article, "The *Dasavatara-Stotra* of Sri Jayadeva's *Gita-Govinda*: A Vaishnava Perspective,"[16] and so there is no reason to reiterate that information here.

Particularly significant, however, is the temple art and other artifacts found in the Upper Mahanadi Valley of Orissa. This is because the area is inextricably connected to Jayadeva (circa twelfth century), whose composition on the ten incarnations is arguably the most famous of all renditions. Consequently, in Orissa we find an elaborate display of Daśāvatāra visuals ranging from the eighth century to the seventeenth century and beyond. Similarly, Daśāvatāra sculptures have been identified in early temples of western Orissa and Chhatisgarh as well as in those of Gandharadi (Boudh District) and elsewhere.

DAŚĀVATĀRA AND EVOLUTIONARY THEORY

A surprising if much documented aspect of Daśāvatāra lore is its connection with evolutionary theory. For those who don't know, biological evolution is the slow process of change that is said to occur in living organisms, adapting to new environments over billions of years. Evolutionists claim that we all arise from a single common ancestor, and like the branches of a tree, species separate from each other over time—even if growing from the same tree.

Interestingly, Charles Darwin (1809–1882), the first major proponent of this theory, was foreshadowed by the Purāṇas of ancient India, which, though few know it, had already proffered a teaching of evolution. But rather than claiming that one species evolves into the next, the Purāṇas tell us that all species were created simultaneously, and that each eternal living being evolves through the various species until it reaches perfection. In other words, the original theory involved an evolution in consciousness, not physical forms.

Explaining this Puranic point of view, Swami Prabhupāda writes as follows:

> It is confirmed in *Padma Purana* that the species of life evolved from aquatics to plants, vegetables, trees; thereafter insects, reptiles, flies, birds, then beasts, and then human kind. This is the gradual process of evolution of species of life. . . . But we do not accept Darwin's theory. According to Darwin's theory, homo sapiens came later on, but we see that the most intelligent personality, Brahma, is born first. So according to Vedic knowledge, Darwin or similar mental speculators are rejected so far as the facts are concerned.[17]

Prabhupāda's point is augmented by his disciple Richard L. Thompson (1947–2008), who received a PhD in mathematics from Cornell University:

> The Hindu text known as the *Padma Purana* provides an example of the idea of evolving consciousness. This traditional texts posits a gradual evolution of souls by transmigration through 8,400,000 different forms of life. This process is generally progressive, although reversals are admitted. Remarkably, the

> evolutionary succession is given as aquatics, plants, insects and reptiles, birds, beasts, and human beings. . . . This parallels the paleontological succession of marine life, terrestrial plants, insects and amphibians, reptiles, birds, advanced mammals, and finally humans. The parallelism is so close that the modern Vaishnava teacher Bhakivedanta Swami Prabhupada saw the *Padma Purana* as anticipating Darwin's theory of evolution.[18]

How does all of this relate to Daśāvatāra? Evolutionary theory, when viewed from a certain perspective, neatly intersects with the ten incarnations. Man's origins in the waters is evoked by the pisciform nature of Matsya. Then come the tortoise and the boar, taking us from amphibians to land animals. This is followed by a therianthropic form (Nṛsiṁha), and then homo sapiens proper, and so on.[19] Eventually we arrive at humans endowed with wealth, values, and spiritual knowledge. In fact, numerous Hindu teachers—and some from the West as well—have noted the correlation.

C. Mackenzie Brown, Professor of Religion at Trinity University, Texas, for instance, writes prodigiously about "avataric evolutionism"—the idea that Vishnu's ten incarnations anticipated Darwinian evolution. According to Brown, "the late nineteenth-century origins of the theory [are to be found] in the works of Keshub Chunder Sen and Madame Blavatsky." He also cites Narayana Bhavanrao Pavgee, known as one of the "Vedic fathers of geology," and Aurobindo Ghose, Indian nationalist turned philosopher, as early proponents of the idea.[20]

In Vaishnava circles, Bhaktivinoda Ṭhākura (1838–1914), the Bengali reformer and devotional exemplar of the Gaudiya tradition (who was in fact one of Keshub Chunder Sen's schoolmates) was the first to align *avatāras* with evolution, as can be seen in his book *Śrī Krishna-saṁhitā* (chapter 3, verses 1–11).[21] Bhaktivinoda's thoughts on the subject were elucidated by his son and successor Bhaktisiddhānta Sarasvatī Ṭhākura (1874–1937) as follows:

> We can notice the different stages of animal life from the invertebrates to the fully-grown human beings. These stages have been classified by the Indian sages of a scientific outlook in ten orders, viz, (1) the invertebrate, (2) testaceous or shelly, (3) vertebrate, (4) erectly vertebrate (as in the combined form of man and beast), (5) mannikin, (6) barbaric, (7) civilised, (8) wise, (9) ultra-wise and (10) destructive. These are the historical stages of *jivas* [souls]. According to the gradation of these stages as indications of evolution of the serving mood of the *jiva* soul, there are manifested the ten Incarnations of God, viz., Matsya (fish), Kurma (Turtle), Varaha (Boar), Nrishmha (Man-Lion), Vamana (Dwarf), Parasu-rama, Rama, Krishna, Buddha and Kalki, as worshippable Deities with eternal transcendental Names, Forms, Attributes and Sports.[22]

A modern extension of this theme was presented by controversial guru Sathya Sai Baba (1926–2011), who envisioned it as the evolution of the soul through a single life:

> See, when the child is in the womb as the embryo, it is like a fish swimming in the fluid (Matsya). Then, the fluid slowly dries up and the embryo moves to the tortoise stage (Koorma). Slowly, it takes the shape of a boar which is Varaha. When the delivery takes place, the little human comes out. That is Vamana. Like Vamana, you too must grow such that you cover the entire three worlds. Then alone will human life find its meaning and purpose."[23]

To be clear, the Vaishnavas do not accept evolutionary theory as it is commonly understood. They agree that initially the earth was covered with water, and that then gradually with the emergence of land new species manifest themselves. But the species are not "created" at that time, even if the bodies gradually arise according to necessity. As Prabhupāda says, "The species already exist, and the living entity simply transfers himself from one womb to the next, just as a man transfers himself from one apartment to another. Suppose a person comes from a lower-class apartment to a first-class apartment. The person is the same, but now, according to his capacity for payment—according to his karma [action/reaction schema]—he is able to occupy a higher-class apartment. Evolution does not mean physical development, but development of consciousness."[24]

In other words, the species are created to *accommodate* different levels of consciousness. Living beings are placed in appropriate bodies according to their awareness level and evolve upward or downward according to their activities and mental disposition. That is to say, the species are static, but the evolution or devolution of consciousness is dynamic. The reason for the 8,400,000 forms of life is to accommodate all the possible forms of consciousness that develop in the course of *saṁsāra* or repeated birth and death.

Thus, the teachings of Vaishnavism, even though sometimes framed in terms of evolutionary discourse, as seen above, is distinct from the modern scientific perspective, stressing evolution of consciousness and not the emergence of bodies or species arising from each other. Instead, Vaishnavism teaches that each living being transmigrates through the species according to an inner development (or regression) of consciousness, not through a biophysical evolution. The Lord, in his compassion, then incarnates in these species as well, just to sanctify all life-forms for the purpose of spiritual elevation—this is the esoteric meaning of Daśāvatāra in a nutshell.

CONCLUSION

One might ask, "Why did all of these manifestations of God appear so long ago? True, there is Buddha, who appeared earlier in this age, and Kalki, who is yet to come, but the vast majority seem to only manifest in the distant past, thousands if not millions of years ago. Why are there no *avatāras* today?"

According to the tradition, it is difficult to understand the qualifications of an *avatāra* and to locate such a being at any given point in time; one desiring to do so requires vast scriptural learning and the spiritual insight that comes from studying under a bona fide spiritual master. In fact, the scriptures and gurus of the Vaishnava tradition have enumerated other incarnations who are more recent, the most significant of which is Śrī Chaitanya Mahāprabhu (1486–1533), who is known as "the master of the holy name."

Interestingly, one of Śrī Chaitanya's primary teachings is that in this age of Kali, Krishna mercifully descends in the sound of his own name, and that this, indeed, is the *avatāra* of our age. This is confirmed in the *Caitanya-caritāmṛta* (1.17.22). In the same text (3.20.16), we also learn that the combined power of all God's many potencies can be found within the name, because Krishna and his names are non-different. One need simply chant with proper consciousness, under the direction of an accomplished master. This is a special benediction for our very difficult age.

Along these lines, the *Bhāgavata Purāṇa* (12.3.51) tells us: "My dear King, although Kali-yuga is full of faults, there is still one good quality about this age. It is that simply by chanting the holy name of Krishna, one can become free from material bondage and be promoted to the transcendental kingdom."

The mystery of God's descent has baffled theologians and practitioners for centuries—whether he appears in the form of exotic, otherworldly beings or in a simple sound vibration. And yet who can deny that this very mystery is among the many characteristics that qualify him as God? Could God, when all is said and done, be anything other than the ultimate mystery? Ravīndra Svarūpa Dāsa, a leading theologian in the modern Gauḍīya Vaishnava tradition, sums up:

> So we encounter God in many forms. He descends, for example, as Matsya, the leviathan who saved the Vedas from the deluge even as He sported in the vast waters; as Varāha, the boar who lifted the fallen earth from the abyss and vanquished her violator in single combat; as the sage Nārada, the eternally wandering space traveler who migrates from planet to planet throughout the universe preaching and singing the glories of the Lord; as Nṛsiṁha, the prodigious man-lion who in an awesome epiphany of power succored His devotee, a boy of six, by slaying—spectacularly—his torturer, a God-hating interplanetary tyrant who was the boy's own father; as Vāmana, the beautiful dwarf who

> traversed the whole universe in three strides; as Paraśurāma, the axe-wielding scourge of kings who punished twenty-one generations of royalty for deviating from the principles of godly rule; as Lord Rāmacandra, the exemplar of godly rule, perfect king and personification of morality in office; and as many other awesome and unforgettable personalities who appeared to teach, shelter, lead, and inspire humanity. . . . All this may be so amazing it commands incredulity. Yet consider: Isn't God, by definition, the most amazing being of all? If so, our principle should be: the more amazing the report, the more open we should be to it. Why demand that God reduce Himself to fit the range of our pedestrian understanding? The more amazing He is, the more Godlike He is.[25]

Let us end with that thought, with the recognition of God's amazing, inconceivable nature. Indeed, if we say that he can't descend in the form of a fish, a boar, a man-lion, and so on, aren't we limiting the unlimited? Wouldn't it behoove us to admit that he can do whatever he likes, as Ravīndra Svarūpa writes, "by definition"? If nothing else, this is one of the major teachings of the Daśāvatāra narratives. And why should we assume that God can be contained within the parameters of what we consider rational? After all, we are finite, whereas the Daśāvatāra are ten from infinity.

NOTES

1. See Paul W. Fairman (Ivar Jorgensen), *Ten From Infinity* (New York: Monarch Books, 1963).

2. See the translation and commentary of His Divine Grace A. C. Bhaktivedanta Swami Prabhupada, *Bhagavad-gītā As It Is* (Los Angeles, Bhaktivedanta Book Trust, 1984, reprint). In his *Essays on the Gita*, published in 1922, Sri Aurobindo Ghose (1872–1950) comments on *Gita* 4.6–8, and in so doing hints at Daśāvatāra's evolutionary dimension (as discussed later in this article): "In some such spirit some would interpret the ten incarnations of Vishnu, first in animal forms, then in the animal man, then in the dwarf man-soul, Vamana, the violent Asuric man, Rama of the axe, the divinely-natured man, a greater Rama, the awakened spiritual man, Buddha, and preceding him in time, but in final place, the complete divine manhood, Krishna."

Elsewhere, Aurobindo writes more accurately, "First the Fish Avatar, then the amphibious animal between land and water, then the land animal, then the Man-Lion Avatar, bridging man and animal, then man as dwarf, small and undeveloped and physical but containing in himself the godhead and taking possession of existence. . . . Krishna, Buddha and Kalki depict the last three stages, the stages of spiritual development." (See Aurobindo's "The Purpose of Avatarhood." In Sri Aurobindo, *Letters on Yoga* [vol. 22 of the Sri Aurobindo Birth Centenary Library], part 1, section 7, 401–30. Pondicherry: Sri Aurobindo Ashram, 1971, reprint.) The entire subject of Aurobindo's musings on "Avataric Evolutionism" has been thoroughly researched by Professor C. Mackenzie Brown. See endnote 19.

3. See the translation and commentary of His Divine Grace A. C. Bhaktivedanta Swami Prabhupāda, *Śrīmad Bhāgavatam*, Canto One (Los Angeles, Bhaktivedanta Book Trust, 1972).

There are three incarnations of the Divine that are often considered most important, above and beyond this list of ten incarnations. In the order in which they appeared in the material world, they are Nṛsiṁha, Rāma, and Krishna. Confidential wisdom texts of India describe them as Parāvastha Avatāras, or "perfect" incarnations. Normally, all of God's incarnations are considered equal, as just various forms of one divine being, and yet, according to the *Padma Purāṇa* (Uttara 226.42), the three mentioned here are singled out as most important, as embodying the ultimate and most complete form of divinity.

For the Gauḍīya Vaishnava tradition, this is confirmed in Rūpa Goswāmī's *Śrī Laghu-bhāgavatāmṛta* (1.5.16–64), where he echoes the *Padma Purāṇa* and adds that Krishna, in particular, is *avatārī*, or the source of all incarnations (*Laghu-bhāgavatāmṛta*, 1.5.303–7). For more on these three *avatāras*, see Steven J. Rosen, "The Reincarnation(s) of Jaya and Vijaya: A Journey through the Yugas" in *Religions* 8, no. 9: 178 (2017). https://doi.org/10.3390/rel8090178.

4. For more on the Buddha as an *avatāra* of Vishnu, see Bradley S. Clough, "Buddha as Avatāra in Vaiṣṇava Theology: Historical and Interpretive Issues" in *Journal of Vaishnava Studies* 26 no. 1 (Fall 2017), 161–88. See also Vasudha Narayanan, "A Note on the Buddha and Buddhism from a Vaiṣṇava Perspective" in *Journal of Vaishnava Studies*28, no. 1 (Fall 2019), 183–96.

5. From a personal communication (February 14, 2014) with Vasudha Narayanan, Distinguished Professor, Department of Religion, at the University of Florida. She also notes that, "Periyalvar's rendition of Dashavatara, seen in most temples throughout Tamilnadu, is Matsya, Kurma, Varaha, Narasimha, Vamana, Parasurama, Rama, Balarama (he conflates the last three and just calls them the 'three Ramas'), Krishna, and Kalki."

6. In the sixteenth century, Rūpa Gosvāmī, the great patriarch of the Gauḍīya Sampradāya, offers a list similar to Jayadeva's in the final verses of his composition, the *Śrī Haṁsadūta* (verses 128–37). He refers to this list again in his later work, the *Vidagdha-mādhava* (4.54).

7. According to Śrī Vaishnava authority Dr. Mudumby Narasimhachary, who taught Rāmānujite Vaishnavism at the University of Madras and was affiliated with Oxford Centre for Vaishnava and Hindu Studies, "The Śrīvaiṣṇava system, perpetuated by the mystic saints, āḻvārs and *ācāryas,* accepts Śrī Kṛṣṇa as the most affable and perfect incarnation of Viṣṇu. He is the *purṇāvatāra*." See http://content.iskcon.org/icj/8_2/narasim.html (Accessed February 22, 2014). Of course, not all Śrī Vaishnava would agree with this premise, arguing instead that all forms of Vishnu are equal in terms of being various manifestations of the one Supreme Godhead.

8. See *Gīta Govinda* 1.15, 16: "I offer obeisance to Krishna, from whom the ten incarnations emerge" (*daśākṛti-kṛte kṛṣṇāya tubhyam namaḥ*).

9. In the teachings of Vaishnavism, it is considered inconsequential that some devotees view Vishnu as the source of all incarnations while others see Krishna as the source. Those emphasizing the *Vishnu Purāṇa* will likely embrace the former,

and those who emphasize the *Bhāgavata Purāṇa* will tend to embrace the latter. In the end, both groups take solace in a higher synthesis wherein Vishnu and Krishna are ultimately one. For more, see Freda Matchett, *Kṛṣṇa: Lord or Avatāra?—The Relationship Between Krishna and Vishnu* (Richmond, Surrey: Curzon Press, 2001), 200–1.

10. Under "Ismailis," the *Encyclopedia of Islam* says: "While idol worshipping is condemned, Hindu mythology is accepted. Ali is described as the Tenth Avatar or incarnation of the deity, and the *imams* are identical with him. The *Qur'an* is considered the last of the *Vedas*, which are viewed as holy scriptures whose true interpretation is known to the pirs. The religious role of the pir or guru is extolled. Acceptance of the true religion will free the believer from further rebirths and open Paradise for him, which is described in Islamic terms, while those failing to recognize the imams must pass through another cycle of rebirths." See http://www.mostmerciful.com/book-6.htm (Accessed February 21, 2014).

11. Joan Cummins, ed., *Vishnu: Hinduism's Blue-Skinned Savior* (Ahmedabad, India, Mapin Publishing, in association with Frist Center for the Visual Arts, 2011), p. 115. Actually, the *Bhāgavata Purāṇa* (1.3) lists twenty-five *avatāras*.

12. Some scholars argue that the Daśāvatāra list in the *Mahābhārata* is a later addition. For more on this, see the Critical edition, *Śanti-parva* 326, footnote to verse 71.

13. The tradition itself, of course, would push the date of these texts back further, to approximately five thousand years ago, when the current age, Kali-yuga, began. But academics tend to date this literature much later, based on linguistic style and internal (if debatable) evidence.

14. See http://hinduphilosophyholypilgrimage.blogspot.com/2013/01/holy-pilgrimage-temples-in-madhya.html (Accessed February 22, 2014).

15. Ayush Goyal, "The *Dasavatara-Stotra* of Sri Jayadeva's *Gita-Govinda*: A Vaishnava Perspective," *Journal of Vaishnava Studies* 22, no. 1 (fall 2013): 55–68.

16. Ibid.

17. The specific quote found here is from Swami Prabhupāda's letter to his disciple Hayagrīva Dāsa (Los Angeles, March 9, 1970), available at http://krishna.org/we-accept-evolution-but-not-darwins-theory/ (Accessed February 20, 2014).

18. See Richard L. Thompson, *Maya: The World as Virtual Reality* (Alachua, FL: Govardhan Hill Publishing, 2003), 254.

19. Although Daśāvatāra is sometimes presented in terms of evolution, the Purāṇas inform us that, at the dawn of cosmic creation, the fish incarnation was not alone, but rather he was accompanied by humans, plants, animals, sages, the *Vedas*, and so on, making this theory incompatible with the understanding of evolution as we know it today.

20. See C. Mackenzie Brown, "The Western Roots of Avataric Evolutionism in Colonial India." *Zygon* 42, no. 2 (June 2007): 423–47. Also see C. Mackenzie Brown, "Colonial and Post-Colonial Elaborations of Avataric Evolutionism." *Zygon* 42, no. 2 (September 2007): 715–47.

21. See Bhaktivinoda Ṭhākura, *Śrī Krishna-saṁhitā*, trans., Bhumipati Dasa (New Delhi: Vrajraj Press, 1998), 87–89. The book was originally published in 1880, making Bhaktivinoda's articulation of the theory contemporaneous with that of the

Theosophists and Keshub Cunder Sen, often seen as its originators. Others associate the idea with the famous scientist J. B. S. Haldane (1892–1964), but he would have expressed his notions about the subject a little later than the others, and, besides, as of the writing of this article I could not find any substantial evidence indicating that he wrote about it at all.

22. This expression of Daśāvatāra in relation to evolution comes from a conversation between Bhaktisiddhānta Sarasvatī Ṭhākura and Albert E. Suthers (1887–1984), the latter being affiliated with the history of religions department at Ohio Wesleyan University. Their discussion originally appeared in the January 1929 issue of *The Harmonist* (*Sree Sajjanatoshani*). See Rupa Vilasa Dasa, *A Ray of Vishnu* (Washington, MS: New Jaipur Press, 1988), 99.

23. See http://aravindb1982.hubpages.com/hub/Theory-for-Evolution-by-Sathya-Sai-Baba (accessed February 20, 2014).

24. See "Srila Prabhupada on Darwinian Evolution." http://iskcontimes.com/srila-prabhupada-on-darwinian-evolution (accessed February 22, 2014).

25. See http://www.krishna.com/descent-god (accessed February 24, 2014).

Chapter Three

Ropes of Love

The Sweet Pastimes of Śrī Śrī Rādhā-Dāmodara

Although the Vaishnava tradition teaches that God descends in any number of forms, he is particularly appreciated as his Deity (an icon made of material elements), for in this way one can interact with him in the material world, developing an intimate relationship with him.

Such Deity forms are based on scriptural narratives that reveal a certain aspect of his nature, trying to recapture intimate "pastimes" (*līlā*) of the spiritual world and thus, under the direction of an adept, enter into them.

One such pastime is called the "Dāmodara-līlā." Cherished by Vaishnavas worldwide, this form of the Lord is particularly favored by those who have a "nurturing" (*vātsalya*) mood toward the Supreme. But as this chapter will show, those who feel a sense of conjugal love (*mādhurya*) may also find deep attraction to Lord Dāmodara.

"Although he is beyond the reach of all senses, his mother endeavored to bind him to a wooden grinding mortar. But when she tried to tie him up, she found that the rope was too short—by two inches."[1]

For Vaishnavas, the above lines can arouse a flood of profoundly sweet emotions and philosophical reflection, because, in its essence, it excavates and displays a storehouse of theological gems hidden in a charming story, vividly recounting the complex, loving exchanges that take place between the Supreme Lord Krishna—appearing in his original form as an all-attractive, ever-youthful cowherd—and his mother, Yaśodā, who is one of his most dear and intimate devotees in the spiritual world.

For the nondevotee, however, the narrative naturally raises a number of challenging questions. To begin with, the scene depicted seems too ordinary, too prosaic. How can an account of bucolic domestic affairs have anything to do with ultimate reality, the Supreme Person, the Absolute Truth?

Additionally, one might naturally wonder at a seeming absurdity: Are we to believe that the Supreme Godhead, the source and origin of all that be, has a mother? Isn't that contradictory? And even if we allow that God can somehow have a mother in some esoteric sense, one might legitimately ask, "Why would God's mother try to bind him with ropes, let alone succeed in doing it?"

During her attempt to bind him, the story continues, he runs away from her in fear. And this of course leads to another question: "Why would the Lord of all fear anyone?" Such questions are entirely logical, but only from an uninformed point of view.

Even a cursory familiarity with Vaishnava theology prepares the reader for a breathtaking excursion into the inner life of the Supreme. The Dāmodara episode makes one privy to profound insights, revelation after revelation, about the emotional and psychological life of God. And it simultaneously makes known the character, the motivation, and the profound emotional and psychological life of His loving devotees as well. In its portrait of village life in Vrindavan, Dāmodara-līlā ushers the reader into an otherwise hidden realm of divine love, wherein God's esoteric nature is fully elucidated and, as the recounting unfolds, simultaneously grants the reader knowledge of just how—and precisely why—the Supreme Person engages with those who love Him in seemingly mundane exchanges that in fact fully nourish His own pleasure, while they fully delight His most confidential associates in the spiritual world.

Let it be clear: According to ancient India's wisdom texts, as per the Gauḍīya Vaishnava tradition, Krishna is the Supreme Personality of Godhead, and although he is the source of everything and the most powerful being in existence, he enjoys having "ordinary," loving exchanges with his dear ones in which he sometimes subordinates himself to them. This is part of his perfection—how boring or unfulfilling it would be to always be the best or the most powerful or always have the upper hand in all interactions with other beings. Therefore, Krishna, in his wisdom, arranges reality so that he can experience playful subservience: He allows his trusted and loving devotees to interact with him as equals—and sometimes as his superiors.

Our relationships in the material world, the sages tell us, are reflections of prototypical relationships in the spiritual world. Thus, in the Kingdom of God, one finds interactions like those of master and loving attendant (*dāsya-rasa*); friendly interchange, as found among equals and with superiors (*sakhya-rasa*); relationships that include a nurturing dimension, such as those involving parent and child (*vātsalya-rasa*); and romantic or conjugal exchanges (*mādhurya-rasa*).

Yaśodā's particular relationship is that of a mother (*vātsalya*), and Krishna, lost in the love of that relationship, allows it to play out as it would in the material world. Her desire to serve him as his mother is so undeviatingly pure that Krishna, to reciprocate her love, plays the role of her son for all eternity. It is within the context of this transcendental relationship that she attempts to bind him with rope, and in which he ultimately accommodates her.

The entire narrative is found in the *Śrīmad Bhāgavatam* (tenth Canto, chapters 9, 10, and the beginning of 11), with added nuance gleaned from traditional commentaries. Supplementary details can be found throughout India's wisdom texts, such as the *Padma Purāṇa,* the *Garga-saṁhitā,* the *Brahma-vaivarta Purāṇa,* the *Bṛhad-bhāgavatāmṛta,* the *Gopāla-Campū,* and the *Ānanda-Vṛndāvana-Campū.* Also significant is Sanātana Gosvāmī's commentary on *Śrī Dāmodarāṣṭakaṃ,* written by Satyavrata Muni.[2] Thus, it is an important part of North Indian Vaishnavism in general and Gauḍīya Vaishnavism in particular.

In South India, too, the Dāmodara-līlā resounds: It is found throughout the *Divya Prabhandam,* or the collected works of the Āḻvārs (the twelve poet-saints who established the philosophical underpinnings of Śrī Vaishnavism). For instance, in Nammāḻvār's *Tiruvāymoli* 1.3, it is identified as a prime example of divine accessibility, in that the Lord allows himself to be bound by his loving devotee. Further, the title of Maturakavi Āḻvār's sole work, which is in praise of his guru, Nammāḻvār, is *Kaṉṉinuṉ Ciṟuttāmpu* ("the short knotted string," or, more fancifully, "the flower-garland rope"), a reference to the rope with which Krishna is bound. The opening words of the poem refer to the story as well. Clearly, the Dāmodara narrative is ubiquitous in the Vaishnava tradition, enjoying pan-Vaishnava status.[3]

MOTHER YAŚODĀ'S DĀMODARA-LĪLĀ

Dāmodara, as one of Krishna's many names,[4] is traceable to the incident of Yaśodā binding him with a cord (*dama*) around the belly (*udara*) when He was an infant. Dāmodara thus means "having a rope on the abdomen," as described in the *Śrīmad Bhāgavatam* (10.9.19): "Then she bound him with a rope to the mortar, as if he were an ordinary child." But there is much more to the narrative than that.

Before summarizing the basic details of the story, it is important to understand the unique position of Mother Yaśodā, who is glorified as being among Krishna's greatest devotees, one of the Lord's paradigmatic associates in the eternal realm of Vraja. The *Bhāgavatam* is clear: "Neither Lord Brahmā, nor Lord Śiva, nor even the goddess of fortune, who is always the better half of the Supreme Lord, can obtain from the Supreme Personality of Godhead, the deliverer from this material world, such mercy as received by Mother Yaśodā" (10.9.20). And Prabhupāda, in his gloss of this verse, makes it clearer still:

> This is a comparative study between mother Yaśodā and other devotees of the Lord. As stated in *Caitanya-caritāmṛta* (*Ādi* 5.142), *ekale īśvara kṛṣṇa, āra saba bhṛtya:* the only supreme master is Kṛṣṇa, and all others are His servants. Kṛṣṇa has the transcendental quality of *bhṛtya-vaśyatā,* becoming subordinate to His *bhṛtya,* or servant. Now, although everyone is *bhṛtya* and although Kṛṣṇa has the quality of becoming subordinate to His *bhṛtya,* the position of mother Yaśodā is the greatest. Lord Brahmā is *bhṛtya,* a servant of Kṛṣṇa, and he is *ādi-kavi,* the original creator of this universe (*tene brahma hṛdā ya ādi-kavaye*). Nonetheless, even he could not obtain such mercy as mother Yaśodā. As for Lord Śiva, he is the topmost Vaiṣṇava (*vaiṣṇavānāṁ yathā śambhuḥ*). What to speak of Lord Brahmā and Lord Śiva, the goddess of fortune, Lakṣmī, is the Lord's constant companion in service, since she always associates with His body. But even she could not get such mercy. Therefore Mahārāja Parīkṣit was surprised, thinking, "What did mother Yaśodā and Nanda Mahārāja do in their previous lives by which they got such a great opportunity, the opportunity to be the affectionate father and mother of Kṛṣṇa?"

Yaśodā's closeness to God is rarely articulated as clearly as it is in the Dāmodara-līlā. In truth, few would be allowed to predominate in their interactions with Krishna as she does when she binds Him with her ropes of love. And so, without any further ado, let us now summarize the basic story from the sources already mentioned.

Krishna, as an infant, desires to interact with Yaśodā by engaging in childlike playful activities, often to the point of being disruptive. While in that mood, he sometimes spoils her stock of butter, breaking pots and distributing the contents to his friends and playmates, including the celebrated monkeys of Vrindavan. Mother Yaśodā, wanting to protect her divine child, and to stop him from causing further mischief, took a rope and threatened to tie him to a large wooden mortar. Seeing the rope in his mother's hands, he began to weep like an ordinary child, with tears rolling down his cheeks. This made his mascara-laden eyes more beautiful than ever before.

Yaśodā quickly realizes that the rope isn't long enough to bind him, and so she gathers more from other rooms in the house. She exhausts herself finding various kinds of rope, but no matter how much she manages to accumulate, it's always too short to actually do the deed. The neighboring *gopīs* try to help. One woman brings in a nice, long piece of rope—somehow, again, it's too short—and another brings more. They tie each piece to the next, but, still, nothing works. "It's downright mystical," they think. No matter how much rope they bring, it's always two inches too short. As long as he doesn't want to be bound, it seems, he will remain free.

His mother reaches the end of her strength, if not her rope. She has to admit defeat, succumbing to utter exhaustion. Her unswerving devotion, matched by her intense effort, is affectionately noted. Seeing his mother's nearly relentless endeavor, he finally gives consent, and she succeeds in binding him. Somehow, what did not work before is now easily achieved.

As for the version found in the *Bhāgavatam*'s Tenth Canto, the last two verses of chapter 9 segue into chapter 10: Krishna is now tied to the mortar, but his ordeal in the courtyard will soon take on new dimensions: He sees in the distance twin arjuna trees, which, he knows, are in fact two nature-spirits (*yakṣas*). They had been cursed by the sage Nārada to incarnate as trees, which is a long story in itself.

Chapter 10 begins by elucidating the *yakṣas'* background and how they came to be cursed. This includes Nārada's fifteen-verse sermon on their salacious behavior, which he explains as being the reason for their current predicament. After this, we witness Krishna scurrying through the courtyard, dragging the mortar behind him, since it is still tied to his waist. He makes his way past the two trees, inadvertently lodging the mortar between them. As he keeps moving, he pulls them down, and the *yakṣas* are liberated.[5]

The whole incident of being tied to the mortar, then, serves an additional purpose, as the heavy wooden cauldron aided the Lord in uprooting the trees, thus freeing the reincarnated *yakṣas*. This scene is followed by a ten-verse prayer addressed to Krishna. The *yakṣas* are repentant, and this is reflected in their words. Chapter 11 completes the narrative by describing how the entire incident is viewed by neighboring cowherds and by Nanda's undoing of Krishna's ropes.

Although, in the Dāmodara-līlā, it is Yaśodā who binds Krishna with ropes of love (*niryoga-pāśa*), it is usually the other way around: Krishna generally binds his devotees with such ropes—in terms of metaphor, at least—but, in this instance, He wanted to be bound in return, fully relishing his mother's maternal affection (*vātsalya-prema-pāśa*).[6]

TWO INCHES TOO SHORT

The "two inches too short" motif is not arbitrary. There is a profound teaching at the heart of this dyadic dimension to the story, and it goes back to the very beginnings of the Gauḍīya tradition: Several early teachers identify these two inches with "faith and works," or "grace and endeavor"—the notion that before one can "bind" God, or tie Krishna with ropes of love, one must secure his mercy and make one's best effort to serve him. As Yaśodā did.

In the sixteenth century, Śrīnātha Chakravartī, who is renowned as the guru of Kavi Karṇapūra, one of Śrī Chaitanya's celebrated associates, offers the "grace and effort" explanation in his *Caitanya-mata-mañjuṣā* (10.9.15, or, in some editions 10.9.15–17). This text is historically important because it is likely the first Gauḍīya commentary on the *Śrīmad Bhāgavatam*.

Śrīla Jīva Gosvāmī echoes this reading of grace and works in both his commentaries on the *Bhāgavatam*'s Tenth Canto: The *Krama-sandarbha* (10.9.18) and *Laghu-vaishnava-toṣaṇī* (10.9.15), when elucidating the two missing inches of Yaśodā's rope, repeat it verbatim: "He [Krishna] is bound by two factors—the effort of the devotee and his own mercy" (*dvābhyām eva baddho bhavati—bhakta-pariśramaḥ svasya kṛpā ceti*).

The view is reiterated yet again by Viśvanātha Chakravartī Ṭhākura, *Bhāgavatam* commentator par excellence, when illuminating the pertinent text (10.9.18). It is worth quoting at length:

> As you cannot tie up His waist even with all the ropes of the house, then it must be concluded that it is His good fortune that it should not be. Listen Yaśodā, give up this attempt!" Though the village women advised in this way, Yaśodā was insistent. "Even if evening comes, and I tie together the rope of the whole village, I must find out just once the extent of my son's waist." If Yaśodā, with desire to do good to her son, and being stubborn, would not give up her attempt to bind the Lord, then between the Lord and the devotee, the devotee's stubbornness prevails. Thus, seeing His mother becoming tired, the Lord gave up His own stubbornness, and by His mercy allowed Himself to be tied. His mercy is the king of all *śaktis*, illuminating all else. It melts the heart of the Lord as if it were butter. Mercy's appearance made the *satya saṅkalpa* and *vibhūta śaktis* suddenly disappear. The shortage of two fingers was filled by effort (*pariśrama*) and mercy (*kṛpā*). The effort and fatigue due to service and worship (the steady faith of the devotee—*bhakta niṣṭhā*), and the mercy of the Lord arising from seeing that effort and fatigue (the steady quality in the Lord—*sva niṣṭhā*)—these two caused the Lord to be bound. As long as these are not there, the rope remains two fingers too short. When these two are there, the Lord is bound. The Lord Himself showed to His mother how only love can bind Him. This is what the pastime illustrates. (translation by Gopīparāṇadhana Dāsa)

Giriraj Swami, an ISKCON leader and articulate spokesperson for the Gauḍīya Vaishnava Sampradāya, writes along similar lines in his essay, "Dāmodara-līlā: Works and Grace":

> Now, if we look closely at the life of the devotee, yes, ultimately the devotee is picked up by the grace of the Lord, but still the devotee makes every effort to serve the Lord, and then the Lord's mercy allows the devotee to bind the Lord—the Lord comes under the control of the devotee's pure love. So if someone thinks he can, as they say, storm the gates of heaven, or reach God by his own endeavor, that is not correct. But then again, if someone says, "Well, I am just going to sit and pray to God to deliver me, and I am not going to make any effort," that also is not complete. We need both: *pariśrama* [intense effort] and *krishna-kṛpā* [the Lord's mercy].[7]

The faith and works doctrine is not peculiar to Gauḍīya Vaishnavism. Aside from its Christian dimensions, which we will address in a moment, the Vaishnavas of South India, known as the Śrī Sampradāya, or the Rāmānuja tradition, explored it as well, underlining a philosophical tension that resulted in two factions. The Vaṭakalai branch, championed by Vedānta Deśika (1268–1368), teaches that salvation or self-surrender comes about when there is both divine grace and human effort, yes, but with a special emphasis on effort. This is comparable, says Deśika, to a mother monkey carrying her baby. The mother does most of the work, but the baby must take some initiative to hang on as well, with its arms wrapped around its mother's neck. On the other hand, the Teṅkalai school, represented by Pi<u>ll</u>ai Lokācārya (1264–1369), claims that God's grace alone saves the soul, much in the way that a cat carries its kitten—the baby kitten is virtually inactive, being propped up in its mother's mouth and exerting no effort of its own.[8]

The Vaṭakalai and the Teṅkalai appreciate both works and faith, but the two schools have built entire philosophical systems according to their particular emphases.

The same tension exists in Christianity: Here, the concern is how the faithful can be saved from sins, enabling them to go to heaven when they die. Early Christian theologians opined that one qualifies for salvation through good deeds, observing sacred rites and pious traditions—ultimately being obedient to the commandments of the Church. Martin Luther (1484–1546), however, held forth that we attain salvation merely through faith in God. This, of course, gave rise to the dogmatic position, so popular among certain Christian groups today, that simple belief in Jesus is enough for salvation.

The scriptural quotes used by both factions are many, but it comes down to the following. On the one hand: "For by grace are ye saved through faith; and that not of yourselves: it is the gift of God." (Ephesians 2:8) And yet: "Faith without works is dead" (James 2:26.). Thus, modern Christianity has its own version of the Vaṭakalai/Teṅkalai dichotomy. But in the end, most Christians and Vaishnavas would agree: Faith does not exist where it does not manifest itself in works, even though, in the end, one must attain the grace of God to achieve spiritual perfection.[9]

One may wonder how all this applies to Dāmodara-līlā. "Devotional action" (*bhakti-sevā*) manifests in the process of worship. Activities that bring one closer to God, like Mother Yaśodā giving every ounce of strength to binding little Dāmodara, constitute the effort required to receive God's mercy. This is referred to as steadiness in worship (*bhakta-nisthā bhajanotthā*). The spiritual potency generated from such "works" constitutes the first missing inch of Dāmodara's rope.

The second, in a sense, is often a consequence of the first. That is to say, Krishna's mercy, which is generally evoked when he sees his devotees' relentless effort (*darśanotthā svaniṣṭhā kṛpā*), takes a practitioner the rest of the way. Yaśodā's effort was not enough, though she gave it all she had. It was ultimately Krishna's mercy that allowed her to bind him. It should be understood, too, that while effort is a reliable path in achieving the grace of the Lord, it is, in the end, entirely up to him. Krishna is independent (*svarāṭ*), and his grace manifests according to his sweet (and sometimes unpredictable) will.

As leading ISKCON teacher and Sanskrit scholar Bhanu Swami sums up:

> It is the *bhakta-niṣṭhā*, firm faith of the devotee, seen in his tireless endeavors to worship the Lord, and the *sva-niṣṭhā*, steadiness of the Lord in bestowing his mercy upon seeing the devotee's effort and fatigue, that caused Krishna to be bound. In the absence of these two, the rope would have remained two fingers too short. But when *bhakta-niṣṭhā* and *sva-niṣṭhā* are present, the Lord can be bound. In this pastime, Krishna showed Yashoda and the whole world that only love can bind the Supreme Lord.[10]

A philosophical addendum may be pertinent here, though not directly related to the "two inches" motif: In the *Bhagavad-gītā*, Śrī Krishna talks at length about the "three modes of material nature" These are subtle forces that influence our behavior as well as every aspect of our physical, mental, and emotional experience. The Sanskrit term for these forces is *guṇa*, which can be translated as "rope," and the *Gītā* explains how this rope pulls us to act in various ways, even, sometimes, against our better judgment. The effects of *sattva-guṇa*, the mode of goodness, are seen when an atmosphere of peace, serenity, and harmony prevails in our environment and in our overall way of being. *Rājo-guṇa*, the mode of passion, is felt as gnawing desire for temporary things, an insatiable striving, and consequent dissatisfaction. *Tamo-guṇa*, the mode of ignorance, is characterized by laziness, depression, intoxication, and lack of clarity. "All men are forced to act helplessly according to the impulses born of the modes of material nature," Krishna notes in the *Gītā*, "and therefore no one can refrain from doing something, not even for a moment" (3.5). This applies to everyone: "No being existing, anywhere in the material world, is free from the three modes of material nature" (18.40). Krishna, however, is naturally distinguished from all other living entities in that He is never bound by these ropes—or any ropes, for that matter (7.13). On an esoteric level, that is among the many implicit meanings of Dāmodara-līlā.

ŚRĪ RĀDHĀ'S ROPES OF LOVE

One may wonder how the Yaśodā-Dāmodara-līlā connects to Śrī Rādhā, or the Feminine Divine. After all, the famous Rādhā-Dāmodara Deities in Vrindavan and Jaipur (and elsewhere), to be discussed below, are forms of "Rādhā"-Dāmodara, not "Yaśodā"-Dāmodara. Indeed, the focus on Rādhā speaks to the fundamental predilection of the Gauḍīya tradition, which is Rādhā-dāsyam, that is to say, love of Krishna is eclipsed by love for Rādhā: It should be noted that she is considered the female manifestation of God—Krishna's other half—just as much as she is his greatest devotee and *hlādinī-śakti*, his original internal pleasure potency. Krishna's very existence, say the great Gauḍīya teachers, has little meaning without her. What is the value of the sun, they ask, without sunshine?

Accordingly, the eighth and culminating verse of Satyavrata Muni's famous "Dāmodarāṣṭaka" might serve as a bridge from Yaśodā-Dāmodara-līlā, which is the tenor of the entire poem, to Rādhā-Dāmodara, thus subtly connecting Śrī Rādhā to the Dāmodara-līlā: "O Dāmodara, I offer my respectful obeisances to the celebrated rope binding Your belly, for it is an abode of brilliant effulgence. I offer my respectful obeisances to Your belly, which supports the entire universe of moving and non-moving entities. I offer my respectful obeisances again and again to Śrīmatī Rādhikā, Your most beloved, and I offer my respectful obeisances to You, my divine Lord who performs unlimited transcendental pastimes" (*namas te 'stu dāmne sphurad dīpti-dhāmne/ tvadīyodarāyātha viśvasya dhāmne// namo rādhikāyai tvadīya-priyāyai/ namo 'nanta-līlāya devāya tubhyam//*).

Indeed, there is abundant Gauḍīya poetry that makes suggestive links to Śrī Rādhā in terms of the Dāmodara-līlā. For example, in the *Śrī Rādhā-rasa-sudhā-nidhi* (text 174), Prabodhānanda Sarasvatī speaks of Rādhā and Krishna as "tied [to each other] with the knot of deep love" (*gāḍha-snehānubandha-grathitam*). He further writes that Śrī Rādhā "subdues and binds Krishna, who is like an elephant—her helpless pet—just by virtue of her playfully amorous glances" (text 188).[11] But Śrī Rādhā's place in Dāmodara-līlā goes beyond figurative speech.

Her more overt connection with the story reaches back to the Uttara-kāṇḍa of the *Bhaviṣya Purāṇa*: "Once, in the auspicious month of Kārttika,[12] Krishna came late for a rendezvous with Rādhārāṇī in her *kuñja*. In loving anger, Śrī Rādhā looked at Krishna with frowning eyebrows. Using some golden vines, she then tied a rope around Śrī Krishna's belly to punish him for not showing up as promised. Krishna said he was late because Mother Yaśodā kept him home for a festival. Seeing her mistake, Rādhā quickly untied her beloved Dāmodara."[13] Thus, Mother Yaśodā's pastime of binding Krishna with her love (*vātsalya-bhāva*) has a parallel in the conjugal exchange (*mādhurya-bhāva*) of Rādhā and Krishna, and in this way Gauḍīya Vaishnavas cherish an esoteric dimension to the Dāmodara episode.[14]

In fact, according to Jīva Gosvāmī, the exchange with Śrī Rādhā is the prototype for the exchange with Yaśodā:

> *tasmin dine ca bhagavān rātrau rādhā-gṛhaṁ yayau* |
> *sā ca kruddhā tam udare kāñcī-dāmnā babandha ha* ||121||
> *kṛṣṇas tu sarvam āvedya nija-geha-mahotsavam* |
> *priyāṁ prasādayāmāsa tataḥ sā tam amocayat* ||122||
> *idaṁ covāca tāḥ kṛṣṇaḥ preyasī prīta-mānasaḥ* |
> *kāñcī-dāma tvayā tanvi udare yan mayārpitam* ||123||
> *dāmodareti me nāma priyaṁ tena śubhānane* |
> *nātaḥ prītikaraṁ nāma mama lokeṣu vidyate* ||124||
> *nityam etat prajapatāṁ sarva-siddhir bhaviṣyati* |
> *bhaktiṁ ca durlabhāṁ prāpya mama loke mahīyate* ||125||
> *ulūkhale yadā mātrā baddho'haṁ bhavitā priye* |
> *udare dāmabhir loke tadā vyaktaṁ bhaviṣyati* ||126||

> "That day (in the spiritual world, before Govardhana-pūjā) Bhagavān went late at night to meet Śrī Rādhā at her home. [Since he was late], she was angry and bound him by her golden girdle belt. Krishna pleaded in front of her and narrated everything about the great festival at his home (which caused his late arrival). Thus he placated her and she let him go.
>
> Then Krishna being pleased at mind said to her, "The golden girdle belt which you have offered to me around my stomach will cause me to be known as 'Dāmodara.' There is no name dearer to me in all the worlds. Those who chant this name always will achieve all perfections. Having obtained the rarest gift of my *bhakti*, they will achieve my abode.
>
> Dear Rādhā! I will manifest this pastime in the material world when I will be bound by my mother to a mortar using various ropes."[15]

Vraja tradition further reveals that the *gopīs* sometimes sit near Mother Yaśodā just to hear her sing Krishna's glories. In those moments, Rādhārāṇī, especially, listens closely, particularly when Yaśodā recites the Dāmodara pastime. Enveloped by Dāmodara's mood of surrender, when he acquiesces to Mother Yaśodā's love, Śrī Rādhā feels deep affection, remembering when she, too, was able to bind him in this way (as described above by Jīva Gosvāmī). More, she longs to once again bind Krishna with her love, resolving to do whatever might be necessary to win his affections. The notion of "Rādhā-Dāmodara," then, refers to Rādhārāṇī's mood of intense attraction for this totality of loving affection, and how it was achieved by Mother Yaśodā.

To highlight this mood, Rādhikā even performs Kātyāyanī-vrata in the month of Kārttika, honoring a set of vows usually performed by women who want a particular husband.[16] Of course, she has no need to pray for enhanced intimacy with Krishna, but in her humility—and in her desperation to do anything for closeness with the Lord of her life—she says the appropriate prayers and undergoes the standard austerities, just to solidify her loving exchange. To this day, during Kārttika, the priests of Vrindavan's Rādhā-Dāmodara temple tie a golden rope from Rādhā's waist to Krishna's stomach, indicating the esoteric dimension of Dāmodara-līlā and the deep love that abides between Rādhā and Krishna.

THE RĀDHĀ-DĀMODARA TEMPLE OF VRINDAVAN

In the sixteenth century, Śrī Chaitanya Mahāprabhu sent his chief followers to Vrindavan to write treatises on the acme of spiritual life and to unearth the lost holy places associated with Krishna's pastimes. The central figures in Vrindavan's restoration were Sanātana Gosvāmī and Rūpa Gosvāmī, as well as their illustrious nephew Jīva Gosvāmī, who followed close behind.

Sanātana and Rūpa established the first major temples in Braj—Madan-Mohan and Govindadeva, respectively, along with their presiding Deities, Śrī-Śrī Rādhā-Madan-Mohan and Śrī-Śrī Rādhā-Govinda. Following in the tradition of his uncles, Jīva Gosvāmī established a temple dedicated to Śrī-Śrī Radha-Damodara, a Deity fashioned for him by his uncle, Śrī Rūpa, in 1542 CE.[17]

Dāmodara is a mere eight inches high—just as the Lord in the heart measures eight inches (*Śrīmad Bhāgavatam* 2.2.8–11). Beautifully carved from a rare form of black marble, originally imported from Central India's Vindhya Range, He became the Lord of Śrī Jīva's life.

Contemporary Gauḍīya Vaishnava guru Radhanath Swami gives a sense of the intimacy Jīva Gosvāmī enjoyed with the Lord of his heart:

> The *Bhakti-ratnakara* explains a few incidences of the nature of Jiva Goswami's love. Lord Damodar was so pleased with Jiva Goswami's devotion that He would speak to Jiva Goswami! He would say, "Please give Me bhoga, I am hungry." We just understand the time of offering of the *bhoga* by the clock, knowing that Krishna's expecting it. But for Jiva Goswami, because of his love, Damodar would actually call him when it was coming close to the time offering. I guess there were not any clocks in those days. The devotees would understand quite precisely when offering is to be made. But Damodar would say, "I am hungry Jiva, I am hungry, please feed Me *bhoga*." And, Jiva Goswami would personally prepare the *bhoga*, and offer with his own hands with love and devotion.

> By Damodar's mercy, Jiva Goswami with his own eyes would see Damodar eating the *bhoga*. . . . One time, Jiva Goswami heard a flute playing, and then Damodar called out and said, "Jiva! Come, I am playing the flute for you." And, Jiva Goswami came to the altar and there he saw Damodar dancing! The Deity of Damodar was dancing!! His three-fold bending form, playing upon His flute, beautiful sweet music for the pleasure of His devotee. Jiva Goswami saw the beautiful form of Damodar, whose eyes were like lotus petals, His head was decorated with a peacock feather, a garland of beautiful forest flowers was around His neck, and lovely ornaments decorated His body. He was dancing and singing, playing sweet, sweet melodies on His flute for His devotee. Jiva Goswami fell unconscious in ecstasy, and when he came back to consciousness, he could only weep, cry in ecstatic love. These were some of the pastimes that Sri Jiva Goswami performed with Sri Damodar, who is worshiped here. . . . It is believed that Emperor Akbar, once, when he came to Vrindavan-Dham, had the *darshan* of Jiva Goswami and the *darshan* of Jiva Goswami transformed his heart. He was given such a vision of appreciation of Vrindavan, that under Jiva Goswami's instruction, he as well as many of his generals and ministers became very active in developing Vrindavan as a very great holy place. They helped in the construction of Radha-Govindaji Mandir, Radha-Damodar Mandir, Jugal-kishor-Mandir, and Radha-Gopinath Mandir."[18]

Originally, the Gosvāmīs worshipped their Deities in a simple way, often informally, and in the hollow of a tree, or in small, enclosed, thickly wooded areas. At first, they only established Krishna Deities, without a visible form of Rādhā by his side. Even "Rādhā-Dāmodara," in those days, referred to Dāmodara Himself. The Rādhā *mūrti* was added later. One may wonder, given the Gosvāmīs' stated ontological position as Śrī Rādhā's intimate maid-servants, why they did not establish Rādhā Deities as well.[19]

The answer is that they were concerned with the gradual unfolding of ontological truth (*tattva*), as required by practitioners. In other words, one must understand the importance of worshipping Krishna before introducing the esoterica of Rādhā Tattva.[20] In the end, of course, Rādhā is always side by side with Krishna, especially as he was presented in the teachings of the Six Gosvāmīs, and this is understood as a fundamental principle in Gauḍīya *siddhānta*.[21] Thus, she is implicit whenever Krishna is properly worshipped.

Nonetheless, Śrī Jīva worshipped his Krishna Deity with great enthusiasm, and many devotees came to worship with him and to see his uncommon devotion.

Soon, a temple was needed, and Sevā Kuñj seemed the natural choice. This is the holiest of holy lands, where Krishna had engaged in his Rāsa-līlā, the dance of love, enacted with his loving cowherd maidens, and, more, where he had submitted to Rādhā by serving Her lotus feet.[22] In fact, Śrī Jīva had already been worshipping his small Dāmodara Deity there, and the area had by now been renamed Jīva Gosai Kuñj.

The Rādhā-Dāmodara temple was built by Maharaja Man Singh of Amber (1550–1614), one of Akbar's most trusted generals and a servant of the Vaishnavas.[23] Although, externally, it is a humble dwelling, especially when compared to the more elaborate Govindadeva Mandir, also built by Man Singh, it is considered one of the most important temples in Vrindavan.[24]

The sacred images currently worshipped there are Lord Dāmodara with two *gopīs* on either side.[25] On the altar, too, are the larger Rādhā-Vrindavan Chandra, said to be the Deities of Krishnadāsa Kavirāja Gosvāmī; the Radha-Madhava Deities of Jayadeva Gosvāmī; and the Rādhā-Chailacikana Deities of Bhūgarbha Gosvāmī. Additionally, Lord Jagannātha has a presence here, as do Deities of Gaura-Nitāi, like Śrī Chaitanya and Nityānanda Prabhu. Also on the altar is Sanātana Gosvāmī's Girirāja-charan-śilā, said to have been given to him by Śrī Krishna Himself. The *śilā* has Krishna's footprint and several other distinguishing marks indelibly etched on its face.

The temple is famous for its many *samādhis* or burial places, such as those of Krishnadāsa Kavirāja Gosvāmī; Rūpa, Jīva, and Bhūgarbha Gosvāmīs; King Vīra Hāṁvīra of Vana Vishnupura and his wife; and numerous flower (*puṣpa*) *samādhis* of other, more contemporary saints. Alongside these various burial places are hallowed meditation areas, particularly the famous "Bhajan kutir" of Rūpa Gosvāmī, where he contemplated the deep pastimes of Rādhā and Krishna in the most profound of meditative states.

Significantly, Śrī Jīva's temple also housed the most thorough collection of Vedic and post-Vedic works of its time, including diverse literature that nourished Vedic learning. According to Dr. Tarapada Mukherjee, who catalogued many of the Vrindavan Research Institute's manuscripts, the bulk of their holdings came from this collection of the Rādhā-Dāmodara temple. Jagadananda Das (Jan Brzezinski) writes:

> Mukherjee spent many years researching the Gauḍīya manuscripts found in the Vrindavan Research Institute [VRI], most of which came from the Rādhā Dāmodar temple library, i.e., Jīva Gosvāmī's personal collection. . . . Rūpa stayed at Rādhā Dāmodar in his last days and his *samādhi* is on the temple grounds. One would naturally expect that he should give his collection of manuscripts to his nephew, disciple and successor, Śrī Jīva. From several *dalils* (testimonials) of the period, it is clear that the official library (*puṣtak ṭhaur*) of the school was there.[26]

Brzezinski's work on the life of Jīva Gosvāmī gives a sense of both Jīva's important place in the annals of Gauḍīya Vaishnava history[27] and the significance of his Rādhā-Dāmodara temple for Mahāprabhu's mission in Vrindavan:

> Not long after Jīva's arrival in Braj, he started engaging in land transactions, making several in association with Raghunāth Dās at Arith. In 1558 he bought land for the Rādhā Dāmodar temple from a certain Alisha Chaudhurī. . . . Later, this temple was to contain the library of the Gosvāmīs Rūpa and Sanātan, who bequeathed their collections to Jīva. In the remnants of the library now in the collection of the VRI, Jīva's last will and testament and a copy thereof written sometime later, as well as [manuscripts] with Rūpa's signature, etc., have been found. . . . Jīva appears to have been greatly concerned that the properties that had been accumulated by him and his uncles should remain under the stewardship of the Gauḍīya Vaishnavas. In the VRI collection, there is an important *farman* dated AH 976 (AD 1568) issued by the emperor Akbar. In this document, Akbar gives official recognition to the custodians of the Govinda Deva and Madana Mohan temples in response to a petition from Raja Todar Mall on behalf of Jīva Gosvāmī . . . in whose care the temples had been left. This date would appear to confirm Rūpa Gosvāmī's death in that year. Rūpa Gosvāmī's *samādhi* is maintained at the Rādhā Dāmodar temple. . . . The numerous other transactions recorded in land deeds found in the Rādhā Dāmodar temple library include properties in Vrindavan acquired in 1572 and 1601 and in the Rādhā Kuṇḍ area between 1577 and 1579. In 1584, Raghunāth Dās bequeathed his worldly possessions to Jīva with the following words: "dictating the document to Kavirāj on my deathbed, I, the blind and lowly Raghunāth Dās, zealous for the service of Sri Rādhā Kuṇḍ, do hereby place the whole of my property at the lotus feet of the deity worshiped by Jīva," i.e., to the Rādhā Dāmodar temple.[28]

Finally, Swami Prabhupāda lived at Vrindavan's Rādhā-Dāmodara temple for six years, from 1959 to 1965, just before traveling abroad and founding ISKCON. It was at Rādhā-Dāmodara that he translated and wrote commentaries on the first three volumes of the Śrīmad-Bhāgavatam, and, taking inspiration from the eternal presence Rūpa, Jīva, and others, planned his journey west. While there, Prabhupāda used two rooms: his living quarters and a kitchen, both preserved to this day by his disciples. Upon entering his quarters today, one sees a life-sized mūrti of him, sitting at his desk, pen in hand. The room is small, but his time here was sweet. The kitchen, a few feet away from his room, includes a small window that looks out at Rūpa Gosvāmī's samādhi. Prabhupāda spent many months in this place, sitting and watching, planning his approach, thinking how he would spread the Bhakti Movement worldwide. "I live eternally," he once remarked, "in my rooms at Rādhā-Dāmodara temple."[29]

THE RĀDHĀ DĀMODARA TEMPLE IN JAIPUR

More than half a century after Śrī Jīva's time on Earth, North India was thrown into difficult circumstances: Even while Vrindavan was thriving spiritually, a deepening of political tensions was on the horizon. This involved already-existing Rajput kingdoms and chieftaincies, the newly ascendent Moghuls, and the developing Kachwaha kingdom in the west. The common narrative is descriptively recounted in a recent *Vrindavan Today* article:

> The year: AD 1669. King Mirza Rajah Jai Singh, who was at the Mughal court, sends a messenger to the temple priests at Vrindavan with some chilling news. The emperor Aurangzeb has turned his vengeful gaze towards Vrindavan. In short order, his army will invade the temples and destroy everything inside, including the precious *murtis* of Krishna.
>
> Flee, says the Rajput king to the temple pandit, Shiva Ram Goswami. Take the *murtis* and flee. Go via adjoining Bharatpur. The hardy Jat king, Surajmal, will give you safe passage. Once you get to Jaipur, the *murtis* will be safe. Aurangzeb's army dares not invade Rajputana.
>
> Threatened by Muslim raids, each of the temple priests grabbed a *murti* of Krishna, wrapped them with diaphanous white *dhotis* and fled into the mists of the night. After a treacherous journey where they travelled by bullock cart and camel in the stealth of the night, hiding in caves during the day, the priests and five *murtis* reached Jaipur, where they make their home and are worshipped under the names of Govind Dev, Radha Gopinath, Radha Damodar, Madan Mohan and Vinodi Lal.[30]

Tradition offers several variations on the story, but the basics are now well known: The destructive raids on temples in nearby Mathurā—and in Benares as well—resulted in a prompt exodus of Vrindavan's most important Deities, with only the miniature Rādhā-rāmaṇa remaining, hidden from public view. By 1670, before the soldiers arrived, Lord Dāmodara was already on his way to Jaipur, where he is worshipped to this day.[31] Thus, as it now stands, Vrindavan is mainly home to replica Deities (*pratibhū mūrtis*),[32] while their prototypical counterparts, including Dāmodara, are to be found in Rajasthan.

Although duplicate Deities were gradually established, one can only imagine the heartbreak in having to relocate the prominent Krishna images that had been worshipped in Vrindavan for so long, so dear to the devotees and pivotal for their everyday practice. The tradition does not take such relocation lightly (though, of course, in such extreme circumstances, exceptions can be made): The *Śrīmad Bhāgavatam* (11.27.13) tells us, "The Deity form of the Lord, who is the shelter of all living entities, can be established in two ways: temporarily or permanently. But a permanent Deity, having been called [installed], can never be sent away, My dear Uddhava" (*calācaleti dvi-vidhā/ pratiṣṭhā jīva-mandiram// udvāsāvāhane na staḥ/ sthirāyām uddhavārcane//*).[33]

In the Gauḍīya tradition, this idea was further developed in the *Hari-bhakti-vilāsa* (chapter 19): After explaining how to install both types of Deities—movable and immovable, temporary and permanent—the text informs us that these Deities have to be re-installed if they are broken, dropped, moved, and so on. The movable are usually those made of metal or wood and not permanently fixed in a particular location, while the immovable are the marble or granite Deities that are permanently fixed and/or cemented into place. Dāmodara would have been considered a permanent Deity, made of black marble, and long established in his temple. Thus, moving Him caused great anguish, and tension thus mounted between the aggressors and those seeking only to serve their Deities.

While the role of Aurangzeb (r. 1658–1707) is indisputable in the displacement of Krishna images from Braj in the 1660s and 1670s, resulting in Rādhā-Dāmodara's long journey to Jaipur, his involvement should not be overstated and was perhaps more nuanced than generally supposed.[34] Nonetheless, it was he who gave the decisive order in 1669, mandating the destruction of temples in Vrindavan, Mathurā, and other regions in his domain. This, again, forced local priests to shift the Deities westward, toward Rajasthan, protecting their much-cherished forms of Krishna from Moghul forces—the Kachwahas of Amber had the facility, financially and otherwise, to build temporary temples, offering sanctuary and protection to the Deities as they traveled, which took years. Their ultimate destination was Jaipur, where they would find permanent shelter.

Śrī-Śrī Rādhā-Dāmodara, specifically, came to Jaipur in 1733 and was installed in a preexisting *havelī*, one of the earliest buildings in the city. Local records explain that the land was donated by Himmatram Nazir, who was so taken by the Deities that he offered them his own home.[35] Malay Goswami, present Mahant of the Rādhā Dāmodara Temple in Jaipur, informs us that the Rādhā Deity was added later, when Sawai Jai Singh, the Rajput ruler, "had a dream to install Deities of Rādhārāṇī along with Govindaji, Gopinathaji and Damodarji Deities."[36]

Indeed, Jai Singh became an outspoken advocate for all of Vrindavan's Deities and helped to establish permanent temples for Them in Jaipur, where, today, the original Dāmodara still resides: He is worshipped at Chaura Rasta Road, Tripolia Bazar, Modikhana, a mere ten-minute walk from the famous Rādhā-Govinda temple. At Rādhā-Dāmodara Mandir (Jaipur), there are two sets of Deities on the main altar, the smaller of which includes Jīva Gosvāmī's original Rādhā-Dāmodara from Vrindavan, though he is now flanked by two *gopīs*.[37] The larger Deities on the altar behind Rādhā-Dāmodara are Rādhā-Vrindavanchandra, the original Deities of Krishnadāsa Kavirāja Gosvāmī.[38] To the left of the Deities is a Govardhan-śilā said to have been worshipped by Sanātana Gosvāmī.[39] Additionally, on a separate altar to the left of the main worship area are the Deities of Lakṣmī-Narasiṁha, accompanied by Prahlāda Mahārāja, the paradigmatic young devotee who is the very emblem of Vaishnava devotion.

It is stunning to think that Rādhā-Dāmodara, so loved in Vrindavan, took the long westward journey to Rajasthan. But there is more to the story. Just as Jīva's Deity eventually went in a westerly direction, his teaching traveled eastward, and that in his own lifetime. Several years before his passing, he had called a meeting at his Rādhā-Dāmodara temple in Vrindavan.

At that time, he officially announced that he would be sending three of his best students to Eastern India to share the literature of the Gosvāmīs. Śrīnivāsa Ācārya would focus on West Bengal; Śyāmānanda moved toward Orissa; and Narottama Dāsa made his field East Bengal (present-day Bangladesh). But initially, they would travel together. Jīva had arranged a bullock cart and packed it with the best of all possible cargo: a large chest full of Gosvāmī manuscripts.

"The first traveling *saṅkīrtana* party (TSKP) leaves Rādhā-Dāmodara Mandir as a *padayātrā* heading East," writes Vaiyasaki Das, noted *kīrtaniya* and author of *Rādhā-Dāmodara Vilāsa*. "Ten soldiers accompany the party to guard the precious scriptures. Crossing the breadth of India without any incident, the party finally arrives in the province of West Bengal. They pass the night on the bank of a lake on the outskirts of Vana Vishnupur, rejoicing to be back in the holy land of Śrī Chaitanya's appearance."[40]

The die was cast. All of India would eventually benefit from these books—as would the entire world, in due course. In Bengal, His Divine Grace A. C. Bhaktivedanta Swami Prabhupāda had made this literature the focus of his entire life and work, and he took it west, just as the Deity had gone west earlier. But this was not westward as in Rajasthan—as in the initial journey of Śrī Jīva's Dāmodara Deity—but as in the "big" West, the Western world, the ready and waiting land across the ocean.

ŚRĪ-ŚRĪ RĀDHĀ-DĀMODARA IN AMERICA

Jīva Gosvāmī's Deity never left India, but Prabhupāda did, and in establishing his worldwide preaching mission, he brought the entire Gauḍīya tradition with him. This naturally included Rādhā-Dāmodara. But if Śrī Jīva's Deity traveled the subcontinent for a particular set of reasons, ostensibly as a result of the Moghul invasion, the Rādhā-Dāmodara Deities in America would have an entirely different agenda, resulting in the worldwide proliferation of "Krishna Consciousness."

The unfolding of Dāmodara's sojourn in the Western world begins soon after Prabhupāda founded his movement in 1966. Only four years later, the temple president of ISKCON's DC temple (not surprisingly, a devotee named "Dāmodara Dāsa") had purchased Rādhā-Krishna Deities in Benares, arranging for them to be shipped to his temple in the nation's capital. However, without the required number of Brahmins to worship them properly, the Deities who would soon be Rādhā-Dāmodara sat in a closet for over six months.

Nonetheless, their beauty was uncanny, and all the local devotees noted it, even if they were simply unequipped to accommodate them:

> The silver-blue body of Dāmodara was made of German silver, while Rādhārāṇī's golden-hued form was fashioned from a combination of eight metals. Dāmodara's red-soled lotus feet rested upon a high silver base, on which His name was carved. The redness was visible on His palms, lips, ears, and eyes as well. He had an especially bewitching smile, and His eyes were wide and lotuslike, reaching almost to His ears. He was dressed in a rich gold- and green-colored silk brocade. From head to toe He was covered with flowers and jewels, some of which resembled elephants, calves, and peacocks. He was playing on a short flute, His right arm resting upon a staff, with a buffalo horn hanging from His waist. I had never before seen such a wonderfully attractive form of Krishna. While Dāmodara was thirty inches in height, Śrīmatī Rādhārāṇī was slightly smaller. Her color was as effulgent as bright molten gold. She had eyes like lotuses, similar to Dāmodara's. Her cheeks were very high and Her smile slightly hidden. Her regal appearance in every way substantiated that She was the queen of Vrindavan, the greatest of all the *gopīs*. Nevertheless, in Her right hand She held a bouquet of fresh flowers to be offered to Dāmodara, indicating Her constant meditation as His eternal servant. . . . As beautiful as Rādhā-Dāmodara were when fully dressed and jeweled, this was surpassed by Their natural beauty. Dāmodara's bluish-silver body had a carved *dhotī* with a *cādar* that flared on both sides. He also had natural bracelets, as well as a beautiful *mukuṭa*. Rādhārāṇī wore a finely decorated natural *sārī*. These were all unusual features, for normally Deities made of metal lacked such detailed ornamentation. How special Rādhā-Dāmodara were in every way![41]

Not wanting their exquisiteness to go unnoticed, Kīrtanānanda Svāmī (1937–2011), a leading devotee of the time, took them out with him in 1971, as he and a handful of talented devotees staged an ongoing "Transcendental Rock Opera" throughout the country. It was a Krishna-conscious traveling road show, known as "Every Town and Village"—complete with colorful dramatic performances, *kīrtana*, and philosophical discourse. This traveling show marked the beginning of a touring bus party that evolved into a major book distribution campaign.

When first brought aboard the unsteady old school bus, Rādhā-Dāmodara had to be tied with ropes to secure them in place. Prabhupāda approved and eventually named them "Rādhā-Dāmodara," remembering the Lord being tied with Mother Yaśodā's ropes of love.

Soon, the charismatic Vishnujana Swami (1948–1976) allied with the fledgling bus party, and his euphonious singing voice and overall loving nature encouraged other devotees to join as well. It was he who built a stable altar for Rādhā-Dāmodara, so that they no longer had to be tied in place. Under his influence, the party gradually evolved from its "rock opera" styling to a more traditional approach. The original group disbanded, and Vishnujana Mahārāja established it anew as the "Rādhā-Dāmodara Traveling Saṅkīrtana Party" (RDTSKP). College campuses, festival grounds, state parks, and various other public venues thus became privy to *kīrtana*, Krishna-conscious philosophy, and the distribution of sacred vegetarian food (*prasādam*)—as only Vishnujana could provide it.

By 1974, his old friend Tamāla Krishna Gosvāmī had returned to America (from serving as one of Prabhupāda's leading devotees in India), and offered his managerial skills to the Rādhā-Dāmodara party. Together, Vishnujana Mahārāja and Tamāla Krishna Gosvāmī were the consummate team, and devotees—both well-established and newcomers—flocked to them like bees to honey.

But the two leaders were clearly not the focus—the focus, always, were the Deities. And Rādhā-Dāmodara were indeed special. Unlike most Rādhā-Krishna Deities, which could largely be found only in temples, they shared Their mercy freely, "taking it to the streets." Like Lord Chaitanya and Prabhu Nityānanda, Rādhā-Dāmodara were "mercy incarnations," regularly appearing in public places to bestow their grace upon people in general. This naturally led to a perpetual increase in followers.

Those joining would be divided into two groups: Those going out with Vishnujana and Tamāla Krishna, along with the Deities, for *kīrtana* and *prasādam* distribution, or those going off on satellite parties to distribute books, an innovation to extend the concept of *saṅkīrtana* conceived by Prabhupāda's guru Śrīla Bhaktisiddhānta Sarasvatī—if *kīrtana* meant sharing the holy name of Krishna with others, he reasoned, then distributing books would share this holy name to an even greater degree. If a *mṛdaṅga* could be heard for a few city blocks, then the printed word—the *bṛhat mṛdaṅga*, or the "great drum"—could be heard around the world.[42] Says ISKCON guru and early Prabhupāda disciple, Satsvarūpa Dāsa Gosvāmī:

> Śrīla Prabhupāda took personal interest in the party and approved loans from the BBT [Bhaktivedanta Book Trust] for the purchase of more buses, thus creating a *saṅkīrtana* army traveling in renovated Greyhound buses. By the end of the year [1974], the Rādhā-Dāmodara party had five buses, a fleet of vans, and one hundred and four men. "I am glad that you have understood the importance of my books," Prabhupāda wrote, "therefore I am stressing it so much. Let everyone take these books." Śrīla Prabhupāda encouraged the Rādhā-Dāmodara party to expand to hundreds of buses and thus fulfill the message of Śrī Chaitanya Mahāprabhu to bring Krishna Consciousness to every town and village. Prabhupāda called the buses "moving temples" and he urged the Rādhā-Dāmodara devotees to continue their program with certainty that they were pleasing Lord Chaitanya.[43]

In the end, Rādhā-Dāmodara TSKP was the most prodigious traveling *saṅkīrtana* initiative the world had ever seen, before or since, comprising numerous large buses with a legion of extension vans and cars that traversed the North American continent time and again. The dedicated devotees who affiliated themselves with this party distributed millions of Prabhupāda's books and inspired other ISKCON projects around the world to do the same—all in the name of Rādhā-Dāmodara. While Jīva Gosvāmī's original Deity and his replica can be found in India's holy places Vrindavan and Jaipur, providing shelter and inspiration for the multitudes who come to see them on a regular basis, their mercy incarnation in the forms of ISKCON's Rādhā-Dāmodara extended their assets to an often materialistic or godforsaken land steeped in all modernity has to offer, both good and bad.

But road life doesn't last forever. After traveling for the bulk of the 1970s, Śrī-Śrī Rādhā-Dāmodara were ready for a temple environment, where souls aspiring for Krishna Consciousness could come to see them and find a home at their lotus feet. This would be Gita Nagari, a 350-acre farm community in Port Royal, Pennsylvania, established by Śrīla Prabhupāda's disciples in in 1974, long before Rādhā-Dāmodara arrived there.

Modeled on Prabhupāda's by then thriving New Vrindaban community and on his own anticipatory text about "Geeta Nagari," written in the 1950s—and the way Indian villages have traditionally been run for centuries—he envisioned an environment of peace and prosperity, where devotees could live simply, close to the land, imbibing cow's milk along with the principles of Krishna consciousness. The community would be centered on its cows and bulls, whose virtues were well known in ancient India.

In its initial years, Gita Nagari met with mixed results. Caring for cows was always a central concern, and for a time numerous success stories appeared in ISKCON periodicals. But in due course it was found that manpower was lacking, and the community went through hard times. Still, in 1977 they managed to build their own temple, with the beautiful Deities of Śrī-Śrī Rādhā-Dāmodara taking center stage, inspiring the devotees who tended the farm. Prabhupāda himself had planned to come and visit that year, as he had the year before, but declining health prevented him from doing so. Later in 1977 he would depart for Krishna's kingdom in the spiritual world. Nonetheless, Rādhā-Dāmodara were now there to stay. Śrī Rādhā's associate *gopīs*, Lalitā and Viśākhā, eventually came to be by their side, and Gaura-Nitāi Deities are now also in place to share Their abundant mercy.

In the mid-1980s, Bhakti Tīrtha Swami (1950–2005), a leading ISKCON guru and High Chief in Warri, Nigeria, West Africa, started the Committee for Urban Spiritual Development, attracting a large number of newcomers to Krishna Consciousness. Inner-city endeavors, combined with welfare work and *prasādam* distribution, usually through opening restaurants, became a mainstay of his work. His restaurant in Washington, DC, was particularly successful. But perhaps his most prominent accomplishment in America was his founding, in 1988, of the Institute for Applied Spiritual Technology (IFAST), dedicated to presenting Krishna Consciousness to new age spiritual seekers around the world. One of the aims of the Institute was to establish self-sufficient farm communities, and to that end he rejuvenated ISKCON's Gita Nagari project in Port Royal, along with increasing the worship of Śrī-Śrī Rādhā-Dāmodara. With this project, the Swami found an attentive audience among professionals—high-powered doctors, lawyers, and others who saw truth in his message. He stationed himself in Gita Nagari until his passing in 2005. Today, his memorial exists right outside Rādhā-Dāmodara's temple in Pennsylvania, so far from Vrindavan and Jaipur—and yet, spiritually, these places share the same soul.

CONCLUSION

In traditional India, three Deities are said to represent the truths of Krishna Consciousness, or the path of Bhakti-yoga: Sanātana Gosvāmī's Madan-Mohan represents *sambandha*, or the genesis of reestablishing our relationship with Krishna. This is the beginning part of the devotional process. Rūpa Gosvāmī's Govinda Deity represents *abhideya*, or the path through which one attains true Krishna Consciousness. Finally, Madhu Paṇḍita's Deity, Gopīnātha, represents *prayojana*, or the ultimate fruit of the path of *bhakti*, love of God.

"These three Deities," Śrīla Prabhupāda writes, "have very specific qualities. Worship of Madan-Mohan is on the platform of reestablishing our forgotten relationship with the Supreme Personality of Godhead. In the beginning of our spiritual life we must worship Madan-Mohan so that He may attract us and nullify our attachment for material sense gratification. This relationship with Madan-Mohan is necessary for neophyte devotees. Then, when one wishes to render service to the Lord with strong attachment, one worships Govinda on the platform of transcendental service. When by the grace of Krishna and the other devotees one reaches perfection in devotional service, he can appreciate Krishna as Gopījanaballabha [Gopīnātha], the pleasure Deity of the damsels of Vraja."[44]

Jīva Gosvāmī's Dāmodara Deity—especially in his Western manifestation—may represent a fourth aspect: *saṅkīrtana*, or *distribution* of love of God. In other words, one discovers the path of Krishna Consciousness (*sambandha*); engages in devotional practices with full determination (*abhideya*); achieves the goal, or at least moves in the direction of achieving the goal (*prayojana*); and then one naturally seeks to share it with others (*saṅkīrtana*). This is what we find in the Deity of Dāmodara.

Indeed, the original Rādhā-Dāmodara temple, it is said, was a meeting place for the Six Gosvāmīs, where they would plan the propagation of Krishna-bhakti, amass a comprehensive library, and send delegates to share their literature in other parts of India. Soon, Śrīla Prabhupāda would reside at that same temple, and, taking inspiration from Śrī Rūpa, Śrī Jīva, and the other Gosvāmīs, conceive tangible plans for going abroad and spreading Mahāprabhu's mission ubiquitously. In the end, Prabhupāda achieved the impossible, with disciples who would take his teachings everywhere, as exemplified in the American (yet transcendental) adventure of Rādhā-Dāmodara TSKP, an act of compassion that continues to reverberate throughout the world. This author benefited from that compassion.[45]

In conclusion, then, a personal prayer is in order, for I too am bound by ropes, though not the kind that restrain Śrī Krishna.

As Raghunāth Dāsa Gosvāmī humbly says in his *Śrī-Śrī Vraja-Vilāsa-Stava* (verse 1): "I am bound by the ropes of the desire for distinction, thrust upon me by 'highwaymen' like lust. May the heroic devotees of Śrī Krishna save me by cutting these ropes and destroying them."[46] Dāsa Gosvāmī had earlier referred to these same highwaymen in *Manaḥ Śikṣā,* telling us that they live to accost travelers, stealing all their wealth and leaving them penniless. Enemies such as lust and anger rob the practitioner of his accumulated riches—his ability to properly worship—leaving him bereft of devotional treasure.[47] Dāsa Gosvāmī is obviously referring to the six standard enemies of spiritual life: lust, anger, greed, illusion, madness (pride), and envy (*kāma-krodha-lobha-moha-mada-mātsarya*).[48] I know these enemies all too well.

In Rūpa Gosvāmī's *Stavamālā*, he also uses Dāmodara-līlā to ask for edification, praying that just as Krishna brought down the twin Arjuna trees with the grinding mortar tied to His belly—and liberated the two *yakṣas* within, turning them into devotees—so too does Śrī Rūpa humbly wish that he will be similarly blessed and protected: "You pulled down the two *arjuna* trees and were pleased by the *yakṣa*s' prayers. You made the *yakṣa*s into your own devotees. Mādhava [Krishna], protect me, too" (*kṛta-yamalārjuna-bhaṅga guhyaka-nuti-dhṛta-raṅga/ nija-bhaktī-kṛta-yakṣa mādhava mām api rakṣa//*).[49]

Śrīla Prabhupāda alludes to a similar prayer in his masterwork *Nectar of Devotion* (chapter 4r):

> During the month of Kārttika, Dāmodara is prayed to as follows: "My dear Lord, You are the Lord of all, the giver of all benedictions." There are many demigods, like Lord Brahmā and Lord Śiva, who sometimes offer benedictions to their respective devotees. For example, Rāvaṇa was blessed with many benedictions by Lord Śiva, and Hiraṇyakaśipu was blessed by Lord Brahmā. But even Lord Śiva and Lord Brahmā depend upon the benedictions of Lord Kṛṣṇa, and therefore Kṛṣṇa is addressed as the Lord of all benefactors. As such, Lord Kṛṣṇa can offer His devotees anything they want, but still, the devotee's prayer continues, "I do not ask You for liberation or any material facility up to the point of liberation. What I want as Your favor is that I may always think of Your form in which I see You now, as Dāmodara. You are so beautiful and attractive that my mind does not want anything besides this wonderful form." In this same prayer, there is another passage, in which it is said, "My dear Lord Dāmodara, once when You were playing as a naughty boy in the house of Nanda Mahārāja, You broke the box containing yogurt, and because of that, mother Yaśodā considered You an offender and tied You with rope to the household grinding mortar. At that time You delivered two sons of Kuvera, Nalakūvara and Maṇigrīva, who were staying there as two *arjuna* trees in the yard of Nanda Mahārāja. My only request is that by Your merciful pastimes You may similarly deliver me."[50]

Finally, the contemporary guru Gour Govinda Swami (1929–1996) draws on Dāmodara-līlā as well, revealing the ultimate secret for achieving Lord Dāmodara's mercy, which can be found only at the feet of a bona fide spiritual master. "Guru has descended here with the one end of that rope that is known as *prema-bhakti sūtra*, the rope of *prema-bhakti*," says the Swami. "The one end of the rope is tied to the lotus feet of Krishna there in Goloka Vrindavan. With the other end of that rope, guru has come here and sees who has fallen in the deep dark well, *andha-kūpān*, who have been suffering and crying for many lives. Seeing you crying, his heart bleeds, so he drops that rope. Catch it up, hold it very tightly—no slackness! Then he will pull you out of the deep dark well. That is guru. That other end is tied to the lotus feet of Krishna. Now you will go to Krishna."[51] I pray to one day latch onto that rope.

NOTES

1. See A. C. Bhaktivedanta Swami Prabhupāda, *Kṛṣṇa Book*, chapter 9 (Bhaktivedanta Book Trust, 2008, reprint). Some translations of the Dāmodara story refer to the two inches as "two fingers," and Prabhupāda, in various instances, does the same. In ancient India, small length measurements, such as an *aṅgula* (finger) or a *mutthi* (fist) were used to determine length and breadth. In fact, one can find the rough equivalent of an inch by measuring from the top knuckle of one's thumb to the thumb tip. Two of those, of course, will constitute two inches. The "digit" is sometimes referred to as a finger or fingerbreadth, because it was originally based on the dimensions of a human finger.

2. "Dāmodarāṣṭakam" is a famous Sanskrit *stotra* attributed to the *Padma Purāṇa* and originally written by Satyavrata Muni.

3. Important modern retellings of the entire Dāmodara-līlā in English include: Śivarāma Swāmī, *Śrī Dāmodara Jananī*, Kṛṣṇa in Vṛndāvana series vol. 4 (Budapest: Lāl Publishing, 2016); B. G. Narasingha Maharaja, ed., *Śrī Dāmodara Kathā* (Vrindavan: Gosai Publishers, 2008); Śrī Śrīmad Bhaktivedānta Nārāyaṇa Goswāmī Mahārāja, *Dāmodara-Līlā-Mādhuri*, Volume One (Singapore and Kuala Lumpur: Sri Caitanya-Mudrani Publications, 1999); Vaiyasaki dasa Adhikari, *Śrī-Śrī Rādhā-Dāmodara Vilāsa (The Inner life of Vishnujana Swami & Jayānanda Prabhu)*: Volume One 1967–1972 (Vrindavan: Ras Bihari Lal and Sons; 2009, reprint; original printing, 1999); Mahanidhi Swami, *Prabhupāda at Rādhā Dāmodara* (India, n.p., 1990); Gour Govinda Swami Maharaja, chapter 4, "Bound by Love," in *Mathura Meets Vrindavan* (Bhubaneswar, Odisha: Gopal Jiu Publications, 2003); and Shubha Vilas, *Two Fingers Short* (Mumbai: Tulsi Books, 2015). Vallabhācārya's commentary on the *Śrīmad Bhāgavatam* is also available in an English edition with the full Dāmodara-līlā as one separate volume: *Sri Subodhini: Commentary On Śrīmad Bhāgavata Purāṇa, Text and English Translation, Canto Ten Chapters 9 To 11* (Delhi: Sri Satguru Publications; 2003).

4. The name Dāmodara occurs as name 367 in the *Viṣṇusahasranāma* ("Thousand Names of Vishnu").

5. When the trees were uprooted, the forms of Nalakūvara and Maṇigrīva, the *yakṣas* in question, emerged, offering prayers to the Lord. Receiving Krishna's benediction, they were reinstated in their previous divine position. Only Krishna and some neighboring children saw them, and when the elders arrived, they were amazed at how the divine infant could knock down two large trees, even with a heavy grinding mortar. Their plight as trees was now a thing of the past, and Krishna returned to his usual exploits in Vrindavan, playing with his friends and exchanging pastimes of love with his many devotees.

6. The term *niryoga-pāśa* is interesting: There is a method in Vrindavan for milking cows in which their legs are tied to protect them from overreacting and hurting themselves during the procedure. Following this technique, when Krishna milks his cows, he sometimes ties their hind legs with ornamental rope, which he keeps on his shoulders or places in his turban when his hands are not free. The rope is called

niryoga-pāśa. Symbolically, this rope is said to represent the ropes of love with which Krishna binds his devotees.

7. See Giriraj Swami, "Damodara-lila: Works and Grace": (http://www.girirajswami.com/?p=4949).

8. See Patricia Y. Mumme, "Grace and Karma in Nammālvār's Salvation" *in Journal of the American Oriental Society* 107, bo. 2 (April–June 1987), 257–66. See also "Balancing Faith and Works: To Whom is God's Grace Given?" in *The Agni and the Ecstasy: The Collected Essays of Steven J. Rosen (Satyaraja Dasa)* (London: Arktos, 2012), 86–88.

9. Ibid.

10. See "Short by Two fingers: Srila Viśvanātha Chakravartī Ṭhākura *Sārārtha Darśinī* commentary on *Śrīmad Bhāgavatam* 10.9.18," translated by Bhanu Swami (taken from http://www. granthamandira.com) and also published in *Sri Krishna Kathamrta Bindu*, No. 263 (November 2011).

11. See *Śrī Rādhā-rasa-sudhā-nidhi*: *vicchedābhāsa-mātrād ahaha nimiṣato gātra-visraṁsanādau, dīpyat-kalpāgni-koṭi jvalitam iva bhaved bāhyam abhyantaraṁ ca | gāḍha-snehānubandha-grathitam iva yayor adbhuta-prema-mūrtyoḥ, śrī-rādhā-mādhavākhyāṁ param iha madhuraṁ tad dvayaṁ dhāma jāne* ||174|| *yayonmīlat-kelī-vilasita-kaṭākṣaika-kalayā, kṛto vandī vṛndā-vipina-kalabhendro mada-kalaḥ | jaḍībhūtaḥ krīḍā-mṛga iva yad-ājñā-lava-kṛte, kṛtī naḥ sā rādhā śithilayatu sādhāraṇa-gatim* ||188||

12. The month of Kārttika—also known as the month of Dāmodara, and corresponding to the time between mid-October and mid-November—is elucidated in Gopāla Bhaṭṭa Gosvāmī's *Hari-bhakti-vilāsa* (chapter 16). For dedicated Vaishnavas, the text recommends that during this particular month it is particularly effective to recite the "Dāmodarāṣṭakam," mentioned above. Other austerities and vows enunciated in this text are considered highly auspicious during this month as well. The name "Kārttika" is derived from that of Rādhārāṇī's mother, whose name is Kīrttikā (or Kīrtidā). Rādhārāṇī thus became known as Kārtikī, which means, "born of Kīrttikā." At the beginning of his *Dig-darśinī-ṭīkā* on Śrī Dāmodarāṣṭakam, Śrīla Sanātana Gosvāmī includes the following verse as his *maṅgalācaraṇam*, highlighting Śrī Rādhā's connection to the Dāmodara-līlā: "Bowing before Śrī Dāmodara-īśvara, who is accompanied by Śrī Rādhā, I now commence my commentary of Śrī Dāmodarāṣṭaka entitled *Dig-darśinī*." (*śrī rādhā-sahitaṁ natvā śrī-dāmodaraṁ īśvaram, dāmodarāṣṭaka-vyākhyā digeṣā darśyate'dhunā*) Similarly, he closes his commentary on the last verse (16.206) as follows: "Everything I have I offer to you, Śrīmad Dāmodara, Lord of Śrī Rādhā's life, and I also offer it all to Chaitanya-deva and my guru." (*śrī-rādhā-prāṇa-nāthāya śrīmad-dāmodarāya te, sarvaṃ caitanya-devāya gurave 'rpitam eva me*).

13. The Uttara-kāṇḍa is sometimes published as a separate book known as the *Bhaviṣyottara Purāṇa*. The original Sanskrit for this verse is *saṅketāvasare cyute praṇayataḥ saṁrabdhayā rādhayā/ prārabhya bhrū-kuṭiṁ hiraṇya-raśanā-dāmnā nibaddhodaram// kārttikyāṁ jananī-kṛtotsava-vara-prastāvanā-pūrvakaṁ/ cāṭūni prathayantam ātma-pulakaṁ dhyāyema dāmodaram//*. (Cited in the commentary on *Krishna-Karṇāmṛta* by Śrīla Krishnadāsa Kavirāja Goswāmī, verse 110.) The English rendering is from Mahanidhi Swami, *Radha Kunda Mahima Madhuri* (Vrindavan:

Ras Bihari Lal and Sons, 2009), 50. Jīva Gosvāmī repeats this story in his *Priti Sandarbha* (367) as well.

14. There are numerous hints of Rādhikā's Dāmodara-līlā throughout India's wisdom texts. Another example occurs in the *Nārada-pañcarātra* (chapter 5), in a section called the "Śrī Rādhā Sahasranāma. There we learn that among Śrī Rādhā's many names are Dāmodara-priyā ("dear to Dāmodara," text 13) and Śṛṅkhalā ("the shackle that binds Krishna," verse 111). Both hint at the *mādhurya* aspect of Dāmodara-līlā.

15. See Jīva Gosvāmī, *Śrī Rādhā-kṛṣṇārcana-dīpikā,* texts 121–26, translated by Hari Parshad Das. Published in *Sri Krishna Kathamrta Bindu*, No. 263 (November 2011).

16. It is sometimes suggested that Rādhā and the *gopīs* worshipped Kātyāyanī in the usual fashion, viewing her as a manifestation of Durgā, or Devī, the goddess of the material world. While it is true that they sometimes worshipped both Śiva and the goddess for the sake of their service to Krishna, they did not see these deities in the usual way: The *Bhāgavatam* (12.13.16) says, "Lord Śiva is the best of all devotees" (*vaiṣṇavānāṁ yathā śambhuḥ*), and that's how the *gopīs* viewed him—not as God but as the greatest among the Vaishnavas. Similarly, because they worshipped Kātyāyanī, or Durgā, with the intention of attaining the favor of Krishna and not for material benefits, they understood the goddess as an incarnation of Yogamāyā. Thus, Rādhā and the *gopīs* worshipped Yogamāyā to attain Krishna as their husband. (See *Caitanya-caritāmṛta,* Madhya 8.90 and Madhya 9.360, purport)

17. Śrī Rūpa's fashioning of this Deity is revealed by Rādhākrishna Gosvāmī, a leading priest of Rūpa's own Govindadeva temple in the seventeenth century. In his book *Sādhana-dīpikā* (chapter 8), Rādhākrishna tells us, "Out of compassion, Śrī Rūpa Gosvāmī carved with his own hands the Deity of Dāmodara and presented him to Jīva Gosvāmī." The same text tells us that the Deity was installed in the presence of Rūpa, Sanātana, and Jīva himself on *śukla-daśami* in the month of Māgha (January/February) 1542, seven years after Śrī Jīva's arrival in Vrindavan. See also *Bhakti-ratnākara* 4.286.

18. See Radhanath Swami, "Journey to Spiritual Places with Radhanath Swami: Radha Damodar Temple." (http://radhanathswamiyatras.com/vrindavan-town/7-main-temples/radha-damodar-temple/).

19. All Six Gosvāmīs are, in their original forms, *mañjarīs*, meaning that their focus in the spiritual realm is Rādhikā even more than Krishna. In *Bhakti-rasāmṛta-sindhu* (1.2.299), Rūpa Gosvāmī states: *tad-bhāvecchātmikā tāsāṁ bhāva mādhurya kāmitā*, i.e., "The devotional attitude of wanting to assist Śrī Rādhā and other *yūtheśvarīs* (leading *gopīs*) in meeting Śrī Krishna for amorous exchanges, rather than enjoying with Krishna personally, is called *tad-bhāvecchātmikā* or *sakhī-bhāva*." This is a *mañjarī.*

20. In the practice of Krishna-*bhakti*, one must first establish the supremacy of Krishna as Bhagavān, or the Supreme Lord. This is why the Gosvāmīs initially focused on Krishna. Once Krishna is established as Bhagavān, then Rādhā Tattva can be understood. Jīva Gosvāmī implicitly shows this stepwise progression in the sequence of his six comprehensive volumes, the *Ṣaṭ-sandarbha,* also called *Bhāgavata-sandarbha.* The first four Sandarbhas are devoted to *sambandha-tattva,*

which establishes Krishna as the highest Deity and the most exclusive object of worship. The *Bhakti-sandarbha* deals with *abhidheya-tattva*, which is *bhakti* (devotion to Krishna), and the *Prīti-sandarbha* is concerned with *prayojana-tattva*, pure love of God. This can also be understood as follows: Śrī Jīva begins with the initial *Tattva* (offering various scriptural *pramāṇas* and other evidences showing that Krishna is Supreme, as introduced by the *Śrīmad-Bhāgavatam*) and then methodically moves to *Bhagavat* (understanding the three varieties of Godhead, i.e., Brahman, Paramātmā, and culminating in Bhagavān, more thoroughly). He then looks at *Paramātmā* and its implications (the living being in connection to Krishna), and, following this, Krishna's ultimate identity (as *svayam bhagavān*, the original Godhead). Finally, he explores *Bhakti* (the means to attain Krishna), and, after that, Śrī Rādhā (as found in *Priti-sandarbha*). The *Ṣaṭ-sandarbha* thus presents the entire philosophy and theology of Gauḍīya Vaiṣṇavism in systematic format.

21. For example, the tradition teaches: "There is no Lakṣmī devī without Vishnu and there is no Hari without Padmajā (Lakṣmī), for such is the verdict manifested in the *Hayagrīva-pañcarātra*." (*na viṣṇunā vinā devī na hariḥ padmajāṃ vinā/ hayagrīva-pañcarātram iha prakaṭitaṃ yataḥ//*) The same verse is also in Jīva Gosvāmī's *Rādhā-kṛṣṇārcana-dīpikā.*

22. Regarding the Six Gosvāmīs meeting at the Rādhā-Dāmodara temple to discuss their plans, Prabhupāda says, "they developed this Kṛṣṇa consciousness movement by sitting together in Vṛndāvana. And not only in Vṛndāvana, in that very particular place, Rādhā-Dāmodara temple, where we have got a little space. That you have seen, Rūpa Gosvāmī's tomb, that space. All the six Gosvāmīs, they used to sit down and discuss *Śrīmad-Bhāgavatam*. Gopāla Bhaṭṭa Gosvāmī was reading, and all the other Gosvāmīs, Rūpa, Sanātana, they were hearing, and Jīva Gosvāmī was writing comment. That is the comment of *Kṛṣṇa-sandarbha.* So that place in Vṛndāvana, Rādhā Dāmodara Temple, is very sacred place. So they were practicing this Kṛṣṇa consciousness" (*Nectar of Devotion* lectures Jan. 8, 1973).

23. Man Singh of Amber was a disciple of Raghunātha Bhaṭṭa Gosvāmī (1505–1579) and was behind the building of Rūpa Gosvāmī's massive Govindadeva temple.

24. Prabhupāda considered this as one of the most important temples in Vrindavan, and from the time he initially stayed there in the late 1950s enjoyed a special relationship with both the Deity and the temple environment. Among his many letters about this temple, he writes to his disciple Shivananda (November 11, 1968): "Regarding Radha-Damodara temple, because it is one of the most important temples in Vrindaban, I took shelter in this temple." And further to Nripen Babu (March 18, 1967): "As you are going to restore order in the temple I am always with you because Srila Jiva Goswami's temple is my heart and soul. I think with your cooperation I shall be able to render some genuine service to the Gosvamis who are staying in the temple." As far as the Rādhā-Dāmodara temple being a humble dwelling, it was apparently easy to miss when Moghul troops came to the area to destroy Vaishnava Deities: "[It is said that] during the infamous attacks on Vrindavana's temples in 1670, the Moguls went straight past Radha-Damodara, mistaking it for a private residence and sparing the temple from attack. Out of fear of the Moguls, the temple priests had already moved the original Radha-Damodara Deities to Jaipur, a stronghold of Krishna devotees,

where the Deities remain today." See Vrindavani Devi Dasi, "The Hub of the Spiritual World" (http://www.krishna.com/hub-spiritual-world).

25. In Vrindavan's Rādhā-Dāmodara Temple, the *gopīs* to the left and the right of Lord Dāmodara are said to be Śrī Rādhā and Lalitādevī, respectively. The local priests tell a popular story about the origin of these Deities, passed down, it is said, from the recently departed Acharya Sri Nirmal Chandra Goswami, who was the fifteenth *sevāita ācārya* of the Rādhā-Dāmodara Temple. His ancestry can be traced to Krishna Dāsa, a direct student of Jīva Gosvāmī. In other words, his family has been involved in the worship of these Deities from just after the time of Śrī Jīva. The story may be summarized as follows: One day, a fisherman in Bengal, out for a normal fishing adventure, caught two deities instead of fish. Confused, he gave the two sacred objects to the king. That very night, the king had a dream in which he was told that he should send these Deities to Jīva Gosvāmī in Vrindavan, which he did. Śrī Jīva happily received the Deities but was unsure who they were. That night, Rādhikā herself came to him in a dream and revealed their identities. Heeding the words of the Goddess, Śrī Jīva placed Rādhikā on the left of Lord Dāmodara and Lalitā on right, and so their service began.

26. See Jagadananda Das, "The Authenticity of the *Caitanya-Caritāmṛta-Mahā-Kāvya*, Part I" (2015). (http://jagadanandadas.blogspot.com/2015/10/the-authenticity-of-caitanya-caritamrta.html).

27. It should be said too that Jīva's vast learning was without equal. He was considered one of the greatest philosophers of his time, perhaps of any time, and, apropos of this, he established the Viśva Vaishnava Rāja Sabhā (World Vaishnava Association) and the Rūpānuga Vidyāpitha, educational facilities for Gauḍīya Vaishnavas to study the works of Rūpa, Sanātana, and others. He is renowned for formulating the Vedāntic system of Acintya-bhedābheda, and is a prolific author, with Sanskrit tomes ranging in content and style from treatises on theology and philosophy; scriptural commentaries and hermeneutics; and works on grammar and poetics, including detailed analyses of the most esoteric and sublime philosophy.

28. See Jan Brzezinski, "Jiva Goswami: Biography and Bibliography," in *Journal of Vaishnava Studies* 15. 2 (Spring 2007), 51–80.

29. See Vrindavani Devi Dasi, "The Hub of the Spiritual World" (http://www.krishna.com/hub-spiritual-world).

30. Shoba Narayan, "Krishna, laddoos and rabdi in Jaipur," October 24, 2015 (https://www.livemint.com/Sundayapp/viC4qQ3kxa6NF6DaxVI0gN/Krishna-laddoos-and-rabdi-in-Jaipur.html) See also "Vrindavan deities in Jaipur," October 26, 2015 (https://vrindavantoday.com/vrindavan-deities-jaipur/).

31. Though the common understanding is that the original Deities are still in Jaipur, the official website of the Rādhā-Dāmodara Mandir in Vrindavan has another story to tell (http://www.radhadamodarmandir.com/history.htm), claiming that the original Deities made their way back to Vrindavan and, having returned, never left. Others say that the Deities, once having arrived in Jaipur, never again returned to Braj. Still others claim that the Deities returned to Vrindavan in 1796—and in 1821 were brought back again to Jaipur, where they still remain (http://www.radhadamodarji.com/Festivals.htm). It is unlikely that anyone knows for sure. In the end, it matters

little, for Krishna is Krishna, and whether it is the original Deity or a facsimile, the potency to purify all onlookers and worshippers is the same. However, it is likely that the original Deity is the one currently in Jaipur. The late Alan Entwistle, who is renowned for his knowledge of Vrindavan, supports the view that Rādhā Dāmodara had temporarily returned to Vrindavan in 1796 but was returned to Jaipur in 1821. See Asim Kumar Roy, *History of the Jaipur City* (Delhi: Manohar, 1978), 27–28. Quoted in A.W. Entwistle, *Braj Centre of Krishna Pilgrimage* (Groningen: Egbert Forsten, 1987), 219, fn471.

This particular version of the story—that after several decades in Vrindavan, the original Rādhā-Dāmodara Deities ultimately returned to Jaipur—is supported by documentary evidence: "In 1796 Śrī-Śrī Rādhā-Dāmodar returned to Vrindāvan for some unknown reason. In 1821, Govinda Lāl Gosvāmī, the *sevādhikārī* of Rādhā-Dāmodar temple in Vrindāvan, received a number of [requests] from various government ministers (Raoul Bairīsāl and Sanghi Jhuthārām) expressing the desire of the Mahārājā that Śrī-Śrī Rādhā-Dāmodar return to Jaipur. . . . A few months [later], Śrī-Śrī Rādhā-Dāmodar returned to Jaipur on the eleventh day of the dark fortnight in the month of Māgh. This time they received a royal reception. They were met on the outskirts of the city by a royal procession consisting of elephants, soldiers, vassals, feudal princes and chieftains to escort their Lordships to the city. After first offering a tribute in the form of a coconut and a golden coin [as per the custom], the Deity's palanquin was hoisted onto the back of one of the elephants. The son of Govinda Lāl Gosvāmī also rode on the back of an elephant. With the elephants in front, the festive procession made its way to the king's palace." See Asimkumar Ray, *Vṛndāban theke Jaipur* ("From Vrindāvan to Jaipur"), Bengali edition, ed., Kiran Candra Rāi (Calcutta: Jijnasa, 1985). Śrīla Nārāyaṇa Mahārāja also confirms that the original Deities are currently in Jaipur. See B. V. Nārāyaṇa Mahārāja, *Śrī Braja Maṇḍala Parikramā* (Delhi: Gaudiya Vedanta Publications, 2001, reprint), 441.

32. Monier Williams defines *pratibhū* as follows: "to be equal to or on a par with." A variation is *pratimā*, "an image, likeness"—a synonym for "a Deity." See Monier-Monier Williams, *A Complete Sanskrit-English Dictionary* (Oxford: The Clarendon Press, 2002), 668. Traditionally, a *pratibhū* Deity is considered non-different from the original. Teachers of the tradition often quote the *Bhāgavatam*'s Rāsa-līlā (10.33.19) to give a sense of just how identical the *pratibhū* is to the original: "Expanding himself as many times as there were cowherd women to associate with, the Supreme Lord, though self-satisfied, playfully enjoyed their company" (*kṛtvā tāvantam ātmānaṁ/ yāvatīr gopa-yoṣitaḥ// reme sa bhagavāṁs tābhir/ ātmārāmo 'pi līlayā*). In other words, Krishna himself was with each cowherd woman, individually.

33. Prabhupāda teaches much the same: "According to Vedic culture, once worship has begun a deity may not be moved. Therefore if ISKCON does not own the property, then there may be an unacceptable risk that the deities will have to be moved in the future. This is particular relevant for the worship of Rādhā-Kṛṣṇa and large marble deities." (http://www.deityworship.com/installation-guidelines.html).

34. The usual Hindu view of Mughal history positions Akbar (r. 1556–1605) as a liberal, pluralistic leader in contrast with Aurangzeb, who is generally seen as little more than a bloodthirsty, sectarian tyrant. However, recent research—using

vernacular texts from Aurangzeb's own time period, written by both supporters and adversaries—has determined that he was not the vicious autocrat people think he was. Yes, during his reign there were clearly isolated instances of iconoclasm, such as dismantling a portion of the Govindadev Mandir and virtually destroying the Keshavadev temple in Mathurā, but his violent work, it seems, was not as extensive as suggested by colonial-era scholarship. Moreover, his reign was not altogether different than that of his peers: It was instigated by political, financial, and other concerns, as opposed to trite bigotry or religious hatred. It is now known that his exaggerated reputation as a religious bigot was largely constructed by the British according to their methods of "divide and conquer" (*divide et impera*), meant to pit Hindus against Muslims and vice versa.

In fact, Aurangzeb followed the specific Islamic law, well established by his time, of granting protection to non-Muslim religious leaders and institutions. Again, recent findings reveal that his policies toward Hindu temples were more focused on state security than religious preference. Contrary to the long-standing view of Aurangzeb as a mastermind behind temple demolition, it is now known that he patronized thousands of Hindu temples, many of which thrived under his rule. Evidence also shows that Aurangzeb granted land to build both Hindu and Jain structures and sometimes even castigated his fellow Muslims if they disturbed local Brahmins.

Some may argue that this newfound view of Aurangzeb is merely an attempt to be politically correct, pushing back against Hindu nationalism and anti-Muslim sentiment. Indeed, no one would question that he was almost constantly at war, that he expanded the Mughal empire to its greatest extent, and that it collapsed soon after his demise due to his extremism. All that being said, the recent scholarship on this subject is too extensive to not take seriously and further research. See Audrey Truschke, *Aurangzeb: The Life and Legacy of India's Most Controversial King* (Stanford University Press 2017); Audrey Truschke, "A Much-Maligned Mughal" in *Aeon* (April 2017), https://aeon.co/essays/the-great-aurangzeb-is-everybodys-least-favourite-mughal; I. Habib, "Dealing with multiplicity: Mughal administration in Braj Bhum under Aurangzeb (1659–1707)," *Studies in People's History* 3, no. 2 (1996): 151–64; Heidi Pauwels and Emilia Bachrach, "Aurangzeb as Iconoclast? Vaishnava Accounts of the Krishna Images' Exodus from Braj" in *Journal of the Royal Asiatic Society*, Series 3, 28, no. 3 (2018): 485–508; Heidi Pauwels, "A Tale of Two Temples: Mathurā's Keśavadeva and Orcchā's Caturbhujadeva," in *South Asian History and Culture* 2, no. 2 (April 2011): 278–99; Richard Eaton, "Temple Desecration and Indo-Muslim States," *Journal of Islamic Studies* 11, no. 3 (2000): 283–319. Special thanks to Heidi Pauwels and John S. Hawley for the fruits of their research and personal correspondence.

35. See Amy Joy Hirschtick, "The Krishnas of Jaipur" PhD thesis, Department of Religious Studies, Indiana University (June 2017), 64.

36. Personal correspondence with Malay Goswami on November 27, 2019.

37. Shantanu Bhattacharya, originally from Assam, is currently a leading priest at the Rādhā-Dāmodara temple in Jaipur. "The Deity on the left of Damodaraji is Radhaji," he says. "Sakhi Lalitaji is on the right." This information was confirmed by the main Mahant of the temple, Malay Goswami. Personal correspondence on November

28, 2019. That fact that Rādhā *and* Lalitā accompany Dāmodara—in both Vrindavan and Jaipur—has important implications for the Gauḍīya Sampradāya, particularly those who see themselves as Rūpānuga Vaishnavas: Such devotees follow in the footsteps of Rūpa Mañjarī, who is the chief assistant of Lalitādevī.

38. "Present with Śrī-Śrī Rādhā-Dāmodar in Jaipur are Śrī-Śrī Rādhā-Vṛndāvancandra. It is not certain who established the worship of these Deities or when. They came from Vrindāvan to Jaipur in the year 1765. On the plea of one gentleman named Harsahāy, a decree was issued on the third day of the bright fortnight in the month of Kārtika, stipulating a daily stipend of Rs.1 for the *bhoga* offering and Rs.100 annually for attire. It is mentioned in the decree that Śrī-Śrī Rādhā-Vṛndāvancandra hailed from Vrindāvan. . . . Later, the expenses for all the Deities (Śrī-Śrī Rādhā-Dāmodar, Śrī-Śrī Rādhā-Vṛndāvancandra, Govardhan-śilā and Narasiṁhadev) were merged into one leasehold, issued in 1883 Samvat." See Asimkumar Ray, *Vṛndāban theke Jaipur* ("From Vrindāvan to Jaipur"), Bengali edition, ed., Kiran Candra Rāi (Calcutta: Jijnasa, 1985).

39. The presence of Sanātana Gosvāmī's Girirāja-charan-śilā in Jaipur is interesting. According to the editor of Asimkumar Ray, *Vṛndāban theke Jaipur* ("From Vrindāvan to Jaipur"), Bengali edition, ed., Kiran Candra Rāi (Calcutta: Jijnasa, 1985): "When Śrī-Śrī Rādhā-Dāmodar were brought to Jaipur this *śilā* accompanied them. [Editor's note: During the present day, there are Govardhan śilā*s* both in Jaipur and Vrindāvan, both purported to be the *śilā* given by Śrī Kṛṣṇa to Sanātana. Both of the *śilās* have the impressions of Kṛṣṇa's foot, as well as his flute, cane and the impression of the hoof-print of a calf. The relief work of the *śilā* in Jaipur is pronounced, more so that the one in Vrindāvan, almost as though it has been carved by an expert stonemason. The *śilā* in Vrindāvan does not have the same distinguishing features or definition.]"

40. See Vaiyasaki Das Adhikari, *Śrī-Śrī Rādhā-Dāmodara Vilāsa (The Inner life of Vishnujana Swami & Jayānanda Prabhu)*: Volume One 1967–1972 (Vrindavan: Ras Bihari Lal and Sons; 2009, reprint; original printing, 1999), 49. For the entire story of the manuscripts getting stolen in Vīra Hāṁvīra's kingdom and Śrīnivāsa's retrieval of them, see Steven Rosen, *The Lives of the Vaishnava Saints* (Vrindavan: Rasbihari Lal & Sons, 2002, reprint; original printing by FOLK Books, 1998); also see Tony K. Stewart, *The Final Word* (Oxford University Press, 2010), especially chapter 1.

41. These are the words of Tamāla Krishna Gosvāmī (1946–2002), a highly regarded ISKCON guru and scholar who, although not part of the original road show, later joined Rādhā-Dāmodara TSKP and, along with Vishnujana Mahārāja, became one of its foundational members and abiding inspirations. For the exact quote and elaboration, see Tamal Krishna Goswami, *Servant of the Servant* (Los Angeles: Bhaktivedanta Book Trust, 1984), 391–92.

42. See "Srila Bhaktisiddhanta Sarasvati Thakura" (http:// harmonist.us/2016/12/srila-bhaktisiddhanta-sarasvati-thakura/).

43. See Satsvarūpa Dāsa Goswāmī, *"Distribute books, Distribute Books, Distribute Books!": A History of Book Distribution in ISKCON, 1970–1975* (Port Royal, PA: Gita-nagari Press, 1982), 46–47.

44. *Caitanya-caritāmṛta* Ādi 1.19, purport.

45. I was a monk on that Rādhā-Dāmodara party in the years 1974 and 1975.

46. *pratiṣṭhā rajjūbhir baddhaṁ kāmādyair vartma-pātibhiḥ chittvā tāḥ saṁharantas tā-naghāreḥ pāntu māṁ bhaṭāḥ.* ||1||

47. *asac-ceṣṭā-kaṣṭa-prada-vikaṭa-pāśālibhir ihaprakāmaṁ kāmādi-prakaṭa-patha-pāti-vyatikaraiḥ |gale baddhvā hanye'ham iti bakabhid-vartmapa-gaṇekuru tvaṁ phutkārān avati sa yathā tvāṁ mana itaḥ* ||5||

48. The standard Ariṣaḍvarga ("the group of six foes") is alluded to by Krishna in the *Bhagavad-gītā* (3.37, 16.11–12, and 16.21). However, its earliest source may be the *Maitreya Upaniṣad* 3.18 (*ṣaḍ vikāra vihīno'smiṣaṭ kośa rahito'smy ahamari ṣaḍ varga mukto'smiantarād antaro'smy aham*), whose commentary (*ṭippanī*) lists all six (*kāma krodhau lobha mohau mado mātsaryam eva ca, ete'riṣaṭakāḥ' iti*). The same listing is also found in the *Varāha Upaniṣad* (1.10) and the *Artha-śāstra* (1.6.1–11).

49. This is a verse from Śrī Rūpa's *Stavamālā*, in a section called "Chandoṣṭādaśaka." This particular poem, the *Yamalārjunabhañjanam,* is the third in a series of eighteen. See David Buchta, "Pedagogical Poetry: Didactics and Devotion in Rupa Gosvāmin's *Stavamālā*," PhD thesis, (University of Pennsylvania, 2014), 240. This is Buchta's translation.

50. His Divine Grace A. C. Bhaktivedanta Swami Prabhupada, *Nectar of Devotion*, "Chapter Four: Devotional Service Surpasses All Liberation" (Boston: ISKCON Press, 1970), 40–41. He is referring to the penultimate verse of the Dāmodarāṣṭakam prayers: *kuverātmajau baddha-mūrtyaiva yadvat/ tvayā mocitau bhakti-bhājau kṛtau ca// tathā prema-bhaktim svakām me prayaccha/ na mokṣe graho me 'sti dāmodareha//* ||7||

51. Sri Srimad Gour Govinda Swami Maharaja, "Guru's Rope" in *Sri Krishna Kathamrta Bindu,* issue 462 (from a lecture in Seattle, May 18, 1993), 2.

Chapter Four

Radha Raman

Three Deities in One

Poised at the summit of ecstasy in a singularly enchanting threefold bending form, Radha Raman (Rādhārāmaṇa) has for centuries drawn countless pilgrims to his abode, Śrī Radha Raman Mandir, one of Vrindavan's most famous and respected Vaishnava temples. A magnet for pilgrims, scholars, and spiritual connoisseurs alike, he is deeply revered and much loved. But who is he?

Of course, all know that he is Krishna: Nanda Lāl, the darling of Vrindavan, the lover of the *gopīs*. But this chapter will show that there is more to him than meets the eye. The Deity of Radha Raman has secretly hidden within his slender, alluring form, his transcendental counterpart, Śrī Rādhā, the Original Goddess, who is residing in the selfsame body as her beloved Śrī Krishna.

Additionally, we will show that Radha Raman is a manifestation of Śrī Chaitanya Mahāprabhu (1486–1533), the *channa* ("hidden") manifestation of the Supreme Lord. According to the tradition, he is God himself, appearing in the form of his own devotee.

Thus, the apparently lone Deity of Radha Raman is, in actuality, three Deities in one.

Interestingly, this preeminent Gauḍīya-Vaishnava Deity from the North has his genesis in the South, not in terms of origin or worship, but in terms of backstory and predecessor tradition. The story of Radha Raman begins with the lineage of Śrīvaishnavism in its holy environment of Śrī Raṅgam, arguably the crest jewel of all such sacred shrines, and it begins not with Radha Raman himself, but with another Krishna Deity altogether.

In the days when South India's bountiful Kāverī River was the lifeline that nourished the ancient kingdoms and cities that bejeweled Tamil Nadu, this sacred temple town was sought after by sages and pilgrims from all quarters. Scintillating in the Kāverī's fertile delta, this small, celebrated center of learning and worship drew multitudes to its famed Mandir each day. They came from hundreds of miles to relish the sight of Śrī Raṅganāth, also known as Raṅganāthaswāmy, or Periya Perumāḷ, the large, recumbent Krishna/Nārāyaṇa Deity whose extraordinary beauty graces the temple's innermost sanctum.[1]

In 1511,[2] among its many pilgrims, a *sannyāsī* like no other arrived. His presence and his unprecedented beauty, learning, and influence were unique, even among the hosts of great souls who came to visit Śrī Raṅgam.

The *sannyāsī* would eventually be known as Śrī Chaitanya Mahāprabhu, mentioned above. He had come to Śrī Raṅgam without fanfare to quietly spread his unique brand of divine love, even if his soft and humble presentation was often counterbalanced by passionate dialogue and the enthusiastic singing of Krishna's name.

While in Śrī Raṅgam, Mahāprabhu graced the home of Vyeṅkaṭa Bhaṭṭa, head priest of the temple, and he enjoyed intimate friendship with Bhaṭṭa and his two brothers, as will be described below. These three vastly learned *brāhmaṇas* warmly welcomed the traveling *sannyāsī* as an honored guest. Their exchanges were many, since the Lord stayed for a full four months (during Chāturmāsya, the monsoon season), as recorded in Krishnadāsa Kavirāja Gosvāmī's *Caitanya-caritāmṛta* (Madhya 1.107–8 and Madhya 9.79–165).

Significantly, it was at this time that Śrī Chaitanya also met Vyeṅkaṭa's young son, Gopāla Bhaṭṭa, who, in mature years, would become Gopāla Bhaṭṭa Gosvāmī (circa 1503–1578),[3] one of the famous Six Gosvāmīs of Vrindavan. Śrī Chaitanya's stay in Śrī Raṅgam was thus pivotal in the history of Gauḍīya Vaishnavism and significant in the primal origins of the Radha Raman Deity. We will therefore circuitously approach the story of Radha Raman through a brief look at Śrī Raṅgam.

LORD RAṄGANĀTH

Located in the Tiruchirappalli (Trichy) district of Tamil Nadu, Śrī Raṅgam is widely renowned as the largest temple complex in all of India. Although it dates to antiquity, with a past that includes stories of both the first created being, Brahmā, at the dawn of time, and Lord Rāma in a previous world age, its current manifestation is traceable to the time of the Pandyas and Cholas—South Indian dynasties that replaced the Pallavas in the ninth century. Visually stunning, the island of six hundred acres is home to this massive tribute to Vishnu, with its seven huge concentric walls radiating outward from the inner sanctum like divine water towers, showering blessings on all who visit.

Within the temple compound, one invariably finds throngs of pilgrims meandering through crowded lanes with village-like homes, shops, and assorted frenetic activity. Communal gatherings and festivals are held on a nearly daily basis. The temple's twenty-one ornate *gopurams* (entrance towers) that surround the immense complex rise high into the sky, evoking awe and reverence for the Deity who inspires such devotion. The most esteemed shrines are within the inner four boundary walls, though there are many deities and much to see before one reaches that most sacred of all areas. Mahāprabhu would have seen all of this, and then, too, he would have relished the Deity.

It is said that during his four months in Śrī Raṅgam, Mahāprabhu sang and danced before Lord Raṅganāth on a daily basis.[4] He was enamored by the altar for his entire stay: the main Deity, the *mūla-mūrti,* is a two-armed form of Lord Vishnu,[5] Lord Raṅganāth, reclining on the divine serpent Ananta Śeṣa.[6] In front of the imposing, majestic Lord Raṅganāth, who is some fourteen to sixteen feet in length,[7] is the much smaller *utsava-mūrti* (proxy icon) called "Namperumāḷ," Vishnu in a standing pose, and it is this smaller form that, for practical purposes, is taken on procession and served as representative of the main Deity. Small Deities of Śrī and Bhū—Lakṣmī, the Supreme Goddess, and her expansion, the Earth Goddess—flank Namperumāḷ, the smaller Deity, on his right and left, respectively. On the altar one can also see a golden basket of *śālagrāmas* (fossilized, aniconic shell or rock manifestations of Vishnu) behind Bhūdevī. To the right there are two smaller Deities of Vishnu, which are customary Bali Bera and smaller Snapana Bera Deities, i.e., movable icons used for daily offerings (rice, water, etc.) to various demigods and for daily bathing ceremonies.[8]

In addition to the main sanctum, numerous altars stipple the Śrī Raṅgam environment, with at least fifty other shrines in the same temple complex. Some of these already existed in Mahāprabhu's time; others were added later. Particularly significant is the *samādhi* (tomb) of Śrī Rāmānujācārya (1017–1137), the systematizer of the entire Śrīvaishnava tradition, which was already in place when Mahāprabhu arrived. Pilgrims from around the world now visit to pay their respects.

Though the Śrī Raṅgam temple had, in the past, come under attack by Muslim forces, this had all occurred centuries before Mahāprabhu. By the time of his visit to Veṅkaṭa Bhaṭṭa's home, the temple was once again thriving, and the level of Deity worship would have been restored to the highest standards of Vaishnava practice, with no hindrance whatsoever from hostile elements.

The story of the Muslim invasion is interesting for historical context. The temple was invaded in 1311 by Mālik Kafūr and again in 1323 (some say 1331) by Ulugh Khan (Muhammad Bin Tughlak). The latter was highly posted in the Delhi sultanate and, upon invading South India, managed to establish the Madurai Sultanate to the dismay of resident Vaishnavas. Thus, while the former had merely plundered riches, the latter had caused devastation, disrupting lives and worship in a major way. The processional Deity itself had to be moved to safety in Tirupati by a band of courageous devotees headed by Piḷḷai Lokācārya (1205–1311), a prominent Śrīvaishnava *ācārya.*

Restoration began in 1372 with a major Southern conquest by Vijayanagar armies. Vedānta Deśika (1268–1369), foremost of the scholarly followers of Rāmānuja, returned to Śrī Raṅgam at that time, inspired by the reconsecration of his beloved Deity. The bulk of the Śrīvaishnava community returned during this period as well.[9] The temple was more thoroughly rebuilt toward the end of the fourteenth century and embellished and expanded upon with many new *gopurams* in the sixteenth and seventeenth centuries and continued to be refurbished into the modern era. The main southern entrance—a thirteen-story *gopuram*, called the Rāja-gopuram—is the largest in India at 235 feet high. It was finished in 1987 and is now a major pilgrimage attraction for the entire Vaishnava world.

MEETING THE BHAṬṬA BROTHERS

By Mahāprabhu's time, the Muslim invasion would have been a thing of the past, with Śrī Raṅgam already largely rebuilt, invigorated, and animated in its worship of Lord Raṅganāth. Indeed, it is reported that when Śrī Chaitanya arrived, he visited Raṅganāth's temple and was overwhelmed with divine love (Madhya 1.107). He lived at Vyeṅkaṭa Bhaṭṭa's home for the four months of the rainy season, as already mentioned, and blissfully sang and danced at the temple on a daily basis.

But even more important, perhaps, was his interaction with his hosts: Vyeṅkaṭa, Śrī Raṅgam's chief priest, and his two learned brothers, Prabodhānanda Sarasvatī and Tirumalla Bhaṭṭa (also known as Trimalla). The three of them relished and deeply benefited from Mahāprabhu's association. Young Gopāla Bhaṭṭa, Vyeṅkaṭa's son, was also in attendance, serving the Master with great enthusiasm. When Mahāprabhu would take bath in the Kāverī River, for example, Gopāla Bhaṭṭa used to go with him, holding his clothes and doting on him in every way. He would oversee the cooking for Mahāprabhu, too, and render all services with great love, going beyond the call of duty. The Lord became pleased with him, and marked him as a special devotee.[10]

It was around this time too that young Gopāla Bhaṭṭa is said to have taken initiation from his uncle, Prabodhānanda Sarasvatī, who was one of the greatest scholars of his time. Indeed, both *Hari-bhakti-vilāsa* (1.2) and *Bhakti-ratnākara* (1.151) indicate that Gopāla Bhaṭṭa was his disciple, even if initiation as such is not clearly mentioned.[11]

Prabodhānanda Sarasvatī gradually moved from the worship of Lakṣmī-Nārāyaṇa, which is a form of devotion more characteristic of Śrīvaishnavas, to the worship of Rādhā-Krishna, the prerogative of Gauḍīya Vaishnavism. His later writings, such as *Rādhā-rasa-sudhā-nidhi* and *Vṛndāvana-mahimāmṛta*, show that he became fully ensconced in the Gauḍīya mood, with both Rādhā-dāsyam and Braj-bhakti permeating his poetry and prose.[12] This transformation took place in large measure because of his conversation with Mahāprabhu in Śrī Raṅgam, and it matured further when he later traveled to Vrindavan.[13]

Although that conversation is too detailed to reproduce here, its essential features may be summarized as follows.

It is to be remembered that Vyeṅkaṭa and his brothers were prominent members of the Śrī Sampradāya. This is a particular Vaishnava lineage that emphasizes awe and reverence, focusing, as it does, on Lakṣmī and Vishnu (Nārāyaṇa) as opposed to Rādhā and Krishna. Kavirāja Gosvāmī gives a detailed account of Mahāprabhu's discussion with Vyeṅkaṭa, especially regarding the nature of their respective Deities, Vishnu and Krishna. These manifestations of divinity, Mahāprabhu and Vyeṅkaṭa admit, are in essence one. However, when forms are diverse, as these two are, there must be nuances of difference as well. Those differences were explored in this conversation.

Through numerous lighthearted arguments, delivered in a friendly, loving way, Mahāprabhu shows Vyeṅkaṭa and his brothers the importance of intimacy over power, sweetness over awe and reverence. While Mahāprabhu clearly has respect for Vyeṅkaṭa's dedication to Lakṣmī-Vishnu, and says as much,[14] he wants to leave him with the understanding that love displaces majesty, Krishna supersedes Vishnu. Mahāprabhu thus makes evident, using scripture and logic, that Vishnu's magisterial bearing (*aiśvarya*) is subservient to Krishna's sweet and intimate nature (*mādhurya*), even while both are in essence the same divinity.

Vyeṅkaṭa understands Mahāprabhu well and praises his insight. The essence of Vyeṅkaṭa's realization, having heard the truth from Śrī Chaitanya, might be summarized as follows: "Vyeṅkaṭa Bhaṭṭa continued, 'According to transcendental realization, there is no difference between the forms of Nārāyaṇa and Krishna. Yet in Krishna there is a special transcendental attraction due to the conjugal *rasa*, and consequently he surpasses Nārāyaṇa. This is the conclusion of transcendental philosophy in terms of Rasa Tattva'" (Madhya 9.117).

While thoroughly explaining the subtleties of *rasa* (spiritual relationship) over *tattva* (objective truth), Mahāprabhu affirms Vyeṅkaṭa's realization in Madhya 9.153–54. In fact, he says it is offensive to see distinctions between any of God's many forms (*īśvaratve bheda mānile haya aparādha*). Still, his point was made, showing the glory of Krishna, and all of this was to have a deep influence on the youthful Gopāla Bhaṭṭa.[15]

GOPĀLA BHAṬṬA'S DREAM

While serving Mahāprabhu in Śrī Raṅgam, Gopāla Bhaṭṭa lamented his plight of seeing him only as a *sannyāsī* and not as a young householder. He wondered about Mahāprabhu's beautiful form and pastimes in Navadvīpa, where he had associated with those closest to him and chanted the holy name with great abandon. He thus prayed before Mahāprabhu with pronounced emotion, "O Providence, why was I born in this distant place? Why was I forced to only see my Lord after his renunciation, so far from Bengal?"

As soon as these thoughts crossed his mind, says the *Bhakti-ratnākara* (1.100–22), Gopāla Bhaṭṭa had a vision in which he witnessed Mahāprabhu's many pastimes in the land of his youth, and, due to mystical accomplishment, Gopāla was actually able to enter into them: Nityānanda, Advaita, and others lovingly welcomed him into the sacred precincts of Navadvīpa. Furthermore, Mahāprabhu revealed his form as Vrajendranandana Krishna, dark blue like a newly formed rain cloud and incomparably beautiful. The vision quickly faded, and Mahāprabhu stood before Gopāla Bhaṭṭa in his golden form as Śrī Chaitanya, his identity now fully revealed.[16]

At that time, Mahāprabhu offered Gopāla Bhaṭṭa direct instructions, telling him to go to Vrindavan and to work closely with the two valuable jewels—the two brothers known as Rūpa and Sanātana—which he did, in due course. Mahāprabhu specifically told him to help them in compiling scriptures and uncovering the holy places of Braj. Most importantly, Śrī Chaitanya said he would come to be with him in Vrindavan and that he should make arrangements for his stay. Excited that the Lord had now promised his association in the land of Krishna, Gopāla Bhaṭṭa was more anxious than ever to go there.[17]

Mahāprabhu stayed a few more days in Śrī Raṅgam, inspiring devotees with the holy name and his discourses on ultimate reality. Feeling separation from Lord Jagannātha, Baladeva, and Subhadrā, the forms of Krishna, Krishna's immediate expansion (brother), and his divine energy (sister), respectively, that had captured his heart in Purī, he is said to have carved duplicate images with his own hands while in Śrī Raṅgam, and those very forms are worshipped there to this day.[18]

Fully aware that Śrī Chaitanya would soon leave Śrī Raṅgam to continue his South Indian travels, Gopāla Bhaṭṭa asked if he could accompany him and then return with him to Vrindavan. But Mahāprabhu reminded the boy that his parents were Vaishnavas, and that he should stay and assist them for the remainder of their lives. With that instruction, Mahāprabhu was gone, and Gopāla Bhaṭṭa felt bereft in his absence.[19]

Taking the instruction to care for his parents to heart, Gopāla Bhaṭṭa responsibly looked after them for many years in Śrī Raṅgam and, while there, excelled in learning the ways of the Śrīvaishnavas, fully imbibing the intricate rules and regulations that he would eventually compile into his famous *smṛti* text, the *Hari-bhakti-vilāsa*, an authoritative tome that elucidates the traditions, customs, and preferred conduct of practitioners in the Vaishnava tradition.

Before Vyeṅkaṭa and his wife left this world, they blessed their only son, saying, "Gopāla, you have our blessings to go to Vrindavan and to serve Śrī Chaitanya."

Gopāla Bhaṭṭa left Śrī Raṅgam and, after arduous travels, arrived in the land of Lord Krishna. He immediately located his spiritual brothers, Rūpa and Sanātana Gosvāmīs, falling at their feet with great respect and offering them warm embrace. Although Mahāprabhu was in Purī at the time, Rūpa and Sanātana kept Him informed by letter, and because he is the Supreme Lord, he understood well that Gopāla was in Vrindavan and what this meant for his movement. In fact, he sent Rūpa and Sanātana a letter, saying, "I am very pleased that Gopāla has finally arrived. Consider him to be your younger brother." Along with that letter, especially for Gopāla, he sent his own wooden seat (*āsana*) and personal clothes (*dor-kaupīna* and *bahir-vāsa*), items cherished to this day at Radha Raman Mandir.[20]

BECOMING RADHA RAMAN

Soon after Gopāla Bhaṭṭa arrived in Vrindavan, Mahāprabhu appeared to him in a dream, saying, "If you want my *darśana*, go on pilgrimage to Nepal."[21]

So he did. Rūpa and Sanātana encouraged him as well. The three Vaishnava leaders were confident that Gopāla would see his Lord in the north, as promised, and so he trekked well beyond the difficult regions that *yogīs* and pilgrims normally attend for purification and enlightenment.

After long and demanding travel, he came to the far northern banks of the Gaṇḍakī River, to an area called Dāmodara-kuṇḍa on what is now the Tibetan border of Nepal's Mustang District. When he could go no farther, he set up camp and took his bath.

Just then, a *dāmodara-śālagrāma-śilā*,[22] less than twelve inches in size, appeared in his waterpot. He was not expecting to see Krishna in the form of a stone and so didn't give it much thought. Consequently, he placed the *śilā* back in the water and refilled his pot again, continuing to bathe as if nothing had happened. But to his surprise, mysteriously, the *śilā* appeared in his waterpot once more—and again after that.[23]

He then smilingly recalled Mahāprabhu, and thought to himself, "What is too amazing for my Lord?" Remembering both Śrī Chaitanya's promise that he will see him again and the Lord's instruction to worship Krishna in Vrindavan, he finally accepted the recurring *śilā* as a sign from Krishna and brought it back to Vrindavan, along with eleven other *śilās* he had found on the same day.

On his return journey, he traveled though Saharanpur District in Uttar Pradesh and gradually came upon a town now called Deoband. Although he was anxious to see Vrindavan again, he paused for some time in that town, initiating three noteworthy disciples: Gopīnātha and his younger brother, Dāmodara, and, according to some, their cousin Śrī Hit Harivaṁśa as well.[24]

Arriving in Braj, he began worshipping his *śālagrāmas* with great affection. It became an everyday occurrence, and a sight most cherished by the townspeople: Gopāla Bhaṭṭa and his twelve *śilās*—they were the Lords of his life, and everyone in Braj knew it. Many would congregate in the shady, sylvan glade that became known for his presence, and they would see him worshipping under the same tree, every day. They would witness his profoundly alluring worship of Lord Krishna and become inspired.

But when Gopāla Bhaṭṭa considered the other Gosvāmīs—how they lovingly interacted with personalized forms of the Lord, forms with arms, legs, and a face, more than just the nondescript form of a rock—his aniconic worship became somewhat troubling to him. He imagined what it would be like to dress his Lord in the way that Rūpa and Sanātana dress Govindadeva and Madan Mohan, respectively, and to adorn them in ways that only a personal form would allow.

"After many years of worship," notes Margaret Case, who lived among the Radha Raman Gosvāmīs and was given access to their temple documents, "it is said that Gopāla Bhaṭṭa became discouraged because Śrī Caitanya's promise that he would have his *darśana* (or perhaps that of Śrī Krishna) . . . had not been fulfilled. On the eve of Buddha Jayanti, Vaiśākha-pūrnimā, V. S. 1599 (AD 1542), [Gopāla Bhaṭṭa] was reading about *bhakta* Prahlāda on the occasion of Vishnu's manifestation as Nṛsiṁhadeva, when [he] realized that this young boy had the good fortune to see the Lord himself through the power of devotion. . . . A basket holding the precious *śālagrāmas* was hanging from a branch overhead. When he awoke, he noticed that the lid of the basket had come open a bit. Fearing that a snake had entered, he tried to push the basket's lid down, but it resisted. Then he looked inside and found, instead of the *śālagrāmas*, a small black triple-bent figure playing a flute. This, as it turns out, is today the deity that stands in the Rādhāramaṇa temple. . . . Two facts are cited as proof that this deity is in fact a self-revealed figure from a *śālagrāma*: the image is said to bear on its back the imprint of the original Dāmodara *śālagrāma*; and a *śālagrāma* cannot be carved, since because of its composition it will simply flake away if cut."[25]

Tradition has it that Gopāla Bhaṭṭa's Deity had self-manifested under a very special Peepul tree—it was a tree that had witnessed the sacred Rāsa Dance some 4,500 years earlier, in which Śrī Krishna and his beloved *gopīs* enjoyed pastimes of love. The story runs as follows: Initially, just as the Rāsa Dance was about to begin, Krishna suddenly left all the *gopīs*, who had become prideful that he was meeting with them in a private place. He took only Rādhikā with him, so that they might have intimate moments together in a private bower. At that time, all the *gopīs* naturally lamented, and Rādhārāṇī became proud that she alone was Krishna's chosen one. To curb this pride, and to increase her love for him, he immediately disappeared from her, too, in the same way that he had previously disappeared from the other *gopīs*. Consequently, Rādhārāṇī began to feel anguish, just as the *gopīs* had when Krishna ran away with Rādhā. Significantly, when he vanished from that spot, Rādhā called out to him using the Name "Ramaṇa," which means lover, dear one, one who is pleasing, delightful, charming.[26] He was "Rādhā's Ramaṇ." Thus, the Gosvāmīs named Gopāla Bhaṭṭa's Deity—who they recognized as this self-same Krishna—"Radha Raman."

The tale of Radha Raman's appearance is a poignant one, and from beginning to end it is told in various ways, with diverse nuances, depending on the affiliation and leaning of the person conveying the story. Professor Kenneth Valpey (Krishna Kshetra Swami), using traditional sources, gives an eloquent summary of *śālagrāma*'s transformation into Radha Raman, in all its transcendental complexity. He refers to the Hindi work *Śrī Gopālabhaṭṭa Gosvāmī* of Gaurakrishna Gosvāmī, a present-day retired Rādhāramaṇa priest. Drawing on this source, Valpey begins by telling us that after Gopāla Bhaṭṭa had obtained *śālagrāma* stones from Nepal and returned to Vrindavan, he worshipped Madana-mohana, Govinda, and Gopīnātha, along with his own *śālagrāma* stones. The other Gosvāmīs, we are told, noted Gopāla's expert and devotionally infused way of dressing and ornamenting the Deities, even while he privately hankered to worship his divine stones in this same way, with clothing and assorted ornaments. Meanwhile, Gopāla also suffered due to his separation from Chaitanya. This is made more poignant by a message from Puri, which arrived with special gifts, informing him that the Master was about to leave the world. He had promised that he would appear to Gopāla in the sacred *śālagrāma* stone, but this had not yet transpired. Valpey continues:

> In Gopāla's anguish of separation he compares his plight to that of the *gopīs* in their disappointment on being turned away by Krishna in the forest prior to the rāsa dance (according to BhP 10.29.18–28). . . . Gopāla's overwrought condition comes to a head in the year 1542 on the day for celebrating the Nṛsiṁha *avatāra*'s appearance, to be observed at dusk by performing ablution of a *śālagrāma* stone as a *mūrti* of the half-man, half-lion form of the Lord. At that time, while concentrating on the form of Vishnu as Nṛsiṁha and addressing him by *mantra,* he thinks of the Lord's form in the stone and exclaims (citing BhP 7.8.17), "This very day the Lord appeared before Prahlāda, fulfilling the latter's statement that he can appear anywhere by appearing from a stone pillar. Can he not similarly appear again in his extraordinary form from my *śālagrāma*?" . . . Eventually he performs the *abhiṣeka* [bathing ceremony], but after its completion he is awarded a vision of the Lord as Ghanaśyāma, Krishna, the dark and beautiful divine cowherd of Vrindavan, within the stone. Now emotions overwhelm him as never before, spilling forth as solicitous pleas and fainting spells.
>
> The denouement (or "charismatic moment") occurs the next morning, when the Lord calls the now sleeping Gopāla to awaken and encounter him in the form Gopāla has so longed to behold. After awakening and bathing, Gopāla finds in the basket holding the *śālagrāma* stones a "bluish shining" image from which spread "countless rays of light." Gopāla is confounded by what he sees. . . . The magnetic force of Gopāla Bhaṭṭa's *bhakti* had become irresistible to its Object, who then appears directly out of the *śālagrāma* stone (once again confirming Prahlāda's statement that the Lord can appear anywhere). This shiny black image is delicately formed yet consists of the same (brittle, humanly uncarvable) material as the *śālagrāma* from whence it had apparently come. . . . In Gaurakrishna Gosvāmī's account the Vaishnava community of Vrindavan is thrilled and only too willing to acknowledge that Gopāla Bhaṭṭa's "years of practice have today become complete." [27]

All of Vrindavan rejoiced upon witnessing Radha Raman, noting that he encompassed the best of the three established Deities—Śrī Madan Mohan, Śrī Govindadeva, and Śrī Gopīnātha. According to the *Bhakti-ratnākara* (4.320–22) Radha Raman's beautiful face was comparable to Govindadeva's, while his chest was like Gopinātha's and his feet were like Madan Mohan's. (*śrī govinda, gopīnāth, madan-mohan; krame e tiner mukh, vakṣa, śrī caraṇa*) These three manifestations of Krishna, we are told, were all apparent, at least according to aficionados, in the form of Radha Raman. Indeed, tradition asserts that the merits of seeing these Deities are all achieved upon taking *darśana* of Radha Raman, whose beauty is unsurpassed.

Cynthia Packert, Christian A. Johnson Professor in the History of Art and Architecture at Middlebury College, describes the otherworldly radiance that is Radha Raman:

> When they are not overly obscured by dress and ornamentation, one can see that the toes on his feet are individually articulated, and there is a flexible dancer's bend to his crossed front leg. His thighs are smooth and shapely, tapering into tight hips, a narrow waist, and a triangular torso canted to the side that is surprisingly muscular in effect. His arms are energetically lifted across his body, fingers bent in readiness to accept his flute. A full neck supports a lightly tilted square head with round cheeks, upon which is etched a full mouth curved into a smile that just hints at a private joke, or perhaps satisfaction at the world he beholds and the loving attention that is continually lavished upon him. A dimple in his chin is ornamented with a jewel. When particularly delighted, he does show his teeth. A small, perfectly proportioned nose and lightly curved eyebrows frame the curving, cat-shaped enamel eyes that are his special defining feature. In the summer, his skin gleans with the high sheen of a special *itr*, scented oil that is specially selected for its seasonal appropriateness; in the winter, the oil is dampened down to a pleasingly matte surface through which the delicacy of his features become somewhat clearer to the eye. The radiant power of this stylish and diminutive body is hard to explain, but it is palpable.[28]

"This self-manifesting Deity," writes Howard Wheeler (Hayagrīva Dāsa), an early disciple of Śrīla Prabhupāda, who also captures the beauty of Radha Raman in this brief description, "is only about twelve inches high. He is finely contoured, especially at the chin-line and mouth, and He has big lotus eyes, curved upward a bit. The heavy epicanthic folds remind me of Nepalese Buddha eyes. He stands in His *tribhanga* position, a threefold bending curve, one leg crossed over the other, a stance that is Lord Krishna's famous trademark. This beautiful shiny black Deity is remarkable, especially considering that He's not sculptured by anyone's hand. . . . A silver crown on a small throne is placed on His left for Radharani. Since Radha Ramana is self-manifested, the devotees feel that it would be inappropriate to put a sculptured Deity of Radharani next to Him, although the Deity is the same whether sculptured or self-manifesting. The *pujaris* have prepared a place for Radharani just in case She wishes to appear. 'She is visible in your heart,' they reply when asked about Her presence."[29]

RADHA RAMAN IS ŚRĪ CHAITANYA

Although most other Krishna Deities in Vrindavan enjoy having Rādhā by their side, Radha Raman is apparently alone. Before explaining why that is—or perhaps in partial explanation of why that is—it is important that the reader understand the Mahāprabhu component. Make no mistake: Radha Raman is a manifestation of Śrī Chaitanya, and this was revealed to Gopāla Bhaṭṭa Gosvāmī by the Lord himself. Remember: Mahāprabhu had promised Gopāla

Bhaṭṭa (when the latter was but a youth in Śrī Raṅgam) that they would see each other again while in Vrindavan, and he also told him that Hari would manifest to him while in Nepal̄. Both promises were brought to fruition in the form of Radha Raman.

The *Bhakti-ratnākara* (4.345) reveals that Radha Raman and Śrī Chaitanya are one: "Śrī Rādhāramaṇa, who was ever bound by the love of Śrī Gopāla Bhaṭṭa Gosvāmī, took pleasure in revealing himself as Śrī Gaura Sundara." (*gopālera premādhīna śrī rādhāramaṇa; śrī gaurasundara mūrti hailā sei kṣaṇa*)[30] From the earliest days of the tradition, then, it was understood that Radha Raman and Śrī Chaitanya interpenetrate each other, confirming that Radha Raman is a special manifestation of Krishna. Śrī Chaitanya is seen as a particularly esoteric divinity. He is Rādhā and Krishna lovingly fused into one form (*jugalāvatāra*). The tradition makes this clear, as articulated in the well-worn verse, "Śrī Chaitanya Mahāprabhu is none other than Rādhā and Krishna combined." (*mahāprabhu śrī caitanya, rādhā-krishna nahe anya*).[31] Thus, not only is Radha Raman a form of Mahāprabhu, but he is ipso facto both Rādhā and Krishna, three Supreme entities in one.

In this way, Gopāla Bhaṭṭa did indeed see Mahāprabhu again, as per the Lord's promise—but this time in the form of Radha Raman, not as Śrī Chaitanya. It should additionally be pointed out that, according to the Radha Raman Gosvāmīs, Radha Raman is unique among all Deities of Krishna, for only he manifests the personality and *śakti* of Śrī Chaitanya.[32]

Confirmation of Radha Raman's identity with Śrī Chaitanya comes from deep within the tradition. According to Madhusudana Goswami's *Shri Radharaman Prakatya*, "Sanatan said that he could see Chaitanya Mahaprabhu in Radharaman. A wave of happiness filled the devotees when they realized that they were being blessed with the *darshan* of Krishn [sic] and Gaur in one form."[33] As Vaishnavacharya Chandan Goswami, disciple and successor of Padmanabh Goswami, a central figure at the Radha Raman temple, confirms: "For the love of Gopal Bhatt Goswami, Shri Chaitanya Mahaprabhu appeared as Radharaman. *Gaur holo Radharaman.* Chaitanya Mahaprabhu is the joint Incarnation of Radha and Krishn [sic]. The ancient deities of Vrindavan had Names like Govind, Gopinath and Madanmohan, but later when Shri Radha's deities were installed in those temples, they became known as Radha-Govind, Radha-Gopinath, Radha-Madanmohan, and so forth. But Shri Radharaman Dev is Radha and Krishn [sic] in a single form, non-different from Shri Chaitanya Mahaprabhu."[34]

Following traditional accounts, the modern academy often articulates these same truths regarding Radha Raman: "There is yet another image," writes Margaret Case, "that is closely associated with Śrī Caitanya Mahaprabhu: the image of Rādhāramaṇa, 'he who enjoys Rādhā,' said to be another form of the incarnation of Rādhā and Krishna in one body, and whose appearance was invoked by Gopāla Bhaṭṭa. Whereas in Caitanya, Rādhā was on the outside [visible in his golden complexion] and Krishna inside, in the black stone image of Rādhāramaṇa, Krishna is outside, Rādhā inside. . . . This is the image whose home is in Rādhāramaṇa temple. It is understood that he is the same as the deity Gopāla Bhaṭṭa had longed to see—Śrī Caitanya Mahāprabhu, the incarnation of Rādhā and Krishna in one body."[35]

Similarly, we find in Kenneth Valpey's *Attending Krishna's Image*: "Rādhā-ramaṇa as the combined form of Rādhā and Krishna renders a separate image of Rādhā superfluous. . . . [There] is a sense of fluidity in Rādhāramaṇa's identity giving place for varied moods and expressions of devotion from his *bhaktas*. This fluidity is underscored by the soft contours of the Rādhāramaṇa image, countering the hardness of the stone material. He is Krishna, but also Rādhā; and as both combined he is Caitanya, whose life embodied the constant ebb and flow of intense spiritual emotion."[36]

This selfsameness of Radha Raman and Śrī Chaitanya is summed up in a beautiful contemporary prayer by prominent Radha Raman Vaishnavacharya Chandan Goswami:

śhrī rādhāramaṇ hamāre ishṭ /prabhu kṛshṇchaitanya yugal-var mūrat madhu mahishṭ

sarvopari hai dhām manohar vṛndāvipin varishṭ /

kuñjkeli kautuk kālindī keli karat ati mishṭ //mand pavan pulakit pakshī sukh pāvat premāvishṭ /lāl sayut lalitādi lalit alil tan lakhat ratinishṭh //

gāvat jinko śhrī-āchāraj rūp-sanātan śhishṭ /

guru-gopāl bhaṭṭ gosvāmī guṇmañjarī garishṭ //

"O Rādhāramaṇ, you are the one I worship. You are Rādhā and Krishna in one form, who appeared as the Lord of love, Śrī Chaitanya Mahāprabhu. Your home, Vṛndāvan, is the crown of all holy places, where Yamunājī longs to drink the sweetness of your pastimes. The gentle breeze in this sacred land makes even the birds blissful with love. Your body glows like bejeweled ornaments and looks very graceful in the presence of Prīyājū, Lalitājī and the other *sakhīs*, whose only purpose is to give you pleasure. Our worshipable guru Gopāl Bhaṭṭ Goswāmī (Guṇa-mañjarī), Rūp, Sanātan and the other *āchāryas* always sing your glories."[37]

WHERE IS RĀDHĀ?

Given this background—that Radha Raman is non-different from Śrī Chaitanya—it becomes easy to understand why, unlike other Krishna Deities in Braj, there is no overt Rādhā by his side: She is already there as part of Radha Raman's intrinsic identity.[38] Still, although there is no need for a separate Rādhā *mūrti*, Braj devotees relish seeing the Divine Couple together, as evidenced by the vast majority of Vrindavan's altars. For this reason, there have been several attempts to "show" Rādhā's presence next to Radha Raman.

The phenomenon goes back to just after the time of Śrī Chaitanya, perhaps 450 years ago, when Jāhnava Mātā, Nityānanda Prabhu's widow, brought a Rādhā Deity to Gopāla Bhaṭṭa for his altar. The Bhaṭṭa was, of course, fully aware that Rādhā was already present in his beloved *mūrti*, but he nonetheless graciously accepted Jāhnava's offering, so deeply did he respect her. However, over time, the Rādhā image would have to find an alternate home. Vaishnavacharya Chandan Goswami tells the story well:

> Upon visiting Vrindavan, Shrimati Jahnava Mata brought a solid gold deity of Radharani for Radharamanji. However, Shri Gopal Bhatt Goswami did not wish to place the deity next to him, because . . . Radharamanji is [already] the combined form of Radha and Krishn [sic]. Nevertheless, Gopal Bhatt Goswami felt unable to deny Jahnava Mata's request, so the deity brought by her was installed anyway.
>
> When the temple opened the morning after the ceremony, the golden deity was not there, and it was later found in some lonesome corner of the temple. But the next day, she went missing yet again. This continued for several days until Radharamanji came in Gopal Bhatt Goswami's dream. He said, "That deity is not Radha. She is my sister, Yogamaya. Every night you put me to sleep next to my sister, and every night I have to send her out! You must take her somewhere else."
>
> Thus the deity was taken to the place now known as Gurugram (Gurgaon, near New Delhi). She is called Sheetla Mata and she is the kuldevi of the Radharaman Goswamis.[39]

The Rādhā *mūrti* that was once worshipped with Radha Raman is in fact now found in a famous temple just outside of Delhi, revered as Durgādevī, not Rādhā.[40] Since the time of her removal, Śrī Rādhā has been represented on Radha Raman's altar by a small, decorated assemblage of paraphernalia on his left side, replete with elegant ornamentation and special ritual adulation. As Cynthia Packert reports,

> Radharamana's symbolic partner, though but a petite mounded shape, is always beautifully dressed in a *sari*, its border seemingly framing Radha's face as she gazes upon her beloved. A cascade of miniature jewels is arranged as if for forehead and nose ornaments, and the top of Radha's head is adorned with her special mango-bud shaped crown. Necklaces and floral garlands are expertly positioned, and the rest of the *sari* is elegantly draped around the base of the form. Radha's costuming and ornamentation is equally elaborate as Radharamana's, and in the hands of a skilled temple Goswami, her presence can be just as visually vibrant. In fact, in many ways, Radha's presence here is made even more potent because her full presence is by necessity imaginatively conjured through mental recreations of her beauty and actions that are elaborately evoked through aesthetic theory, song, poetry and memory."[41]

"On the altar," writes Padmanabh Goswami, one of the head *mahānts* at the Radha Raman temple, "we put the dress and ornaments, crown, over the sacred name of Srimati Radharani. The name is under it. It is written on a gold plate. No one knows how long that plate has been there. They consider it to have been there since the very beginning of Radharaman's worship. It says, 'Shri Radha' on it in Devanagari script. There is a crown and nose ring, also, and these items indicate the presence of Radha next to Krishna."[42]

The presence of Śrī Rādhā's name is significant: In Gauḍīya Vaishnava thought, when it comes to Divine Personhood, each part of God's spiritual body—and every other aspect of his being—is equivalent to every other part. In other words, every component of Divine Being is absolute, with an interchangeability that functions according to his sweet will. The arms can perform the function of the eyes, and so on. In this way, Krishna can "taste" a food offering, for example, by merely looking at it, or be present for his devotee in the mere chanting of his name. This is referred to as *sa-viśeṣābheda* (*viśeṣa* for short)—the non-difference of an entity with his or her own attributes.[43]

Accordingly, in regard to Krishna, it is often said that there is no difference between the name (*nāma*) and the named one (*nāmī*).[44] The same is true in regard to Rādhikā, and so her presence on the altar in the form of her name is consistent with Vaishnava philosophy.

Furthermore, Gauḍīya Vaishnavism views the chanting of Rādhā's name as the pinnacle of spiritual achievement. Her name, in its way, is equal to Krishna's, a fact that was evident from the earliest days of the tradition. In Rūpa Gosvāmī's play *Vidagdha-mādhava* (Act VI), for example, Krishna's close friend Madhumaṅgala promises to bring Rādhā, who is in hiding, to Krishna's side. But instead he brings a leaf with the two syllables of her name inscribed on it (not unlike the golden plate at the Radha Raman temple).

Krishna is thoroughly pleased by this gift—as pleased as he would be by Rādhā's actual presence—indicating the non-difference between the name and named one. He proceeds to praise her name, in fact, much as Paurṇamāsī,

Madhumaṅgala's grandmother, had previously glorified his. Paurṇamāsī then extols Rādhā's name as well, knowing this to be the only way to get Krishna's attention.[45]

Among all such texts that focus on Rādhā's considerable magnificence, and there are many, the *Śrī Śrī Rādhā-rasa-sudhānidhi* stands supreme. Written by Prabodhānanda Sarasvatī,[46] who, we will remember, is the uncle and spiritual master of Gopāla Bhaṭṭa Gosvāmī, this text explains the supreme position of Śrīmatī Rādhikā, not just in terms of abstract philosophy but even in relation to Krishna himself: He—God—is fully enticed only by her love, and is motivated only by the sound of her name.

"O my heart," the text advises, "please turn from great things of this world and run to Vrindavan, where the great treasure, the nectar flood that liberates the devotees from this world, is Śrī Rādhā's name" (Verse 9).

It goes on: "May the two wonderful syllables *Rā-dhā*, which immediately attract even the king of Gokula, which teach the love-laden devotees that all material goals are simply petty and inconsequential, and which are chanted by Lord Krishna himself, even though he is already the husband of the goddess of fortune, appear before me (verse 95). May the two-syllable mantra 'Rādhā'—which Lord Hari, sitting like the king of *yogīs* in a cottage by the Kālindī's shore, meditating on her lotus feet, overcome with unequalled bliss and sweet love, and his eyes filled with tears, always chants—always appear in my heart" (verse 96).

> "The nectarean word 'Rādhā,' which goes beyond even the demigods, the liberated souls, the devotees, and the kindly persons who are friends to all, which when spoken with love brings a flood of blissful affection, and which Lord Hari, tears coursing down his face, happily hears, chants, and sings in the company of the *gopīs*, is my life and soul." (Verse 97)

Prabodhānanda's advice: "Chant the holy name of Rādhā every day, abandoning millions of other great spiritual practices. The most profound goals of life are merely performing *āratī* to the nectar of Rādhā's lotus feet. . . . Millions of wonderful spiritual perfections set themselves at the feet of Śrī Rādhā's maidservants (verse 144). O Rādhā, when a person once tastes the nectar of your holy name, Lord Krishna becomes filled with love for that person, makes no record of his offenses, and considers giving him the greatest gift. Who, then, can touch the pinnacle of the glory possessed by persons whose only thought is to serve you?" (verse 155). The Gauḍīya teaching is clear: "The greatest treasure of all is the name of Rādhā." (*rādhā nāma parama sampad*).[47]

But at Radha Raman temple, it is Radha Raman himself that is front and center, standing boldly, as he does, on a small embossed golden platform, which is itself propped up on a silver throne, elegantly sculpted with lion feet.

Overhead one sees a small golden umbrella, protecting and containing the Lord on his altar, and just beneath this central throne, keeping Radha Raman company, are various well-chosen statuettes, such as cows, swans, and so on, along with cups and plates; all are silver in color. These are strategically arranged for the Lord's pleasure by his ever-dutiful priests, who care for him throughout the day.

To Radha Raman's left is his loving consort, who is both there and not, as already described. She, too, is shaded by a small golden umbrella.

To Radha Raman's right but hardly visible to the many pilgrims who press in to see him, off to the side of the inner sanctum, is yet another golden umbrella—this one intended for the eleven *śalagrāmas* that Gopāla Bhaṭṭa brought back with Radha Raman from the Gaṇḍakī, those many years ago.

Still farther back, completely out of sight, is a small throne with Śrī Chaitanya's wooden sitting place and other items ready for worship, the ones that had been gifted to Gopāla Bhaṭṭa by the Lord himself. Radha Raman, the *śalagrāmas*, Rādhikā's representational presence, and Mahāprabhu's seat are regularly offered worship in quick succession during the *āratī* ceremony, which we will discuss below. But the *āratīs* would be less spectacular without a temple, and so before elucidating Radha Raman's daily service, we should briefly explore the origins of the environment he now calls home.

THE TEMPLE

When Radha Raman first appeared to Gopāla Bhaṭṭa Gosvāmī, the latter worshipped him in a simple way, just as the other Gosvāmīs had initially worshipped their *mūrtis*, before they had constructed temples. For Gopāla Bhaṭṭa, it was a straightforward, humble, and personal *pūjā*, outdoors—right beneath the tree where Radha Raman saw fit to manifest his divine form. In due course, a simple dwelling was built, and that initial structure, or some refurbishment of it, is now the kitchen area of the larger Radha Raman complex, just behind the current temple.

The Mandir today stands outside the sacred Nidhivan area,[48] if also ensconced in the crowded shopping district of Loi Bazaar, or, more directly, Gopinath Bazaar.[49] A narrow but busy alley leads to an intersection famous among Gauḍīya Vaishnavas, for it spills into the main gateway of the Radha Raman temple. Although an assortment of monkeys (rhesus macaque) famously greets all visitors—and not always with the best intentions—discerning pilgrims are far more interested in what lies beyond the promising Mughal architecture just ahead.

Constructed under the auspices of Shah Behari Lal, the banker grandfather of Shah Kundan Lal and Shah Fundan Lal, from Lucknow, this nineteenth-century structure is home to the hero of our story, though Lal's original architectural scheme was at first far too grandiose, as we shall see.[50] The present Radha Raman temple was built in 1826 at the cost of some eighty thousand rupees, and the original endeavor, with its baroque and modern-classical architecture, became the now-famous Shahji Temple. Margaret Case summarizes the somewhat elaborate story. In the nineteenth century, she tells us, Vrindavan would become the beneficiary of much wealth, with Rādhāramaṇa finding particular favor with Shah Kundan Lal, finance minister of Wajid Ali Shah, the last Nawab of Avadh, who built a most beautiful temple for the Deity. But the leading Gosvāmīs of the Rādhāramaṇa temple did not want their beloved Deity in such a lavish temple, for this ran counter to his simple and delightfully down-home mood. It was at this time, Case tells us, that Shah Kundan Lal acquiesced and began construction on the modest sandstone temple that is now Rādhāramaṇa's home. Says Margaret Case: "The gaudy marble Shahji Mandir, which stands on the other side of Jaisingh Gherā from Rādhāramaṇa Gherā, and whose massive courtyard walls tower over the street that leads from Jaisingh Gherā to the bazaar, is maintained chiefly as an attraction for pilgrims and tourists. As such, the ambience of a busy pilgrim site prevails: stalls with mementos crowd around the courtyard entrance, including four or five that sell cassettes with songs celebrating Rādhā and Krishna, set to popular and filmi tunes, competing with each other in a decibel war that deafens the passerby."[51]

Margaret Case also describes the home he soon built for Radha Raman proper:

> The temple is built around an inner courtyard about thirty-five feet square, partially open to the sky but at night and in bad weather covered by a sliding tin roof. This style of temple architecture, known as the haveli style, derives from a common form of domestic architecture in the region—one, two, or three stories built around an inner courtyard. The floor of Rādhāramaṇa temple is a checkerboard of black and white marble. On the left as you enter, there is a marble platform about four and a half feet high, and behind it is the inner sanctum. The courtyard is surrounded on the other three sides by porticos, each with three arches that were recently painted a slightly surprising bright pink and green. Even when the doors to the inner sanctum are closed, and the deity is not visible, a few devotees are usually to be found sitting in the porticos or standing around in the courtyard, perhaps chatting with one another. In the rear (east) portico, facing the sanctum, a singer sits in the morning and evening with a harmonium, perhaps with a *tabla* (drum) player or with other devotees who keep time with hand-cymbals as he sings chants of praise to Krishna. . . . The raised platform that serves as the antechamber to the inner sanctum also has three cusped arches, these of unpainted sandstone; at the rear is an embossed silver double-leaved door leading to the sanctum. There the deity stands facing east.[52]

Worship at this temple—or at its earlier constructions, mounted in the same area, just behind the current shrine—has been going on for nearly five hundred years, almost exactly as it appears today, and while most of the other famous Deities of Vrindavan had to journey to far-off lands during the Mughal invasions, Radha Raman has remained in Braj, without leaving.[53]

But Gopāla Bhaṭṭa Gosvāmī knew that to ensure the continued worship of his beloved Radha Raman, he would need to place others in charge, creating a succession that would do the needful into posterity. He felt that celibate monks, such as himself, were duty-bound to wander and preach, and that they were otherwise disinclined to stay in one spot, tending to the logistics of everyday temple finance. To this end, he conferred temple *sevā* upon his married disciples, hoping they would care for the Deity generation after generation.[54]

Gopīnātha Dāsa Gosvāmī was the first *pūjārī* and Gopāla Bhaṭṭa's initial choice, but when asked to marry and have children to continue the lineage in the future, he declined. Gopīnātha then pointed to his younger brother, Dāmodara Gosvāmī. This became a workable solution, for Dāmodara was both highly qualified and married as well. Dāmodara's three sons were Harinātha, Mathurānātha, and Harināma, and it is from these glorious personalities that the current Radha Raman families descend.[55]

Thus, Śrī Dāmodara Gosvāmī, Gopāla Bhaṭṭa's disciple, carried on the lineage. Initially, Dāmodara handed the mantle to Harinātha Dāsa Gosvāmī, but then the line splits into two, nurtured by Harinātha's sons: One branch stemmed from Vrajbhooshan Das and the other from Janardhan Das. The genealogical tree of Vrajbhooshan gives us Purushottam Goswami, whose sons are Shrivatsa Goswami and Venu Gopala, renowned contemporary representatives of Radha Raman.

The Janardhan branch gives us Madusudana Lal (esteemed author of *Shri Radharaman Prakatya*) and, a generation later, Vishwambhar Goswami (who, from 1953 to 1957, was mayor of Vrindavan). Vishwambhar's sons are Padmanabh Goswami and Padmalochan Goswami, and Anupam (Chandan Goswami) is Padmanabh's son. Additionally, there are many other luminaries who have carried on the Radha Raman tradition, with some fifty families connected to the daily *sevā* of the temple.[56]

WORSHIPPING RADHA RAMAN: AN INNER DIMENSION

The worship of Radha Raman, or any other authorized Vaishnava Deity, may at first seem primitive, without logical basis or theological sophistication. But nothing could be further from the truth. Vaishnava texts, in fact, offer much in the way of explanation,[57] and the practice itself, traditionally employed throughout the centuries, has been effective: those who regularly worship the Deity in the temple inevitably draw closer to Krishna, God, in due course. And this is understandable: Their ability to interact with divinity is enhanced by access to a personal form. As Lord Krishna says in the *Bhagavad-gītā* (12.2), "He whose mind is fixed on my personal form, always engaged in worshiping me with great and transcendental faith, I consider to be most perfect." And, three verses later, "For those whose minds are attached to the unmanifested, impersonal feature of the Supreme, advancement is very troublesome. To make progress in that discipline is always difficult for those who are embodied."[58] Thus, Deity worship has pragmatic application and is invaluable in the life of the practitioner.

Pūjārīs, temple priests who serve the Deity on the altar—as well as the multitudes who come to offer their worship, whether by singing, dancing, or other heartfelt endeavors—will benefit from the Deity's presence, advancing toward spiritual perfection. Indeed, simply witnessing the Deity (which is called "taking *darśana*"), or admiring his form, will aid in one's spiritual progress. In most Vaishnava temples, this opportunity is available throughout the day.

Traditionally, the Lord is served on the altar through various types of *pūjā*, or worship, particularly with a ceremony known as *āratī*, a Sanskrit word derived from *ārātrika*, referring to the removal of *rātri*, or night (or, more colloquially, "darkness"). The idea is not only that the Deity is "awakened" in the temple to start his day after a long, playful night with his consort,[59] which we will soon explain, but that witnesses to this event will similarly be awakened from the "nighttime of the soul," allowing them to overcome material conditioning and "awaken" their spiritual consciousness.

Symbolically and literally, then, altar service emphasizes the offering of a lamp, usually a lighted ghee wick, for the Lord's pleasure.[60] Other items are offered as well, all of which are meant to engage each of our senses in full "Krishna consciousness": Sight (seeing the Deity), hearing (the sound of the mantras, the ringing of a bell), taste (food offerings, water), smell (incense, flowers), and touch (all offered items). The ceremony begins with the blowing of the *śaṅkha*, or conch shell, a sign of auspiciousness, and culminates, especially in summer months, when the Lord is fanned with peacock feathers and a yak tail, to cool him off and to ward off all unwanted material misconceptions for the practitioner.[61]

In any given Vaishnava temple—and Radha Raman is no exception—there are various services that prepare for such worship, and these are generally grouped in five divisions as follows: (1) *Abhigamana*, or cleansing the temple and taking away offerings from a previous ceremony, such as older garlands; (2) *Upādāna*, or gathering flowers and Tulasī leaves and other assorted items for Deity worship; (3) *Yoga*, or the inner contemplation of oneself as spirit-soul, beyond the body, or, on a deeper level, in one's pure spiritual form as the eternal servant of the Supreme Lord in the spiritual realm; (4) *Svādhyāya*, the practice of chanting of the holy name and one's guru-given mantra (fully considering its meaning), while reciting prayers and studying of the scriptures; and (5) *Ijyā*, contemplating how one could best serves one's own worshipful Deity in a variety of ways relevant to that particular divinity. "This Pañcāṅga, or five-branched Deity worship," writes Śrīla Bhakti Prajnāna Keśava Gosvāmī Mahārāja (1898–1968), a leading spiritual master in the Gauḍīya Sampradāya, "is not of the nature of non-eternal, fruitive activity, but is eternal and pure, and is a branch of pure devotional service which helps one attain the direct association of the Supreme Lord."[62] Below, we would like to focus on the esoteric nature of yoga as part of this fivefold schema, particularly because it is an important part of Radha Raman Deity service and central to Gauḍīya *siddhānta.*[63]

From an external perspective, *āratī*, as already stated, is a ceremony in which one greets and worships the Lord in his Deity form by offering him a glowing lamp, along with incense, water, a fine cloth, a fragrant flower, a peacock feather, and a yak-tail fan, all accompanied by bell-ringing and devotional chanting. The specifics may vary from temple to temple, both in terms of the number of *āratīs* offered throughout the day and the items being offered at each *āratī*, according to standards set by one's individual lineage and tradition. But the point here is this: *āratī*, or Deity-sevā, has inner meaning, even if its practice accompanies the devotee through all levels of devotional life, ranging from the most rudimentary to the most advanced, from ritualistic formality to spontaneous intimacy, from Vaidhī-bhakti to Rāga-mārga.[64] When one worships the Deity on the platform of Rāga-mārga, certain esoteric meditational principles, such as the eight periods of Krishna's day (*aṣṭa-kālīya-līlā*), make their way into daily *sevā*, revealed in the temple for those who have eyes to see.

Gauḍīya Vaishnavas consider Deity service (*arcana*) a limb of Vaidhī-bhakti. Thus, *arcana* is generally kept in the realm of *śāstra-vidhi*, or the injunctions of the scriptures, even if inner meditations awaken in an advanced stage of spiritual development. Again, the process of Deity service is such that it caters to both neophyte and advanced practitioners, without any need to change the specific rituals according to one's *adhikāra* (qualifications). Thus, while externally observing the same activities, i.e., offering food, incense, and all the other usual *āratī* items, the ceremony can appear in diverse ways according to one's inner meditation and devotional predilection. If outwardly a practitioner is offering the same *pūjā* as they would in Vaidhī-mārga, but internally they are remembering *aṣṭa-kālīya-līlā* according to the principles of Rāga-mārga, it is called "*vaidhī-saṃvalita-rāgānuga,*" which is *vaidhī* combined with *rāgānuga.*[65] "This development of conjugal love," writes Śrīla Prabhupāda in *Nectar of Devotion*, chapter 16, "can be possible only with those who are already engaged in following the regulative principles of devotional service, specifically in the worship of Rādhā and Kṛṣṇa in the temple. Such devotees gradually develop a spontaneous love for the Deity, and by hearing of the Lord's exchange of loving affairs with the *gopīs*, they gradually become attracted to these pastimes."[66]

When taking *darśana* with such cultured perception, or eyes smeared with the salve of love, one can perceive the correlations between the Deity's daily *āratī* activities with the daily "life-cycle" of Krishna in the spiritual realm. By adjusting one's vision in this way, through inner meditation and studying well-established guidebooks, devotees gradually transform their vision from the *laukika* ("mundane") to *alaukika* ("transcendent"), and then from Vaidhī (following rules and regulations) to Rāga-mārga (the path of spontaneity). In the Puṣṭimārga tradition, for example, the term *darśana* resonates with the term *jhankī*, denoting "a mere glimpse of something divine." The idea is that while taking *darśana* of the Deity in the temple, or performing service to an image of Krishna in a household shrine, the contemplative devotee "strives to enter into the *līlā*, to actualize, with heart, mind, and soul, the sublime experience of sharing space with Krishna as the supreme ontological reality. As *darśana* is a reciprocal process of vision, the devotee sees the divine, and the divine . . . also sees the devotee."[67] One thereby enters Krishna's reality.

To understand how the process of Deity service is viewed by accomplished devotees—including those of the Radha Raman temple—it would be worthwhile to briefly look at the "eight times of Krishna's day."

The seed concept is originally found in early post-Vedic wisdom texts, such as the *Padma Purāṇa* (*Patala khaṇḍa*, chapter 52) and the *Sanat-kumāra-saṁhitā* (chapter 36), where Krishna's typical day in celestial Braj is broken down into distinct periods for meditative purposes.[68] These texts offer a sampling of God's average day in the spiritual world. In this way, accomplished devotees on the path might learn to further focus on the Lord's intimate pastimes, and, through the process of *rāgānuga-sādhana*, enter into them. This eightfold meditation, again, came to be called *aṣṭa-kālīya-līlā*, or "the eightfold daily pastimes."

Kavi Karṇapūra, an early Gaudīya Vaishnava poet, elucidated this eightfold schema in his *Kṛṣṇāhnika-kaumudi*, and so did Gauḍīya mystic Dhyānachandra Goswāmī in his *Smaraṇa-paddhati.* A short poem written by Rūpa Goswāmī, *Aṣṭa-kālīya-līlā-smaraṇa-maṅgala-stotra* conveyed the essence in summary form, which was later elaborated upon by Krishnadāsa Kavirāja Goswāmī, in his classic, *Govinda-līlāmṛta.* This became the main text of the *aṣṭa-kālīya-līlā* tradition (and is used by the Radha Raman Goswamis to this day). Viśvanātha Chakravartī elaborated further in his *Śrī Krishna Bhāvanāmṛta Mahāvākhya*, and others followed suit.

Although one can consult any of the above works for detailed specifics, *Govinda-līlāmṛta* (1.4), in one verse, offers a much abbreviated summary of what goes on during Krishna's day: "May Krishna, who at the end of night goes from the bower to the cowherd village, who in the morning and evening performs the pastime of milking cows and taking his meals, who herds the cows and plays with his friends at milking time, who at noon and at night plays in the forest with Rādhā and who in the afternoon goes back to the village and in the evening gives joy to his friends, be pleased with us."[69] Using this—along with the added nuance found in the books that support it—practitioners of Gaudīya Vaishnava devotion who are engaged in *smaraṇa*, or meditational remembrance, focus on the eight periods of Krishna's day as follows: (1) *niśānta-līlā,* pastimes at the end of night (3:36 a.m.–6:00 a.m.); (2) *prātaḥ-līlā,* pastimes at dawn (6:00 a.m.–8:24 a.m.); (3) *pūrvāhna-līlā,* morning pastimes (8:24 a.m.–10:48 a.m.); (4) *madhyāhna-līlā,* midday pastimes (10:48 a.m.–3:36 p.m.); (5) *aparāhna-līlā,* afternoon pastimes (3:36 p.m.–6:00 p.m.); (6) *sāyāhna-līlā,* pastimes at dusk (6:00 p.m.–8:24 p.m.); (7) *pradoṣa-līlā*, evening pastimes (8:24 p.m.–10:48 p.m.); and (8) *rātri* or *nakta-līlā,* midnight pastimes (10:48 p.m.–3:36 a.m.).[70]

It is not difficult to see how Deity worship, at least for the seasoned practitioner, lends itself to this inner meditation. Punctuality is essential in worshipping the Deity, as it must be executed at very specific times of day. So, too, does *aṣṭa-kālīya-līlā* meditation. Moreover, the specific services traditionally rendered to the Deity at various *āratīs* correspond, in a general sense, to Krishna's divided day, as suggested above.

Śrībhaṭṭa (c. 1440–1510) of the Nimbārka Sampradāya may well be the first Brajbhāṣā author to write on the phenomenon of *aṣṭa-kāliya-līlā* in relation to *āratī*.[71] The importance of his work, known as the *Yugalaśataka*, should not be underestimated. "The innovation of Śrībhaṭṭa," writes Vijay Ramnarace (Brahmachari Sharan), Director for Dharmic Life and Hindu Spiritual Advisor, Georgetown University, and scholar of Braj tradition, "lies in his presentation of the *aṣṭayāma-līlā*, perhaps the earliest description of the complete daily pastimes (for the eight watches of a twenty-four hour day, each lasting three hours), and specifically the [temple] *sevā* that occurs during those periods: *maṅgalā* (pre-dawn), *śṛṅgāra* (bathing and dressing), *vana-vihāra* (forest-grove sojourns), *rāja-bhoga* (midday meal and ensuing siesta), *utthāpana* (waking and afternoon snacks), *sandhyā* (sunset), *śayana* (bedtime) and *rāsa*." In other words, Śrībhaṭṭa connects *aṣṭa-kāliya-līlā* to Deity-sevā, specifically to *āratīs*.[72]

A general outline of how *āratī* corresponds to *aṣṭa-kāliya-līlā* might be rendered as follows:

Yāma 1: Maṅgalā—Maṅgalā Āratī (1)
Yāma 2: Śṛṅgāra—Śṛṅgāra Āratī (2)
Yāma 3: Vana-vihāra
Yāma 4: Rāja-bhoga—Rāja-bhoga Āratī (3)
Yāma 5: Utthāpana
Yāma 6: Sandhyā—Sandhyā Āratī (4)
Yāma 7: Śayana—Śayana Āratī (5)
Yāma 8: Rāsalīlā

Here we can see how the eight periods of Krishna's day (*yāmas*) overlap with the standard five *āratīs*. Of course, the number of *āratīs* will vary from lineage to lineage, and exactly how *āratī* lines up with *aṣṭa-kāliya-līlā* will also vary. But the above can serve as an overall example.[73]

To summarize: *Āratī* proper is done whenever an "audience" is held. Maṅgalā-āratī, for example, is when the *sakhīs* want to see and serve their Lordships, and we, the general audience, can view them at this time as well.[74] Then, just before the Deities go about their day, they are bathed and dressed with all the fanfare suited to a king and queen. Consequently, Śṛṅgāra-āratī becomes a luxurious event, which is often more elaborate than the earlier *āratī*. Now, according to the above outline, Vana-vihāra is when Krishna journeys out to roam the forests, or perhaps to tend cows, and so, for this, there is no *āratī* as such. (These periods are referred to in various ways, depending on the Vaishnava tradition to which one adheres.)[75] Next, Rāja-bhoga is when Krishna returns to have lunch, and so the *sakhīs* are eager to see a satisfied Divine Couple, well-fed. The noon Rāja-bhoga offering is a full meal, the main meal of the day, corresponding to Krishna's *aṣṭa-kāliya-līlā* lunch extravaganza—a forest feast sent by Mother Yaśodā for his pleasure. This is also a period of amorous pastimes with Śrī Rādhā and her associate *gopīs* in the many wonderful groves of Rādhā-kuṇḍa.

After enjoying their meal, they take rest once again. When they are awakened in the afternoon, a simple *dhūpa* (incense) ceremony takes place, often along with an offering of fruits. At this time, no formal *āratī* is necessary, though some temples will engage it according to their means.[76]

The Divine Couple then moves out for further adventures in the forest. According to many, Sandhyā, then, is the most important time of the Vaishnava day, and in the Nitya-līlās this is reflected in the Sandhyā-bhoga-āratī: the Divine Couple is offered an elaborate meal, after which we find them in the Śayana period—the official end of their day, when they are relieved of their ornamentation and heavy clothing. Everyone leaves, and the Deities are alone: Thus, the Rāsa-līla takes place at midnight, with no "audience" in sight; consequently, there is no *āratī*. In this way, the above scenario accommodates the five traditional *āratīs* found in most temples along with the confidential periods in which the Deity is said to relish the company of his closest associates, especially Rādhikā, particularly at the end of the evening when he enjoys His Rāsa-līlā.

How is all of this played out at the Radha Raman temple? "Sevā of Rādhāramaṇ," writes Margaret Case, "involves service to the deity throughout the day by priests who are mindful of his eternal, daily activities, which are considered to take place at specific times during the eight periods or watches into which the day is divided."[77] She continues:

> The temple is opened before dawn; the first *āratī, maṅgala-āratī*, is at 4:45 or 5:00 A.M. in the summer, 5:30 A.M. in winter. The temple is locked at night, and the key is in the safekeeping of the Goswami who is in charge of sevā at the time. . . . The *darśana* at midmorning (*dhūpa-āratī*), after Rādhāramaṇ is dressed for the day, is eagerly anticipated by the devotees. . . . The *āratī* at this time is offered with a cotton wick light, and also with aloe and sandalwood charcoal incense (*dhūpa*), and again the bells are rung. For each successive *darśana* (viewing the deity, both during *āratī* and otherwise), Rādhāramaṇ's basic costume remains the same, but details of adornment change, and in the evening lush garlands of flowers may be added. . . . The *āratīs* conducted later in the day are more elaborate than the first two in the morning.[78]

Vaishnavacharya Chandan Goswami's official Radha Raman website offers a list of temple āratīs, and non-āratī darśanas, too, along with his commentary, which harkens to the principle of aṣṭa-kāliya-līlā:

1. Mangla Aarti
2. Dhoop Aarti Sandarshan
3. Srngaar Aarti Sandarshan
4. Rajbhog Aarti Sandarshan
5. Evening Dhoop Aarti Sandarshan
6. Sandhya Aarti Sandarshan
7. Aulai Sandarshan
8. Shyan Aarti Sandarshan

"As the first rays of morning light spread across the sky," writes Chandan Goswami, "Shri Radharaman (Shriji) awakens. Soon, eager devotees swarm into the temple, to quench their thirst for the nectar of His beauty at the auspicious time of Mangla Aarti. Shriji's attendant Goswami waves the lamp in graceful rings, binding the divine Youth with the protection of his love, and dispelling any negative energy that might bring Him harm. . . . Then the curtain falls. After the eternal Youth brushes His teeth, He is bathed and dressed with greatest care by His Goswamis. Finally the curtain parts, revealing the glory of Shriji's handsome Form, amidst the spreading aromatic smoke of the Dhoop Aarti. . . . Now Shriji is ready to go and graze the cows, but not before His mother and the gopis serve Him privately with a lavish breakfast. Once fed and fully dressed, He sets out with His cows and cowherd friends. Finding any opportunity, Shriji slips away to meet His Beloved, Shri Radharani, and Her friends (*sakhis*) under the shade of the forest trees, flowers and creepers. The sakhis decorate this moment by performing Srngaar Aarti, an auspicious ritual to keep the Sweethearts safe throughout the day. The curtain is drawn. Shriji rejoins His friends and walks and wanders through the forest. Later, He meets up again with His Soul Mate, Shri Radharani, and when He feels tired and hungry, She serves Him delicious, rich dishes prepared with greatest care by Her sakhis. The royal plate is filled with the flavours of their love. After enjoying Their midday meal, both Radha and Her Raman find Themselves in a relaxed mood. The Lovers are greeted with Rajbhog Aarti. Soon after, Shri Radharamanji with His Sweetheart retire to rest in a nearby grove. The evening sandarshan starts with the Dhoop Aarti again, filling the entire atmosphere with aroma, and then fruits, refreshments and snacks are offered to Shri Radharamanji. The sun is now sinking: Krishn, His big brother Balram and their cowherd friends return home, along with the cows. Thereupon Mother Yashoda welcomes her children by performing Sandhya Aarti. The boys return by the end of the day, covered with dust spread by the cows. After bathing, they dress in comfortable evening attire, and hungrily demand their dinner. 'My dear Boy please be patient,' answers Mother Yashoda as she brings the evening meal. When the time comes for sleep, the last aarti of the day is offered, called Shyan Aarti. In perfect silence the devotees worship Shriji with their eyes, while His attendant Goswami delicately waves the lamp. The bamboo flute plays, and the gong quietly sounds the most gentle lullaby."[79]

In a personal letter, dated January 6, 2020, Chandan Goswami wrote to me as follows, confirming the clear connection between Radha Raman Deity service and the *aṣṭa-kāliya-līlā*: "Ashtayam-lila or *ashta-kaliya-lila* is followed in many temples in Braj, and in other places where the pure Braj traditions are followed. In the Shri Radharaman Temple, worship is done according to *Govind Lilamrit*. Just as in *Govind Lilamrit*, Krishn [sic] goes to the pastureland with cows and has lunch near Radhakund, similarly, there is a separate space in the temple where Radharaman goes for Rajbhog (lunch). . . . In our tradition, there are so many beautiful Brajbhasha songs about the eternal *lila* based on *Govind Lilamrit*. We have recently published a book of such songs with their English translations. These songs were written by one of the pillars of our tradition, Shri Gunmanjari Das Goswami, and they have been sung in the temple for over a century. *Lila-kirtan* is used to connect every moment of temple worship to the *ashta-kaliya-lila*."[80]

CONCLUSION

We began this chapter with the notion that Radha Raman is three Deities in one, namely, Śrī Rādhā, Lord Krishna, and Śrī Chaitanya. But there is another way in which we may understand Radha Raman to be three Deities in one: We earlier cited the *Bhakti-ratnākara* (4.320–22), which states that Radha Raman embodies Vrindavan's three main Krishna Deities, Śrī Madan Mohan, Śrī Govindadeva, and Śrī Gopīnātha. This, then, is a second way that he manifests as a triadic group of divinities, and it is especially significant, for it suggests yet a third notion of trinity situated at the very core of the Gauḍīya Vaishnava tradition.

Vrindavan's three Deities are overt manifestations of a three-tiered theological concept, i.e., *sambandha* (Madan Mohan), *abhidheya* (Govindadeva), and *prayojana* (Gopīnātha), representing the full trajectory of spiritual practice. *Sambandha* refers to relationship with Krishna, or the dawning of awareness that such a relationship even exists. *Abhidheya* is the phase in which one begins to employ the time-honored skillful means by which that relationship reaches perfection. And, lastly, *prayojana* is the culmination of that relationship, when the longing for unalloyed spiritual affection is fulfilled by its transformation into consummate love of God. In other words, Radha Raman, in his simple, playful, threefold-bending form, represents the entire path of Vaishnava spirituality, from beginning to end.

In the Gauḍīya Vaishnava tradition, these three terms—*sambandha, abhidheya*, and *prayojana*—are used prodigiously, and are particularly noteworthy in Jīva Gosvāmī's *Tattva-sandarbha* (anuccheda 9) and Krishnadāsa Kavirāja's *Caitanya-caritāmṛta* (see especially Ādi 7.146, and Madhya 6.178, 20.124, 20.125, 20.143, 25.102, and 25.131).

The same words, along with their deepest possible implications, are also used throughout Bhaktivinoda Ṭhākura's massive literary oeuvre, and upon reading these works we become privy to inner meaning and Vaishnava context. Prabhupāda himself draws on Bhaktivinoda's understanding, as we see in his *Caitanya-caritāmṛta* commentary:

> Worship of Madana-mohana is on the platform of reestablishing our forgotten relationship with the Supreme Lord. In the material world we are presently in utter ignorance of our eternal relationship with the Supreme Lord. . . . In the beginning of our spiritual life we must therefore worship Madana-mohana so

> that He may attract us and nullify our attachment for material sense gratification. This relationship with Madana-mohana is necessary for neophyte devotees. When one wishes to render service to the Lord with strong attachment, one worships Govinda on the platform of transcendental service. Govinda is the reservoir of all pleasures. When by the grace of Kṛṣṇa and the devotees one reaches perfection in devotional service, he can appreciate Kṛṣṇa as Gopījana-vallabha, the pleasure Deity of the damsels of Vraja.[81]

This is all true of Radha Raman as well. Being the combined manifestation of all three, he is capable of bringing his worshippers beyond the realm of *māyā* (illusion) from the very beginning of their devotional journey. Merely seeing him can awaken one to his/her true nature, which is, first of all, one's identity as spirit-soul, and then to one's eternal relationship with Krishna (*sambandha*). By such awakening, one very quickly adopts the process of devotional service (*bhakti*), enabling one to traverse the spiritual path in earnest (*abhidheya*). If one determinedly continues on this path, under the guidance of a genuine spiritual preceptor, one achieves the goal, which is Krishna-premā, or love for Krishna (*prayojana*).

This tripartite schema—*sambandha* (relationship), *abhidheya* (execution), and *prayojana* (goal)—has special meaning on the path of *bhakti*, and consequently in the context of understanding Radha Raman. In fact, on one level, all three phases can be seen as permutations of *bhakti*: (1) God is love, as it is said,[82] and so Krishna, with whom one seeks relationship (*sambandha*), is himself the embodiment of *bhakti* (this is especially so when he is viewed as Śrī Chaitanya or in relation to Śrī Rādhā); (2) *bhakti* is the means (*abhidheya*) by which one attains Krishna, i.e., the practices of *bhakti* allow that relationship to unfold; and (3) the goal (*prayojana*) is devotion in all its fullness, the natural end-result of following the path with faith and sincerity.[83]

Radha Raman, then, is *bhakti* personified, for, as we have seen, he is Śrī Rādhā, Mahāprabhu, Krishna, and the three prominent Deities of Braj as well.

We thus end with two contemporary prayers in his honor, glorifying both the Deity himself and the eternal associate of the Lord, Gopāla Bhaṭṭa Gosvāmī, who brought him to our three-dimensional world and thus within the purview of our vision:

madana mohana caraṇāmbujam

vistīrṇa vakṣaḥ-sthala gopīnātham

govinda su-smera mukhāravindam

rādhāramaṇa praphulla svarūpam

"Śrī Radha Raman is the fully blossomed form of Madana-mohana, Gopīnātha, and Śrī Govinda. He has the lotus feet of Madana-mohana, the broad chest of Gopīnātha, and the beautiful smiling face of Govinda."

vraje vilāsam sadā ramantah ānanda-samudra magnāḥ

śrī rūpa mañjarī preṣṭha-sakhī gosvāmī anyatamam

śrī gopāla bhaṭṭa dāsanam daso'ham śaraṇaṁ prapadyam

sarvātma snapanaṁ paraṁ vijayate śrī rādhāramana satataṁ namāmi

"I take shelter of those who call themselves the servants of the servants of Gopāla Bhaṭṭa Gosvāmī, the foremost of self-controlled saintly personalities. He is an intimate sakhī of Śrī Rūpa Mañjarī, and is always playing in Braj, drowning in an ocean of bliss. I perpetually offer my obeisance to Śrī Radha Raman, who awards supreme victory over māyā and who establishes the eternal identity of the soul, fully bathing that spiritual entity in the nectar of divine service to His lotus feet."[84]

NOTES

1. Although Lord Raṅganāth is generally seen as Vishnu, he is also acknowledged as a form of Krishna, and this is accepted throughout the Śrīvaishnava tradition. Thus, Mahāprabhu's attraction to him can be adjudicated in terms of the Gauḍīya point of view (in which Krishna is lauded over Vishnu). Of course, Vaishnava tradition—whether Śrīvaishnava or Gauḍīya—accepts the oneness of Vishnu and Krishna, both being acknowledged as forms of the same supreme Godhead, especially in terms of *tattva* or ontological truth (even if, according to Gauḍīyas, the two divinities are different in terms of *rasa*, i.e., inner, transcendental relationship, with Krishna taking a predominant role).

Still, it is clear from the Śrīvaishnava tradition itself that Lord Raṅganāth can be seen as Krishna. For example, one of the 12 Āḻvārs, Tiruppanāḻvār, writes about the Deity as "tasting butter," a clear allusion to his manifestation as Krishna. This is further confirmed in the traditional and much-lauded commentary of Periavāchān Piḷḷai, where Raṅganāth is directly stated to be a manifestation of Dāmodara. Nonetheless, Raṅganāth is also identified as Rāma in the same poem, and as other forms of God as well. Further, "The Moolavar at Śrī Raṅgam is Dāmodara Krishnan, with the welt marks from his mother's tying him up to a mortar. The *utsava-mūrti* is traditionally recognized as Śrī Rāmachandra" (See http://www.ibiblio.org/sripedia/oppiliappan/archives/apr07/msg00177.html). Sometimes, the opposite is stated, with the main Deity as Rāma and Namperumāḷ, the smaller Deity, as Krishna. Tradition has it that the latter still shows signs of having had a rope tightly tied around his waist. So when he is bathed, the priests make sure not to show that part of his body (https://www.srivaishnavasri.com/namperumal-thirumanjanam-kaili). Similarly, Āṇṭāḷ Āḻvār adores Lord Raṅganāth as Krishna in her famous *Tiruppāvai* (5), also including the name Dāmodara. It is clear from her writing that Raṅganāth is identifiable as Lord Krishna. Finally, Lord Raṅganāth's appearance day is listed as Āvaṇi Rohiṇī or Krishna Janmāṣṭami. Āvaṇi is the Tamil solar month and Rohiṇī is the star under which Lord Krishna was born. All this being said, Śrīvaishnavas tend to view all forms of Vishnu as various faces on the same ultimate divinity, with a fluid conception encompassing all Krishna/Vishnu forms according to each devotee's personal emotion (*bhāva*).

2. Although the year of Mahāprabhu's journey to Śrī Raṅgam is sometimes listed as 1510 CE (and sometimes 1512), it is most commonly said to be 1511, the difference justified by how one correlates the Indian dating system to the Western calendar. According to Bhaktisiddhānta Sarasvatī Ṭhākura: "In the beginning of the Śaka year of 1433 (1511 AD), on the pretext of a pilgrimage, Śrī Krishna Caitanya Mahāprabhu distributed his mercy to the devotees [in Śrī Raṅgam]." See "Prabodhānanda Sarasvatī" by Bhaktisiddhānta Sarasvatī Ṭhākura, published in *Viveka-śatakam: A Hundred Verses of Wisdom*, edited and translated from the original Sanskrit by Demian Martins (Surat: Bhakti Vikas Trust, 2017), xi. The essay by Sarasvatī Ṭhākura was originally published as an introductory note in his editions of Prabodhānanda's *Caitanya-candrāmṛta* and *Navadvīpa-śatakam* (Gaudiya Matha, Kolkata, dates unknown). His Divine Grace A. C. Bhaktivedanta Swami Prabhupāda also writes, "From historical records it is found that Śrī Caitanya Mahāprabhu traveled in South India in the year 1433 Śakābda (1511 AD) during the Cāturmāsya period, and it was at that time that He met Prabodhānanda, who belonged to the Rāmānuja-sampradāya." (See *Caitanya-caritāmṛta* Ādi 7.149, purport) Prabhupāda also mention the year 1511 in *Caitanya-caritāmṛta* Ādi 10.105, purport.

3. The dates I have supplied for Gopāla Bhaṭṭa Gosvāmī (1503–1578) come from Bhaktivinoda Ṭhākura. See Bhaki Pradip Tirtha Swami, *Sri Chaitanya Mahaprabhu* (Calcutta: Gaudiya Mission, 1947), appendix III, 98, quoting Bhaktivinoda's *Sajjana-toṣaṇī*, Vol. II, 1882. Other authorities supply alternate dates, such as 1500–1586. This much we know: Gopāla Bhaṭṭa Gosvāmī would have been anywhere from seven to eleven years old when Mahāprabhu visited Śrī Raṅgam.

4. *Caitanya-caritāmṛta* (Madhya 9.87): "[He] visited the temple of Śrī Raṅgam daily and danced in ecstasy." (*śrī-raṅga darśanapratidina premāveśe karena nartana*) His love for the Deity while chanting and dancing is also noted (Madhya 9.81): "In the temple of Raṅganāth, Śrī Chaitanya Mahāprabhu chanted and danced in ecstatic love of Godhead (*prema-āveśe*). Seeing His movements, everyone was struck with wonder."

5. Vishnu is generally depicted with four arms or more. His most typical iconographical image might be rendered as follows: His chest is adorned with Śrīvatsa, a lock of hair that represents Śrī, the Goddess, and the brilliant Kaustubha jewel, along with beautiful and fresh garlands (*vanamālā*). His four hands hold *śaṅkha* (conch), *chakra* (discus), *gadā* (mace), and *padma* (lotus), while his dark blue complexion is always illuminated by his armlets, jewels, earrings, and long dark hair. In addition

to all this, he is traditionally described as having four arms. Less commonly, he is depicted with two. But, again, given the poetry of the Āḻvārs and the tradition maintained to this day in Śrī Raṅgam as briefly elucidated in Endnote 2, the Deity's two arms can easily be construed as an allusion to his identity with Lord Krishna. Nonetheless, for Śrīvaishnavas, as already explained, the distinction between Krishna and Vishnu is theologically inconsequential, at least when compared with the Gauḍīya perspective.

6. In the Puranas, Śeṣa is a thousand-headed serpent who holds all the planets of the universe on his hoods while singing the glories of the Lord from his numerous mouths. He is sometimes referred to as Ananta Śeṣa, or the "endless-serpent." Śrīla Jīva Gosvāmī, in his *Krishna-sandarbha*, has described Śeṣa Nāga as follows: "Śrī Anantadeva has thousands of faces and is fully independent. Always ready to serve the Supreme Personality of Godhead, he waits upon him constantly." He is a manifestation of Balarāma, Krishna's elder brother, who serves the Lord's every need. The word *Śeṣa*, in fact, also means "servant."

7. Most scholarly literature on Śrī Raṅgam informs us that the central Deity is roughly eighteen feet in length, but in personal correspondence, Murali Battar Rangaraja (January 10, 2020), the present-day descendent of Vyeṅkata Bhaṭṭa and currently leading priest at the Śrī Raṅgam temple, opines that an estimation of fourteen to sixteen feet would be more accurate.

8. According to Greg Jay (Gaura Keśava Dāsa), independent researcher, ritualist expert, *pūjārī*, and longtime resident of Śrī Raṅgam, Lord Raṅganāth is made of stucco (brick and mortar), even if many think he is made of black stone. "I was present one year when they did the re-plastering of the main Deity as part of the twelve-year re-consecration rituals," says Jay, in a personal letter to me, dated December 30, 2019. "Namperumāḷ (the smaller altar Deity) and Ubhaya Nācchiārs (Śrī and Bhū) are Chola-style forms, made of five metals. The composition is laid down in the *Śilpa-śāstra*, a collection of ancient texts that describe arts, crafts, and various design rules and standards for divine images. Apart from that, the *śālagrāmas* are stone."

9. Śrīla Prabhupāda mentions the Muslim invasion of Śrī Raṅgam, "There was also a celebrated disciple of Rāmānujācārya's known as Kūreśa. Śrī Rāmapillā was the son of Kūreśa, and his son was Vāgvijaya Bhaṭṭa, whose son was Vedavyāsa Bhaṭṭa, or Śrī Sudarśanācārya. When Sudarśanācārya was an old man, the Mohammedans attacked the temple of Raṅganātha and killed about twelve hundred Śrī Vaiṣṇavas. At that time the Deity of Raṅganātha [Namperumāḻ, the *utsava-mūrti*] was transferred to the temple of Tirupati in the kingdom of Vijayanagara. The governor of Gingee, Goppaṇārya, brought Śrī Raṅganātha from the temple of Tirupati to a place known as Siṁha-brahma, where the Lord was situated for three years. In the year 1293 Śaka (1372 AD) the Deity was reinstalled in the Raṅganātha temple. On the eastern wall of the Raṅganātha temple is an inscription written by Vedānta-deśika relating how Raṅganātha was returned to the temple." See *Caitanya-caritāmṛta* (Madhya 9.79, purport).

10. Because of the intimate relationship between Śrī Chaitanya Mahāprabhu and Gopāla Bhaṭṭa, it is sometimes claimed that Mahāprabhu initiated him while in Śrī

Raṅgam, but there is no direct evidence of this. According to the larger tradition, Mahāprabhu is not known to have formally initiated anyone. Still, the Radha Raman Gosvāmīs, in an attempt to prove their contention, cite a famous verse from Gauḍīya Vaishnava literature: "I praise the soles of my Guru's feet that are an abode of Chintamani gems. She is the ocean of mercy and a mine of all jewel-like qualities. The remembrance of the daughter of Ācārya Prabhu, named Śrīla Hemalatā, bestows all siddhis. Seeing me fallen in the darkness of ignorance, she was so kind to anoint me with the ointment of divine knowledge. By her grace my eyes were enlightened and all darkness went far away. I praise Śrī (Śrīnivāsa) Ācārya Prabhu, the master of my master. I offer millions of obeisances at his lotus-feet. I praise the abode of *prema* for Rādhā-Kṛṣṇa, named Gopāla Bhaṭṭa, my great grand Guru. I praise prabhu Gauracandra, the source of all transcendental bliss, who is my *parameṣṭi* Guru [great great grand guru]." (*vando guru padatala, cintāmaṇimaya sthala, sarva guṇakhani dayānidhi// ācārya prabhura sutā, nāma śrīla hemalatā, tāhāra smaraṇe sarva siddhi// ageyāna andhakāre, patana dekhiyā more, jñānāñjanā dilā doyā kori// tāhāra karunā hoite, netra hoilo prakāśite, dūre gelo andhakārāvali// vando śrī ācārya prabhu, amāra prabhura prabhu// tāra pade koṭi paraṇāma, vando gopāla bhaṭṭa nāma, rādhā-kṛṣṇa prema-dhāma// parāpara guru kṛpā dhāma, vando prabhu gauracandra, sakala ānanda kanda, parameṣṭi guru tiho hoy//*) See Yadunandana Dāsa, *Govinda-līlāmṛta, padyānuvāda*, in Bengali (Calcutta: Caitanya-candrodaya-yantra, 1774 Śaka era [1861 CE], English rendering by Advaita Das), 3.

It must be noted that the word *dīkṣā*, initiation, does not occur in this verse. In fact, it is a common device in various Guru-praṇālis that Mahāprabhu is claimed as the Guru of the *prāṇa-puruṣa*, or arch father, of their particular lineage. The same can be seen in Lokanātha Gosvāmī's Guru-praṇāli and in several others as well. Also interesting is that the same Yadunandana Dāsa who wrote the above verse describes the meeting between Mahāprabhu and young Gopāla Bhaṭṭa in detail (in his book *Karṇānanda*). But in this text, too, he offers no direct statement to the effect that Mahāprabhu gave *dīkṣā* to Gopāla Bhaṭṭa, and this would have been an appropriate place to do so. Rather, he merely notes that the two luminaries saw each other in their original forms, that Mahāprabhu gave him *kaupīna* and *bahirvāsa* as gifts, and told him to go to Vrindavan and initiate Śrīnivāsa in future (*Karṇānanda*, chapter 5). Additionally, Gopāla Bhaṭṭa does not mention Mahāprabhu as his *dīkṣā-guru* in the *Hari-bhakti-vilāsa,* despite the traditional custom of crediting one's guru in any major writing endeavor.

This being the case, the Radha Raman Gosvāmīs often quote a more pointed verse to make their conclusion inescapable: "Chaitanya Mahāprabhu gave shelter to Gopāla Bhaṭṭa by initiating him with the Gopāla Mantra. He taught him the philosophy of Vaishnavism and the essence of devotion. Mahāprabhu instructed him to go to Vrindavan and live there" (*tin kah prabhu dīkṣā tab dīnī, śrī gopāl mantra ras bhīnī kahī karahu vṛndāvan vāsā, vaiṣhṇav dharm tattva parakāsā*). This verse was penned by one of the greatest scholars of the Radha Raman lineage: Sarvabhaum Shri Madhusudan Goswami (1858–1929 CE). It is found in his Brajbhasha work, *Shri Radharaman Prakatya*, and it is also inscribed on the temple wall. (See Vaisnavacharya Chandan Goswami, trans., *Shri Radharaman Prakatya* [Anupam Goswami: 2018],

60.) Although the word *dīkṣā* does indeed occur in this verse, the *Shri Radharaman Prakatya* is deemed internal literature and is not generally accepted outside the specific Radha Raman tradition. In the end, then, it should be acknowledged that there are instructing spiritual masters (*śikṣā-gurus*) and initiating spiritual masters (*dīkṣā-gurus*), and, barring any additional evidence, it is likely that Mahāprabhu was the former in regard to Gopāla Bhaṭṭa Gosvāmī.

11. That Gopāla Bhaṭṭa was initiated by Prabodhānanda Sarasvatī is confirmed by Śrīla Prabhupāda: "Śrī Gopāla Bhaṭṭa Gosvāmī was later initiated by his uncle, the great *sannyāsī*, Prabodhānanda Sarasvatī" (*Caitanya-caritāmṛta* Ādi 10.105, purport). And further, "Prabodhānanda Sarasvatī was the uncle and spiritual master of Gopāla Bhaṭṭa Gosvāmī" (Madhya 17.104, purport).

12. For more on Prabodhānanda Sarasvatī, see Jan K. Brzezinski, "Prabodhānanda Sarasvatī: From Benares to Braj," in *Bulletin of the School of Oriental and African Studies,* University of London 55, no. 1 (1992): 52–75. See also Brzezinski, "Prabodhānanda, Hita Harivaṃśa and the '*Rādhārasasudhānidhi*,'" in *Bulletin of the School of Oriental and African Studies* 55, no. 3(1992): 472–97. Prabodhānanda eventually relocated to the Braj area and Gopāla Bhaṭṭa eventually followed suit: "Giving up Srirangam," writes Bhaktisiddhānta Sarasvatī, "he [Prabodhānanda] first took shelter of Lord Chaitanya, and keeping in mind his desired mode of worship, without delay he went to live in Kamyavana in the Mathura district. Meanwhile, Gopala Bhatta also gradually developed an intense desire to live in Vraja-dhama and later followed in his uncle's footsteps." See "Prabodhānanda Sarasvatī" by Bhaktisiddhānta Sarasvatī Ṭhākura, reprinted in *Viveka-Satakam: A Hundred Verses of Wisdom*, edited and translated from the original Sanskrit by Demian Martins (Surat: Bhakti Vikas Trust, 2017), op. cit., xiv.

13. According to Bhaktisiddhānta Sarasvatī, "[Mahāprabhu's visit to Śrī Raṅgam] resulted in the conversion of [Vyenkata's] brother Prabodhananda, a *tridandi sannyasin*, and his son Gopala Bhatta, who turned out to be one of the six principal disciples at Vrindavan." See Bhaktisiddhānta Sarasvatī Ṭhākura, *Rai Ramananda* (http://www.krishnapath.org/Library/Goswami-books/Bhaktisiddhanta-Sarasvati-Thakura/Bhaktisiddhanta_Sarasvati_Thakura_Rai_Ramananda.pdf) Thus, by Sarasvatī Ṭhākura's account, it seems that while Prabodhānanda and Gopāla Bhaṭṭa became Gauḍīyas, Vyeṅkaṭa and Tirumalla Bhaṭṭa continued in their loving service to Lord Raṅganāth at Śrī Raṅgam.

14. Mahāprabhu was happy (*prabhura tuṣṭa haila mana*) with Vyeṅkata's devotion (Madhya 9.109): "Being a Vaishnava in the Rāmānuja-sampradāya, Vyeṅkaṭa Bhaṭṭa worshiped the Deities of Lakṣmī and Nārāyaṇa. Seeing his pure devotion, Śrī Caitanya Mahāprabhu was very much satisfied."

15. Gauḍīya Vaishnavas accept the notion that all forms of the Lord are one. According to *Caitanya-caritāmṛta* (Ādi 5.128–32), there is no difference between all incarnations or manifestations of the Lord and the source of all incarnations and manifestations, i.e., Krishna (*avatāra-avatārī-abheda*). "In whatever form one knows the Lord, one speaks of him in that way. In this there is no falsity, since everything is possible in Krishna." (*yei yei rūpe jāne, sei tāhā kahesakala sambhave kṛṣṇe, kichu mithyā nahe*) Still, Gauḍīyas see Krishna as the source of all incarnations and

manifestations, as per *Bhāgavata Purāṇa* 1.3.28—"All of the above-mentioned incarnations are either plenary portions or portions of the plenary portions of the Lord, but Lord Śrī Krishna is the original Personality of Godhead (*kṛṣṇas tu bhagavān svayam*)." Additionally, Gauḍīyas point out that of all incarnations and manifestations of the Supreme, Krishna embodies the zenith of all loving intimacy, personhood, and sweetness (*mādhurya*), which eclipses power, awe, and reverence (*aiśvarya*). Mahāprabhu expressed these truths to Vyeṅkaṭa Bhaṭṭa.

16. Mahāprabhu shows Gopāla Bhaṭṭa his own Navadvīpa pastimes and revealed himself to be Krishna. But this revelation is not given to just anyone. Indeed, Gopāla Bhaṭṭa is a special personality, an intimate associate of Śrī Rādhikā. In the *Gaura-gaṇoddeśa-dīpikā* (184) it is mentioned that, "his previous name in the pastimes of Lord Krishna was Anaṅga Mañjarī [Rādhikā's younger sister]. Sometimes he is also said to have been an incarnation of Guṇa Mañjarī." His humility is also beyond compare: Gopāla Bhaṭṭa's name is found in only four different instances in the *Caitanya-caritāmṛta* (Ādi 1.36–7, 9.4, 10.105, and Madhya 18.49), but little information of a biographical nature can be gleaned from these verses. Later authors, including Narahari Chakravartī, ascribe this lacuna to the humble Gopāla's own request to remain anonymous (cf. *Bhakti-ratnākara* 1.222), and, in their boldness, attempt to add the missing data to the biographical record.

17. See *Bhakti-ratnākara* (1.141–44) wherein Mahāprabhu assures Gopāla Bhaṭṭa that his desires would soon be fulfilled, and that they would both be together in Vrindavan.

18. The three Deities carved by Mahāprabhu in Śrī Raṅgam are unusual forms of Jagannātha, Baladeva, and Subhadrā, and local residents have built a temple to honor them, with worship being conducted on a daily basis. Jagannath Mutt (Matha), as the temple is called, can be found on North West Chitra Street opposite the home of Murali Bhattar and family, where Vyeṅkaṭa lived in Śrī Chaitanya's time. The Mutt or temple is under the management of Sri Ranganatha Devasthanam (the main temple) in conjunction with the HR&CE (Hindu Religious and Charitable Endowments Department), a government institution that manages and controls the temple administration for the state.

Prominent personalities in the Śrī Sampradāya today confirm the story of Mahāprabhu's visit and his carving of the Deities, including Vasudevan Lakshmikumara Tattacarya (Sanskrit Scholar, Professor, Sastra University, Tanjavur, Tamil Nadu), a descendant of the original Nāthamuni, one of the originating patriarchs of the Śrīvaishnava tradition, and Murali Bhattar, the current head priest of the main temple and modern-day descendent of Vyeṅkaṭa Bhaṭṭa. Murali Bhattar authenticated these Deities in a personal letter to me dated December 24, 2019. Thus, while Mahāprabhu's carving of these Deities may not be mentioned in the traditional biographies, the event falls into the category of *aitihya pramāṇa* ("expert testimony, established historical tradition"), and is tacitly accepted in both Śrīvaishnava and Gauḍīya Sampradāyas.

19. Śrī Raṅgam is a stronghold of the Rāmānuja tradition, with little evidence of Mahāprabhu's sixteenth-century visit. Aside from the Jagannath Mutt, mentioned above, there are few other indications that he was ever there: One commemorative

item would be the marble footprints of Mahāprabhu within the Śrī Raṅgam temple area on Amma Mandapa Road, leading away from the temple in a southerly direction toward the Kāverī. These footprints were installed in 1958 by Bhakti Vilas Tirtha Maharaja, a prominent disciple of Bhaktisiddhānta Sarasvatī. In 2020, a *mūrti* of Śrī Chaitanya was added by current Gaudiya Matha devotees, Gopananda Bon Maharaj and B. S. Damodar Maharaja, to augment the glory of these footprints. The worshipful *maṇḍap* is managed by ISKCON devotees in Śrī Raṅgam, who manage a small temple nearby as well.

20. It should be noted that while the *Bhakti-ratnākara* (1.193–5) says that Śrī Chaitanya sent his personal garments and his wooden seat to his followers in Vrindavan to bless them, there is no specific indication (in that particular text) that these items were meant for Gopāla Bhaṭṭa Gosvāmī alone. That said, we learn from both Yadunandana Dāsa's *Karṇānanda* (chapters 5 and 6) and Nityānanda Dāsa's *Prema-vilāsa* (chapter 1) that the items were indeed meant for Gopāla Bhaṭṭa. These texts tell us that in addition to *kaupīnas* and the wooden seat, a sacred thread and a *bahirvāsa* (upper cloth worn by *sannyāsīs*) were included as well. But what do these gifts signify beyond the Master's deep appreciation of Gopāla Bhaṭṭa? The present-day Radha Raman Gosvāmīs claim that the paraphernalia was sent to him as a special blessing and even somehow indicate that he is Śrī Chaitanya's unique successor because of it. The power of this argument is minimized by the fact that Mahāprabhu also gave his Govardhana-śilā and *guñjā-mālā* as loving gifts to Raghunātha Dāsa Gosvāmī, as we learn from *Caitanya-caritāmṛta* (Antya 6.287–307). [Govardhana is Krishna and *guñjā-mālā* is Rādhikā, respectively.] There are other instances of such special mercy as well, with Rūpa and Sanātana getting Mahāprabhu's attention as few others did.

It might be argued that there is distinct meaning in Mahāprabhu offering to Gopāla Bhaṭṭa his "seat," in particular. Normally, according to traditional texts, one is not permitted to use the shoes, sitting place, etc., of the guru, even when presented as a gift, unless the recipient is inheriting the spiritual master's mantle. The sitting place of the guru is known variously as *vyāsāsana* or *pīṭham*, and is considered especially sacred. So one might see the offering of the guru's seat in almost metaphorical terms: If the guru gives his sitting place to the disciple indicating that he should use it, as Mahāprabhu does to Gopāla Bhaṭṭa in both *Prema-vilāsa* and *Karṇānanda*, then he is indicating the disciple's ascension to the position of master, as a representative of Vyāsa. There is no doubt that Śrī Chaitanya Mahāprabhu considered Gopāla Bhaṭṭa such a special soul and as being among his eminent successors, but that the position was *uniquely* Gopāla Bhaṭṭa's remains in question. The conclusion, then, is that one must acknowledge the profound love that Mahāprabhu had for Gopāla Bhaṭṭa Gosvāmī—and the special position afforded him—without reading into it in a sectarian way. As an addendum: The items that were given to him are still privately worshipped at Radha Raman Mandir regularly and are on display on six occasions annually: (1) Śrī Radha Raman's appearance day. (2) the day of Gopāla Bhaṭṭa Gosvāmī's disappearance and (3) the day after that; (4) Śrī Krishna Janmāṣṭamī and (5) the next day, Nandotsava; and (6) Mahāprabhu's appearance day (Gaura Pūrṇimā).

21. Although there are various versions of this story, explaining just how and why Gopāla Bhaṭṭa decided to go to Nepal, the narrative replicated here is the most

common. Moreover, it is the authorized account of the Radha Raman tradition, as articulated by Padmanabh Goswami, head *mahānt* of the current Radha Raman Temple. See *Śālagrāma-śilā: Śāstric Evidence Compiled by Padmanābha Goswami* (Vrindavana: Radharamana Temple, 1993), 1. Additionally, one might ask: when Mahāprabhu appeared in Gopāla Bhaṭṭa's dream and said that he would give him *darśana*—did he mean in his form as Śrī Chaitanya? In his form as Śrī Krishna? The tradition allows for both answers, as we shall see.

22. *Śālagrāma-śilās* are very specific sacred stones that are considered non-different from Vishnu. It is difficult to worship them properly, requiring qualified *brāhmaṇas* who adhere to the strictest standards of the Vaishnava tradition. "*Śālagrāma*" refers to a village on the bank of the Gaṇḍakī in Nepal, from which these sacred stones get the name. The *śālagrāma* is actually an ammonite, the fossilized shell of an extinct species of mollusk, and it will visibly show certain distinguishing characteristics of Vishnu, such as the discus or the *chakra*. Important in the present context is that *śālagrāmas* are natural objects only found in the Gaṇḍakī of Nepal and are never man-made; thus Radha Raman is a self-manifesting Deity, originating as a *śālagrāma* and mystically turning into a three-fold bending Krishna form. A Dāmodara-śilā is a specific type of *śilā*, with special marks or other indications denoting exactly what form of Vishnu it is. They usually have circular fossil formations at the center and an indentation at the top containing a thread of gold. See Allan Aaron Shapiro, "Śalagrāmaśilā: A Study of Śalagrāma Stones with Text and Translation of Śālagrāma-parīkṣā," PhD thesis (Columbia University, 1987).

23. There is a slightly alternate version of this story in which Gopāl Bhaṭṭa knew exactly what to expect. That is to say, when Mahāprabhu appeared in his dream and told him to go to the Gaṇḍakī, he specifically informed him that he would find a Dāmodara-śilā and eleven other *śilās* as well. If this is true, then the initial version, in which the *śilās* miraculously enter his waterpot, not once, but three times before being recognized as a gift from God, would be problematic. Gopāl Bhaṭṭa would have been expecting the *śilās* to appear, not surprised as the first version indicates. This alternate telling is based on *Bhakti-ratnākara* 4.316: "Śrī Gaurāṅgadeva gave an order to Gopāla Bhaṭṭa Gosvāmī: 'You will see Lord Hari in the *śālagrāma-śilā*.'" (*śrī-gaurāṅga-deva ājñā dila gosvāmīre, śālagrāma haite tumi dekhibe harire*) Some take this to mean that Gopāla will go to the Gaṇḍakī and understand that he is seeing Hari there when he first acquires the *śālagrāmas*. Others say that it means he will "eventually" see Hari in the *śālagrāmas*, as in "when Radha Raman manifests through the *śilā* in Vrindavan." This latter version is reiterated in Madhusudana Goswami's *Shri Radharaman Prakatya* [See Vaisnavacharya Chandan Goswami, trans., *Shri Radharaman Prakatya* (Anupam Goswami: 2018), 14, 17. It is also found in O. B. L. Kapoor, *The Gosvāmīs of Vṛndāvana* (New Delhi: Sarasvati Jayasri Classics, 1995), 194. Kapoor goes even further, saying that Mahāprabhu asked Gopāla to go to the Gaṇḍakī and worship *śālagrāma*, and that he would even see Radha Raman, specifically, in the rocklike Deity while there.

24. Gopīnātha and Dāmodara would figure prominently in terms of worshipping Radha Raman and carrying on the lineage, while Hit Harivaṁśa would become the founder of the Rādhāvallabha Sampradāya. The subject of carrying on the tradition

through initiation is complex and viewed variously by competing factions of the lineage. In the end, Gopāla Bhaṭṭa Gosvāmī and Raghunātha Bhaṭṭa Gosvāmī—the two Bhaṭṭas—were expected to be the initiators, since they came from untainted *brāhmaṇa* backgrounds. These were practical considerations. Mahāprabhu wanted his line to be accepted by the larger Hindu tradition of his time, and his other leaders, such as Rūpa and Sanātana, though also from qualified *brāhmaṇa* backgrounds, would be viewed suspiciously due to their association with Muslim political leaders, a fact that compromised their pure brahminical status in the eyes of many. Initially, then, Gopāla Bhaṭṭa was to give *dīkṣā* to those from the western provinces, and Raghunātha Bhaṭṭa to those from the east (Man Singh was among the latter's more famous disciples). This is described in Manohar Dāsa's *Anurāgavallī* (2), paraphrased in O. B. L. Kapoor's *The Gosvāmī of Vṛndāvana* (chapter 6, page 197), op. cit. In addition, Nityānanda Prabhu and Advaita Prabhu (along with their wives) were delegated the task of making disciples, and many others would soon follow suit.

25. See Margaret Case, "Sevā at Rādhāramaṇa Temple, Vrindavan," *Journal of Vaishnava Studies* 3, no. 3 (Summer 1995): 45–46. She adds that "Rādhāramaṇajī is worshiped not only as a manifestation of Śrī Krishna, he is also regarded as a manifestation of Caitanya Mahāprabhu—that is, a manifestation of Rādhā and Krishna in one body. Rādhāramaṇa is reportedly one of only three temples in Vṛndāvana in which there is no separate image of Rādhā." We will discuss this more thoroughly later. The other two temples with no image of Rādhā are Bāṅke Bihāri of the Haridāsī Sampradāya and Rādhāvallabha of the Rādhāvallabha Sampradāya, both famous temples in Braj.

26. See *Bhāgavata Purāṇa* 10.30.39: "O my Lord, O my husband, O most dearly beloved (*ramaṇa*)! O mighty-armed Lord! Where are you? Where are you? O my friend, reveal yourself to your maidservant, who is very much aggrieved by your absence" (*hā nātha ramaṇa preṣṭha/ kvāsi kvāsi mahā-bhuja// dāsyās te kṛpaṇāyā me/ sakhe darśaya sannidhim//*).

27. See Kenneth Russell Valpey, *Attending Kṛṣṇa's Image: Caitanya Vaiṣṇava Mūrti-sevā as Devotional Truth* (New York: Routledge, 2006), 45–48. The detailed elaboration in this lengthy quote comes from the Radha Raman tradition, specifically Acharya Dr. Gaurakrsna Goswami, *Śrī Gopāla Bhaṭṭa Gosvāmī*, in Hindi (Vrindavan: Anilkumar Goswami, 1985). Allan Shapiro tells another side of the story: "The popular version tells that a certain king came to Vrindaban, a place of pilgrimage for devotees of Kṛṣṇa, and determined to donate various items of cloth or ornaments to the images which were being worshipped there. Gopāl Bhaṭṭ had a great desire to be able to adorn Kṛṣṇa (others say it was Kṛṣṇa who had a great desire to be adorned), and from the intensity of this desire, Kṛṣṇa and Rādhā (united in one form or image) appeared from the *śālagrām* and received the largesse of the monarch." See Allan A. Shapiro, "The Birth-celebration of Śrī Rādhāramaṇ in Vrindaban," MA thesis, Columbia University, 1979, 14–15.

28. See Cynthia Packert, *The Art of Loving Krishna: Ornamentation and Devotion* (Bloomington: Indiana University Press, 2010), 49.

29. Hayagriva Swami, *Vrindaban Days: Memories of an Indian Holy Town*, chapter 16 (West Virginia: Palace Publishing, 1988), 103–4.

30. This entire section of the *Bhakti-ratnākara* indicates how in serving Radha Raman, Gopāla Bhaṭṭa's memory of Mahāprabhu was sweetened and enhanced, contextually indicating the oneness of the two Deities: "In service [to Radha Raman] his supreme *ānanda* increased moment by moment; and [because Śrī Chaitanya and Radha Raman are one, by serving Radha Raman], he always remembered the service of Śrī Gaurasundara" See especially 4.342 (*sevāy paramānande bāre kṣane kṣane; śrī gauracandrer sebā sadā pore mone*).

31. For elaboration see *Caitanya-caritāmṛta,* Ādi 1.5.

32. Although Radha Raman's identity with Śrī Chaitanya is important, it should not be overstated. In one sense, since Mahāprabhu is non-different from Śrī Krishna, all Krishna Deities might be seen as embodying Mahāprabhu as well, especially if they show some special dimension of mercy, a defining quality for which Śrī Chaitanya is known. According to each devotee's individual *bhāva*, one can see Mahāprabhu in any given Krishna *mūrti* and Krishna in any given Mahāprabhu *mūrti*. As Gauḍīya poet Vasu Ghosh says about Lord Jagannātha in Purī (*vāsudeva ghoṣa bole kori joḍa hāta, jei gaura sei kṛṣṇa sei jagannātha*—"Vasudeva Ghosh says with folded hands, 'He who is Gaura is He who is Krishna is He who is Jagannātha.'").

Along similar lines, Kāśīśvara's Gaura-Govinda Deity is said to be both Krishna and Śrī Chaitanya. In fact, tradition has it that Śrī Chaitanya came to Western India in the form of this Krishna Deity, which he had given to his great devotee, Śrī Kāśīśvara Paṇḍita (*śrī caitanya śrī kāśīśvarera premavaśe/ śrī vigraha-rūpe āilā paścima pradeśe//*). This Deity is today in Jaipur, sharing the altar with the famous Deity of Govindaji. There are other examples as well. Still, clearly, in Radha Raman there is a special appearance of Mahāprabhu brought out by the love of Gopāla Bhaṭṭa Goswāmī.

Bhaktivedānta Nārāyaṇa Gosvāmī Mahārāja highlights an esoteric aspect of this phenomenon, saying that Gopāla Bhaṭṭa not only saw his Radha Raman Deity as Chaitanya but worshipped him in that way: "Now that the Lord of his heart had come, Gopāla Bhaṭṭa began worshiping Rādhā-ramaṇa as non-different from Gaurāṅga Mahāprabhu. He would dress the deity in *kaupīnas* and because Mahāprabhu is a *sannyāsī*, he did not establish Śrī Rādhā's Deity by his side.

Therefore, Rādhā-ramaṇa stands alone without Rādhārāṇī. Instead, a symbol of Rādhārāṇī in the form of a silver crown is placed on his left side." This explains both why there is no Rādhā Deity with Radha Raman and how his initial worshipper saw him as a manifestation of Chaitanya Mahāprabhu. See Bhaktivedānta Nārāyaṇa Gosvāmī Mahārāja Bhaktabāndhav Śrīla Gurudeva, *Rāgātmikā Vrajavāsī & Prayojana-tattva Ācārya Śrīla Gopāla Bhaṭṭa Gosvāmī* (Vrindavan: Bhaktabandhav, 2018), 24, 29.

33. See Vaishnavacharya Chandan Goswami, trans., *Shri Radharaman Prakatya* (Anupam Goswami: 2018), op. cit., 22.

34. http://www.shriradharaman.com/faq.html.

35. Margaret H. Case, *Seeing Krishna: The Religious World of a Brahman Family in Vrindaban* (New York: Oxford University Press, 2000), 72, 76.

36. Kenneth Russell Valpey, *Attending Kṛṣṇa's Image: Caitanya Vaiṣṇava Mūrti-sevā as Devotional Truth*, op. cit., 70.

37. See Vaishnavacharya Chandan Goswami, *Śrī Rādhāramaṇ Gītā: Nitya Līlā* (Vrindavan: Anupam Goswāmi, 2019), 39–40.

38. Kenneth Russell Valpey writes that there are two other Deities in Vrindavan without Rādhā accompaniment: "Still, as in two other temples of Vrindavan (Bāṅkebihārī and Rādhāvallabha), Rādhā is represented by a *gaddī* (throne or cushion), and her service is *gaddī-sevā* (she appears as a *sari* draped with ornaments propped over a gold plate, or *yantra*, inscribed with her name—*nāma-sevā*). Each of the other main Krishna images in Vrindavan would eventually be accompanied by an image of Rādhā." See *Attending Kṛṣṇa's Image: Caitanya Vaiṣṇava Mūrti-sevā as Devotional Truth*, op. cit., chapter 2, footnote 38, 178. See also endnote 25, above. Outside of Vrindavan, too, there are many Deities, such as Śrī Nāthjī (Vallabha Sampradāya) and Uḍupi Krishna (Mādhva Sampradāya), that are sans Rādhā, but the philosophical reasoning for their omission is very different than that found in Braj.

39. Vaishnavacharya Chandan Goswami, personal correspondence, January 4, 2020. The story is also told on his website (http://www.shriradharaman.com/faq.html).

40. The Sheetla Mata Mandir in Gurgaon, just outside Delhi in Haryana, is now famous. The oral history of the Radha Raman temple portrays Sheetla Mata as "Radha Ramanji's younger sister," while people of Gurgaon have their own local legends about the goddess's origin. They call her "Kripi"—the wife of Droṇācārya, of *Mahābhārata* fame—who is known for her service to sick and suffering children. It is believed that if local children become ill, the goddess will cure them. Additionally, couples come to worship her with the hope that she will bless them with a child. https://vrindavantoday.com/the-vrindavan-roots-of-gurgaons-sheetla-mata/. Philosophically, Yogamāyā expands from Rādhā and is a manifestation of Krishna's spiritual potency (*antaraṅga-śakti*). For Gauḍīyas, Durgā is one of her forms or expansions for governing the material energy (*bahiraṅga-śakti*). Padmanabh Goswami confirmed the Sheetla Mata story to me in a letter dated December 30, 2019: "In Gurugram (Haryana) there is famous old Shitala Mata Temple, which is worshiped as a goddess Durga. We have story that this is the same Radharani deity which was installed next to Shri Radha Raman ji."

41. See Cynthia Packert, "An Absent Presence in Vrindavana," in Harsha V. Dehejia, ed., *Radha: From Gopi to Goddess* (New Delhi: Niyogi Books, 2014), 53.

42. Padmanabh Goswami, from letters dated December 28 and 30, 2019.

43. For further discussion, see Rādhā Dāmodara's *Vedānta-syamantaka* 2.23 and the various works of Baladeva Vidyābhūṣaṇa, particularly *Siddhānta-darpaṇa* 1.18 and *Siddhānta-ratna* 1.15–22 as well as his Vedānta commentaries. The term *viśeṣa*, in this context, is also explained by Bhaktivinoda Ṭhākura in the Introduction to his *Gītā* commentary, *Vidvad-rañjana*. Finally, Jīva Gosvāmī, although he does not specifically address the term as such, indicates his acceptance of it by implication. This occurs, for example, in his *Sarva-saṁvādinī* commentary of the *Bhagavat-sandarbha*, where he gives explicit approval of Madhva's commentary on *Vedānta-sūtra* 3.2.28–31, which deals with *viśeṣa*.

44. The Vaishnava adage is *abhinatvaṁ nāma-nāmīnaḥ*: "The name of Krishna is spiritual substance, identical to Krishna himself." This phrase is originally attributed

to the *Padma Purāṇa*. See *Bhakti-rasāmṛta-sindhu* 1.2.233: "The name of the Lord fulfills all desires like *cintāmaṇi*. It is the very form of Krishna. It is full of consciousness and *rasa*. It is complete, pure, and eternally liberated. This is because of the non-difference of Krishna and his name." (*nāma cintāmaṇiḥ kṛṣṇaś caitanya-rasa-vigrahaḥpūrṇaḥ śuddho nitya-mukto 'bhinnatvān nāma-nāminoh*).

45. *Vidagdha-mādhava* (Act VI), texts 23–25: *Madhumaṅgalaḥ: gheppijja{u} esā | (iti rādheti varṇa-dvayī-bhājāṁ patra-lekhām arpayati)* "Madhumangala says: 'You should now accept Rādhā.' (He gives Krishna a leaf with the syllables Rādhā written on it.)" *Kṛṣṇaḥ (smitvā): sakhe, satyam anenāpi bhavad-arpitena tarpito'smi | yataḥ-kramāt kakṣām akṣṇoḥ parisara-bhuvaṁ vā śravaṇayor manāg adhyārūḍhaṁ praṇayi-janānām akṣara-padam | kam apy antas-toṣaṁ vitarad-avilambād anupadaṁ nisargād viśveṣāṁ hṛdaya-padavīm utsukayati ||24|| (iti parāvṛtya dakṣiṇato vikāśantam aśokam avalokya sa-vismayam)*: "(Smiling) Krishna says, 'O friend, I am truly satisfied with your offering because the syllables of the lover's name, when they come near the eyes or ears of the beloved, even for a moment, they immediately give an indescribable inner satisfaction, delighting the hearts of all the world at every moment by their very nature.'" See also Donna M. Wulff, *Drama as a Mode of Religious Realization: The Vidagdhamādhava of Rūpa Gosvāmī* (Chico, CA: Scholars Press, 1984), 124–25.

46. Some say Hit Harivaṁśa was the author of this text. See Jan K. Brzezinski, "Prabodhānanda, Hit Harivaṁśa and the *Rādhā-rasa-sudhānidhi*," *Journal of Vaishnava Studies* 7, no. 1 (Fall 1998): 19–61.

47. See Prabodhānanda Sarasvatī, *Śrī Śrī Rādhā Rasa Sudhā Nidhi: The Nectar Ocean of Sri Rādhā's Flavours* (Transliterated Text, Word-to-Word Meaning, Translation and Detailed Commentaries), trans., Śrīla Bhaktivedānta Nārāyaṇa Gosvāmī Mahārāja (Vrindavan: Bhaktabandhav, 2016). I have adapted the translations for readability.

48. In the Vaishnava tradition, Nidhivan ("forest of treasures") is among the most sacred of all sacred places. It is known to be the Rāsa-sthālī ("the place of the Rāsa Dance"), which refers, of course, Krishna's most intimate pastime with the *gopīs*, thus explaining why Nidhivan is so revered. Rādhā and Krishna are given their due privacy to conduct this dance nightly, even today, and so after dusk, pilgrims are advised to leave the Nidhivan area. The main temple currently identified with Nidhivan is Bāṅke Bihārī, though most of Vrindavan's major temples are nearby, including Radha Raman.

Nidhivan also means "forest of sleep." *Nidhi* means sleep and *vana* means forest. Along these lines, in Nidhivan, there is a famous temple called Ranga Mahal, indicating an area where Rādhā and Krishna take rest. There is a small bed inside the temple, daily decorated by the attending priest, who supplies flowers, incense, and assorted accouterments for the pleasure of the Divine Couple. Today, the main section of Nidhivan is still a very beautiful *kuñja* of small trees, even if signs of modernity have infiltrated as well. According to Viśvanātha Chakravartī, Nidhivan is the place where Lord Krishna left the Rāsa Dance to find his beloved Rādhikā.

49. Radha Raman temple is specifically located down the narrow lane from Chir-ghāt adjacent to the banks of the Yamunā, just in between the Rādhā-Gopīnātha and Rādhā-Gokulānanda temples, and is right next door to the latter.

50. As for the closely related Shahji temple, it was completed in 1867, engaging an unusual mixture of Indian and European architecture. The Shah brothers' Deity—"Choto Radharaman"—now presides at the Shahji Mandir, and the brothers' burial places are also there, just outside of the temple's main entrance. They were disciples of Shri Radha Govinda Goswami of the Radha Raman temple and were poets who composed under the pen names Lalit Kishori (Kundan Lal) and Lalit Madhuri (Phundan Lal). See https://vrindavantoday.com/shahji-mandir-and-shah-kundan-lal/.

51. See Margaret H. Case, *Seeing Krishna: The Religious World of a Brahman Family in Vrindaban,* op. cit., 80–81.

52. Ibid., 81–82. She continues: "The compound courtyard is lined with the houses of Gosvāmīs. To the left, just inside the gate, is a small passageway that gives access to a red sandstone archway and a shrine marking the spot where Rādhāramaṇa revealed himself." Believers say that the initial flame that Gopāla Bhaṭṭa used to prepare his first food offering for Radha Raman was never extinguished and continues to burn in the kitchen to this day.

53. There are other noted Deities who remained in Vrindavan, such as Śrī Bāṅke Bihārī (from the Haridāsī Sampradāya), but as far as Deities that are specifically in the Gauḍīya Vaishnava lineage, Radha Raman may be unique. Tradition tells us that Krishna never leaves Vrindavan. (See Śrīla Rūpa Gosvāmī, *Śrī Laghu-bhāgavatāmṛta* [1.5.461] and Krishnadāsa Kavirāja Gosvāmī, *Caitanya-caritāmṛta* [Antya 1.67].) From the theological perspective of the Gosvāmīs, we learn that when Krishna ventures off into Mathurā and Dvārakā, for example, he actually remains in Vrindavan in an unmanifest state, while his first "expansion," Vāsudeva, moves into those other areas. This phenomenon is important in that it highlights the inseparability of Vrindavan and the original form of Krishna, who is known as Vrajendranandana ("the child of Braj"). For the Radha Raman Gosvāmīs, this is often cited as among the exclusive characteristics of Radha Raman.

54. This is not uncommon in the Gauḍīya Sampradāya. Though Sanātana Gosvāmī initially gave responsibility for Madan Mohan to *vairāgīs*, or renunciants, internal conflict soon arose and, after several generations, his disciplic descendants adopted the same method as Gopāla Bhaṭṭa. A family lineage took responsibility, and this continues to the present day. Overall, the seminal *paramparā* system has proven to have more social stability. Raghunātha Bhaṭṭa Gosvāmī's line, Jīva Gosvāmī's line, and the service of Śrī Nāthjī (transferred from Raghunātha Dāsa Gosvāmī to Viṭṭhalanātha, the son of Vallabhācārya) follow this same tradition. (Before Śrī Jīva's disappearance, he left his Deities and library in the care of his successor Śrī Krishna Dāsa, the head *pūjārī*, and the present *sevāites* are his descendants.) By way of partial explanation: Temple Deities are served in the style of *rāja-sevā*, as one would serve a king, which entails dealing with money, assets, and other material amenities. Traditionally, *vairāgīs* would avoid financial dealings and delegate responsibility to married devotees, who are more inclined to such things.

According to Jan Brzezinski (Jagadananda Das), "Subsequent to Chaitanya, initiation in Bengali Vaishnavism was more or less a monopoly controlled by those whom Bhaktisiddhānta disparagingly called *jāti gosāñi*. These were members of *brāhmaṇa*, or less frequently *vaidya* or other families, who traced their lineage to direct associates of Chaitanya Mahāprabhu. Chief among these was the family of Nityānanda, who according to the *Nityānanda-vaṁśa-vistāra* was instructed by Chaitanya himself to marry and establish a family precisely as an institutionalization of the succession. . . . Where they established temples, they assured the continued service to the deities by turning them over to householders who were expected to maintain them through the generations. These families, centered around the great temples, also became important initiating spiritual masters of the *sampradāya*. . . . In his *Hari-bhakti-vilāsa*, on the other hand, Gopāla Bhaṭṭa Gosvāmī uses the word *āmnāya-gata* ('coming in sacred tradition') in connection to the guru, which Sanātana glosses as *kula-kramāgata* ('coming in a family line') or *veda-vihita* ('ordained by the scripture')." See Jan Brzezinski, "The Parampara Institution in Gaudiya Vaishnavism (Part II)" (http://jagadanandadas.blogspot.com/2018/08/the-parampara-institution-in-gaudiya_29.html). In the end, Gauḍīya Vaishnavism recognizes that disciplic lineages can be either familial (seminal) or based on teacher/student relationships, depending on which branch of the tradition one favors.

55. Vaishnavacharya Chandan Goswami writes (personal letter, January 6, 2020): "About the 'Goswami' term [as used in the Radha Raman tradition], it is both an attainment and a surname, and similarly, one can say the lineage is both seminal and preceptorial. This is because Shri Gopal Bhatt and other *acharyas* of his time personally selected our ancestor, Shri Damodar Das Goswami, as the next guru on Mahaprabhu's seat, along with his children and future descendants, to take care of his beloved Radharaman and preach Mahaprabhu's path of love. His blessing is eternal and remains upon our family through every generation. However, one usually needs to study the scriptures and perform strict spiritual *sadhana* in order to embody the intention of that blessing to the fullest extent possible."

56. And the lineage continues. According to Vaishnavacharya Chandan Goswami in a letter dated January 25, 2020: "There are plenty of figures who are in active preaching, [including] Padmanabh Goswami, me (Anupam), Pushpang Goswami, Kartik Goswami, Devanshu Goswami, Pundrik Goswami, Vasudev Goswami, Keshav Dev Goswami, Narsingh Dev Goswami, Shrivatsa Goswami, Venu Gopal Goswami, Chaitanya Kumar Goswami, Alok Kumar Goswami, Anil Goswami, Dinesh Chandra Goswami, Abhishek Goswami, Aditya Goswami and some of my cousins who are stepping in slowly."

57. It is significant in this regard that our own Gopāla Bhaṭṭa Gosvāmī was the author of several books addressing this very subject. Perhaps his most famous work is *Hari-bhakti-vilāsa*, which primarily deals with ritual performance and standards of Vaishnava behavior. It was originally a manuscript prepared by Sanātana Gosvāmī but finished by Gopāla Bhaṭṭa, who also wrote *Sat-kriyā-sāra-dīpikā* and its supplement, *Saṁskāra-dīpikā*, the former being primarily a guide for householders and the latter for renunciants. All three of these works detail the specifics of Vaishnava ritual, particularly in relation to Deity-sevā, and practical matters of Vaishnava etiquette.

Gopāla Bhaṭṭa Gosvāmī also wrote an introduction to Jīva Gosvāmī's *Ṣaṭ-sandarbha*, and a commentary on Bilvamaṅgala Ṭhākura's *Krishna-karnāmrita*. For more on Gopāla Bhaṭṭa's literary work, see Bhaktivedānta Nārāyaṇa Gosvāmī Mahārāja Bhaktabāndhav Śrīla Gurudeva, *Rāgātmikā Vrajavāsī & Prayojana-tattva Ācārya Śrīla Gopāla Bhaṭṭa Gosvāmī, op. cit.* For a contemporary study on the philosophy of Deity worship, see Kenneth R. Valpey, *Kṛṣṇa-Sevā: The Theology of Deity Worship in Chaitanya Vaishnavism* (Berkeley: Graduate Theological Union, 1998).

58. His Divine Grace A. C. Bhaktivedanta Swami Prabhupāda glosses these verses as follows: "There is evidence in the Vedic literature that worship may be *saguṇa* and *nirguṇa*—of the Supreme possessing or not possessing attributes. Worship of the Deity in the temple is *saguṇa* worship, for the Lord is represented by material qualities. But the form of the Lord, though represented by material qualities such as stone, wood, or oil paint, is not actually material. That is the absolute nature of the Supreme Lord. . . . This *arcā-vigraha* [Deity in the temple] is an incarnation of the Supreme Lord. God will accept service through that form. The Lord is omnipotent and all-powerful; therefore, by His incarnation as *arcā-vigraha*, He can accept the services of the devotee, just to make it convenient for [one] in conditioned life." I have only quoted the pertinent section of his commentary. There are many other texts endorsing Deity worship, such as *Bhāgavata Purāṇa* (7.5.23–24), which mentions it as being among the nine standard processes of *bhakti*: "Hearing and chanting about the transcendental holy name, form, qualities, paraphernalia and pastimes of Lord Vishnu, remembering them, serving the lotus feet of the Lord, offering the Lord respectful worship with sixteen types of paraphernalia, offering prayers to the Lord, becoming His servant, considering the Lord one's best friend, and surrendering everything unto Him (in other words, serving Him with the body, mind and words)—these nine processes are accepted as pure devotional service." The element of "offering the Lord respectful worship," as stated above, refers to *arcanaṁ* and is understood as Deity-sevā. Moreover, Rūpa Gosvāmī, in his *Bhakti-rasāmrta-sindhu* (Pūrva-vibhāga 1.2.90–92) lists *arcanaṁ* as essential to the practice of Vaishnavism.

59. Obviously, not all Krishna Deities have a consort, but we are discussing standard Gauḍīya Vaishnava worship, leading, gradually, to a discussion of Radha Raman specifically.

60. Or camphor. In some temples, they use oil lamps (sesame oil is usually favored in South India, while mustard is preferred in the north). Parenthetically, the use of fire in worship services is not peculiar to *āratī,* nor even to Indian tradition. In Judaism, for example, flame is taken as a metaphor for God's presence, and lit candles are therefore used in numerous ceremonies. We illumine our eyes, we "awaken," the tradition teaches, by lighting celebratory candles on special holy days, whether Shabbat, Hanukkah, or generic memorial celebrations.

61. On a practical level, fan and yak *cāmara* are meant for cooling and keeping off flies, respectively. They are two elements of Rāja-upacāra or kingly service, as is expected in Deity-sevā.

62. See Śrīla Bhakti Prajnāna Keśava Gosvāmī Mahārāja, "Introduction: The Deity and Deity Worship," in *The Process of Deity Worship (Arcana-paddhati)*, translated by Jai Sacīnandana Dāsa (Los Angeles: Bhaktivedanta Book Trust, 1978), xiv

(accessed January 2020: http://www.prabhupada-books.de/pdf/Arcana-Paddhati.pdf). See also Śrī Śrīmad Bhaktivedānta Nārāyaṇa Gosvāmī Māhārāja, *Acrana-dīpikā: The Light That Illuminates the Process of Deity Worship* (New Delhi: Gaudiya Vedanta Publications,1999), 9.

63. By yoga we are not here talking about postural yoga in any of its popular modern formations. Rather, we refer to a particular type of deep meditation that allows true unity with God, entering into profound relationship with him through personal practice. This meditation is known as *līlā-smaraṇam,* or "remembrance of God's eternal pastimes."

64. Briefly, Vaidhī-bhakti and Rāgānuga-bhakti are both forms of *sādhana*, or practice, but whereas Vaidhī is preliminary, infused with awe and reverence for the Deity and based on the need to follow rules and regulations (in service to Vishnu), Rāgānuga consists of following in the wake of those who have spontaneous devotion, and its practitioners are more inclined to intimacy with the Deity, focusing on his sweetness and informal personhood (as in the personality of Krishna). Part of this latter practice involves an inner meditation that we will now briefly describe. Thus, Deity-sevā can range from the most fundamental, basic kind of devotional practice to involving complex meditational techniques that will lead one to the inner precincts of Vrindavan, the highest portion of the spiritual realm.

65. Regarding "*vaidhī-saṃvalita-rāgānuga*," Vaidhī combined with Rāgānuga, see *Bhakti-sandarbha* (Anuchedda 312). Interestingly, the word *arcana* appears in English as *arcana* (är-kānə), meaning "a deep secret, a mystery," through the Latin *arcānum*, the neuter of *arcānus*, "secret." For Gauḍīyas this would suggest that the deep secret of Deity worship awaits practitioners who delve deeply.

66. Prabhupāda is very clear that one should not take this inner meditation lightly, and that to graduate from ordinary Deity service to one involving deeper meditation is only for advanced practitioners. See *Śrīmad Bhāgavatam* (4.24.45–46), purport: "Generally the worship of the Lord begins with the worship of Nārāyaṇa, or Viṣṇu, whereas the worship of Lord Kṛṣṇa and Rādhā is most confidential. Lord Nārāyaṇa is worshipable by the *pāñcarātrika-vidhi,* or regulative principles, whereas Lord Kṛṣṇa is worshipable by the *bhāgavata-vidhi*. No one can worship the Lord in the *bhāgavata-vidhi* without going through the regulations of the *pāñcarātrika-vidhi*. Actually, neophyte devotees worship the Lord according to the *pāñcarātrika-vidhi,* or the regulative principles enjoined in the *Nārada-pañcarātra*. Rādhā-Kṛṣṇa cannot be approached by the neophyte devotees; therefore temple worship according to regulative principles is offered to Lakṣmī-Nārāyaṇa. Although there may be a Rādhā-Kṛṣṇa *vigraha*, or form, the worship of the neophyte devotees is acceptable as Lakṣmī-Nārāyaṇa worship. Worship according to the *pāñcarātrika-vidhi* is called *vidhi-mārga*, and worship according to the *bhāgavata-vidhi* principles is called *rāga-mārga*. The principles of *rāga-mārga* are especially meant for devotees who are elevated to the Vṛndāvana platform. . . . One should strictly follow the *vidhi-mārga* regulative principles in the worship of Lakṣmī-Nārāyaṇa, although the Lord is present in the temple as Rādhā-Kṛṣṇa. Rādhā-Kṛṣṇa includes Lakṣmī-Nārāyaṇa; therefore when one worships the Lord according to the regulative principles, the Lord accepts the service in the role of Lakṣmī-Nārāyaṇa."

67. While the language here is taken from a work specifically about Puṣṭi-mārga, the same truths exist for all Vaishnava traditions coming out of Braj. See Ankur Vijay Desai, "Visions of Grace: Svarūpa Imagery and Veneration in the Puṣṭimārga Sampradāya," MA thesis (The Ohio State University, 2011), 56.

68. It should be reiterated that *līlā-smaraṇam*, particularly as it applies to *aṣṭa-kālīya-līlā*, is not generally associated with a meditation focusing on the Deity in the temple, nor is it a common part of *āratī* in the usual sense. For most Gauḍīya Vaishnavas, *aṣṭa-kālīya-līlā* is an internal meditation that forms a part of Rāgānuga-sādhana. Applying it to Deity-sevā is an esoteric practice, mainly found in Bengal and Braj, though it does have application elsewhere. For more on its connection to *āratī* see A. W. Entwistle, *Braj: Centre of Krishna Pilgrimage* (Groningen: Egbert Forsten, 1987), 82.

69. See Bhanu Swami, trans., *Govinda Līlāmṛta* (*kuñjād goṣṭhaṁ niśānte praviśati kurute dohanānnāśanādyāṁ, prātaḥ sāyaṁ ca līlāṁ viharati sakhibhiḥ saṅgave cārayan gāḥ | madhyāhne cātha naktaṁ vilasati vipine rādhayāddhāparāhne, goṣṭhaṁ yāti pradoṣe ramayati suhṛdo yah sa kṛṣno'vatān naḥ*)

70. According to the *Aṣṭa-kālīya-sūtra*: The eight time periods of the day shall be known in this sequence—*niśānta* (end of night), *prātaḥ* (morning), *pūrvāhna* (forenoon), *madhyāhna* (midday), *aparāhna* (afternoon), *sāyāhna* (early evening), *pradoṣa* (nightfall), and *rātri* (night). The *madhyāhna* and *rātri* time periods each last for six *muhūrtas* [1 *muhūrta* = 48 minutes, so 6 *muhūrtas* = 4 hours, 48 minutes) and the others all last for three *muhūrtas* each (2 hours, 24 minutes) (https://www.radha.name/sites/default/files/documents/1278/Gaura%20Govindarcana%20Smarana%20Paddhati.pdf).

71. Śrībhaṭṭa referred to it as *aṣṭa-yāma-līlā*. *Aṣṭa-yāma* = *aṣṭakālīya* = *aṣṭakāla*. The concept involves a division of *kāla* (time) into eight watches (*yāmas*). When the day and night are divided into eight parts, each part is known as a *yāma*. There are three *yāmas* during the night, three during the day, one at dawn, and one at dusk. Bhaktivinoda Ṭhākura's *Bhajan Rahasya* also uses the term *aṣṭa-yāma,* and he describes it as an esoteric practice. His book shows how to use Śrī Chaitanya's eight prayers (Śikṣāṣṭaka) and the Hare Krishna Mahā-mantra to gradually evolve to the point of remembering the Lord's eight daily periods, and, indeed, enter into them. Bhaktivinoda divides his book into eight *sādhanas*, or practices, that correspond to the eight periods of the day, and he names the chapters as various *yāmas* as well. These eight periods, he says, are together known as *aṣṭa-kāla,* or *aṣṭa-yāma*, terms that are explained by Śrīla Bhaktisiddhānta Sarasvatī in the Preface. Bhaktivinoda further writes that one should remember the Śikṣāṣṭaka and practice *smaraṇa* and *kīrtana* according to the methods of the *ācāryas*, and only then might *aṣṭa-kāla* service gradually and genuinely awaken in one's heart.

72. I am indebted to Brahmachari Sharan for this information both in personal correspondence and through his PhD thesis. See Vijay Ramnarace, "Rādhā-Kṛṣṇa's Vedāntic Debut: Chronology & Rationalisation in the Nimbārka Sampradāya," PhD dissertation (The University of Edinburgh, 2014), 277. Brahmachari Sharan adds, "Harivyāsa's *Mahāvāṇī* expands upon Śrībhaṭṭa's theory concerning the *sakhīs*. Harivyāsa would have also been witness to the developments in *mādhurya-rasa*

aesthetic theory made by Rūpa and Sanātana Gosvāmin, and the work of Harivyāsa seems to contain definite parallels with them." See p. 289 of his dissertation.

73. In ISKCON, there tend to be six *āratīs*. According to my correspondence with Kulapradipa Dasa, January 20, 2020: "4:30 am—Mangal ('auspicious') Arati; 7:15 am—Sringar ('beautiful') Arati; 12:30 pm—Rajbhog ('Kingly offering') Arati; 4:15 pm—Dhupa ('incense') Arati; 7:00 pm—Sandhya ('evening' or 'twilight') Arati; 8:30 pm—Shayana ('rest') Arati."

74. Interestingly, in Bhaktivinoda Ṭhākura's famous song, "Śrī Yugala-āratī," he mentions in the very first verse that Lalitā-sakhī performs the *āratī* ceremony, and in the fifth verse that Viśākhā leads the *kīrtana*. This underscores the fact that *āratī* is initially and internally performed by eternal associates of Rādhā and Krishna, and that by performing similar activity practitioners can enter their realm.

75. For Nimbārkīs, for example, it is referred to simply as "*vihāra*," or "*nikuñja-vihāra*." As Brahmachari Sharan says, "Non-āratī periods are when [the Deities] go off for confidential sports or play: *vihāra* means 'sport, play, pastime, enjoyment, pleasure'—it is used usually to denote an 'excursion for recreational purposes' in the Nimbārkī theories of the *nityalīlā*. It refers to evening excursions, and excursions in Nikuñja." Personal correspondence with Brahmachari Sharan, January 28, 2020. He further notes that: "*Ashta-kala-seva* seems to be a common theology expressed liturgically amongst members of the Pushti Marg, Nimbark Sampraday, Radha Vallabh Sampraday, Haridasi Sampraday, and Gaudiya Sampraday. Braj Vaishnavas seem to have chosen this method over the more traditional Pancharatra system of the south as evinced in the antecedent *Kramadipika*, for example, which is the basis for the quotidian worship cycle of Jagannatha in Puri. Even the Swaminarayans now have it and it is adopted, according to the *Shikshapatri*, from the Pushtimarg. It is a basic part of Braj Vaishnavism. *Ashta-kala-seva* can be seen in the *Yugala Shataka* of Shri bhatta, the *Kelimal* of Swami Haridas, the *Seva Pranaali* of the Haridasis, and the *Ashtayama Seva* of the Pushti Marg, among others." Personal correspondence dated January 25, 2020.

76. By early ISKCON standards, there can be as few as three or four *āratīs* in a day: See Prabhupāda, Room Conversations (April 22, 1972, Japan):

Sudāmā: And how many full *āratīs* should we perform, Śrīla Prabhupāda?

Prabhupāda: Three main: *maṅgala-āratī, bhoga-āratī* and *sandhya-āratī*. These are main. Then you can offer *śayana-āratī* before going to bed. *śayana-āratī*. And these four, and *dhūpa-āratī* just after lighting, or before lighting. Then, after rest in afternoon, *dhūpa-āratī*. After dressing, *dhūpa-āratī*. So two, three *dhūpa-āratī,* and three, four full *āratīs*. Three must be, and four also, four, full *āratīs*. And *dhūpa-āratī* at least three, four. In this way.

Bhānu: The full *āratī* will be in the morning, *maṅgala-āratī,* there will be the noon *āratī*, supposed to be one in the evening. When should the other full *āratī* be?

Prabhupāda: When the Deities are going to bed. Before going to bed. Yes. *śayana-āratī*, it is called *śayana-āratī. Sundara-āratī, bhoga-āratī, maṅgala-āratī.* You write down. *Maṅgala-āratī* early in the morning, *bhoga-āratī* at noon, offering *prasādam*, then *sundara-āratī* just after half an hour or one hour sunset, then *śayana-āratī*." ISKCON gradually increased its standard.

77. Margaret H. Case, *Seeing Krishna: The Religious World of a Brahman Family in Vrindaban*, op. cit., 82.

78. Ibid., 82, 87–89, 91–92.

79. Adapted text from Chandan Goswami's official Radha Raman website: http://www.shriradharaman.com/daily-worship.html.

80. For more on *aṣṭa-kālīya-līlā* in relation to *āratī* in the Gauḍīya tradition in general, see "Eleven Points of Arati" by Mahanidhi Swami (http://moodsofvraja.blogspot.com/2016/01/eleven-points-of-arati.html). He writes as follows: "While *arati* is a ritual that purifies the heart, a ritual leading to higher reality, it is also a reality unto itself. Such is the nature of *bhakti*, for devotion is both means and end. As we have heard, even the *gopis* perform *arati*, thus there is *arati* for the *sadhaka* and *arati* for the *siddha*. The Gaudiya Vaishnava lineage advocates the *raga-marga*, the path of passionate love of Godhead. As the *sadhaka* qualifies himself for *raganuga-sadhana*, his orientation toward the rituals of devotion changes. The path of *raga* requires that the *sadhaka* regularly contemplate the eternal *lilas* of Radha-Krsna, and thus in the beginning stages of *raganuga-bhakti,* the *sadhaka* thinks of the *arati* ceremonies throughout the day in relation to the eightfold daily pastimes of Radha-Krsna. Indeed, it is from these pastimes that the *arati* ceremony derives."

81. See *Śrī Caitanya-caritāmṛta* (Ādi 1.19, purport).

82. I mention the truism "God Is Love" (1 John 4:7–21). There are at least three ways to understand this: (1) God is an impersonal abstraction, the force of love that penetrates the hearts of all good souls; (2) divinity manifests as pure love of God, again an abstraction, in which the soul who is spiritually accomplished engages in intimate exchanges of deep affection with his Maker; and finally (3) particular manifestations of the Supreme that exude love and distribute love to such a degree that they are commonly identified as embodiments of love. It is this final concept to which I refer. In the Vaishnava tradition, Rādhā, Krishna, and Śrī Chaitanya have all been so identified, as perfected emblematic representations of love personified.

83. While this explanation of *sambandha, abhidheya,* and *prayojana* in terms of *bhakti* is useful in our present context, I am well aware of its limitations. After all, in an ultimate sense, Rādhā/Chaitanya is *prayojana-tattva*, not *sambandha*. ("Rādhārāṇī is the embodiment of *mahābhāva*." See Cc, Ādi 4.69–70. Additionally, "Lord Śrī Krishna is the reservoir of all pleasure, and Śrīmatī Rādhārāṇī is the personification of ecstatic love of Godhead." See CC Madhya 8.282.)

However, it is not incorrect to say that Rādhā/Chaitanya are exemplars of *bhakti* as well, and thus they too are paradigms of relationship with Krishna (*sambandha*). For example, it is said that the *gopīs* are most advanced among the devotees, and that Rādhikā is most advanced among the *gopīs*. See Prabhupāda's *Nectar of Instruction* 10: "The *gopīs* are exalted above all the advanced devotees because they are always totally dependent upon Śrī Kṛṣṇa, the transcendental cowherd boy. Among the *gopīs*, Śrīmatī Rādhārāṇī is the most dear to Kṛṣṇa." And in Prabhupāda's gloss on this verse: "In this way, Śrīla Rūpa Gosvāmī gradually concludes that Śrīmatī Rādhārāṇī is the most exalted devotee of Kṛṣṇa."

Regarding Śrī Chaitanya, Prabhupāda writes: "Lord Chaitanya Mahāprabhu should not be considered to be one of us. He is Krishna Himself, the supreme living entity and as such He never comes under the cloud of *māyā*. Krishna, His expansions, and even His higher devotees never fall into the clutches of illusion. Lord Chaitanya came to earth simply to preach Krishna-bhakti, love of Krishna. In other words, He is Lord Krishna Himself teaching the living entities the proper way to approach Krishna. He is like a teacher who, seeing a student doing poorly, takes up a pencil and writes, saying, 'Do it like this: A, B, C.' By this, one must not foolishly think that the teacher is learning his ABC's. Although He appears *in the guise of a devotee*, we should always remember that Lord Chaitanya is Krishna (God) Himself teaching us how to become Krishna conscious, and we must study Him in that light." (A. C. Bhaktivedanta Swami Prabhupada, *The Teachings of Lord Chaitanya*, from the Introduction, italics added) Prabhupāda also writes, "The symbol of devotional service in the highest degree is Rādhārāṇī" (*Nectar of Devotion*, chapter 1).

Clearly, then, Śrī Rādhā and Mahāprabhu are embodiments of *bhakti*. Thus, all three terms, *sambandha, abhidheya*, and *prayojana*, can be appropriately applied to them.

84. See Bhaktivedānta Nārāyaṇa Gosvāmī Mahārāja Bhaktabāndhav Śrīla Gurudeva, *Rāgātmikā Vrajavāsī & Prayojana-tattva Ācārya Śrīla Gopāla Bhaṭṭa Gosvāmī* (Vrindavan: Bhaktabandhav, 2018), Introductory Prayers.

Chapter Five

Jagannāth

The Entire Universe in a Block of Wood

The image of Jagannāth—superficially reminiscent of Native American totem poles, and indeed traceable to tribal origins—is revered among Vaishnavas as God in the form of wood. While scholars have referred to the "unfinished, premature, aboriginal, savage, exotic look"[1] of Jagannāth, devotees have praised this simple and unrefined form—with his reddish crescent-moon smile, jutting arms, rectangular, legless torso, and large, perfectly symmetrical black-and-white eyes—as the epitome of beauty. For Vaishnavas, He is God in a most confidential and intimate feature.

The ancient literary backdrop for Jagannāth goes back to the *Ṛgveda* (10.155.3): "In the beginning, the primeval Lord manifested as the transcendental *dāru-brahman* on the shore of the ocean. Those who take shelter of this Supreme Personality are delivered from all difficulties" (*ado yād dāru plāvate sindhoh pāre apūruṣām/ tādārabhasya durhaṇo tena gaccha parastarām//*).

The famous Vedic commentator Sāyaṇācārya (1300–1387 CE), who flourished under King Bukka Raya of the Vijaynagara Empire, writes in reference to this verse: "On the seashore, in a place that is not accessible by material vision, God, who is beyond the perception of the senses, the self-born who is without any human component, exists in a wooden form and is named Puruṣottama [a common name for Jagannāth]. He delivers His devotees from the ocean of material sufferings. O learned persons, take shelter of that wooden form of the Lord, and through His worship attain the supreme abode of Vishnu."[2]

As the centuries passed, Jagannāth indeed became synonymous with *dāru-brahman*, the term suggested in the above statement from the *Ṛgveda*, and devotees today know him as the only major manifestation of God made from wood.

The word "Jagannāth" literally means "Lord of the Universe." It refers to the wooden Deity of Krishna who for centuries has been worshipped and adored at Purī's main temple, located in the State of Odisha on the eastern coast of India. It is significant that the name "Jagannāth" gives us the English word "juggernaut," which means "a massive and unstoppable force."

Modern science recognizes an all-pervasive energy at the core of the universe, a "force," if you will, often divided into four distinct categories: (1) gravitational force, (2) electromagnetic force, (3) weak nuclear force, and (4) strong nuclear force.[3] While the specifics of these energies are complex and beyond the scope of this chapter, it should at least be understood that these fundamental forces inform the entire theoretical dynamics of the material universe. Nonetheless, they do not account for the subtle nuances of life itself—they do not account for consciousness—and so scientists search for a unifying force, a fifth force, something that speaks to larger and more subtle issues that undergird the mysteries of the mind and the heart. Some have called this fifth force "Quantum Brahman,"[4] but it could just as easily—and in some ways most appropriately—be called "Jagannāth."[5]

This "unstoppable force," without direct reference to Jagannāth, of course, has been the subject of much scientific discussion, the roots of which draw on a well-known philosophical conundrum: "The Irresistible Force Paradox." Typically expressed as "What happens when an unstoppable force meets an immovable object?" we are faced with an unresolvable contradiction: After all, if a force is unstoppable, how can something that meets it be an immovable object, and vice versa?

In regard to Jagannāth, however, all paradoxes are easily resolved. He is indeed an unstoppable force, as in the first part of the stated paradox, and the living entity—you and I—can easily be compared to an "immovable object." We exhibit, according to Gauḍīya Vaishnava texts, a causeless unwillingness to submit to the Lord of the Universe. Nonetheless, by the mercy of a pure soul, we ultimately succumb, showing that we are not truly unmovable, especially when penetrated through the region of the heart. This happens through a process called Bhakti-yoga, the Yoga of Devotion. The present chapter will explicate both the specifics of that unstoppable force, i.e., God in the form of Lord Jagannāth, and his relation to the surprisingly "movable" object known as the spirit soul, or all living beings who are fortunate enough to become privy to his existence.

THE ESSENTIAL NARRATIVE

There are various versions of the Jagannāth story, contrasting perspectives meant to capture him from different angles. Some are related in scriptural texts; others are the product of personal realization, articulated by devotees who love him in their own unique way; while still others take liberties with the details in an attempt to bring out an inner teaching. Slightly divergent versions appear in the *Skanda Purāṇa* (*Utkal Khaṇḍa*, chapters 1–19); the *Brahma Purāṇa* (part 2, chapters 41–47); the *Nārada Purāṇa* (*Uttarābhaga*, chapters 53 and 54); the *Kāpila Saṁhitā* (texts 1.12–2.30); Sāralā's Odia *Mahābhārata* (*Vāna-parva* and *Musali-parva*)[6]; the *Mādaḷā-pāñji* ("The Drum Chronicle"), a twelfth-century Odia text that purports to be the earliest records of the Jagannāth temple itself; and the *Deula Tolā* ("construction of the temple"), which are seventeenth-century elaborations on the early history of the Deity, including alternate versions by Nīlāmbara Dās and Śiśu Krishna Dās, two respected Odia poets. There are several other versions as well.

Thus, anyone researching the story of Lord Jagannāth will likely encounter variations and differing nuances. But in the end these differences matter little, for the same picture ultimately emerges, as any summary makes clear. It should also be mentioned that there are two parts to the Jagannāth story, one that tells His "origin," how he manifested in the material world, and another explaining his unique look, so different from Lord Krishna's form as a blue cowherd playing on his flute. Both parts of the story are necessary to understand the Jagannāth Deity,[7] and a brief summary of each might be rendered as follows.

Long ago, during the epoch of world history known as Satya-yuga, Indradyumna Mahārāja was King of the Sūrya dynasty. He ruled in Avantipura (Ujjain), which was then associated with the country of Mālava. After meeting a traveling Vaishnava who happened into his royal assembly, exclaiming about the beauty and excellence of Nīla-Mādhava, the "Blue Lord," Indradyumna became obsessed with seeing this divine entity for himself.[8]

Thus, the king sent numerous Brahmins in search of the Lord. Unfortunately, each one soon returned to the capital, without success. Only the royal priest known as Śrī Vidyāpati was unaccounted for. Vidyāpati was relentless, and he eventually found himself in the midst of obscure jungle tribesmen in the hills of Odisha. They were known as Śabaras.[9] To his surprise, the Śabaras were secretly worshipping Nīla-Mādhava deep in a nearby forest. After a complex series of events, including his own marriage to one of the Śabara people—it was tribal chief Viśvāvasu's daughter, Lalitā, in fact—Vidyāpati returned to Indradyumna's kingdom, announcing that he had found the Deity for whom the King searched.

Indradyumna was thrilled and set off with Vidyāpati to see the Deity.

It was a long journey to where Nīla-Mādhava stood. The wise Vidyāpati had sprinkled mustard seeds to secure his path, so that he might trace it later, and those seeds had grown into mature plants, which were easy to follow. Consequently, he and the King were able to find their way to Lord Nīla-Mādhava.

But all was not so simple. Indradyumna was not able to see the Lord, even though he was brought to the exact spot. The Deity had been moved. At that point, the King's life lost meaning: Like the yogi-king that he was, he decided to fast until death. But the Lord would not have it. He appeared to Indradyumna in a dream, insisting that his lamentation was needless—"Build a large temple for Me on top of Nīla Hill in Purī. There you will see me, not as Nīla-Mādhava, but in a form made of wood."[10] God himself promised to appear as wood (*dāru*), and thus, in Purī, he is called *dāru-brahma* ("wood-spirit").

In due course, Indradyumna waited by Purī's ocean, at the Bay of Bengal, where the Lord soon presented himself as a giant log floating toward the beach.

When the massive wooden cylinder arrived, the King appointed Viśvakarmā, architect of the gods, to do the needful.[11] But the eccentric Viśvakarmā gave him a stipulation: he would only carve the Deity if he could remain undisturbed for twenty-one days (according to some, it was fifteen days). If anyone were to interrupt him before that allotted time, he said, he would simply leave, even if his work had remained unfinished. The King consented, and the divine carpenter toiled behind closed doors.

After some time, however, Indradyumna's curiosity got the better of him, though alternate versions say it was Queen Guṇḍicā, his wife, who could wait no longer. Whatever the case, the royal doors were flung open, and Viśvakarmā, true to his word, disappeared from the room. In his place were three unfinished Deities: Jagannāth, Baladeva, and Subhadrā, i.e., Krishna, the Supreme Lord; his brother Balarāma (an alternate name for Baladeva); and his sister Yogamāyā.[12] They had no hands or feet[13]—and they didn't look like Krishna, Vishnu, or any divinity with whom Indradyumna was familiar.

Still, because both Indradyumna and the sculptor had exhibited passion (*rāga*) and divine love (*premā*) for the Deity, and because they both had the proper conception (*bhāva*), which allowed for the flow of devotion (*bhakti*), the Lord agreed to fully manifest in the unfinished Deities. This is instructive. Deity worship, in reality, is not about the technicalities of how the icon is fashioned, nor is it about the rules governing his worship. Rather, it is about the internal emotion and the devotional heart of the dedicated worshipper.

The above story of Jagannāth's origins is often coupled with another about his specific countenance. In addition to the sculptor leaving prematurely, thus accounting for the Deity's odd, unfinished features, there is an esoteric narrative that more thoroughly explains Jagannāth's unique morphology. While the genesis of this latter tale is shrouded in mystery, many attribute it to a direct associate of Śrī Chaitanya Mahāprabhu: Kāhnāi Khuṭiyā, a sixteenth-century Odia poet, who, among other distinguished honors, was head priest of the Jagannāth Mandir in Mahāprabhu's time. In Khuṭiyā's classic drama, entitled *Mahābhāva-prakāśa*,[14] he opines that Jagannāth's form is actually Śrī Krishna in the mood of acute separation from Rādhā, his female counterpart. It is a form of Krishna that is transformed by emotional intensity.[15]

The narrative is told in various ways. The most common might be rendered as follows: Once, Rohiṇī Devī, the mother of Lord Balarāma,[16] came to Dvārakā, and Krishna's many wives took the opportunity to gather around and ask about his time in Vrindavan, which occurred long before his married life in Dvārakā. They said, "Sometimes, we hear him talking in his sleep. With a sweet voice, he calls out names of his friends like Śrīdāma and Subāla, and the names of his cows. At times, he shouts, 'Oh Lalitā, Viśākhā; Oh Rādhikā!' Or he says, 'Mother, where is my fresh butter today?' Sometimes he cries in his sleep, and then he wakes up, sobbing for hours. How special are those residents of Vraja! Please tell us everything about them."

Seeing their love for Krishna, Mother Rohiṇī agreed to describe his wonderful pastimes for them. But she stipulated that Krishna and Balarāma should not hear these talks under any circumstances, lest they become unnecessarily self-conscious. She suggested that she meet with the other queens when the two divine brothers are not in proximity.

And so, one day when Krishna and Balarāma were busy with other concerns, all the queens gathered in a huge lecture hall, anxious to hear Mother Rohiṇī revel in Krishna's Vrindavan pastimes. This she did, but not before instructing Subhadrā to keep guard at the front door, to make sure that Krishna and Balarāma do not come back unexpectedly and perchance overhear their discussion.

As Mother Rohiṇī rapturously communicated the childhood pastimes of Krishna, the queens listened with full attention, never once becoming distracted from the nectar that engulfed their ears. Even Subhadrā, who was at the door, became completely absorbed in hearing the narration, and though she tried to be conscientious about the task given to her, she found that after some time, she had failed: Krishna and Balarāma suddenly appeared, standing directly in her midst. No matter. The three of them found themselves ecstatically engrossed in Mother Rohiṇī's words, and mystical transformations began to transform them into unrecognizable beings. Their eyes became oversized and dilated; their hands and legs withdrew into their bodies. They became Jagannāth, Balarāma, and Subhadrā as they now appear in Purī.

While They were exhibiting these ecstatic forms, the great sage Nārada Muni appeared. Overwhelmed and delighted to witness these new manifestations, he approached them with great love. Acknowledging Nārada's presence, Krishna, along with his brother and sister, came to their senses, thus resuming their usual appearance. Nārada was initially speechless but then managed to speak, begging the Lord to again appear in this special form somewhere—anywhere—so that others could benefit from seeing it on a regular basis. This *Mahābhāva-prakāśa-rūpa*, said Nārada, should be seen by one and all. To fulfill the desire of his pure devotee, Nārada Muni, Lord Krishna manifested this form in Śrī Kṣetra, Puruṣottama Dhāma, Jagannāth Purī, where he resides to this day.

WHO IS LORD JAGANNĀTH?

With the above narratives so clearly defining the Jagannāth tradition in Purī, one would think his identity indisputable: He is Śrī Krishna, Lord of the universe. And that is, in fact, the overriding notion in Purī today.

Surprisingly, however, Jagannāth has been identified with other divinities as well, and this phenomenon goes back many centuries. The Lord of Purī has been claimed by Jains, Buddhists, Śaivites, Śāktas, and others, as we will see below, giving new meaning to the words, "Lord of the Universe." That is to say, he is as worshipable by one religious sect as he is by another. Jagannāth is the same one God being adored by various worshippers, according to their particular vision, customs, and rituals.

On one level, the syncretism of the Jagannāth Deity is easy to understand. The diverse conceptions of his identity can be related to Hindu egalitarianism, wherein "both/and" tends to override "either/or." This is common in India, where one "god" is often considered synonymous with every other "god." Thus, the Deities at the Jagannāth temple are sometimes seen as Brahmā (Subhadrā), Śiva (Balarāma), and Vishnu (Krishna), and/or any other combination of those three. This holds true even while Vaishnava monotheism tends to have votaries see him as Śrī Krishna, plain and simple.

But Jagannāth syncretism is also a product of political reign and conquering regime. The administrators of the Jagannāth temple, over its long history, have been aligned with various kingships and dynasties, and have consequently identified Jagannāth with whatever divinities those in power held dear. For example, Anantavarman Chodaganga, the twelfth-century founder of the current Jagannāth temple, to be discussed below, was originally a Śaivite, even if he became a Vaishnava in his later career.[17] Thus, his initial religious allegiances led to the popularization of Śaivite and Śākta worship at the time, as he foisted the particularities of those gods upon the Deities in Purī.

Moving to yet another tradition, Jainism was widespread in Odisha during the immediate pre-Christian era, with its rule and dominion engulfing the Jagannāth temple. Kharavela was a notable Jain emperor during that period, conquering lands that included Purī and Cuttack. As a result, to this day, many local Jains say that Jagannāth, Balarāma, and Subhadrā are personifications of Samyak-darśana (correct view); Samyak-jñāna (correct knowledge); and Samyak-caritra (correct conduct), configurations of Jain philosophy.[18]

Similarly, and perhaps most famously, Buddhists in the area claim the Jagannāth Deities as their own. From their perspective, the Deities represent the "three jewels" of Buddhist philosophy: Buddha (the enlightened one), Dharma (the Path), and Sangha (holy association).[19] This appropriation began with Buddhist rulers in India soon after the time of the Buddha himself. Along similar lines, Buddhists claim that Ratha-yātrā, the now famous Jagannāth cart festival, was originally a Buddhist celebration, and that the holy if undisclosed substance hidden in Jagannāth's navel is in actuality the Buddha's tooth, preserved for the last 2,500 years.[20]

Although endnote 6 discusses this "undisclosed substance" in some depth, it might be worthwhile to revisit the subject here, for it plays a significant role in understanding just who Jagannāth is and how he is worshipped to this day. It centers on Lord Jagannāth's "rejuvenation" ceremony, when his older body is replaced by a newer one.[21] The ceremony itself is called "*Nava-kalevara*" (or, in the local dialect, Nabakalebara), which literally means "new body." Approximately every twelve to nineteen years, the transcendental bodies of the Lord and his associates (Balarāma and Subhadrā) are changed: New trees are brought in and the Deities are made afresh.[22]

Most aspects of the Nava-kalevara ceremony are conducted secretly. Only special priests, or *paṇḍās*, descendants of Viśvavāsu and Vidyāpati, are allowed to preside at this ceremony. Other preconditions are equally rigorous. For example, the Deities must be fashioned from the wood of very specific neem trees (*Azadirachta indica*), indigenous to particular villages in Odisha. Each year, the village is different, and the priests must locate them as specified in the *Nīlādri-mahodaya-śāstra*, an ancient text written on palm leaves thousands of years ago. Using this text, they hunt for the exact location of the trees for each Nava-kalevara festival, and they must do this each time the Deities undergo new incarnation.[23] These are just a few of the ceremonial caveats, but there are many. The entire ritual is complex and esoteric, and all of the many prerequisites must be followed to the letter for the spirit of Jagannāth to embody the Deities.

The most confidential part of the ceremony is the transferral of the "undisclosed substance" mentioned above; this is the *nābi-brahma* that is placed inside of Jagannāth's abdomen with each new "incarnation." The priests carefully remove it from the old Deity and place it into the new one. They are blindfolded and cloth is wrapped around their hands, so that they avoid touching the substance directly. No one is allowed to see or feel the *nābhi-brahma*, and, consequently, to this day no one knows what it looks or feels like.[24] Be that as it may, for Vaishnavas, the substance is viewed as Lord Jagannāth's "life force."[25]

But the entire notion of the Nava-kalevara ceremony, and others like it, can be misleading. It can give the appearance that Lord Jagannāth's worship is dependent upon external ritual and family priests, that he is limited by the parameters of man-made religious customs and visible only if one journeys to far-off Purī. In other words: Is Jagannāth merely the wooden form that one sees in pictures or at the temple in Purī—or even in the many replicas now worshipped around the world, for that matter—or is he the Supreme all-pervading Godhead, the ultimate spiritual entity, the unlimited force of the universe, simply allowing himself to be worshipped in this way by those who have the vision to see him?

In the end, Vaishnavism teaches that he is both. For while it is clear that the Jagannāth tradition, with its many narrative tales and complex ritual theology, is not to be taken lightly, there is an underlying truth that transcends the particularity of Odia Vaishnavism. That is to say, to truly understand Lord Jagannāth, one must delve into his essential spirit and not merely the external form. Unless one knows who Jagannāth really is—the Lord of the Universe—and what that means on an esoteric level, one will miss the real import of his worship. This secret can only be penetrated through the practice of Bhakti-yoga under the guidance of someone who is already an accomplished practitioner.

Nonetheless, prior to achieving the inner realization that comes from practice, one can know the basics of Jagannāth's identity through Vaishnava teaching.

The theological implications of the Jagannāth Deity include Vedic, Purāṇic, and Tantric ideologies. Accordingly, Jagannāth embodies the Vedic Puruṣottama, or the nurturing oversoul of the universe, the original and supreme controller of all that be; the Purāṇic Nārāyaṇa, or the all-pervading Supersoul of the cosmos, who interpenetrates all aspects of reality; and the Tantric Bhairava, or a form of Śakti and Śiva, the ultimate destructive force of material existence. Jagannāth's elder brother Balarāma is his immediate expansion, facilitating each and every aspect of his divine activity. Balarāma is the embodiment of all existence and spiritual knowledge, and, through this existential knowledge, he leads one to the truth of Jagannāth. Subhadrā, for her part, is Krishna's divine energy, manifesting in narrative traditions as his younger sister. She is the very source of all pleasure (*ānanda*), since she is an expansion of Śrī Rādhikā, Krishna's feminine counterpart and complete pleasure potency. Thus, the Jagannāth triad is suggestive of *sat-cit-ānanda*, eternity, knowledge and bliss, and they infuse their worshippers with the essence of these qualities as well. Indeed, as is often said, Jagannāth is *chaitanya* ("consciousness"), Balarāma is *jñāna* ("knowledge"), and Subhadrā is *śakti* ("energy").[26]

For Gauḍīya Vaishnavas, then, the main Deities on the Jagannāth altar—aside from being God himself—evoke the Lord's internal energy, which makes him the overarching force of the universe: "Svarūpa-śākti" or "Antaraṅga-śakti"—the force of Lord Jagannāth—is said to have three aspects, *sandhinī, saṁvit*, and *hlādinī*, corresponding to *sat-cit-ānanda*, mentioned above. By his *sandhinī* potency, God upholds his own existence and that of others. By *saṁvit*, he knows and allows others to receive knowledge. By *hlādinī*, he enjoys and facilitates others in their enjoyment of bliss. Jagannāth, Balarāma, and Subhadrā (as an expansion of Rādhikā) are represented by these three potencies.[27] Theologically, all of the above summarizes the truth of these Deities, though there are certainly variations on this theme.

For instance, the great Vaishnava reformer Bhaktivinoda Ṭhākura (1838–1914) explains the Jagannāth Deities in yet another way:

> In the middle room [there is] an elevated seat on which stand four different forms, viz., Jagannātha, Balarāma, Subhadrā, and Sudarśana. According to Vedānta, God is one without a second, but He has infinite energies and attributes which are not fully known to man. . . . [M]an perceives only three energies in God, because he has no [way] to understand the other powers. From one of the energies proceeds matter in all its different forms and properties and this energy is styled Māyā-Shakti of God. From the second energy proceeds all spiritual creation, in all its relations and phases. This power is entitled the Jīva Shakti of God. The third energy perceivable by man is the energy of Will, which is called Chit-Shakti. God moving in creation is what is meant by this infinite energy. Jagannātha is the emblem of God having no other form than the eyes and the hands. They mean to show that God sees and knows and creates. Balarāma is the Jīva-Shakti of God; Subhadrā, the Māyā-Shakti; and the Sudarśana is the energy of Will. We cannot form any idea of God as separated. We form all ideas of these energies and hence it is that the worship of Jagannātha depends upon the collection of these four forms on the same platform. Here we see God analyzed in the shape of forms for the sake of those who want to conceive of Him. It is the same thing to see Jagannātha as to study the Vedānta in all its branches. The temple and its institution appeared to me to be a book for those who can read it, to the foolish the institution is certainly useless except as a means of reminding one of the Deity who created the world."[28]

In this paragraph, Bhaktivinoda Ṭhākura draws on the specificity of Jagannāth and his associate Deities but also explicates the inner truth of who they are in relation to the perceivable world. To be sure, this inner truth has been variously expressed by other Gauḍīya teachers according to differences in relationship (*rasa*) or the particular lessons to be conveyed, as shown above. But the important point is this: The value of the external form is highlighted here, even as those forms are seen as a bridge to more esoteric reality. The forms themselves are thus crucially important.

In the end, however, it needs to be said that Lord Jagannāth, like his alter ego, Śrī Krishna, is considered the source of all Incarnations, the Supreme Divinity and Manifestor of all other *avatāras*. This is confirmed by the most senior of the six Gosvāmīs, Śrīla Sanātana Gosvāmī: "His transcendental form, the one source of all incarnations (*eka nidhāna*), expands all of his various pastimes. Whichever of his forms a devotee finds attractive, that form the Lord shows Him."[29]

Without further ado, then, let us explore the specifics of the Jagannāth temple and the very special Deities waiting therein. Once apprising ourselves of this information, we may pray to one day fully understand it and to enter into it by rendering devotional service under a pure Vaishnava.

THE DEITIES AND THE TEMPLE

No description of Lord Jagannāth is complete without some background on the temple and its altar. As the story goes, an ancient shrine was built by King Indradyumna where the current temple now stands. However, that original temple was destroyed by the sands of time. In the current era, Devendravarma Rajaraja of the Ganga dynasty ruled Kalinga, Central Odisha, from 1070 to 1078 of the Common Era, and after his death, his son, Ananta Chodagangadev (r. 1077–1150), became king at a very young age. It was Chodagangadev who built the present temple.[30]

However, tradition holds that the sanctuary was left incomplete in his lifetime. It was then that King Ananga Bhima Deva II (1170–1198), Chodagangadev's son, continued the work of his father, bringing the temple to completion. He built the massive walls around the temple as we see them today, as well as the numerous shrines within the temple compound. He also did much to establish the temple's regulations and standards of Deity service.

Śrī Mandir, as Lord Jagannāth's temple is called, is traditionally divided into four sections: (1) Mūla-Mandira, (2) Mukha-śālā, (3) Nāṭya-mandira,[31] and (4) Chatra Bhoga Maṇḍapa. A brief description of these four would begin with the temple's central feature: The Mūla-mandira is the main Deity room, where multitudes enter daily to worship Lord Jagannāth. The altar itself is called the Ratnavedī, the bejeweled throne of the Lord. It is a raised platform, roughly sixteen feet long, thirteen feet wide, and more than six feet high. There we find Balarāma, Subhadrā, and Jagannāth, from left to right, their colors white, yellow, and black, respectively. Next to Jagannāth, slightly behind him, is a red pole called Sudarśana, who is approximately the same height as Balarāma.[32] He is carved from wood, like the three main Deities, and clothed daily, unlike his traditional representation as a *cakra* (discus) in other Vishnu temples.[33]

Sudarśana is usually depicted as circular, and the story of how he became a "pillar" is intriguing: Tradition draws on the narrative, mentioned above, wherein Jagannāth, Balarāma, and Subhadrā achieve their current forms. Rohiṇī Devī, it may be remembered, shared the stories of Krishna's Vrindavan pastimes with all the queens of Dvārakā, when the tripartite divinity, who were all present, became ecstatic upon hearing her narrations. They consequently assumed the unusual forms we now know as Jagannāth, Balarāma, and Subhadrā. The little-known addendum is this: Sudarśana, too, was present, and he melted with the mood of transformative love, literally dripping into the form of a staff.[34]

Along with these four major Deities are the smaller metallic Deities of Śrī and Bhū, the Lord's manifest consorts, also known as his internal and external energies.[35] Near Śrī one also sees a Deity known simply as "Madhava." This is a small Jagannāth replica said to evoke the presence of the original Nīla Madhava Deity on the altar. This form, along with Śrī and/or Bhū, are brought out of the temple for public festivals.[36] The above Deities are called the "seven-fold form" (*saptadhā mūrti*), and one who sees them properly, says the Jagannāth tradition, has actually seen the face of God.

Near the main altar is the door of the Deity room. This leads to the Mukha-śālā, which is an entrance hall, of sorts, or a waiting room to view the Deity. Next to that is Nāṭya-mandira. This is where major dance and dramatic performances take place, and where devotees more generally gather to chant and dance in glorification of Lord Jagannāth. To the east of Nāṭya-mandira, one finds the Chatra Bhoga area, where numerous temple servants help share the food (*prasāda*) offered to Jagannāth, strictly vegetarian spiritual nourishment for the millions who visit the temple. However, the Chatra Bhoga Maṇḍapa is only for offerings brought to the temple from Purī's various indigenous religious institutions, including offerings from common visitors, patrons, and well-wishers in general; the offerings given by the king, which also arrive regularly, are reserved for the Deity room and is given special treatment.

But the most sought-after *prasāda* comes from the "Rosaghara," which is Lord Jagannāth's own kitchen. No longer explicitly part of the main temple area, this is where Jagannāth is served by hundreds on a daily basis.[37] It is said to be the world's largest kitchen, with no other food establishment coming even close (it engages some six hundred chefs and four hundred assistants every day). From here the famous fifty-six varieties of gourmet (cooked) food are regularly offered to the Lord. Much of it is given away freely and some is sold on temple grounds. More than five thousand to ten thousand people are fed daily and over ten million on special occasions.[38]

Numerous shrines surround the main temple as well. To the south, for example, we find a temple of Madana-Mohana and the Lakṣmīdevī Mārjana *maṇḍapa*, where the Goddess Lakṣmī is bathed weekly. In the north we find a temple of Bhāṇḍāra-Lokanātha, a deity who is said to be in charge of Jagannāth's storeroom. In the Chatra Bhoga Maṇḍapa stands the Garuḍa *stambha,* or column, from which vantage point Mahāprabhu was known to stand and gaze at the Deity. On an elevated platform to the southeast of the main temple is a Deity of Śrī Ṣaḍbhūja Mahāprabhu, Lord Chaitanya's six-armed form, with his own arms, the bow-and-arrow-clutching arms of Rāma, and the flute-bearing arms of Krishna. It was installed some time after Mahāprabhu's appearance to commemorate his importance in the worship of Lord Jagannāth. There are several others of him in the main temple area as well. There are also three Piḍha-Deula or sub-temples north, south, and west of the main temple: Śrī Varāhadeva, Śrī Vāmanadeva, and Śrī Nṛsiṁhadeva reside in these three temples, respectively.[39] Numerous other shrines dot the region as well.

Nṛsiṁhadeva, the half-man/half-lion Deity of Vishnu, is especially important at the Jagannāth temple. Śrī Chaitanya showed great reverence for Lord Nṛsiṁha at this temple. As stated in the *Caitanya-caritāmṛta:* "On the southern side . . . is a Deity of Lord Nṛsiṁhadeva. It is on the left as one goes up the steps toward the temple. . . . Śrī Caitanya Mahāprabhu, His left side toward the Deity, offered obeisances to Lord Nṛsiṁha as He proceeded toward the temple. He recited the following verses repeatedly while offering obeisances: 'I offer my deepest respects unto You, dear Nṛsiṁhadeva. You are the giver of pleasure to Mahārāja Prahlāda, and Your nails cut the chest of Hiraṇyakaśipu like a chisel cutting stone. Lord Nṛsiṁhadeva is here and also there on the opposite side. Wherever I go, there I see Lord Nṛsiṁhadeva. Likewise, He is outside and within My heart. Therefore, I take shelter of Him, the original Personality of Godhead.'"[40]

"The extraordinary importance of Narasiṁha for the Jagannātha cult" writes Odia scholar Anncharlott Eschmann, "has been repeatedly remarked upon. . . . Narasiṁha 'is the guardian deity of the temple and all the performances beginning from cooking to Pūjā are preceded by offerings to Narasiṁha first.' During the period of *anavasara* when Jagannātha cannot be seen because of his 'illness,' the main worship is offered to Narasiṁha and the prescribed meditations are focused on him. . . . Khambha Narasiṁha, an image of Lakṣmī-Narasiṁha on the first pillar of the Jagamohana when entering from the south, is the *iṣṭa-devatā* of the Brahmin priests. The initiation of any new *paṇḍā* starts with worshipping this image. Moreover, it seems that the priests, if they want to consecrate *bhoga* at the time of *pāhuda,* that is, when the *garbha-gṛha* is closed, offer the food to this particular Narasiṁha image instead of presenting it to Lord Jagannātha. Narasiṁha plays also an important role in all the texts pertaining to the temple as the 'protector of the wooden figures' who will punish whomsoever laughs at them."[41] Although some of the terminology here might be difficult to penetrate, the essence should be clear: The Jagannāth temple is protected by the divine man-lion, who soothes the pains of the devotees and, through his singular compassion, brings non-devotees to the lotus feet of the Lord.

THE GLORIOUS RATHA-YĀTRĀ FESTIVAL

As should be evident from the above, Lord Jagannāth is enthusiastically worshipped in the Purī temple, rarely going out in public. Consequently, only devout Hindus are allowed to see him, for entry is restricted to believers.[42] But there is a period during each year—in the rainy season, corresponding to June or July—when he is brought out into the street, revealing his form and abundant mercy for all to see.

Millions attend this summer festival, celebrating, singing, and even reciting songs with unabashed devotion, as the Lord of the Universe, along with Balarāma, Subhadrā, and Sudarśana (who shares Subhadrā's chariot), is lifted onto massive Ratha-yātrā carts waiting just outside the temple. There is much history, philosophy, and nuance to this festival, and only the best of Vaishnava scholars would know it all.[43] The rich tradition of Ratha-yātrā includes a vast variety of overarching truths, tangential storylines, and numerous subplots, permeating every aspect of the celebration. For example, both on the initial journey and in returning to his temple, Lord Jagannāth briefly visits the Mausi Mā Temple, about midway to Guṇḍicā, the destination of the carts. At Mausi Mā, he spends time with his aunt (Goddess Ardhāsanī, his mother's sister)—a much anticipated snack stop on his emotionally charged journey. Few will have heard of this detour, and it is not part of the carts' major trajectory.

Here we will summarize only the main parts of the festival.

The name "Ratha-yātrā" is comprised of two words, indicating a "journey" (*yātrā*) of the "chariots" (*ratha*). These chariots—three of them, some forty-five feet high—are made of wood, like Jagannāth himself, and each have at least a dozen large wheels allowing them movement (Jagannāth's has sixteen; Balarāma's, fourteen). Above this frame is a platform with the Deity and his priests, offset by colorful—red, green, and yellow—cloth canopies, stretched high into the sky, elegantly embroidered with simple Odia designs.[44]

The chariots are pulled by thousands of devotees and pilgrims along Grand Road, using long yellow ropes. On a simple level, this "pulling" is a metaphor for pulling the Lord back into one's heart.[45] It is said that merely touching these ropes, or seeing Lord Jagannāth on his cart, is enough to achieve liberation. It is the massive, overpowering visage of these huge chariots that defines Ratha-yātrā—and that prompted the English word "Juggernaut."[46]

The festival commences with the Chera Pahara ("cleansing with water") ritual, wherein the current Gajapati King sweeps the road, humbly making way for the Deities and their chariots.[47] The idea is meant to convey the notion that Jagannāth is the real king of the region, and all must bow down and perform menial service in his presence—even the king.[48] Then, in the midst of intense song and dance, with millions in attendance, the Deities are pulled on their carts from the Jagannāth Temple to the Guṇḍicā shrine, which is two miles in a northeasterly direction.[49] Pilgrims dot the area for as far as the eye can see, not just on the street but on rooftops and terraces, hanging out of windows, cheering and crying.

The Deities stay at Guṇḍicā for nine days.[50] The devotees sing and laugh and feast, while deepening their devotion for Lord Jagannāth. Thereafter, the Deities enjoy yet another journey on their chariots, as the devotees return them to the main temple.[51]

What does this festival really mean, and why is it so important to Gauḍīya Vaishnavas? The esoteric significance in all its richness is eloquently expressed by Ravīndra Svarūpa Dāsa, ISKCON leader and prominent disciple of Śrīla A. C. Bhaktivedānta Swami Prabhupāda:

> The chariot ride of Lord Jagannāth commemorates a particular incident in the pastimes Lord Krishna displayed on earth.
>
> . . .
>
> When Krishna left Vrindavan, he broke the hearts of all the residents. Their grief was beyond bearing, and no one's grief was greater than Śrīmatī Rādhārāṇī's.
>
> . . .
>
> Although Śrīmatī Rādhārāṇī appeared to be suffering in separation, in truth she was neither suffering nor separated from Krishna. In the spiritual realm there is no suffering, for all emotions are varieties of ecstasy.
>
> . . .
>
> Separation intensifies love—that is true even in this world. . . . The Ratha-yātrā festival brought these feelings to their highest pitch. For the festival commemorates the single occasion on which Śrīmatī Rādhārāṇī again met Krishna. For many years Krishna had ruled as King of Dvārakā exhibiting in the splendor of his capital, the power of his army, the brilliance of his court, and the beauty and refinement of his queens all the opulence of Godhead.
>
> Then, on the occasion of a solar eclipse, Krishna left Dvārakā. Riding with Balarāma and Subhadrā at the head of endless columns of chariots, elephants,

> and palanquins, Krishna led his whole royal dynasty to a holy pilgrimage site called Kurukshetra.
>
> . . .
>
> And so Śrīmatī Rādhārāṇī came once more to behold the lover of her youth. . . . Yet, strange to say, the joy of meeting did not vanquish the feelings of separation that had possessed her for years. On the contrary, those feelings became even more intense, even though Krishna—the same Krishna as before—was there. For now he was in royal garb, and all around them were warriors and their horses, elephants, and the rattling of their chariots. As she looked at Krishna, she longed to see him as the simple cowherd boy, carrying his flute, decorated with the forest flowers of Vrindavan—the boy she once knew. . . . She yearned to take Krishna back to Vrindavan.
>
> The Ratha-yātrā celebration, commemorating this event, is really the emotional process of bringing Krishna back to Vrindavan. Purī itself, with its majestic temple, is Dvārakā, and Guṇḍicā, set in rural gardens, is Vrindavan. And as Śrī Chaitanya danced before Lord Jagannāth's chariot on the way to Guṇḍicā, he merged deeper and deeper into the feelings of Rādhārāṇī. He lived through all her feelings for Krishna, and expressed all of them in his ecstatic dancing.[52]

Thus, Ratha-yātrā ranges from being a regional festival, if embraced by literally millions, particularly important to locals and those who make Jagannāth their daily religion, to an esoteric phenomenon, universal in application, embodying the deepest theological implications of the Gauḍīya tradition. "The Rathayatra expands divine love in circles of increasing grace," writes Vaishnava author Chaitanya Charan Das. "First, it expands divine grace from the sacred space of the temple to the rest of the city. The Lord riding atop the majestic chariot offers the blessing of His *darshana* (audience) to one and all—even those who do not come to the temple. The sway of the magnificent chariots, the embellishments with many meaningful motifs, the beauty of the three deities (Jagannatha with His brother Baladeva and sister Subhadra), the symphony of musical eulogies by skilled singers, and the worshipers' heartfelt cries of 'Jaya Jagannatha!'—all such potent devotional stimuli at the Rathayatra kindle life-transforming spiritual experiences. . . . Second, the globalization of Rathayatra expands the grace beyond Jagannatha Puri and even India. In 1967, Srila Prabhupada inspired the first Rathayatra outside India, in San Francisco, which also hosted Jagannatha's first Western temple (New Jagannatha Puri). Since then, the festival has assumed international proportions. Indeed, Jagannatha has become a charming face of the beauty and mystery of Indian spirituality. . . . The Rathayatra expands divine love from the temple to the rest of the city, and indeed the whole world. And it offers us a chance to elevate our devotional love from separation to union, from disconnection from the Lord to reconnection with Him."[53]

THE FORCE MOVES WEST

Śrī Chaitanya Mahāprabhu spent the last eighteen years of his life in Jagannāth Purī. His deep emotional relationship with the Deity serves as a profound template for Vaishnava devotion, embraced by Gauḍīyas for more than five hundred years. The desire to spread the glory of Jagannāth worldwide, in fact, was initially suggested in the *Chaitanya-Bhāgavata* (Antya 4.126), one of Mahāprabhu's earliest biographies, even if Jagannāth is not explicitly mentioned. In that verse, the Lord himself says that, "the chanting of my name will spread to every town and village of the world." The reference to "My name" indicates the names of Krishna, of which "Jagannāth" is prominent. The fateful scenario depicted in that verse would be pushed to the fore some four hundred years later, in the time of Bhaktivinoda Ṭhākura (1838–1914), whose life and work—due to both globalization and his profound spiritual insight—would plant the seed for Jagannāth's journey to the Western world.

Śrīla Bhaktivinoda Ṭhākura, a spiritual exemplar in Mahāprabhu's tradition, was intimately connected to the Jagannāth temple. At one point, he was Deputy Magistrate and Deputy Collector of Purī, and was so trusted that he was asked to oversee the affairs of the Temple in Purī on behalf of the Government.[54] An author of great renown, Bhaktivinoda sent his books to intellectuals in the West, hoping to initiate Vaishnavism's inevitable move to Western shores. His work reached the desks of assorted scholars in the British Empire, including the Royal Asiatic Society of London, in whose journal it received a favorable review. It also arrived and was accepted by several prestigious academic libraries, such as that of McGill University in Montreal, Canada, and the University of Sydney in Australia. The famous American Transcendentalist, Ralph Waldo Emerson, another recipient of Vaishnava literature sent by the Ṭhākura, wrote back to acknowledge his receipt and appreciation.[55]

Bhaktivinoda was so adamant about Gauḍīya Vaishnavism's inherent nonsectarianism and universal nature, he made a prediction that it would become an international phenomenon:

> Lord Chaitanya did not advent Himself to liberate only a few men of India. Rather, His main objective was to emancipate all living entities of all countries throughout the entire universe and preach the Eternal Religion. Lord Chaitanya says in the *Chaitanya Bhagavata* (Antya 4.126): "In every town, country

and village, My name will be sung." . . . Very soon the unparalleled path of *hari-nama-sankirtana* will be propagated all over the world. Already we are seeing the symptoms. Already many Christians have tasted the nectar of divine love of the holy name and are dancing with *karatalas* [hand cymbals] and *mridangas* [drums]. Educated Christians are ordering these instruments and shipping them to England. . . . Oh, for that day when the fortunate English, French, Russian, German and American people will take up banners, *mridangas* and *karatalas* and raise kirtan through their streets and towns. When will that day come? Oh, for the day when the fair-skinned men from their side will raise up the chanting of Jaya Sacinandana, Jaya Sacinandana ki jaya [All Glories to Lord Chaitanya! All Glories to Lord Chaitanya!] and join with the Bengali devotees. When will that day be? On such a day they will say, "Our dear Brothers, we have taken shelter of the ocean of Lord Chaitanya's Love; kindly embrace us." When will that day come? That day will witness the holy transcendental ecstasy of the Vaishnava-dharma [the eternal religion of devotional service to the Lord] to be the only dharma, and all the sects and religions will flow like rivers into the ocean of Vaishnava-dharma. When will that day come?"[56]

If Bhaktivinoda developed the overall vision of sending Vaishnavism to the West—and did so through his books—his son Śrīla Bhaktisiddhānta Sarasvatī Ṭhākura (1874–1937) tangibly put into effect his father's dream by actually sending disciples to the Occident.[57] But in the present context, it is especially significant that Sarasvatī Ṭhākura was precise, mentioning Jagannāth specifically. On May 19, 1934, at the ancient temple of Lord Alarnātha in Brahmagiri, Odisha, near Purī, he said, "We must take Lord Jagannāth in an airplane chariot to Eastbourne and to London" (*ākāśayāna bimāna rathare śrī jagannātha devaṅku iṣṭabarṇa landanaku nebāku heba, seṭhāre ālālanātha heba*).[58] He further opined that the mercy of Jagannāth, as per his name, should be available throughout the "*jagat*" ("universe"), adding that Jagannāth Deities are especially needed outside of India. He was firm on this latter point because Jagannāth, the tradition tells us, is renowned for being kind to those who need him most—in fact, he is popularly known as Patita Pāvana, or "deliverer of the most fallen." People in the Western world, said Bhaktisiddhānta, are generally bereft of Vaishnava teaching and all that it implies, and could thus particularly benefit from Jagannāth's mercy.[59]

The climax of this story, of course, is traceable to Śrīla Prabhupāda, the founder of the Hare Krishna movement, who, at the behest of Bhaktisiddhānta Sarasvatī, brought Vaishnavism to Western shores and established it as an irrevocable fact. It might be added that Prabhupāda was devoted to Jagannāth, in particular, even as a five-year-old child in Kolkata, celebrating Ratha-yātrā by using a miniature, homemade cart, pulling it throughout his neighborhood with local friends. In other words, he had an inborn love for Lord Jagannāth throughout his life. Thus, in 1967, a year after incorporating his International

Society for Krishna Consciousness (ISKCON), he planted the seeds for establishing the festival worldwide—he inaugurated the first Ratha-yātrā in the Western world.

Today, his disciples continue to watch those seeds sprout in cities around the world, as Ratha-yātrā annually makes its way to London, Paris, Sydney, Tokyo, San Francisco, Los Angeles, and on New York's renowned Fifth Avenue, to name a few. The festival not only replicates the mammoth carts and traditional parade of Purī, but it now includes a "Festival of India" in place of Guṇḍicā, with colorful displays, entertainment stages, musical performances, free-feast booths, and a variety of cultural displays and exhibits.

Prabhupāda was obviously aware of Sarasvatī Ṭhākura's statements about Lord Jagannāth and the West. For example, in February 1970, when his movement was already firmly established in the West, Śrīla Prabhupāda wrote to Hanuman Prasad Poddar (the well known founder of "Gita Press" with whom he had a friendly relationship): "The Deities worshipped in ISKCON temples are Jagannath Swami with Balarama and Subhadra and Radha-Krishna. When we first start a temple, we start with Jagannath Swami. My Guru Maharaja recommended temples of Jagannath in these countries, so I was inspired to establish first of all Jagannath Swami because He is kind even to the *mlecchas* [foreigners]. Then, when there is opportunity I establish Radha-Krishna *murti*."[60]

Actually, from the very beginning of ISKCON, Prabhupāda wanted to install Lord Jagannāth in his temples. In a little-known incident, for example, Prabhupāda had asked Brahmānanda Dāsa, one of his first disciples, to help him in this regard, even before there were any actual Deities in the movement. Brahmānanda recalls:

> I had first come to a kirtan in the first week of August, 1966, and was initiated in September (Radhastami). Shortly after this, say in October or November, I was sitting with Srila Prabhupada in his room, and he gave me an assignment. He wanted a statue (*murti*) made from stone. He made a drawing of this flat-headed stubby image with funny arms, which he said was the shape of Lord Jagannath, the primary manifestation of Krishna in Puri as worshiped by Lord Chaitanya—it was "the Lord of the Universe," he said. And he wanted me to go across the street and ask the tombstone seller to carve this shape out of granite. This was Provenzano Lanza Funeral Home, at 43 Second Avenue, directly across the street. It's still there. Anyway, from Prabhupada's point of view, this was a perfectly reasonable request, but I was shocked by it. How could a tombstone seller make this shape he had never seen before, and, more, why should he do it? How could I explain why I wanted this thing? To me it seemed like an untenable idea. At the time, I didn't know that deities are routinely hand-carved from marble slabs in India and then decorated and worshipped. I don't think I had ever seen a photo of a deity at that point of time, only artwork, paintings of

> Krishna. Anyway, I obediently went across the street and carried out the assignment. I was relieved that they didn't give much attention to the strange shape in the drawing and politely explained that they only sell the tombstones and do not manufacture them. And the stonecutters use machines to cut the quarried stone into fixed shapes and sizes and do not do custom hand-carved shapes, especially something as unconventional as this. So, Lord Jagannath did not appear in Srila Prabhupada's movement at this time; it would happen a short time later in San Francisco, where he was provided not only the deities by Malati's grace, but a disciple (Shyamasundara) who could carve and paint large deities out of wood, exactly like the Lord of the Universe at Puri.[61]

The story to which Brahmānanda refers at the end of his quote is interesting. It happened shortly before the first Ratha-yātrā festival in 1967. One day, Śyāmasundara, one of Śrīla Prabhupāda's earliest West Coast disciples, hurried into his teacher's San Francisco apartment, carrying a surprise that could only be described as a product of destiny. He excitedly took a small item out of his shopping bag, and placed it on Prabhupāda's desk for authoritative perusal. "What is this?" remarked the master, his eyes opening wide as he looked down at the three-inch wooden image before him. For Prabhupāda, it was more than a familiar form, but entirely out of context—what was it doing here in San Francisco, in the middle of the Hippie Era? It was his very own Lord Jagannāth, making an unexpected if long-awaited appearance!

Śrīla Prabhupāda immediately folded his palms in traditional *añjali* style and bowed down, offering the exotic figure full Vaishnava respects. Prabhupāda then started reciting melodious Sanskrit prayers and encouraged both Śyāmasundara and Mukunda, another early disciple, also in the room, to bow before little Jagannāth as well. The disciples were shocked, without any knowledge of the rich tradition behind the Swami's actions.

"You have brought Jagannāth, the Lord of the universe," he said, smiling, and delighted beyond words. "He is Krishna. Thank you very much." Prabhupāda was overcome with joy, and proceeded to tell them the Jagannāth story. "But where did you get this Deity?" The boys explained that Mālatī, Śyāmasundara's wife, had found it in a commercial market called Cost Plus Imports. "Bring her to me." And so they did.

> "Mālatī, you have found this?"
>
> "Yes."
>
> "There are others?"
>
> "Oh yes, a whole barrelful."
>
> "No, no. Two others?"
>
> "Yes, two more barrels with different figures."

The Swami held up little Jagannāth and said, "This is Krishna. The other two figures will be his sister, Subhadrā, and his brother, Balarāma. Bring them."

Mālatī and Śyāmasundara rushed to the Imports store and bought the two other figures in the set, as Prabhupāda had directed. They hurried back, and dutifully gave the little statues to their spiritual master. As he placed the three forms on his desk, he looked at them with loving affection. Then he looked up at his disciples and asked if any of them knew how to carve.

By Krishna's divine arrangement, Śyāmasundara had been a wood sculptor by profession. Prabhupāda asked him to carve larger replicas of the little Deities. He did so, and thus Lord Jagannāth manifested in the Western world.[62] And so it was that on March 26, 1967, in San Francisco, Śrīla Prabhupāda conducted ISKCON's first installation ceremony at 518 Frederick Street, effectively bringing the Deities Jagannāth, Balarāma, and Subhadrā to the Western world, as predicted by his spiritual master.[63] At that time, he also introduced ISKCON to a new mantra, *jagannāthaḥ svāmī nayana-patha-gāmī bhavatu me,* which means, "Lord Jagannāth, Lord of the Universe, please be visible unto me."

CONCLUSION

As discussed in an earlier chapter, Vaishnava tradition tells us that there are four divisions of cyclically recurring epochs—or "seasons," if you will—of cosmic time, as indicated early in this book. These distinct seasons are known as yuga cycles, and in each of these, the same one Supreme Lord descends from his transcendental realm to play upon the stage of the world. And in each, he manifests a purely spiritual, humanlike body for his pleasure pastimes.

Now, it is an interesting fact that in each of these transcendental bodies, the Lord exhibits a particular color that matches the scheduled yuga cycle. These manifestations of the Supreme are called *yuga avatāras*. While we have discussed this "color scheme" previously, we ask the reader to bear with us, for this consideration of color will also impact our understanding of Jagannāth and his associated Deities.

In Satya-yuga the Lord appears in a self-manifested body that is of whitish complexion (*śukla*). In Treta-yuga, the same Personality appears reddish in color (*rakta*); in Dvāpara-yuga he appears in a blackish body (*krishna*); and in Kali-yuga He appears in a form that has a yellow cast to it (*pīta*).[64]

Vaishnava tradition goes on to tell us that despite the differences in color, and despite the different specific earthly pastimes presented in the different yuga narratives, it is always the same one God who descends and who is at play. The *yuga avatāras* constitute one Tattva, or Truth. Although they exist in various colors, all are manifestations of the same One Supreme Godhead.

We can attempt to understand this seeming mystery by reflecting on the common, everyday phenomenon of race and bodily color as it presents itself in the world around us. After all, our everyday experience shows us the breathtaking variegatedness of humankind. And yet we know that the host of diverse identities is simply a kaleidoscopic display of different manifestations of one species—Homo sapiens.

Diversity among Homo sapiens is ubiquitous—humans manifest variously as white, red, black, and yellow, just like God—and yet, unequivocally, the species of humankind, also like God, is one. Science attests to this fact, and therefore this division by color, this racialization of human identities, this calling ourselves members of the white race, black race (or sometimes brown), red race, and yellow race is misleading and superficial.

Science has proven that we are not four (or five) races, but one. And our single race transcends ethnicity, culture, geographical origin, and, yes, skin color: we all partake of a single phenotype, even to the point of often having similar anatomical features and exhibiting consubstantial behavior.

Along similar lines, the Lord of the universe (Jagannāth) and his associated Deities (Balarāma, Subhadrā, and Sudarśana), as already mentioned, appear in this same color scheme. Jagannāth is black, Balarāma is white, Subhadrā is yellow, and Sudarśana is red. In other words, all races are represented in Jagannāth's domain. And the meaning here is more far-reaching than in the example of the *yuga-avatāras*: Jagannāth is Lord of the universe. That is to say, he is the Lord of everyone, regardless of caste, creed, gender, and even race.[65]

If this is so, one may rightly ask, why to this day do temple guards and priests keep foreigners out? Why is the Jagannāth temple still known for its racial and religious exclusivity (see endnote 42)? The answer is complicated, involving politics and personalities who do not quite understand what Jagannāth really represents, or what spirituality really means.

But suffice it to say that the philosophy behind the Jagannāth Deity and its underlying Vaishnava tradition do not support the myopic view that would keep foreigners at bay, or that would disallow anyone from entering the temple's holy precincts. Jagannāth's home should feel like home to anyone who wants to visit.

Xenophobia and bigotry run counter to everything Lord Jagannāth stands for. The underlying philosophy of Vaishnavism includes the notion of one's existence beyond the body. We are more than these earthly tabernacles of bile, mucus, and air, says Vaishnava teaching—we are pure spirit-soul. The very first step in self-realization, we learn, is realizing one's identity as separate from the body. "As a person puts on new garments, giving up old ones," the *Bhagavad-gītā* (2.22) tells us, "similarly, the soul accepts new material bodies, giving up the old and useless ones." And further, "As the embodied soul continually passes, in this body, from boyhood to youth to old age, the soul similarly passes into another body at death. The self-realized soul is not bewildered by such a change" (2.13).

Jagannāth's broad smile leads us beyond our differences to the realization that we are linked more than separated, that we have more commonality than divergence. We are all one family, with a spiritual bonding that underscores God's ultimate Fatherhood. This is the teaching of Lord Jagannāth, and it is a force to be reckoned with.

NOTES

1. See Shoba Narayan, "Puri part 3: The contrasting tales of Jagannath's origin" in LiveMint, May 5, 2020 (https://www.livemint.com/Sundayapp/xJTi6ZJaM3Y5ouGO7WNvxJ/Puri-part-3-The-contrasting-tales-of-Jagannaths-origin.html).

2. See *Ṛg Veda Samhita,* Edited by F. Max Muller, Vol. VI (London, 1874), 549. See also *Śrī Kṣetra: Vaikuṇṭha on Earth* (Compiled by Śrīpāda Sundarānanda Vidyāvinoda, produced and published by Īśvara dāsa, translated by Bhumipati dāsa (Kolkata: Touchstone Media, 2017), 44–45.

3. *Encyclopedia Britannica* (https://www.britannica.com/science/fundamental-interaction).

4. See O. B. L. Kapoor, "Bhakti, the Perfect Science" in *Back to Godhead* 1, no. 53 (March 1, 1973). Kapoor also seized upon this phrase in a personal conversation with the present author (correspondence, October 12, 1990). Coincidentally, perhaps, the phrase is also used by Robert E. Wilkinson as the title of his enlightening 1996 article in which he analyzes Quantum Theory in relation to Vedic Cosmology. See Robert E. Wilkinson, "The Quantum Brahman," available at SpiritWeb (www2.eu.spiritweb.org).

5. While "Brahman," the impersonal Absolute, adequately expresses the spiritual dimension of this fifth force of the universe, the word "Jagannāth" goes further, showing that the ultimate spiritual energy is in fact an energetic force (and not mere energy), or the source substance behind the energy. In other words, while "energy" is the impetus behind all motion and all activity, "energetic force" is that which possesses, exerts, or displays energy. It is prior, catalyzing energy to do its work.

6. Sāralā Dās's fifteenth-century Odia version of the *Mahābhārata* corroborates the *Bhāgavatam* narrative (Eleventh Canto, chapter 30 and 31) about Krishna's final pastimes. It states that he completed his Earthly mission when Jarā's arrow pierced his heel, thus ushering in the new if degraded age of Kali-yuga. The hunter had ostensibly mistaken Krishna for a deer. But this was all part of Krishna's plan. The text tells us that the Lord wanted to conclude his terrestrial pastimes and chose Jarā to enact the deed. Thus, when the arrow penetrated its mark, Krishna manifested the four arms of

Vishnu and departed for his own abode. Famed commentator Viśvanātha Cakravartī (*Bhāgavata*, 11.30.33) adds that the arrow did not actually pierce Krishna's body, since the Lord's limbs are completely transcendental. It was a spiritual ruse, the text tells us, created by the Lord's own energy (*māyā*) to accomplish many ends at once. This much is stated directly in both the *Bhāgavatam* and the *Mahābhārata*.

The latter text (Mausala Parva, 7.31), however, also indicates that the Lord, by magical display, underwent some form of cremation. Sāralā's Odia version takes this addendum further, creatively offering that Jarā and Arjuna heard the voice of providence, telling them to cremate the divine body by setting it ablaze on a special wooden log bearing the symbols of Vishnu, i.e., conch, wheel, club and lotus. Upon following these instructions, they found that all but Krishna's navel (*nābhi-brahma*) would burn in the fire. (Some versions poetically say that it was his heart as opposed to his navel, though this is not confirmed by the earlier textual tradition.)

Just then, the voice of providence again spoke, telling them to leave the unfired navel at sea, floating on the sacred log. This navel, tradition teaches, made the long journey from Dvārakā to Purī over millennia and, upon arriving, became identified as Nīla-Mādhava, the "Blue Lord." This in turn led to Dāru-Brahman, the wooden log that eventually morphed into Lord Jagannāth.

Additionally, some say that Jarā, the hunter, was the reincarnated Viśvāvasu, the tribesman who worshipped Nīla-Mādhava until King Indradyumna arrived. It should be added here that this cremation tale seems contrary to the narrative found in the *Bhāgavatam*, which indicates that after appearing in His four-armed Vishnu form, Krishna simply departed for the spiritual world: "Without employing the mystic *āgneyī* meditation to burn up his transcendental body, which is the all-attractive resting place of all the worlds and the object of all contemplation and meditation, Lord Krishna entered into his own abode" (11.31.6). "Just as ordinary men cannot ascertain the path of a lightning bolt as it leaves a cloud, the demigods could not trace out the movements of Lord Krishna as He returned to His abode" (11.31.9).

Regarding the Nīla-Mādhava story, there is a "*nābhi-brahma*" component to Jagannāth even to this day, usually referred to as "a mystical substance" that is buried within the Lord's wooden body: "Some of the popular beliefs are that the *nābhi-brahma* is a special blue sapphire with a Viṣṇu *yantra* engraved on it, that it is a piece of the original Deity of Lord Jagannātha, that it is a Śālagrāma-śilā that was given by the King of Nepal, that it is a tooth of Lord Buddha [to be discussed below], or that it is a piece of Lord Krishna's navel from 5,000 years ago." See Madhavananda Das, "The Life Force of Lord Jagannātha" in *Sri Krishna Kathamrita Magazine,* issue 4 (Odisha, India: Gopal Jiu Publications, 1997).

Śrīla Sanātana Gosvāmī, in his *Śrī Śrī Kṛṣṇa-līlā-stavaḥ* (Text 397.2), seems to favor the Śālagrāma-śilā version: "O You Whose eyes are like fully blossomed lotuses! O You Who are the nectar on the shore of the salty ocean! O You who have a small stone in Your belly—*guṭika-udara*! O enjoyer of varieties of food offerings! Please protect me!" Here, Sanātana Gosvāmī describes Lord Jagannāth as being *guṭika-udara*—literally having a pebble in his belly. This is traditionally accepted as referring to a Śālagrāma-śilā. (See Buddhist section of this chapter under the subheading "Who is Lord Jagannāth?" for an alternate view claiming that Jagannāth's navel houses the tooth of the Buddha.)

7. For the significance of the story having two parts, see Bhaktivedanta Narayana Maharaja, *The Origin of Ratha-Yātrā* (Vrndavana: Gaudiya Vedanta Publications, 2003, 1st Edition edition), 1–40. Here Nārāyaṇa Mahārāja refers to these two parts as "The First History" and "The Second History." For the Gauḍīya vision of Jagannāth as the flute-playing cowherd, see *Caitanya-caritāmṛta* Antya 15.7: Mahāprabhu saw Jagannāth not the way most see him but rather as the darling of Braj, with flute, beautiful bluish skin and lotus-like eyes. In other words, he saw him as the son of Nanda Mahārāja (*sākṣāt vrajendra-nandana*), a fact confirmed in Antya 14.31 and elsewhere. This, then, is the way that Gauḍīya Vaishnavas with enhanced realization perceive Lord Jagannāth.

8. Little is known of the original Nīla-Mādhava, i.e., Jagannāth's precursor, but tradition offers various theories. Clearly, Nīla-Mādhava was a Deity of Vishnu/Nārāyaṇa. And today, in fact, most Deity representations of Nīla-Mādhava have the traditional four arms of Vishnu. This can be seen, for example, both in the Nīla-Mādhava Deity found at the current Jagannāth Mandir and also in the Deity found in Kantilo Odisha, some distance from the state capital Bhubaneshwar. Similarly, the four-armed Deity of Alarnath in Brahmagiri near Purī is also considered a manifestation of Jagannāth/Nīla-Mādhava. As a sidenote, perhaps, there is a regional tradition saying that Kantilo is where the original form of Nīla-Mādhava manifested in the time of King Indradyumna. However, it seems clear that this is just a local legend, if a popular one. More details about Nīla-Mādhava are found in local Odiya literature. For example, "The *Indranilamani Purana* (a secret text used in the temple also known as Sthala Purāṇa) mentions . . . the Deity of Nila Madhava, which he says was eighty-one *angulas* (fingers) tall and standing on a golden lotus flower. Nila Madhava is a Deity of Vishnu, but in one hand instead of the lotus flower He carries Subhadra Lakshmi Devi (who is also called Kamala)." See Parama Karuna Devi and Rahul Acharya, *Puri: The Home of Lord Jagannatha* (Chandanpur, Orissa: Jagannatha Vallabha Research Center, 2009).

9. The story of Jagannāth is incomplete without reference to the Śabaras, for, though simple tribal people, they were the original worshippers of Nīla Mādhava in ancient times. Later, when the Deity worship was established at the temple at Purī, the Lord became known as Jagannāth (though Nīla Mādhava was the precursor). Because the Nīla Mādhava narrative originated with the Śabaras, they were elevated to the position of *dayitās* (servants of Lord Jagannāth), and this currently holds true for all of their descendants. The word *dayitā* refers to one who has received the mercy of the Lord. These fortunate souls do not generally come from high-caste families (*brāhmaṇas, kṣatriyas,* or *vaiśyas*), but because they are engaged in Jagannāth's service, their status is high, and they are respected.

10. The full story is complex, with many plots and subplots. In this article, I have attempted to summarize the various versions for clarity. For the unexpurgated Jagannāth story, see *Śrī Kṣetra: Vaikuṇṭha on Earth*, originally compiled by Sundarānanda Vidyāvinoda (in Bengali), produced and published by Īśvara dāsa, translated by Bhumipati dāsa (Kolkata: Touchstone Media, 2017). Also see Tamal

Krishna Goswami, *Jagannātha-Priya Nāṭakam: The Drama of Lord Jagannātha* (Los Angeles: Bhaktivedanta Institute of Religion and Culture; 1st edition, 1985); Dhruva Mahārāja Dāsa, *Jaya Jagannātha: The Culture and Worship of Lord Jagannātha East and West* (Los Angeles: Bhaktivedanta Book Trust, 2007); Nitai Dasa, "The Appearance of Lord Jagannatha" in *Back to Godhead*, July 197510, no. 7 (http://www.krishna.com/appearance-lord-jagannatha); and Narada Rishi Dasa, "Why Krishna Appears as Jagannatha" in *Back to Godhead*, September/October 2007 41, no. 4 (http://btg.krishna.com/why-krishna-appears-jagannatha).

11. Tradition teaches that King Indradyumna at first called many expert sculptors to carve the form of the Lord. But none of them were able to perform the service properly—as soon as they began their work, their chisels mystically disintegrated in their hands. Finally, says the *Nārada Purāṇa* (Utkala Khanda 54.22–65), Viśvakarmā, the architect of the demigods, was called forth, and he carved the Deities in pursuance of the King's desire. According to alternate versions, the Supreme Lord himself appeared in the guise of an old sculptor named Ananta Mahāraṇa.

12. It might seem strange that God has a "brother" and "sister." In the narrative traditions of India, Krishna's immediate expansion is known as Balarāma, and he functions as the Lord's elder brother as they display their divine pastimes for the Lord's pleasure. Similarly, the Lord's internal energy, known as Yogamāyā, manifests as the his sister. In this way, God expands into numerous forms to enjoy exchanges of love (*rasa*) with his various manifestations and so too with all of his devotees in the spiritual realm.

13. Regarding the Jagannāth Deities' lack of arms and legs, some devotees refer to an esoteric reading of the *Śvetāśvatara Upaniṣad* (3.19): "Without legs and hands, he moves and accepts. Without eyes, he sees, and without ears, he hears. He knows all that is knowable, but no one knows him. He is thus referred to as the original Supreme Person." Even though Lord Jagannāth has a form that is bereft of hands and legs, the tradition muses, he still accepts fifty-six different types of *prasāda* (sacred vegetarian food), offered eight times daily, and he yearly mounts his resplendent Ratha-yātrā cart.

14. There are two forms of *mahābhāva-prakāśa* ("ecstatic manifestation"): Śrī Chaitanya Mahāprabhu's and Lord Jagannāth's, with the former being by far the most well known (as depicted in *Caitanya-caritāmṛta,* Ādi 17.18). This *mahābhāva-prakāśa* occurred in the house of Śrīvāsa Ṭhākura, when Mahāprabhu sat on the throne of Viṣṇu and allowed all the devotees to worship him with Vedic mantras. This was uncommon for Mahāprabhu, for his mission was confidential and, consequentally, he normally behaved as a devotee, not as God. His followers knew this to be his preference and generally interacted with him in that way, if also with extreme reverence. But his *mahābhāva-prakāśa* was an exception. It lasted for seven *praharas*, or twenty-one hours, and during this time the Lord showed a profound level of wild abandon, an ecstasy unknown in this world. Indeed, he took this opportunity to show the devotees that he is the original Personality of Godhead, Krishna, who is the source of all other incarnations. Some devotees call this exhibition of ecstasy *sāta-prahariyā bhāva*, or "the ecstasy of twenty-one hours," and others call it *mahābhāva-prakāśa* or *mahā-prakāśa*.

Just as Śrī Chaitanya showed his divine ecstasy during this *mahābhāva-prakāśa*, so too did Lord Jagannāth, at yet another time. Kāhnāi Khuṭiyā's book, titled, simply, *Mahābhāva-prakāśa,* describes Jagannāth's ecstatic state. Khuṭiyā was one of Mahāprabhu's intimate associates in Purī, as we learn from the *Caitanya-caritāmṛta* (2.15.20 and 30). Significantly, he begins his book by describing that he learned about the *mahābhāva-prakāśa* directly from the lips of Rāmānanda Rāya in the Gambhīra—which is among the best of all possible ways to learn something in the Gauḍīya Vaishnava tradition. (Kāhnāi Khuṭiyā's house still exists today, not far from the Gambhīra.) There are variations on the name Khuṭiyā: Khuntia, Khuntiya, Khutia, Khutiya. The name indicates affiliation with the Khuntia tribe of Purī—they were the Deities' bodyguards in the main temple.

15. The great Vaishnava teacher Gour Govinda Swami (1929–1996), elaborates in his book *Embankment of Separation* (Bhubaneswar, Orissa, Gopal Jiu Publications, 1996), 102: "In that form, he is feeling the acute pangs of separation from Rādhā. That is the form of Jagannātha, *rādhā-bhāva sindhure bhāsamāna*, as if the Lord is a log of wood floating in the ocean of Rādhā's love."

16. One may wonder how it is that Balarāma has a mother named Rohiṇī, since his brother, Krishna, is famously the son of Devakī. Do they not have the same mother? They do not. In fact, Krishna's father, Vasudeva, had sixteen wives, and one of them was named Pauravī or Rohiṇī. She was the mother of Balarāma.

17. Hermann Kulke and Dietmar Rothermund, *A History of India*, Third Edition (London: Routledge, 2002), 175.

18. See Julia A. B. Hegewald and Subrata K. Mitra, "Jagannatha Compared: The Politics of Appropriation, Re-Use and Regional Traditions in India" (https://archiv.ub.uni-heidelberg.de/volltextserver/8015/).

19. See https://www.lionsroar.com/what-are-the-three-jewels/.

20. See Avinash Patra, "Origin & Antiquity of the Cult of Lord Jagannath" (Oxford University Press, 2011), 17. There is a local theory that Purī was once called Dantapura ("land of the tooth"), because, as various Buddhist denominations still claim, the Enlightened One's "tooth relic" was housed in one of area's tiered towers (*pagodas*). From there, many say, the relic was taken to Kandy, Sri Lanka, where it now stands. Most Buddhists accept this version of the story, and do not identify the tooth as the *nābhi-brahma* in Jagannāth's abdomen.

21. Vaishnava philosophy generally teaches that, as a completely spiritual entity, the Lord does not have a material body and thus he does not change bodies like ordinary souls, who perpetually reincarnate until they find perfection, at which time they graduate to the spiritual realm. However, Vaishnavas say that in the form of Lord Jagannāth, God, too reincarnates. Here is the one form of Krishna that takes on one body after the other, much as other souls do. That being said, there is still a difference: regular souls are forced to reincarnate as a result of their *karma* (action/reaction schema), but God does so out of his own sweet will.

22. For more, see Madhavananda Das, "Nava-Kalevara: Lord Jagannātha's 'Change of Body' Pastime" in *Sri Krishna Kathamrita Magazine*, issue 4 (Odisha, India: Gopal Jiu Publications, 1997).

23. Ibid.

24. Because no one has seen or felt the *nābhi-brahma*, diverse opinions about its form and shape continue to exist. Buddhists claim it is the Buddha's tooth, as mentioned above, and a certain contingent of Vaishnavas say it is Krishna's navel. The actual shape and form—and identity—remain a mystery.

25. Madhavananda Das, "Nava-Kalevara: Lord Jagannātha's 'Change of Body' Pastime," *op. cit.* It is said that if one looks at the *nābhi-brahma* directly, one immediately dies. The *paṇḍās* say that many years ago one of the priests looked at the *nābhi-brahma* and indeed quickly passed away. It is considered one of the greatest mysteries in the tradition of Lord Jagannāth.

26. See Bijoy M. Misra, "Shri Krishna Jagannatha: The Mushali-parva from Sarala's *Maha-bharata*," in Edwin F. Bryant (ed.), *Krishna: A Sourcebook* (New York: Oxford University Press, 2007), 139–41.

27. *Vishnu Purāṇa* (1.12.68) names these three functions: "Bliss, substance, and sentience are grounded within that one *śakti*." (*hlādinī sandhinī saṁvit, tvayy eka sarva saṁsthitau*) The Lord's energy is divided into three component parts, namely *sandhinī, saṁvit* and *hlādinī*; in other words, he is the full manifestation of existence, knowledge, and bliss, and this is all manifest in Lord Jagannāth. The great Gauḍīya philosopher B. R. Sridhar Dev-Goswami Maharaj (1895–1988) sums this up nicely: "In our conception of divinity, *purusha/prakriti*, the masculine/feminine, are existing together. Potent and potency, substance and potency, are inconceivably interconnected. Otherwise, if we conceive of the Supreme Soul as existing independent of any potency, that will be the Brahman conception of Shankaracharya: ultimate consciousness as non-differentiated oneness. So the Absolute Truth includes both potent and potency—*purusha/prakriti*—consciousness with energy. Actually there are three main elements to be traced within divinity: *jnana*, *bala*, and *kriya*. The eternal aspect of the absolute whole is divided in three ways: energy, consciousness, and ecstasy. Thinking, willing and feeling. *Sat, chit, ananda. Sat*, the potency for maintaining existence, is the potency of Baladeva (*bala*). *Chit*, the consciousness aspect, is Vasudeva (*jnana*). And *ananda*, ecstatic feeling, is Radhika (*kriya*). *Jnana, bala, kriya* (knowledge, strength, feeling); *sat, chit, ananda* (eternity, cognition, bliss); *sandhini, samvit, hladini* (existence, realization, ecstasy): Baladeva, Krishna, Radharani. These are the three phases of *advaya-jnana*, or the one whole. The one whole can be thought of in its primary evolved stage in three ways: main consciousness, main energy, and main satisfaction. In three phases we are to conceive of that ultimate reality. It is there: *jnana, bala, kriya ca*. Thinking, feeling, willing. *Sat, chit, ananda. Satyam, shivam, sundaram* (eternity, auspiciousness, beauty). And these three principles are expressed through evolution and dissolution in the eternal and non-eternal" (https://mahamandala.com/en/audios/93).

28. Śrīla Bhaktivinoda Ṭhākura, "The temple of Jagannātha at Purī," *Tājpore*, September 15, 1871.

29. See Sanātana Gosvāmī, *Bṛhad-bhāgavatāmṛta* (2.5.211). Similarly, Locanadāsa Ṭhākura writes in his *Caitanya-maṅgala* (*Sūtra-khaṇḍa* 487): "Lord Jagannāth is the resting place of all divine Incarnations." Ultimately, of course, the three main Deities at the Jagannāth temple represent the three Deities of the Mahā-mantra—Hare Krishna, Hare Krishna, Krishna Krishna, Hare Hare/ Hare Rāma, Hare Rāma, Rāma

Ramā, Hare Hare. This is so because the three names in that mantra, Hare, Krishna and Rāma, indicate, consecutively, the energy of the Lord, Rādhā, of whom Subhadrā is an expansion; Krishna, who is nondifferent from Lord Jagannāth; and Rāma, who is often identified as Krishna's elder brother. See Bijoy M Misra, "Shri Krishna Jagannatha: The Mushali-parva from Sarala's *Mahabharata*," op. cit., 142. Earlier, in the time of Mahāprabhu, Achyutānanda Dāsa had theorized slightly differently in his book, *Śūnya-saṁhitā* (chapter 8), opining that Jagannāth was identified with Krishna, Balarāma with Hari, and Subhadrā with Rāma, thus embodying the essential truths of the Mahā-mantra. See "The Hidden Identity of Lord Jagannatha" in *Sri Krishna Kathamrta*, no. 12, p. 28.

Similarly, Lord Jagannāth's abode should be seen as nondifferent from Vrindavan. Purī should not be seen in a one-dimensional way: it is not simply "Dvārakā," even if it functions as such in Ratha-yātrā *līlā*. To see it in its full splendor, one must see its esoteric dimension: "Most people think that Jagannātha Kṣetra is Dvārakā Purī or Vaikuṇṭha," writes Vaishnava savant Premānanda Prabhu (Prabhuji). "This same Jagannātha Purī (Jagannātha Kṣetra) is known as Nīlāñcala or Nīlācala. *Nīlā* means blue, and the extra part of a *sāḍī* that women wear over their heads is known as *āṅcala*. Who is She whose *āṅcala* is blue? She is Śrīmatī Rādhārāṇī. Jagannātha has taken shelter under Rādhārāṇī's blue *āṅcala*. This is the confidential purport of Jagannātha's residence in Nīlācala. . . . It is the place of Śrīmatī Rādhārāṇī's shelter. . . . Do not think that Jagannātha-dhāma is Dvārakā or Vaikuṇṭha-puram. The place of Śrī Caitanya Mahāprabhu cannot be Vaikuṇṭha. He never goes to Vaikuṇṭha. The Gauḍīya-vaiṣṇavas never go to Dvārakā or Vaikuṇṭha, and even if they did, they would bring Vṛndāvana there with them." See *Śrī Guru Darśana* (Vrindavan, UP: Bhaktabandhav, 2015), 1069–70, 1074.

30. "Until the beginning of the twentieth century," writes Madhavananda, "scholars had credited Maharaja Anangabhim II with the building of the Jagannāth temple. But in 1990 two copper plate inscriptions were found in Purī at the Trimali Math. These, together with the copper plates of the Gaṅga King Narasiṁha I, which were found in 1892, clearly identify Maharaja Chodagangadev as the personality behind the construction." See Madhavananda Das, "Regaining a Lost Kingdom: Excerpts from the Life of Maharaja Chodagangadev," in *Sri Krishna Kathamrita Bindu,* issue 6, p. 17 (Bhubaneswar, Odisha: Gopal Jiu Publications, June 2001). See also Kailash Chandra Dash, *Legend, History and Culture of India* (Calcutta: Punthi-Pustak, 1997).

31. The name Nāṭya-mandira will forever resound with the memory of the Devadasis. This refers to the women who danced inside the temple for the pleasure of the Lord, with their descendants doing so generation after generation. They were traditionally viewed as the "wives of Lord Jagannath," and were known as *maharis* (this became the name of their dance technique as well) because they gave their lives to learning the art of Indian dance for the pleasure of the Deities. This was a pan-Indian tradition, reenacted in numerous temples throughout the subcontinent, not just in Purī. In due course, the Devadasis were identified as servants of ill repute, since, according to some, a number of them had had sexual relations with government leaders and unscrupulous priests who instructed them in music and dance. Because of this, the entire genre was marked with disdain and the Devadasis infamously developed the

reputation of being "temple prostitutes." Unlike in other parts of India, however, the Odia Devadasis were not sexually liberal and in general were expected to be celibate. Nonetheless, the Devadasi practice waned in the 1950s, even if the tradition of temple prostitution continued to run rampant. As a result, the government of India illegalized the Devadasi tradition in as far back as 1988, although it continues in parts of the Deccan. The last of the Purī Devadasis, Shashimani, died on March 19, 2015, at the age of 92. See Ellen Barry, "Sashimani Devi, Last of India's Jagannath Temple Dancers, Dies at 92," in *The New York Times* (March 23, 2015).

32. The Deities on the main altar are roughly six feet tall, with Subhadrā being slightly shorter.

33. Sudarśana is traditionally the name of Lord Vishnu's deadly weapon, the circular and sharp-edged *cakra* ("disc"). The Sudarśana in Purī, however, is a pillar, bearing no resemblance to the *cakra* mentioned in Purāṇic literature. Some scholars thus assert that Sudarśana in this case is not meant to represent the *cakra* at all but is simply indicative that Jagannāth is to be identified as Vishnu Tattva. See Anncharlott Eschmann Hermann Kulke, Gaya Charan Tripathi, eds., *The Cult of Jagannath and the Regional Tradition of Orissa* (South Asia Institute, 1978; Delhi: Manohar, 1986), 185. The Nīla Chakra ("blue discus," an eight-spoked wheel) is gloriously mounted on the top Śikhara ("peak") of the Jagannāth Temple. This emblem of divinity embodies the more commonly expected image of Vishnu's traditional weapon, while the pole in the temple is representational. See Pattanaik, Shibasundar, "Sudarsan of Lord Jagannath," in *Orissa Review* (July 2002), 58–60.

34. See Sudarshan Sahoo, "Sudarshan,The King of Wheels" *Orissa Review* (July 2005), 80 (http://magazines.odisha.gov.in/Orissareview/jul2005/engpdf/sudarshan_the_king_of_wheel.pdf).

35. Alternatively, these Deities are sometimes called Lakṣmī and Viśvadhātrī (Sarasvatī), the wives of Lord Jagannāth, and they are placed to his right and left, respectively.

36. Sometimes a Deity known as Madan-Mohan (also called Govinda) is counted among the Deities on the main altar, though he is more often than not only worshipped in a nearby shrine. Occasionally, however, he is placed on the main altar for specific reasons of worship. A small Deity of Krishna playing on his flute, Madan-Mohan is the "*vijaya-vigraha*" of Jagannāth. That is, he is a small temple Deity who participates in festivals on behalf of the larger Deity, who is generally too large to bring out of the temple, except for major celebrations.

37. Says Vaishnava historian and scholar Sundarananda Vidyavinoda, "According to the *Mādalā-pāñjī*, the Bhoga Mandap was built in the seventh year of Puruṣottamadeva's reign, the kitchen in the ninth year. . . . The kitchen used to be attached to the east of the main temple building, but smoke would enter the temple to the great inconvenience of Lord Jagannāth. The former structure was also felt to be too small. As a result, a much larger kitchen was constructed during the reign of Dibyasingha Deva (1690–1713). It was built from donations of Rajendra Raya under the auspices of the minister Govinda Mahapatra." See *Śrī Kṣetra: Vaikuṇṭha on Earth* (compiled by Śrīpāda Sundarānanda Vidyāvinoda, produced and published by Īśvara dāsa, translated by Bhumipati dāsa), op. cit., 42. There are local devotees who eat

fish and other nonvegetarian foods as well, since coastal fishing is indigenous to the area and natural to the inhabitants, but these are never offered at the temple and are considered inferior to the Lord's *prasādam*.

38. Panda Saroj Kumar, *The Kitchen of Srimandir: Biggest in the World* (Bhubaneswar: Department of Information and Public Relations, Government of Odisha, 2006), 80–81.

39. Parts of the above section are adapted from *Śrī Kṣetra: Vaikuṇṭha on Earth* (Compiled by Śrīpāda Sundarānanda Vidyāvinoda, produced and published by Īśvara dāsa, translated by Bhumipati dāsa), op. cit., 57–58; See too Parama Karuna Devi and Rahul Acharya, *Puri, the Home of Lord Jagannatha*, op. cit., 225.

40. See *Caitanya-caritāmṛta*, Antya 16, 50–53. It should also be mentioned that the very first Ratha-yātrā was performed by Prahlāda Mahārāja, Lord Nṛsiṁha's great devotee, in the earliest of world ages: "In the *Bhaviṣya Purāṇa* it is mentioned that in Satya-yuga, Prahlāda first performed Ratha-yātrā. He placed a Deity of Mahāvishnu on a *ratha* and pulled that chariot along. Then the *devatās*, demigods, *siddhas* and *gandharvas* performed Ratha-yātrā. It is also found that in ancient times in the month of Kārtika, on a particular day, there was Ratha-yātrā of Krishna." See Gour Govinda Swami Mahārāja, *The Confidential Meaning of Ratha-Yātrā* (Bhubaneswar, India, Tattva Vicara Publications, 1994), 13. The latter story, which includes a more proper Ratha-yātrā, involving Krishna in the mood of Vrindavan, is elaborated upon in Gour Govinda Swami Mahārāja, *Three Logs of Wood*, excerpted from *The Embankment of Separation* (Bhubaneswar, Orissa: Gopal Jiu Publications, 2004).

41. See A. Eschmann, "The Vaiṣṇava Typology of Hinduization and the Origin of Jagannātha," in Anncharlott Eschmann Hermann Kulke, Gaya Charan Tripathi, eds., *The Cult of Jagannath and the Regional Tradition of Orissa* (South Asia Institute, 1978; Delhi: Manohar, 1986), 112–13. For more on the intimate and yet often understated connection between Nṛsiṁha and Jagannāth, see Sara M. Addams, "From Narasiṁha to Jagannātha," in *Journal of Vaishnava Studies* 17.1, Fall 2008, 5–28.

42. Many temples in India have strict policies regarding non-Hindus and foreigners, not allowing them entrance under any circumstances. Most notorious among these temples is the one in Purī. This is especially confounding because Jagannāth is known as "Lord of the Universe." Why would a universal Lord not accommodate all living beings? Why would a divinity with such an all-encompassing reach not allow certain entities within his domain? Why would the Supreme Father reject any of his children? Yet history relates that the Jagannāth temple has been guilty of this atrocity for generations. Even early in its history, the temple's informal policy was to disallow low-caste people, Muslims, visitors from other countries, and non-Hindus. It was an unofficial social custom based on the caste system. With British domination, a law was enacted against "foreigners" that exacerbated the situation. The official regulation began in 1803 while Odisha was under Maratha rule and continued until Indian independence in 1947. Just prior to Indian independence, Mahatma Gandhi and others began protesting on behalf of the lower castes to be allowed inside the Jagannāth Mandir and other temples of India. Accordingly, in 1948 lower castes were finally admitted into the temple, but the practice of barring various other sections of society continued. This included injunctions against the entry of foreigners. But the obvious

question continued to loom large: Who is a true foreigner? Who is a true Hindu? Devotees—whether born in India or abroad—should not, according to Vaishnava philosophy, be considered foreigners, for they are Jagannāth's own. Thus, on principle, A. C. Bhaktivedānta Swami Prabhupāda, the founder of ISKCON, refused to go into Lord Jagannāth's temple when he visited Purī in January, 1977. Why? Because his disciples were not allowed to enter. They, too, he said, were devotees, and thus "foreigners" only in an external sense. But at the time his protest fell largely on deaf ears. Nonetheless, on July 5, 2018, the Supreme Court of India made a formal request to the management of the Jagannāth temple, asking them to allow, "every visitor irrespective of his faith, to offer respects and to make offerings to the deity." While this is a promising development, time will tell if the longstanding tradition changes. For more, See Madhavananda Das, "Jagannath Puri Dham: Two Opposites in One Container," in *Journal of Vaishnava Studies 27, no. 1 (Fall 2018), 123–5*6.

43. For more on the Ratha-yātrā festival, particularly its inner meaning, see Gour Govinda Swami Mahārāja, *The Confidential Meaning of Ratha-Yātrā*, op. cit.; Śrī Śrīmad Bhaktivedānta Nārāyaṇa Mahārāja, *The Origin of Ratha-yātrā* (Vrindavan: Gaudiya Vedanta Publications, 2003); Bhakti Puruṣottama Swami, *The Mystery of Ratha Yātrā* (Kolkata: ISKCON Mayapur, 2015); Subas Pani, *Ratha Yatra: Chariot Festival of Sri Jagannatha in Puri* (New Delhi: Niyogi Books, 2017).

44. The carts themselves are not ordinary. They are considered a manifestation of Lord Balarāma. Just as the Balarāma Deity is a manifestation of *sandhinī-śakti*, as mentioned earlier, the cart is considered concentrated *sandhinī-śakti* as well. *Sandhinī-śakti* is also known as *dhāraṇa-śakti*, i.e., *dhāraṇa* means "to carry" or "to hold"—it is the existential potency of the Lord that carries the Lord or facilitates His movement in various ways. Therefore, the *ratha* is considered a manifestation of this energy, since it "carries" the Lord during the Ratha-yātrā festival. For more, see Bhakti Puruṣottama Swami, *The Mystery of Ratha Yātrā*, op. cit., 26.

45. Vishnu-jana Mahārāja, a charismatic ISKCON *sannyāsin* in the 1970s, gave a lecture at one of the movement's early Ratha-yātrā festivals in San Francisco (1974). There, he spoke of "pulling Krishna back into one's heart by pulling the Ratha-yātrā ropes" (http://iskconleaders.com/ratha-yatra-lecture-by-vishnujana-swami/). His words echoed that of Bhaktisiddhānta Sarasvatī, who wrote much earlier in a *Sajjana-toṣaṇī* article (Vol. 28, No. 2, July, 1930): "Śrī Chaitanya is delighted, therefore, when He finds the Lord moving towards Śrī Guṇḍicā, which is no other than the heart of the devotee."

The idea of why there are three chariots as opposed to just one has also been explained in the Gauḍīya tradition: There is a phenomenon called *rasa-viparyāya* (a contradiction in moods). Because Rādhikā and the Vraja-gopīs would never meet with Krishna in the presence of Balarāma or Subhadrā, they travel separately. Balarāma leads the way and is followed next by Subhadrā. Krishna cannot act as a lover when surrounded by his brother and sister. See Srila Bhakti Vijnana Bharati Maharaja, "Ratha-yātrā Q and A" (https://www.visuddhacaitanyavani.com/single-post/2018/07/12/Ratha-yatra-QnA).

46. "In the early fourteenth century, Franciscan missionary Friar Odoric brought to Europe the story of an enormous carriage that carried an image of the Hindu god

Vishnu (whose title was Jagannath, literally, 'lord of the world') through the streets of India in religious processions. Odoric reported that some worshippers deliberately allowed themselves to be crushed beneath the vehicle's wheels as a sacrifice to Vishnu. That story was probably an exaggeration or misinterpretation of actual events, but it spread throughout Europe anyway. The tale caught the imagination of English listeners, and by the nineteenth century, they were using *juggernaut* to refer to any massive vehicle (such as a steam locomotive) or to any other enormous entity with powerful crushing capabilities." See "Juggernaut-Definition and Meaning." *Merriam Webster Dictionary* (https://www.merriam-webster.com/dictionary/juggernaut).

47. The sweeping of the road should not be conflated with another cleaning ceremony that occurs just before the day of Ratha-yātrā: Guṇḍicā-marjana, the cleaning of the Guṇḍicā temple. This is in preparation for Lord Jagannāth's arrival—the destination of the Ratha-yātrā carts (symbolizing Vrindavan). Mahāprabhu set the example by cleaning this temple with his own hands, in the association of his loving devotees. The subtext is that by such cleaning the practitioner cleans his own heart. Cleaning the temple, in other words, is a metaphor for inner purification, for cleansing the consciousness in such a way that the Lord feels comfortable taking residence there. Mahāprabhu, in fact, cleaned the temple twice. He used his own garment and rubbed the floor and every other area of the temple profusely, diligently, so that no spot would be left untouched. This, he taught, is how seriously one should take inner purification. See *Caitanya-caritāmṛta* Madhya 1.

48. In Mahāprabhu's time, it was Mahārāja Pratāparudra who was the king who swept the road. (See *Caitanya-caritāmṛta* 2.13.15–18). He is mentioned in all of Śrī Chaitanya's sacred biographies as well as in secular historical records. For example, Prabhat Mukherjee, a noted scholar of Odishan history, has written several books on the Chaitanya tradition, touching on Maharaja Pratāparudra's genealogy and political career. Such historical accounts tell us that the wise king Purushottam Deva ruled Odisha until 1497, when he was succeeded by Pratāparudra, who ruled until 1540, about seven years after Śrī Chaitanya returned to his eternal abode. Following the tradition of kings in his line, Pratāparudra accepted the titles Gajapati and Gaudeshwar. His empire extended from the Ganges in Bengal to Karnataka, with his capital city in Cuttack, Odisha. Documents of the Jagannāth temple inform us that even before meeting Śrī Chaitanya, Pratāparudra followed the custom of sweeping the road before Lord Jagannāth's chariot. It has continued ever since. See Jan Brzezinski, "Pratāparudra Deva and Krishna Chaitanya," in *Journal of Vaishnava Studies* 17, no. 1 (Fall 2008), 123–52. Also see Satyarāja Dāsa, Mahārāja Pratāparudra: Humble Servant in Kingly Dress" (http://www.krishna.com/maharaja-prataparudra-humble-servant-kingly-dress).

49. The Deities stay at Guṇḍicā Ghar for seven days, though it is usually counted as nine, because of the days involving their journey to and fro. Except for these nine days, when Jagannāth is worshipped in Guṇḍicā Ghar, the temple is empty, without worship throughout the year. The shrine is named after King Indradyumna's wife, Guṇḍicā, whose devotion was considered "secret," "concealed," or "esoteric"—all synonyms for the word *guṇḍicā* itself. Because of her concealed devotion, some say, Jagannāth promised to visit her home during Ratha-yātrā, and that tradition continues

to the present day. The shrine is also called *guṇḍicā* because of the esoteric nature of what the temple represents—Vrindavan. While there are numerous festivals held at Guṇḍicā Ghar during the Ratha-yātrā celebrations, and we will mention Hera Pañcamī below, the reenactment of Rāsa-līlā, or the sacred Round-dance of Krishna and the *gopīs*, is perhaps most significant for the Gauḍīya tradition. This, again, is because the tradition views Ratha-yātrā as a pretext for the meeting of Rādhā and Krishna after a long separation. At Guṇḍicā Ghar, Jagannāth is brought into the Rāsa-maṇḍapa where *Gīta Govinda* verses are sung for his pleasure. In days of old, the Devadasis would sing these songs, bringing the verses to life with dramatic performance. But now ordinary temple priests and other devotees chant and recreate the performances according to their abilities. See Pika Ghosh, *Temple to Love: Architecture and Devotion in Seventeenth-Century Bengal* (Bloomington: Indiana University Press, 2005), 49.

50. This is not to be confused with an incident that occurs several days before Ratha-yātrā, where the Lord displays a pastime of being "sick" for a total of fifteen days. There is an esoteric reason for this pastime called Rukmiṇī-haraṇa, or Rukmiṇī-vivāha. This occurs inside the Jagannāth temple, where, though unknown to many, the priests wed Lord Jagannāth (Vishnu, Krishna) to the Goddess Lakṣmī (Rukmiṇī) in an elaborate ceremony. Four days later, the devotees celebrate Snāna-Pūrṇimā, wherein Lord Jagannāth has a public bathing festival. This bathing ceremony commemorates the original installation of Lord Jagannāth in Satya-yuga. At the time, King Indradyumna engaged the demigod, Lord Brahmā, in the installation process, and because this was the beginning of Lord Jagannāth's manifestation in this world, it is often viewed as His "birthday" celebration.

After this bath, using hundreds of pots of water, Lord Jagannāth falls "sick" and goes into seclusion to regain his health. This is called *anavasara*. During this period the newly wedded Lakṣmī acts as the ideal wife, and for the next fifteen days she doesn't sleep and instead prefers to nurse her beloved husband back to health. Finally, due to exhaustion, her eyes close, at which point her newly married husband quietly leaves to secretly meet Rādhārāṇī and the other Vraja-gopīs. He mounts his cart and takes off to meet his lover of old, Rādhikā. This is the inner prequel to the Jagannāth Ratha-yātrā festival. Adapted from Madhavananda Das, "Understanding the Return Ratha-Yatra," Part 1 (https://www.facebook.com/notes/madhavananda-n-krishnakund/understanding-the-return-ratha-yatra-part-1-of-2/10153984017599340/).

Another important festival involving the Lord's wife, Lakṣmī, is called Hera Pañcamī. On the fifth day of the Chariot Festival, while the Lord, along with his brother and sister, is at Guṇḍicā (Vrindavan), Lakṣmī becomes worried and thinks, "Where is my husband? He told me, 'I am going for a change of environment after some days of being sick, and I will soon return.' But it has been five days now, and still He has not come back." Externally, Jagannāth offers the above excuse, but in fact he wants to leave Purī to go to Guṇḍicā, for there he will see Rādhā. Lakṣmī decides to go to Guṇḍicā to call his bluff. She travels on a beautifully decorated palanquin, complete with a colorful procession that is recreated to this day. The devotees taking part in the procession sing a famous Hera Pañcamī song, in which the Goddess's anger towards her husband is expressed. She knows what he is doing there in "Vrindavan." And *he* knows her anger. Thus, Lord Jagannāth, anticipating her arrival, asks his servitors to quickly bolt the doors. Lakṣmī feels insulted, and to teach her husband a lesson, she breaks a part of his Ratha-yātrā cart on her way home. The entire episode, of course, is *līlā*, or mystical sport, meant to show how much Lakṣmīdevī loves the Lord, and how much he is willing to sacrifice to meet with Rādhikā at Guṇḍicā.

51. The Ulta-Ratha-yātrā ("return journey," also called Bahuda-yātrā) is a complex subject. Mahāprabhu without doubt took part in this journey, as is clear from the *Caitanya-caritāmṛta* (Madhya 14.244–45). Madhavananda Das even describes Mahāprabhu's ecstasy during this second part of the festival (https://ebooks.iskcondesiretree.com/pdf/Jagannath_Rath_Yatra/Understanding_the_Return_Ratha_Yatra_Part-02.pdf).

Generally, however, the return journey is deemphasized in the Gauḍīya tradition. Vaishnava stalwart Bhakti Vijñāna Bharati Mahārāja says that it is not a proper mood for Gauḍīyas. Why? The Gauḍīyas are interested in uniting Rādhā and Krishna. The journey to Guṇḍicā represents such unity, whereas returning to the Jagannāth temple reflects his leaving Rādhā and returning to Lakṣmī, at least superficially. See Srila Bhakti Vijnana Bharati Maharaja, "Ratha-yātrā Q and A" (https://www.visuddhacaitanyavani.com/single-post/2018/07/12/Ratha-yatra-QnA). An additional point about the ending of the festival is that Lakṣmī is incensed when Jagannāth finally arrives at home, at the Śrī Mandir. She initially denies him entrance but compassionately acquiesces because of their deep love. It is also said that when Lakṣmī meets him at the temple gate, she throws magical powder on him, making him forget his joyful interaction with Rādhā at the Guṇḍicā Ghar. See Pika Ghosh, *Temple To Love: Architecture And Devotion In Seventeenth-Century Bengal*, op. cit., pp. 49–50.

52. See Ravīndra Svarūpa Dāsa (William Deadwyler), "Lord Chaitanya at Ratha-yātrā," originally published in *Back to Godhead* 19, no. 8 (July 1984) (See http://www.krishna.com/lord-chaitanya-ratha-yatra). It was reprinted under the same name in *Journal of Vaishnava Studies* 17, no. 1 (Fall 2008): 43–56. The truths expressed in this inset quote are at the heart of Gauḍīya Vaishnava mysticism. There is a related story concerning an important verse that Mahāprabhu would regularly chant at the Ratha-yātrā festival every summer. Only His intimate associate Svarūpa Dāmodara Gosvāmī knew the purpose behind this verse and why the Lord chanted it. The verse, drawn from a popular love song at the time, basically expressed the dissatisfaction of a woman in love. She bemoaned the fact that her lover was just not the same, even though many of the externals were still in place. It is a verse that comes to us through Rūpa Gosvāmī's *Padyāvali* (386), and is repeated in both Krishnadāsa Kavirāja Gosvāmī's *Caitanya-caritāmṛta* (Madhya 1.58, 13.121, Antya 1.78) and Jīva Gosvāmī's *Gopāla-campu* (Uttara-campu 36.122), where we are told that the verse was originally uttered by Śrīmatī Rādhārāṇī. After some time, Śrī Rūpa showed awareness of Mahāprabhu's intent in uttering this verse by composing a parallel verse to elucidate its inner meaning: "My dear friend," writes Śrī Rūpa, in the voice of Śrīmatī Rādhārāṇī, "now I have met My very old and dear friend Krishna on this field of Kurukṣetra. I am the same Rādhārāṇī, and now We are meeting together. It is very pleasant, but I would still like to go to the bank of the Kālindī River beneath the trees of the forest there. I wish to hear the vibration of His sweet flute playing the fifth note within that forest of Vrindavan" (Antya 1.79). Śrī Rūpa's verse, to be

clear, is a reenactment and development of *Bhāgavata Purāṇa* 10.82, with additional Gauḍīya nuance. The *Bhāgavata* discusses Krishna's reunion with Śrī Rādhā and the *gopīs* at Kurukṣetra, but only briefly. Śrī Rūpa ingeniously makes use of this to explain the verse chanted by Śrī Chaitanya, thus revealing the Lord's inner intent: Śrī Chaitanya was in the mood of Śrīmatī Rādhārāṇī, and, seeing Jagannāth with all his opulence and kingly brilliance, longed to bring him back to the simple rustic mood of Vrindavan.

53. See Chaitanya Charana Dasa "Rathayatra: When the Lord Comes Out, Let's Invite Him In" in *Back to Godhead* 49, no. 4 (July/August 2015) (http://btg.krishna.com/rathayatra-when-lord-comes-out-let's-invite-him). It should also be mentioned that Śrī Chaitanya enjoyed many pastimes at the Ratha-yātrā festival, often exhibiting miraculous feats of devotion. Several will suffice: Once, during this massive celebration, the cart, moving down the road to Guṇḍicā Ghar, suddenly stopped. No one was able to move it. All the assembled devotees tried with their combined strength to not only pull it with its attached massive ropes, but also to push it forward from behind. But their endeavor proved unsuccessful. The gigantic elephants of Purī's royal house were brought in, but they, too, failed to move the cart. Everyone present was bewildered by this inexplicable course of events, not knowing what to do. Just then, Mahāprabhu arrived and placed his head up against the immovable cart. Applying minimal pressure, the enormous vehicle finally moved forward, to everyone's astonishment. Thousands of devotees shouted "Haribol!" in appreciation of Śrī Chaitanya's miracle. (See *Caitanya-caritāmṛta*, Madhya 13.189–90.)

Similarly, once, at Ratha-yātrā, Śrī Caitanya expanded himself into seven forms so that he could dance in the various chanting parties simultaneously. These expansions were visible only to the pure devotees who were present, including King Pratāparudra. (See *Caitanya-caritāmṛta,* Madhya 13.52.) This miracle is recorded in the *Caitanya-caritāmṛta* and has become a famous part of the Purī tradition. Mahāprabhu's loving interaction with Lord Jagannāth and his transcendentally memorable activities at the yearly Ratha-yātrā festival are the stuff of legend, inspirational to devotees worldwide, both now and throughout history. There is much more to tell about this sublime subject, but this would require a separate volume.

54. See Akinchana Priyabandhu Das, "Lord Jagannatha's Ratha-yatra Worldwide" 50–59 (http://magazines.odisha.gov.in/Srimandir/srimandirenglish/Epdf/Ech15.pdf). Das notes that in 1877 Bhaktivinoda was bestowed the honor of becoming a member of the Royal Asiatic Society for his booklet "Maths of Orissa" (1860, English prose). More on Bhaktivinoda's work in Odisha is mentioned in Fakir Mohan Dās, *Choti, the Native Place of Śrīla Ṭhākura Bhaktivinoda* (Bhubaneswar: Gopl Jiu Publications, 1999).

55. See Shukavak N. Dasa, *Hindu Encounter with Modernity: Kedarnath Datta Bhaktivinoda, Vaishnava Theologian* (Los Angeles: Sanskrit Religions Institute, 1999), 89–92.

56. See Bhaktivinoda Ṭhākura, "Nityadharma Suryodoy," in *Sajjana-toṣaṇī* 4.3, 1885, 8–10. Although Bhaktivinoda had long since passed from this world, his prophetic words—anticipating a time when "English, French, Russian, German and American people will take up banners, *mṛdangas* and *karatālas* and raise

kīrtana through their streets and towns"—indeed came to pass. When Śrīla A. C. Bhaktivedānta Swami Prabhupāda brought Mahāprabhu's mission to Western shores in 1965, such international *kīrtana* became a reality that would have no doubt pleased both Bhaktivinoda and Mahāprabhu himself.

57. In 1933, Sarasvatī Ṭhākura's disciples, Bhakti Pradīpa Tīrtha Mahārāja, Bhakti Hridaya Bon (Vāna) Mahārāja, Bhakti Saraṅga Goswāmī, and Sambidānanda Dās set sail for Western shores and, that very summer, introduced Śrī Chaitanya's teachings to the King and Queen of England, among other prominent dignitaries. Soon afterwards, the first Western *ashram* appeared in London, and, soon after that, in Berlin. For more on this initial journey of Vaishnavism to the West, see Steven J. Rosen, *Śrī Chaitanya's Life and Teachings: The Golden Avatāra of Divine Love* (Lanham, MD: Lexington Books, 2017), 193–207.

58. Bhaktisiddhānta Sarasvatī Ṭhākura, *Paramārthi*, February, 1976 (Cuttack: Sacchidananda Math), 34. This monthly magazine is the Odiya version of the *Harmonist*, initially published in the time of Sarasvatī Ṭhākura. The article was reprinted in 1976. Special thanks to Madhavananda Das for bringing this essay to my attention.

59. See Bhakti Vikasa Swami, *Śri Bhaktisiddhānta Vaibhava*, Volume Two (Surat, India: Bhakti Vikas Trust, 2010), 21. There are interesting reasons that Jagannāth is known as "Patita-pāvana," a title shared only with Śrī Chaitanya bimself: Although Lord Jagannāth is ensconced on his altar for most of the year, he ventures out to bestow his mercy on the masses. Ratha-yātrā is thus a symbol of his mercy and one of the reasons he is known as the savior of the fallen. The flag at the top of the temple, too, near the Nīla Cakra, is called *Patita-pāvana*, for seeing it is considered equal to seeing the Deities. That is Lord Jagannāth's mercy.

Additionally, near the "Lion Gate" of the temple there is an image of Jagannāth on the right side of the doorway. This form of Patita-pāvana is in sculptural relief and situated on his own small altar, which is akin to a box with a gate on it. He is by himself, without his usual accompaniment, and he is just a huge face, sans other bodily parts, making him unique among Jagannāth Deities. He is not carved from wood but is made of frankincense, sandalwood paste, natural camphor, resin, scented oils from *aguru* and *chua* plants, and fragrant musk (https://www.scribd.com/document/222650950/Kk-13-Patita-pavana-Pp-6–9). This form of the Lord is traditionally referred to as Patita-pāvana as well, for here the Lord can even be seen while standing outside of the temple. Low-caste pilgrims and untouchables—the special recipients of the Lord's mercy—though not allowed inside, could pray to Jagannāth through this manifestation, available for all to see.

On a related note, the Vaishnava journal *Sri Krishna Kathamrta*, no. 13, focuses on why Jagannāth is viewed as "deliverer of the most fallen" (Patita-pāvana). Some of the reasons given in this issue of the *Kathamrta* include that Jagannāth appeared in person for Ramachandra Dev II, the devotee king of Purī who was barred from the temple after being forced to convert to Islam; Kavi Salabeg, the famous Muslim poet who was denied entrance to the temple yet achieved the Lord's special mercy; Dasia Bauri, similarly, was denied entrance due to low birth, but was given Jagannāth's special kindness as a result; and even Aurangzeb, the Muslim ruler infamous in Indian history for his iconoclasm, was given a vision of Jagannāth as a sign of the Lord's special mercy on him.

60. Prabhupāda's letter to Hanuman Prasad Poddar, February 5, 1970. In *Srila Prabhupada Sikshamrita*, Vol. 3, p. 2,047 (Los Angeles: Bhaktivedanta Book Trust, 1992).

61. See Steven J. Rosen, *Swamiji: An Early Disciple, Brahmananda Dasa, Remembers His Guru* (Badger, CA: Torchlight publishing, 2014), 67–68.

62. For the entire Mālatī/ Jagannāth story, see Shyamasundar das, *Chasing Rhinos With The Swami—Volume 1* (Self-published, 2016), 117–20.

63. Other early Deities in ISKCON would include Kārtamīśa (whom devotees called "the boss"), alternatively pronounced Kartamaśāyī, Kartā Mahāśaya, and Kārtamaśī. He was a small, piercing-blue figurine of Krishna, his left hand gently placed on his hip. While early ISKCON devotees became quite fond of him, he was never installed according to traditional Vaishnava practice, though he was briefly placed on the altar in San Francisco, even before Jagannāth arrived. Then, too, there were the small metal Rādhā-Krishna images now revered in New York, worshipped alongside the large and resplendent Rādhā-Govinda; these smaller forms were Śrīla Prabhupāda's personal Deities and were installed in New York in April, 1968. Śrī Śrī Rādhā-Madana-Mohan, the beautiful Deities currently worshipped at the ISKCON center in Potomac, Maryland, near Washington, DC, were among the first as well, and while they had a presence at 26 Second Avenue (the first ISKCON temple) even before Lord Jagannāth arrived in San Francisco, they were not installed until the summer of 1973. The Jagannāth Deities were the first who were properly installed and worshipped at an ISKCON temple, on the West Coast. Additionally, Prabhupāda promptly asked Śyāmasundara to make Jagannāth Deities for his temple on the East Coast as well, which Śyāmasundara did, and the Deities were shipped there post haste.

64. "In the four *yugas* (world age cycles)—Satya, Tretā, Dvāpara and Kali—the Lord incarnates in four colors: white, red, black and yellow, respectively. These are the colors of the incarnations in different millenniums." See *Caitanya-caritāmṛta,* Madhya 20.330.

65. For the Jagannāth Deities' racial connection, see Bijoy M Misra, "Shri Krishna Jagannatha: The Mushali-parva from Sarala's *Mahabharata*," in Edwin F. Bryant (ed.), *Krishna: A Sourcebook*, op. cit., 140. See also Manoj Panda, "Jagannatha and Shakti" in Orissa Society of Americas 34th Annual Convention Souvenir: For Annual Convention Held in 2003 at Princeton, New Jersey, re-published as Golden Jubilee Convention July 4–7, 2019 Atlantic City, New Jersey commemorative edition (New Jersey: Odisha Society of the Americas, 2019), 108.

Chapter Six

The Country Charm of Śrī Śrī Rādhā-Vrindaban Chandra

Throughout history, Vaishnava sages have highlighted a distinction between God's majestic feature (*aiśvarya*) and his more intimate, down-home dimension (*mādhurya*), his awesome and powerful nature versus his loving and sweet side. In Indian theological texts, this distinction usually points to Vishnu, as representative of the former, and Krishna, as the epitome of the latter.

Both aspects are necessary in terms of God's completeness—a well-rounded divinity would exhibit both power and charm, majesty and simplicity. However, it is his sweeter side that more thoroughly defines who he is on the deepest of levels: God can be identified with love more readily than with might, his kindness and gentleness are more central to his essential nature than strength or invincibility—though having all these qualities, no doubt, is what makes him God.

When Krishna descended to earth some five thousand years ago, say the Vaishnava sages, he appeared in his original form in Vrindavan,[1] India, which, at the time, was a simple, countrylike village. As he grew in years, he displayed additional pastimes in nearby Mathurā, and here we see him moving toward a more city-oriented atmosphere, even if still largely part of the spiritual greenbelt. Finally, for the latter part of his manifested pastimes, we find him in Dwarka, a metropolis of profound proportions, where he resided in palaces with numerous queens, living a life of royalty.

For the perceptive reader—under the guidance of teachers in disciplic succession—what unfolds in these three glimpses of the Supreme are the various dimensions of God, from his primary form as a youthful and loving cowherd to a secondary manifestation as a complex and royal personage, reflecting majesty and gravitas, yet equally divine.

But not equal on all levels. While Krishna in Vrindavan and Krishna in Mathurā and Dwarka are the same in terms of *tattva* (truth), i.e., they are but various faces of the same divine entity, they are different in terms of *rasa* (or the relationship of intimacy that one might have with them). Vishnu, as already suggested, is worshipped with great reverence, as is Krishna in Dwarka. But Krishna in Vrindavan is another matter: He is intimate and playful, exhibiting a simplicity and loving nature that are in fact representative of his overarching raison d'être, to shower his dedicated practitioners with devotion.

Among the ISKCON Deities established by Śrīla Prabhupāda, Śrī Śrī Rādhā-Vrindaban Chandra—lovingly worshipped in the Appalachian hills of West Virginia, in a town now called "New Vrindaban"—have been singled out by the Guru himself. Why did he praise them so highly? While there are no doubt many reasons, Prabhupāda pointed first and foremost to their simple, unabashed beauty, which is considerable—and fully reflecting their countrified (read: Vrindavan-like) aura.

Indeed, there is a famous story in which Prabhupāda, in conversation with a number of disciples, says as much, securing these particular Deities a special place in the hearts of devotees worldwide:

> Kulaśekhara: Śrīla Prabhupāda, I think Radha-Vrindaban Chandra are more beautiful than the Deities in London.
>
> Prabhupāda: Oh, yes. (laughter) London differently.
>
> Kulaśekhara: They are very beautiful, but Radha Vrindaban Chandra . . .
>
> Prabhupāda: Vrindaban Chandra is village beauty, and He is London beauty. He is town beauty.
>
> Kulaśekhara: I have not seen more beautiful anywhere than Radha-Vrindaban Chandra. The jewelry . . .
>
> Prabhupāda: No. Every one is beautiful, but everyone praise [sic] our London Deity.
>
> Kīrtanānanda: They have not seen Radha-Vrindaban Chandra yet.
>
> Prabhupāda: Hmm?
>
> Kīrtanānanda: They have not seen yet Radha-Vrindaban Chandra.
>
> Prabhupāda: No, they have seen the picture.[2]

In the above exchange, Prabhupāda does not, as they say, take the bait. His disciple Kulaśekhara—who, notably, lived in New Vrindaban—tries to get him to speak in favor of Rādhā-Vrindaban Chandra as the most beautiful of Deities, and while the Master acknowledges the truth of Kulaśekhara's statement, he takes it further, indicating that Krishna is *always* beautiful. Prabhupāda says, "Vrindaban Chandra is village beauty, and He [Rādhā London-Īśvara] is London beauty. He is town beauty."

This harkens to the Gauḍīya Vaishnava distinction between *aiśvarya* and *mādhurya*, i.e., city and country, power and pleasing, as described above. Still, it should be underlined that by worshipping such Deities—whether urban or rustic—one can enter into the mysteries of Bhakti-yoga and thereby achieve the highest levels of Krishna Consciousness, regardless of external considerations. In this chapter, we will briefly offer our readers some background on the very special country Deities, Rādhā Vrindaban Chandra, to whom Prabhupada here refers, along with more universal applications of *aiśvarya* and *mādhurya*.[3]

NEW VRINDABAN: AN INTRODUCTION

Vṛndāvana is Krishna's paradise in the spiritual world, the kingdom of God described in the ancient wisdom texts of India. As mentioned above, a replica of this realm exists even today as a village in the Mathurā district of Uttar Pradesh, where Krishna is said to have walked the Earth some five thousand years ago. This seemingly material domain is considered non-different from Vṛndāvana in the spiritual world, a sort of transcendental embassy for conditioned souls to return to him when and if they qualify themselves, a portal through which one returns "home."

Interestingly, soon after Śrīla Prabhupāda arrived in the West, in 1965, he envisioned yet another replication of Vrindavan—a third one, known as New Vrindaban.[4]

This Western counterpart evolved through the agency of two early disciples, Kīrtanānanda Swami and Hayagrīva Dāsa, who spearheaded the community in the early days of the movement. In the winter of 1968 the two disciples saw a newspaper article by Richard Rose, a landowner with spiritual leanings. The article mentioned that he was looking for people to create an ashram in Marshall County, West Virginia. "The conception is one of a non-profit, non-interfering, non-denominational retreat or refuge," read the article, as if directed by Krishna, "where philosophers might come to work communally together, or independently, where a library and other facilities might be developed."[5]

Several months later, Kīrtanānanda and Hayagrīva, who, for various reasons, had temporarily developed a strained relationship with Śrīla Prabhupāda, set out on their own to visit the land. They negotiated with the owner and reached a temporary agreement. Kīrtanānanda settled there for a few months in a farmhouse in the woods, and Hayagrīva would go back and forth to Ohio, where he was employed as an adjunct English professor.

That summer, Kīrtanānanda and Hayagrīva visited Prabhupāda in Canada to make amends. His Divine Grace "forgave his renegade disciples in Montreal with a garland of roses and a shower of tears."[6] With Prabhupāda's approval, they returned to West Virginia and leased the property. A month later, Prabhupāda wrote to them, "Now we can work with great enthusiasm for constructing a New Vrindaban in the United States of America."[7]

It was while in Canada, in fact, that Kīrtanānanda and Hayagrīva visited a store and procured Jagannāth Deities. "While they were there in Montreal," writes New Vrindaban historian Chaitanya Maṅgala Dāsa, "they went to an Indian import shop, found those Deities, purchased Them and brought Them back to the original farm house of New Vrindaban, today called 'Old Vrindaban' by the devotees who live there. That was the first set of Deities on the property. They appeared in July of 1968."[8]

Less than two months later, before summer's end, New Vrindaban would acquire a second set of Deities. This time, they were small brass forms of Rādhā and Krishna (as opposed to Lord Jagannāth),[9] Deities that would eventually be called "little" Rādhā-Vrindaban Chandra, in anticipation of the larger Lordships yet to come.

What had happened is this: Śrīla Prabhupāda had instructed Brahmānanda and Gargamuni, two brothers who were among his leading disciples, to visit New Vrindaban, to see how his fledgling farm community was coming along. Accordingly, the brothers rented a VW Bug and took the long trek from New York to West Virginia soon after receiving Prabhupāda's instructions. While there, Kīrtanānanda and Hayagrīva gave them a thorough tour of the property, and as a result the brothers reported back to Śrīla Prabhupāda with great enthusiasm.

Consequently, Prabhupāda asked Brahmānanda to write a letter to all of ISKCON (on September 7, 1968)—a handful of temples at the time—inviting them to support the endeavor and, if possible, to take up residence there. Thus, New Vrindaban was established as an indelible part of Prabhupāda's movement.

But in our present context, the significant point is this: It was during this same period that Kīrtanānanda and Hayagrīva visited Śrīla Prabhupāda in New York, since he had just been apprised of how successful New Vrindaban was becoming, and while there the guru gave them further instruction on how to move forward with their burgeoning farm community. Whatever he told them, we know one thing for certain: Upon returning to New Vrindaban they brought back with them the little set of bell-metal Rādhā-Krishna Deities mentioned above, placing them alongside the beautiful Jagannāth Deities in the old farmhouse on the initial property.

Soon after, Śrīla Prabhupāda wrote to Kīrtanānanda, referring to an early ill-fated trip to India in 1967, in which Kīrtanānanda would have to return West prematurely: "Because you went to Vrindavan, but circumstantially you could not live there and you left, Krishna has now given you New Vrindaban and, out of His good will, He has come to you. It is very surprising. So please welcome these Deities and install Them on a nice throne."[10]

Further, among the several farm projects/rural communities started by Śrīla Prabhupāda in the early days of the movement, only New Vrindaban was given the mandate to build replicas of Vrindavan's holy places: "There will be seven principle temples, namely, Govinda, Gopinatha, Madana-Mohana, Syamasundara, Radha Ramana, Radha-Damodara, and Gokulananda."[11] The idea, in essence, was to re-create Vrindavan in the West.

THE FORESTS OF BRAJ[12]

The devotees of New Vrindaban took this mandate to heart, trying to recapture the mood of Vrindavan in their humble Western hamlet. One of the ways they sought to do this was to name the various farms of New Vrindaban after the twelve forests of Vrindavan: Madhuvana, Tālavana, Kumudavana, Kāmyavana, Bahulāvana, Bhadravana, Khadiravana, Mahāvana, Lohajaṅghavana (Lohavana), Bilvavana, Bhāṇḍīravana, and Vṛndāvana.[13] Thus, each time new farmland was purchased in the New Vrindaban area, augmenting the original property, the devotees would christen it with a new name, just to remind them of Vrindavan in both India and the spiritual world.

Śrīla Prabhupāda comments on the twelve forests in his purport to *Caitanya-caritāmṛta* 2.17.193: "Vṛndāvana is the name given to the forest where Śrīmatī Vṛndā-devī (Tulasī-devī) grows profusely. There are twelve such *vanas* in Vṛndāvana. Some are located on the western side of the Yamunā and others on the eastern side. The forests situated on the eastern side are Bhadravana, Bilvavana, Lohavana, Bhāṇḍīravana, and Mahāvana. On the western side are Madhuvana, Tālavana, Kumudavana, Bahulāvana, Kāmyavana, Khadiravana, and Vṛndāvana. These are the twelve forests of the Vṛndāvana area."

Lord Chaitanya Mahaprabhu, the *avatāra* of Krishna from some five hundred years ago, himself visited the twelve tracts of land: "Thus I have written a description of the ecstatic love Lord Chaitanya manifested in one of the places he visited while walking through the twelve forests of Vṛndāvana,"

Kṛṣṇadāsa Kavirāja Gosvāmī tells us. "To describe what he experienced there would be impossible."[14] Wandering through these forests while in a heightened state of spiritual awareness bestows nothing less than pure love of God. Indeed, attaining proximity to these forests—even while spiritually immature—can catapult one to higher levels, in which one can experience spiritual ecstasy.

The concept of the twelve forests is deep, and it is perfect for meditation purposes, particularly as one chants *japa*, or the soft regulated chanting that one does on beads. As the Braj historian David L. Haberman writes,

> The path of the journey through the twelve forests is circular. This circular path can be visualized as a *jap-mala,* a wooden-beaded rosary used in India to meditate on a deity. Each site visited on the circular journey represents a "bead" to be fingered and provides an occasion to learn or remember an episode connected with a particular site.[15]

On the highest level, the twelve forests are considered non-different from Krishna himself, and New Vrindaban residents were indeed encouraged to see the Lord in every square acre of land—in West Virginia as much as in its original prototype in India.

The Gauḍīya teacher Nārāyaṇa Bhaṭṭa, who flourished in the time of the Six Gosvāmīs, tells us about the forests' true significance. "The Braj Mandal [Vrindavan] is an essential form of the Lord consisting of organs and limbs," writes Nārāyaṇa Bhaṭṭa in his *Vraja-bhakti-vilāsa.* He describes the various parts of Krishna's body by identifying them with the twelve major forests and other important sites in the Vrindavan area: "Mathura is his heart; Madhuban is his navel; Kumudban and Talban are his two breasts; Vrindavan is his brow; Bahulaban and Mahaban are his two arms; Bhandiraban and Kokilaban are his two legs; Khadiraban and Bhadrikaban are his two shoulders; Chatraban and Lohaban are his two eyes; Belban and Bhadraban are his two ears; Kamaban is his chin; Triveni and Sakhikupaban are his two lips; Svarna and Vihval are his two rows of teeth; Surabhiban is his tongue," and so on.[16] In this way, an entire meditation can be constructed.

This is not to overstate their manifestation in New Vrindaban, which was meant to be a semblance of the original, inspiring devotees to go further in their practice. As land was added to the original New Vrindaban acreage, it seemed like a good idea to use the "ban" (Skt: *vana*, "forest") schema to correlate the new community with its counterpart in India, particularly because Prabhupāda had made the initial connection, asking them to "re-create" Vrindavan in the West. It was not that there were particular reasons for adding these specific names to specific land areas—at least as far as we know—but it did work as a way to identify newer and more fully developed regions, creating moods for each part of New Vrindaban as it developed. Most of all, it reminded the Western devotees of Krishna about Vrindavan and its theological implications, which was their main goal.

And so the original farm (133 acres), leased in 1968, was called, simply, "Vrindaban." The second farm, purchased in 1971, was referred to as Madhuban (ninety acres). Later that same year, a third farm was called Bahulaban (151 acres), and so on throughout the 1970s, with Kadiraban, Mahaban, Talaban, Bilvaban, and Bhadraban, among others, following close behind.[17]

In fact, along these same lines, numerous New Vrindaban locations were named after other regions in the Braj area of India:

- Guruban (comprising 109.4 acres), purchased in 1973, would eventually become the site of Prabhupāda's Palace and Rādhā Vrindaban Chandra's current Temple Complex. (To my knowledge, "Guruban" is unique to the West Virginia manifestation of Vrindavan, without a counterpart in India.)
- Radha Gopinath Mandir (still under construction across from Prabhupāda's Palace)
- Nandagram (farm currently managed by ECO-Vrindaban)
- Radha-kunda (two locations, one at Bahulaban, and another near what is currently identified as Radha Gopinath Mandir)
- Shyama-kunda (two locations, one at Bahulaban, and one near Radha Gopinath Mandir)
- Lalita-kunda (near Radha Gopinath Mandir)
- Kusum Sarovara (lake near Radha Vrindaban Chandra Temple)
- Chaitanya Ghat (smaller reservoir, located in front of the big Gaura Nitai sculptures at main lake)
- Govardhan Hill (two locations, one at the original farm, and one near Radha Gopinath Mandir)
- Govindaji Hill (hilltop above Bahulaban)
- Keshi Ghat (in valley between Vrindaban and Madhuban)
- Yamuna River (Otherwise known as "Big Wheeling Creek")

In this way, the holy precincts of Vrindavan are gradually being re-created by the highly dedicated devotees of New Vrindaban.

OF FORESTS AND DEITIES

The large Rādhā-Vrindaban Chandra Deities, beautiful white marble forms of Rādhā and Krishna, procured by Prabhupāda himself from a master

Deity-maker in Jaipur, India, are the true proprietors of New Vrindaban. They were installed on Janmāṣṭamī (Krishna's Appearance Day), 1971, soon after they arrived in Baltimore, from whence they were brought to their loving devotees in the Appalachian Mountains.

Several months earlier, in March of that year, large Jagannāth, Baladeva, and Subhadrā Deities would serve to prepare their way. (It may be remembered that smaller Jagannāth Deities arrived soon after Kīrtanānanda and Hayagrīva had relocated to West Virginia—these later manifestations were different.) The large Jagannāth Deities were carved from a tree from the original New Vrindaban property. Nara Nārāyaṇa carved Jagannāth, while Bhāgavatānanda carved the other two Deities. Originally, they were all housed at the original Vrindaban farmhouse.

In May 1972, when the new farmhouse at Bahulaban was opened, the large Rādhā-Vrindaban Chandra Deities, as well as their smaller counterparts, were moved there, i.e., from "Old" Vrindaban to the new location. This became the main temple area, where most of New Vrindaban's activities took place. Then, in 1973, two other important sets of Rādhā-Krishna Deities emerged in New Vrindaban: Rādhā-Mādhava and Rādhā-Vrindaban Nāth. The weekend of June 2 witnessed the groundbreaking ceremony for Prabhupāda's Palace of Gold (on land that is currently called Guruban, also purchased in 1973)—which would officially open some six years later—as well as the installation of the two new sets of Deities.

Along with these festivities, the small Govindaji Temple was built on a nearby hill, where Prabhupāda had lectured a year earlier. It was here that these two sets of Deities were installed in the midst of a huge festival—the kind for which New Vrindaban has since become famous: That day there were four colorful fire *yajñas* performed at four different locations, with devotees enthusiastically chanting Krishna *kīrtana*. A huge feast of Krishna *prasadam* would feed hundreds, accommodating the many newcomers who were joining and watching the community as it grew exponentially. After the festival, New Vrindaban would have three active temples with installed Deities, and excitedly engaged devotees who were ready, willing, and able to supply the necessary manpower.

New Vrindaban began to grow beyond anyone's expectations. But with growth one naturally endures growing pains. And in 1973, the community indeed underwent several important challenges, not least the one involving a small motorcycle gang that came through looking for the leader's daughter, who, they had heard, had come to live in New Vrindaban. Although the interaction between the devotees and these intruders is somewhat complex, with gunfire, the death of a devotee, and even the damage of the main Deities there, the net result was a deepening of the devotees' resolve, and their relationship with Rādhā-Vrindaban Chandra blossomed as never before.[18]

Although the subsequent years would see other such hardships, such as the downfall of prominent community leaders, New Vrindaban is ultimately a success story, with a Palace that would bring countless tourists and produce a generation of new dedicated devotees,[19] including a management team that continues to watch the community rise to new heights.

> While it is indisputably true that a New Vrindaban highpoint was reached with Prabhupāda's Palace in 1979, it could be argued that this transcendental victory was surpassed on July 4, 1983, when the Deities were moved from Bahulaban to their current temple in Guruban.

A huge New Vrindaban festival ensued. All the Deities that were at Bahulaban were carried in procession on a magnificent teakwood chariot (which to this day has its place in the temple). This procession, it might be said, was the culmination of a long journey, a special journey that Krishna chose to enact in New Vrindaban—the Deities that were initially at Old Vrindaban farm and then at Madhuban were consolidated and brought to Bahulaban in the late 1970s. It was there that they were worshipped until that fateful fourth of July weekend in 1983, when Krishna in all His forms were settled at the new temple.

On the central altar of the New Vrindaban temple today stand Śrī Śrī Rādhā Vrindaban Chandra. They are accompanied by Deities of Rādhā Mādhava, Rādhā Vrindaban Nāth, Gopāla Nāthjī, Gaura-Nitāi, and others. As one circles the temple room, one sees other altars for Jagannāth, Baladeva, and Subhadrā, and Nṛsiṁhadeva and Prahlāda as well. Additionally, the Six Gosvāmīs of Vrindavan have their own altar, and Prabhupāda's Vyāsāsana stands as a lasting tribute to the personality who inspired it all. Clearly, New Vrindaban is focused on Rādhā and Krishna—both in their Deity forms and as a central focus of meditation—but in the end it is more than anything else a tribute to the spiritual master who brought Vrindavan, in all its rural splendor and transcendence, to the Western world.

NOTES

1. In this chapter, we spell the various manifestations of Vrindavan in three different ways. Following Prabhupāda, we spell the extraterrestrial Vrindavan as "Vṛndāvana"; its facsimile in India is "Vrindavan"; and the West Virginia property is "New Vrindaban." Special thanks to New Vrindaban historian Chaitanya Maṅgala Dāsa for his expertise and archival research.

2. See https://vanisource.org/w/index.php?title=760624_-_Conversation_A_-_New_Vrindaban,_USA.

3. It would be prudent to note that, while traveling throughout the movement, Śrīla Prabhupāda would often describe the Deities at any given temple as being "most" beautiful, a phrase that was *not* only applied to Rādhā-Vrindaban Chandra. Since all these Deities of Krishna were tangibly different, one might wonder how each of them could be the "most" beautiful. The answer is simple and often articulated by Prabhupāda himself: Krishna, as God, need not conform to our laws of logic, wherein it might be said that only one set of Deities can be "most beautiful" while others must occupy a secondary position. No. As the creator of logic, Krishna is not bound by it. Indeed, he stands outside of it. All of his forms can be "most beautiful" simultaneously. However, if we insist on understanding this from *within* the realm of logic, Prabhupāda offer a hint on how one might do so: Each Deity is most beautiful *in his own way*.

4. The notion of "New Vrindaban" is not a new idea. For example, in Sanātana Gosvāmī's sixteenth-century *Bṛhad-bhāgavatāmṛta* (1.7.7–8), he tells us that in Dwarka, there is also a "Nava (New) Vrindavan," where Krishna assuages his intense separation from the land of his youth. The same Nava Vrindavan is mentioned in Rūpa Gosvāmī's play *Lalita Mādhava* (Act 6, Scene 1, texts 41–42). Additionally, Sanātana and Rūpa created a facsimile of Vṛndāvana in Rāmkeli, West Bengal, where they lived while working for the sultan.

5. See Richard Rose, *The San Francisco Oracle*, December 1967.

6. Hayagriva Dasa, "Chant," *Brijabasi Spirit*, November 1981, 20.

7. Letter from Prabhupada, 8/23/68. Quoted in Hayagriva Dasa, "New Vrindaban," in *Back to Godhead* 1, no. 23)Feb. 1, 1969). Online version: http://www.backtogodhead.in/new-vrindaban-hayagriva-dasa/.

8. Personal correspondence with Chaitanya Maṅgala Dāsa, October 4, 2021.

9. A pattern seemed to emerge in ISKCON, with the early temples first worshipping Jagannāth and then Rādhā and Krishna. Prabhupāda had written about this to the popular Indian publisher Hanuman Prasad Poddar, as cited in our Jagannāth chapter.

10. Śrīla Prabhupāda had referred to the West Virginia property as New Vrindaban in an earlier letter. But this is the first one specifically in reference to the Deities. See letter to Kīrtanānanda Swami, September 22, 1968.

11. https://vanisource.org/wiki/680823_-_Letter_to_Kirtanananda_and_Hayagriva_written_from_Montreal.

12. The original twelve forests are described in the *Gopāla Tāpanī Upaniṣad*, Uttara-tāpanī 28 and later in 31–32, where we learn that they can be conceived in terms of two rather than twelve: Bhadravana and Krishnavana, distinguished by their relationship with either Rāma or Krishna. Those on the eastern side of the Yamunā are more closely associated with Rāma (Bhadravana) and those on the western with Krishna (Krishnavana). The forests are also detailed in the Mathurā Māhātmya of the *Ādi-Varāha Purāṇa* and the Vṛndāvana Māhātmya of the *Padma Purāṇa,* Finally, one finds them fully developed in the *Bhakti-ratnākara* (Fifth Wave) and in other writings of the *ācāryas*, particularly Nārāyaṇa Bhaṭṭa's sixteenth-century work, the *Braja-bhakti-vilāsa* and Rūpa Gosvāmī's *Mathurā Māhātmya.*

13. The overall area of the twelve forests is commonly referred to as Vrindavan. Nonetheless, to be absolutely accurate, "Vrindavan" is only one of the twelve, although

arguably the most important one: This particular forest is named after Vṛndā-devī, the personification of the Lord's energy, who specifically arranges for Krishna's pastimes with Rādhārāṇī, many of which occur in this forest. Vṛndā's expansion is the *tulasī* plant, whose leaves and flowers, so dear to Krishna, are used as valuable offerings for the Lord. Vrindavan is her land. The Yamunā River, whose soft waters are said to immediately release one from sin, embraces Vrindavan on three sides. Her banks hold memories of the pastimes with which Krishna graced the earth, such as his play with Balarāma, wherein they are accompanied by cows and calves and surrounded by cowherd boys. Most importantly, it was in Vrindavan that Krishna called forth all the *gopīs* with his flute, leading to their legendary dance on a special full-moon autumn night. This Rāsa dance, as it is called, represents the highest exchange of love between God and devotee, portraying the ultimate goal of Gauḍīya Vaishnavism.

14. See *Caitanya-caritāmṛta,* Madhya 17.230 and 17.146–18.146. See also *Caitanya-bhāgavata*, Ādi-khaṇḍa 9.111.

15. See David L. Haberman, *Journey through the Twelve Forests: An Encounter with Krishna* (New York and Oxford: Oxford University Press, 1994), xvi.

16. Nārāyaṇa Bhaṭṭa, *Vraja-bhakti-vilāsa* 1.93, as quoted in David L. Haberman, *Journey through the Twelve Forests*, ibid., 126.

17. As of this writing, to the best of my knowledge, the remaining four Vrindavan forests have not yet been identified in New Vrindaban (Kamyaban, Kumudaban, Bhandiraban, and Lohaban).

18. For a detailed account of New Vrindaban's horrific encounter with the motorcycle gang in 1973, see Vaiyasaki Das Adhikari, *Radha-Damodara Vilasa*, Volume 2, Fifth Wave ("Bikers and Brahmanas"). I have also interviewed Varshana Swami, Kiranash, Kuladri, and others who were personally present. All attest to the fact that the trauma of witnessing Deity damage, combined with the waiting period of gradually seeing Rādhā-Vrindaban Chandra back on the altar, regaining their rightful place of worship, was in the end a positive experience, deepening the community's attachment and affection for the Deities.

19. See Satyarāja Dāsa, "A Facelift for Prabhupāda's Palace of Gold," *Back to Godhead*, May/June 2016 (https://btg.krishna.com/facelift-prabhupadas-palace-gold).

Chapter Seven

The Intimate Majesty of Śrī Śrī Rukmiṇī-Dvārakādhīśa

India's ancient wisdom texts reveal that Śrī Krishna—the playful flute-wielding cowherd boy who enjoys loving exchange with his associates in the free-spirited, rustic atmosphere of Vṛndāvana—is the Supreme Lord himself. He is God in his original, highest feature, paramount among innumerable manifestations of the one Supreme Godhead.

Krishna is God as he appears in his own element, simple and unpretentious, comparable to a great stately personality in his intimate, home environment. This down-home and uncomplicated image of God is counterbalanced by his awe-inspiring manifestation as four-armed Vishnu, the opulent source of all beings, lying in the Causal Ocean while uncountable universes emanate from his pores. So says the Vaishnava tradition.

Vishnu is an expansion of Krishna. That which is great and awesome is subservient to the basic and unadorned, for we cherish simplicity over complexity, love over might. Still, both are genuine aspects of the Supreme. The Vishnu feature resides in the Vaikuṇṭha planets, the kingdom of God, and in the material cosmos as its Oversoul. Vishnu is comparable to God at work, as opposed to God at home.

In other words, Krishna is the more intimate Supreme Being, without any formal affectations, whereas Vishnu is how he appears in his role as the supreme controller of all that is.

Krishna in Dvārakā lies somewhere in between, embodying a portion of the intimacy and sweetness of his original Vṛndāvana form—with two arms, like the original Personality of Godhead—but also displaying the royalty, grandeur, and majestic bearing of four-armed Vishnu.

The regions known as Vṛndāvana, Mathurā, and Dvārakā—the sacred stages upon which Krishna plays—exist in the spiritual sky even as they manifest as regions of India in the material world.

These are the highest portions of Vaikuṇṭha, where Vishnu is displaced by Krishna, where power (*aiśvarya*) is eclipsed by sweetness (*mādhurya*), as mentioned previously. Of course, on the spiritual platform all forms of God are equal, as are his abodes, and in that sense Vishnu and Krishna are merely various faces of the same one Lord, with nuances of difference that mainly exist to facilitate relationship, as suggested above.

In His earthly pastimes, when, for example, Krishna leaves Vrindavan to go to Mathura and, later, to Dwarka, he expands into subsidiary versions of himself. When he does this, he mystically remains in Vrindavan in his original form, in an unmanifest state, and his appearance in both Mathura and Dwarka are facilitated by plenary portions. With these "portions," he exhibits transcendental pastimes infused with formality and opulence—a mood that is alien to Vṛndāvana, but very much in line with the lordship of Vaikuṇṭha. In Mathura and Dwarka, Krishna is in his work clothes, so to speak, and while these secondary manifestations are fully transcendental, they do not fully reflect his original personality of intimacy and love.

Indeed, Krishna prefers that his devotees worship him in his original form: "Knowing My opulences, the whole world looks upon Me with awe and veneration," Krishna says. "But devotion made feeble by such reverence does not attract Me."[1] This is because awe and reverence tend to dilute intimacy, as we see even in this world. For this reason, Krishna wants us to know him as he is, penetrating his identity beyond his "vocation" as Supreme Lord. Thus, worship of any of Krishna's forms should be accompanied by a sense of who he really is in terms of his original, intimate personality, for this leads to the unfolding of eternal relationships.

These relationships (*rasa*) manifest either as servant (*dāsya*), friend (*sakhya*), parent (*vātsalya*), or lover (*mādhurya*), and self-realization involves finding our place in this varied interpersonal schema.[2] Those blissfully ensconced in such relationships are, interestingly, oblivious of Krishna's Godhood—by design—for awareness of his divinity would result in formal and reverential exchanges, which, again, are contrary to the loving affairs cultivated in the supreme paradise.[3]

Those lesser, more ceremonious moods, exalted though they are, exist only in the other Vaikuṇṭha planets and are usually categorized as neutrality (*śānta-rasa*), servitude (*dāsya-rasa*), and lower-echelon friendship (*sakhya-rasa*), wherein one has a personal relationship with God but largely in a formal capacity. That is to say, in Vaikuṇṭha, awareness of Vishnu's supreme position is paramount, disallowing more intimate exchanges of love. There are of course certain exceptions. The queens of Dvārakā, for example, experience the conjugal mood as part of their service to Krishna. Even there, however, their love is tinged by awe and reverence, not quite approximating the *gopīs* of Vṛndāvana.

Nonetheless, because of these varieties of loving exchanges, the full spectrum of relationship can be found in the kingdom of God, from formal (in Vaikuṇṭha) to intimate (in Goloka Vṛndāvana), and they all have a place in pleasing Krishna.

Again, Krishna in Dvārakā is more akin to Vishnu in Vaikuṇṭha, while also incorporating aspects of the more intimate loving moods of Vṛndāvana as well. Sometimes, in fact, Krishna in Dvārakā is indistinguishable from his primary form in Vṛndāvana, as we shall soon see.

THE KINGDOM OF DWARKA

When Krishna leaves Vrindavan in India to become ruler in the great kingdom of Dwarka, as he did some five thousand years ago, he is still Krishna, even if he manifests in a so-called secondary form. For Krishna, who is absolute, there is in reality no first or second. Krishna is always Krishna, "one without a second," as Prabhupāda often said. But he manifests in particular ways for a specific purpose, especially to please his devotees.

To understand Dwarka-Krishna, we must look at Dwarka itself, popularly considered one of India's four most important holy places: Puri (east), Rameswaram (south), Badrinath (north), and Dwarka (west).

The word *dvārakā* is derived from the root *dvāravatī,* "gated [city]," perhaps a reference to the countless gates that encircled its many awe-inspiring buildings and gardens. *Śrīmad-Bhāgavatam* (10.69.1–12) describes Dwarka as a countrified city filled with the sounds of birds and bees, chirping and buzzing as they fly through numerous parks and pleasure gardens. Dwarka's many lakes were filled with a variety of blooming lotuses, the sweet, melodious songs of peacocks, swans, and cranes complementing the sounds of the birds and bees.

Yet it was also a highly developed urban environment of some 900,000 royal palaces, constructed of crystal, silver, and huge emeralds, with wide roads and sophisticated grid street planning.

Architecturally, Dwarka challenges the common notion of what man was capable of at the time, so elaborate were its buildings and engineering accomplishments, including progressive waste disposal and sewage systems. All of this was lost due to the vicissitudes of time and because Dwarka was submerged in much the same way that one might imagine Atlantis was.

Today, the Underwater Archaeology Wing (UAW) of the Archaeological Survey of India conducts research off the west coast of India, near what is said to be the site of Krishna's ancient dwelling, now marked by a small town known as Devabhumi Dwarka, in Gujarat.[4] The UAW is excavating underwater sites and ruins and finding many artifacts that appear to be remnants of a world that transcends time.

Vaishnava sages pass down additional information as well: In the original city of Dwarka there was a private enclave, distinct in its beauty, worshipped by rulers from numerous planetary systems who would periodically visit to make loving offerings. This was the residential area of Lord Krishna himself, an ornately decorated collection of sixteen thousand palaces where the Lord expanded into an equivalent number of forms to live at peace with His queens. These queens, of course, were not ordinary souls, but rather expansions of His internal, spiritual energy (*śakti*), much as he was an expansion of the original Krishna in Vrindavan. Their love is thus wholly transcendental.[5]

Why did Krishna go to Dwarka? There is an esoteric reason articulated only in the Gauḍīya tradition. Having battled with demonic forces in Mathura, Krishna led his troops to Dwarka to protect his clan, the Yādavas, from Jarāsandha, one of his archenemies, who had attacked Mathura while Krishna was there.

Dwarka was a perfect choice, for it was surrounded by the sea, making it an impenetrable fortress. Krishna had other concerns in Dwarka, too, such as an ongoing relationship with the Pāṇḍava princes, and the soon-to-be marriage of Subhadrā (his sister) and Arjuna.

But Dwarka was perfect for another reason as well, one still more esoteric, a reason that highlights Krishna's innate love for Vrindavan. Had he gone back to that bucolic paradise after the battle at Mathura as he desired, Jarāsandha's troops would have followed him there, destroying Vrindavan's beautiful rural atmosphere, quite possibly harming his family, friends, and the district of Mathura, which were all so dear to him.

Thus, out of love for Vrindavan and its neighboring city, the place of his birth, He led his Yādava army to far-away Dwarka, which became his kingdom for the rest of His pastimes in this world. He would now spend almost ninety-seven years in Dwarka. As time went on, Balarāma married a princess named Revatī, and Krishna married numerous queens, as mentioned above. The foremost among them was the extraordinary Queen Rukmiṇī, who was an expansion of Candrāvalī, one of his prominent cowherd girlfriends in Vrindavan. His other primary queen was Satyabhāmā, a manifestation of his unsurpassed lover, Śrī Rādhā. Through these latter marriages he sought to bring the essence of Vrindavan to his new home in Dwarka.[6]

DWARKA TODAY

In Dwarka, Krishna is known as Dvārakādhīśa, "the Lord of Dwarka," for it was here that he manifested his princely side, wearing royal garb and attended by a vast retinue of reverential servants.

To commemorate the Lord's sovereign pastimes in this highly ornate kingdom, his great-grandson Vajranābha built a temple where Krishna's main palace once stood. Today, the modern structure in its place dates back to the sixteenth century and is considered the original site of Lord Krishna's Dwarka home.

The Deity of this temple is dressed with all the opulence of the original Dvārakādhīśa himself. The symbols in the Deity's four hands (conch, club, disc, and lotus), indicating a mood of sovereignty (*aiśvarya*) appropriate for Lord Vishnu, are covered in glittering silver.

Numerous subsidiary shrines are in the same compound, including those dedicated to Lakṣmī, Śiva, Balarāma, Pradyumna, Aniruddha, Jāmbavatī, Satyabhāmā, and Vishnu. The entire temple complex is thus a tribute to *aiśvarya-bhāva*, or the mood of worshipping Krishna in awe and reverence.

There are a few exceptions, such as an altar for Śrīmatī Rādhārāṇī, and, opposite Dvārakādhīśa's main altar, a shrine to Devakī, Krishna's mother, who lovingly gazes upon her divine child from across the way. These exceptions show that, even in Dwarka, the other standard devotional relationships exist as well, indicating that Krishna is the reservoir of all loving exchange (*rasa*), even if awe and reverence are the focus of this particular temple.

The temple is an imposing structure that stands five stories high, its main sanctum surrounded by seventy-two regal pillars. Functioning under the auspices of the Puṣṭi-mārga tradition, the temple conducts its elaborate deity worship according to the Vallabha lineage, popular in this region of India.

Nearly twenty miles from Dwarka is a quaint coastal village named Okha, from which pilgrims take a twenty-minute boat ride to nearby Bet ("island") Dwarka. Here they see the remains of another ancient Dvārakādhīśa temple. Locals refer to this area as the real Dwarka, and it certainly puts visitors in a Dwarka mood.

Halfway to Bet Dwarka, just off the main road, is Gopi Tallav, said to be the lake where Krishna once reunited with the *gopīs* of Vrindavan. Here one finds *gopī-candana*, the yellowish clay that devotees use as *tilaka*, marking their bodies as temples of God. As one approaches Bet Dwarka proper, one comes upon a temple dedicated to Rukmiṇī, Krishna's primary queen, a structure said to date back to the twelfth century.

ISKCON, too, has a temple in Dwarka, owing to a large property that was donated by a prominent well-wisher, Pritish Bharatia, in 1996. The temple is only a three-minute walk from the central Dvārakādhīśa temple, and the Deities of Śrī Śrī Rādhā-Śyāmasundara happily greet their devotees, again combining the awe and reverence of *aiśvarya-bhāva* with the *mādhurya* aspect of worship favored by Gauḍīya Vaiṣṇavas. His Holiness Mahaviṣṇu Goswami oversaw the project until his passing several years ago. Today, ISKCON has plans for expansion that will make its Dwarka temple the premier facility and tourist attraction in the region.

Ishvarbhai Pujari, one of the priests for the Dvārakādhīśa temple and an architect by profession, is designing a new ISKCON temple, with plans for elaborate outdoor dioramas depicting Lord Kṛṣṇa's pastimes from *Śrīmad-Bhāgavatam*. Aside from the main temple, ISKCON Dwarka includes a six-acre *goshala* (cow sanctuary) some eight miles from town, with plans for future expansion.

THE ROAD TO NEW DWARKA

But the real story of ISKCON Dwarka is not to be found in India.[7] Rather, it emerges in Los Angeles at the height of the hippie era as the result of Śrīla Prabhupāda's early efforts in America, along with those of his early disciples.

After establishing themselves in New York in 1966, and then expanding to San Francisco, Santa Fe, and Montreal, Prabhupada's disciples opened a temple in Boston and, soon after, in Los Angeles. These centers were all born in 1967, toward the end of the year.

Once in Los Angeles, the devotees began what was to become their long history in the city by renting a storefront building at 2364 Pico Boulevard in mid-city, an area bordered by Beverlywood and Koreatown. The new "temple," humble though it was, afforded them a makeshift altar, which was essentially two wooden crates covered by a patterned madras. At the very top was a vibrant and colorful poster of a smiling Krishna with his loving arms wrapped around a cow.

Dayānanda Dāsa and his wife, Nandarāṇī Dāsī, were in charge of the fledgling temple, as they and the resident devotees awaited Śrīla Prabhupāda, who was scheduled to arrive in short order. Dayānanda had rented him a separate apartment on Saturn Street, one block away, just so he would be comfortable while in Los Angeles.

Prabhupada visited as scheduled and held popular programs. People joined, the temple grew, and the full-time devotees, although few, would often go out chanting in the neighboring areas, attracting attention. Soon they installed Deities of Jagannāth, Baladeva, and Subhadrā, and their devotional standards blossomed.

They quickly grew out of their little center and moved to busy Hollywood Boulevard, one block from Grauman's famous Chinese Theater.

Being in such a popular area facilitated their rich and enthusiastic public chanting, which became the center of their lives, and they would often stay out until 1:00 in the morning. They would chant with similar enthusiasm at the temple, bringing the party home with them, so to speak, much to the dismay of the neighbors. As a result, they were quickly evicted.

"Out on the sidewalk we went," remembers Dayānanda, "with pots, pans, and bedding, and the Deities of Jagannāth, Baladeva, and Subhadrā in our arms. Luckily, a stranger passing us on the street offered the use of her nearby garage. That was in the Watts district of southern LA."

Although the devotees were comfortable there, Prabhupāda wanted them to have a better facility. His concern was outreach, not personal comfort. He graciously lectured and joined them in *kīrtana* and feasts, but made clear that they should look for a more appropriate temple. Soon after, they found a church for sale with three large adjacent rooms. This was at 1975 La Cienega Boulevard, situated on a major north-south arterial road, centrally located. The devotees moved in and quickly thrived, and no one was happier than Śrīla Prabhupāda.

In fact, he often wrote to his disciples in other centers to describe it, proud of it as a groundbreaking "world headquarters" from which he would guide his followers to open many more. It was at this point that his Los Angeles disciples heard that he had taught the New York devotees how to worship Rādhā-Krishna Deities. Realizing its importance, the Los Angeles devotees wanted to learn this art and science as well. But where would they get Deities of Rādhā and Krishna in America? At that time, they were only available in India. Still, because Prabhupāda and the Los Angeles devotees desired it, small but alluring Rādhā-Krishna Deities—eleven inches and made of brass—mysteriously arrived at their doorstep, delivered by a widow from Vrindavan.

On July 16, 1969, Śrīla Prabhupāda installed the Deities in the temple, allowing the devotees to begin a full schedule of decoration, *ārati*, and food offerings, replicating the methods used in New York. Prabhupāda's disciple Śīlavatī Dāsī learned from him directly and gradually taught others. In ISKCON's early days, she became something of an authority on Deity worship.

To accommodate the newly inaugurated temple program of worshipping the Deities, Śrīla Prabhupāda stopped the late-night *saṅkīrtana* programs, requesting all disciples to attend the daily *maṅgala-ārati* ceremony at 4:30 a.m., which would necessitate retiring early for the night. He established other mandatory programs to be performed later in the morning and in the evening too. These have become standard in all ISKCON temples.

After one year at the La Cienega address, however, the devotees had outgrown their temple. Their Spiritual Sky Incense business was expanding, *Back to Godhead* distribution increased, and the Sunday Love Feast was attended by numerous seekers from both Los Angeles and the newly established outreach temples in Laguna Beach and San Diego. Under the general leadership of Tamāl Krishna Dāsa (soon to be Goswami), the temple thrived. But he relocated to London, where newer services were calling out his name.

Thus, in 1970, when Gargamuni and Dayānanda, both senior devotees in charge of the new temple, found a large and magnificent church—yet again—with an elaborate service building and minister's quarters, Śrīla Prabhupāda negotiated the price with the minister. The elegant edifice would eventually become the movement's most impressive property at the time, the true "Western world headquarters" of the International Society for Krishna Consciousness.

In the weeks that followed, Gargamuni was put in charge of arranging the finances.

"Prabhupāda," says Dayānanda, "was very pleased with him for arranging the purchase and later buying the three wonderful silver altars that would adorn the new temple. Prabhupāda also worked with Gargamuni on the actual purchase and finances."

This would become the majestic temple at 3764 Watseka Avenue, which continues to serve as the Los Angeles temple today. The earliest days at the new facility are remembered by Satsvarūpa Dāsa Gosvāmī in *Śrīla Prabhupāda-līlāmṛta*:

> On the auspicious occasion of Bhaktisiddhānta Sarasvatī Ṭhākura's appearance day anniversary, the Los Angeles devotees received permission to enter their new temple on Watseka Avenue. The rooms had not even been cleaned, and the large hall was bare; but the devotees brought in Prabhupāda's *vyāsāsana* from the old temple on La Cienega, and Prabhupāda had them place on it a large picture of his spiritual master. Standing before his spiritual master, Prabhupāda offered *ārati* while some fifty disciples gathered around him, chanting Hare Kṛṣṇa and dancing in the otherwise empty hall. . . . This large new temple, Prabhupāda said, had been provided by Bhaktisiddhānta Sarasvatī as a gift for the devotees to use in Kṛṣṇa's service. They should not become attached to the opulence, Prabhupāda said, but they should use this wonderful place for preaching. As he spoke, he wept.[8]

April 1, 1970. Working day and night for the move to the new building, the devotees were finally ready to take their Deities and assorted devotional paraphernalia on a long cavalcade to the new location at Watseka Avenue. The Deities were placed on a magnificent palanquin beautifully painted with scenes from Vrindavan, and along with numerous chanting devotees and awestruck guests, the deities trekked through the streets of Los Angeles.

When the chanting party arrived at what would soon be the new temple room, they noticed an old Mission-style pulpit with large arches over it. Seizing the opportunity, they hung large oil paintings of Lord Caitanya and the disciplic succession there, preparing it for the Deities, who were put in place.

In what was still very much a churchlike atmosphere in terms of decor, Śrīla Prabhupāda lectured from the podium while disciples sat in the pews. He expressed his appreciation of this arrangement for guests. But the pews were eventually removed, and the large chanting room began to look like other ISKCON temples, if a tad more opulent.

"As the movement grew," writes frequent *Back to Godhead* author Karuṇā Dhārinī Devī Dāsī, "more and more devotees made their home in what Śrīla Prabhupada eventually named 'New Dwaraka.' They were sculptors, architects, carpenters, designers, musicians, businessmen, managers, accountants, technicians, writers, editors, artists, teachers, seamstresses, jewelers, photographers, film producers, speakers, and actors, and their skills blossomed due to their love for Śrīla Prabhupāda. Much of his legacy was born from the culture of *kṛṣṇa-bhakti* he inspired in LA, including translated and published Vedic scriptures, *kṛṣṇa-līlā* oil paintings, musical recordings, lectures, museum dioramas, festivals, dramatic performance, films, and the standard-setting worship of Śrī Śrī Rukmiṇī-Dvārakādhīśa."[9]

With the opening of Govinda's Buffet in 1982, declared by major cuisine critics as being among the best vegetarian restaurants in all of California, or even the world, and, later, Govinda's Gift Shop, providing devotional items for worship, books, posters, and more, for both devotees and visitors, the New Dwaraka community was complete—a tribute to Śrīla Prabhupāda's Herculean if loving work in the modern world.

WHAT'S IN A NAME?

When the Watseka temple was purchased, due to its opulence Śrīla Prabhupāda named it "New Dwarka" (adding to its magnificence was an entire city block of private devotee apartments, all centered on the temple). When the large marble Rādhā-Krishna Deities were installed in 1971, they were named Rukmiṇī-Dvārakādhīśa in pursuance of His Divine Grace's vision for an opulent temple community.[10] At that time, too, the smaller Deities—then known simply as Rādhā-Krishna—were renamed Rukmiṇī-Dvārakānātha.

Senior disciple Tuṣṭa Krishna Dāsa, who was at one time a personal servant of Śrīla Prabhupāda, tells the story:

> Prabhupāda was giving specific names for deities in nearly every temple he opened at that time. There was Śrī Śrī Rādhā-Vṛndāvana-candra, for instance, of New Vrindaban, or Radha Pārtha-sārathī in Delhi. With this temple being on the west coast just as the Dwarka of India is on India's west coast, it became obvious. The disciples requested Prabhupāda in a letter that the deities be named Śrī Śrī Rukmiṇī-Dvarakādīśa. Śrīla Prabhupāda gave his permission for this. In subsequent letters of instruction to the Los Angeles *pūjārīs*, Śrīla Prabhupāda always referred to the deities as Rukmiṇī-Dvārakādhīśa.[11]

Still, the difference between Krishna in Vrindavan and Krishna in Dwarka should, again, be understood. In Vrindavan, Krishna plays his flute to entice the *gopīs* into higher states of uncompromising love (*mahābhāva*). This is not the case in pastimes with Rukmiṇī and the queens of Dwarka. In fact, Krishna leaves his flute in Vrindavan when he enters Mathura. By the time he reaches Dwarka, the flute is nowhere to be seen.

In Krishna's manifested pastimes, Dvārakādhīśa is never depicted as playing his flute. So one might wonder: Why is the Krishna Deity in Los Angeles holding a flute when the person next to him is Rukmiṇī? This seems to contradict both scripture and the truth (*tattva*) of *krishna-līlā.* In Dwarka, Krishna acts like a *kṣatriya* in the royal order, and flute playing is not a *kṣatriya* activity.

Thus it can be argued that Krishna standing in his threefold bending form, holding a flute, is incompatible with the presence of Rukmiṇī and even with the name, Dvārakādhīśa.

Śrīla Prabhupāda explains this as follows:

> When the *gopīs* sometimes saw Kṛṣṇa in the form of Nārāyaṇa, they were not very much attracted to Him. The *gopīs* never addressed Kṛṣṇa as Rukmiṇī-ramaṇa. Kṛṣṇa's devotees in Vṛndāvana address Him as Rādhāramaṇa, Nandanandana and Yaśodānandana, but not as Vasudeva-nandana or Devakī-nandana. Although according to the material conception Nārāyaṇa, Rukmiṇī-ramaṇa and Kṛṣṇa are one and the same, in the spiritual world one cannot use the name Rukmiṇī-ramaṇa or Nārāyaṇa in place of the name Kṛṣṇa. If one does so out of a poor fund of knowledge, his mellow [*rasa*] with the Lord becomes spiritually faulty and is called *rasābhāsa*, an overlapping of transcendental mellows. The advanced devotee who has actually realized the transcendental features of the Lord will not commit the mistake of creating a *rasābhāsa* situation by using one name for another. Because of the influence of Kali-yuga, there is much *rasābhāsa* in the name of extravagance and liberal-mindedness. Such fanaticism is not very much appreciated by pure devotees.[12]

In short, Rādhārāṇī and her associates are not attracted to Dvārakādhīśa-Kṛṣṇa, nor should they be. They are attracted only to Vrajendra-nandana Krishna, the

Krishna of Vrindavan, and Gauḍīya Vaiṣṇavas, even today, seek to follow in their footsteps. Although Krishna, Dvārakādhīśa, and even Nārāyaṇa are one and the same in terms of ontological reality (*tattva*), they are different by virtue of individualized relationship and taste (*rasa*), and this is the main point.

Nonetheless, with the above as an important backdrop, the excerpts below show Śrīla Prabhupāda's full acceptance of the names Rukmiṇī-Dvārakādhīśa and the divine personalities behind them, directly referring to the deities in LA without hesitation, criticism, or misgivings. Prabhupāda would have clearly spoken out if he disapproved in any way. Indeed, he saw training and correcting disciples as a large part of his mission, and he would not have hesitated to speak up if he detected something inappropriate. Here, then, is a sampling of his quotes of acceptance:

> Thank you very much for the pictures of Rukmini Dvarakadhisa. They are very nice. (Letter, Nov. 24, 1976)

> Please accept my blessings. I am in due receipt of your card dated October 25, 1975, along with the beautiful photographs of Sri Sri Rukmini-Dvarakadhisa of New Dvaraka. (Letter, Nov. 10, 1975)

> It is very encouraging to hear the arrangement you are making for worship of Their Lordships Sri Dvarakadhisa and Rukmini. Please do it very nicely and I shall be glad to see the completed result. (Letter, June 29, 1973)

Adding to this, we may quote the following excerpt from a room conversation recorded in Vrindavan on June 17, 1977. Here Śrīla Prabhupāda recalls communicating with the Deity Dvārakādhīśa in Los Angeles. He describes how he left Vrindavan in 1965 and went to the West, and then how Krishna sent him back to India to establish temples in Mayapur and Vrindavan, but how he then returned soon thereafter to complete his mission.

> Tamāl Kṛṣṇa Goswami: Actually, when you intended to go to America, everyone was advising, "Better not go. It is too dangerous for someone of your age. Do not go." Someone even said that you may not come back.

> Śrīla Prabhupāda: I thought all this. I went to USA not to come back. I left here hopeless. I did not want to come back. I went with determination that, "If I do this job, I will survive." So Kṛṣṇa helped me. . . . I made my headquarters in Los Angeles.

> TKG: Well . . . by your coming here it was wonderful.

Śrīla Prabhupāda: That means Kṛṣṇa desired. Otherwise I had no plan to come back here.

TKG: Your business was in the West. Still it is, you said. Still, whatever we're doing here . . .

Śrīla Prabhupāda: Therefore I took this permanent residency.

TKG: Not intention but . . . Do you regret having come back to India?

Śrīla Prabhupāda: No, it is well. My plan was like that, but Kṛṣṇa's plan was different. When I was coming back, I was speaking to Dvārakādhīśa, "I do not know. I came here to live. Why You are driving me away?" While leaving Los Angeles I was not happy.

TKG: Oh, I remember.

Śrīla Prabhupāda: But He had this plan.

TKG: Pretty nice plan.

Śrīla Prabhupāda: Kṛṣṇa wanted that, "You left Vrindavan. I'll give you better place in Vrindavan. [*Chuckles*.] You were retired in Vrindavan. I obliged you to leave. Now you come back. I'll give you better place." So He has given a temple [Kṛṣṇa-Balarāma Mandir] hundred times better than Los Angeles. Is it not?

TKG: There's nothing comparable in the three worlds.

Śrīla Prabhupāda: *Hmm.* So it is always by His desire.[13]

"Regarding the arrangement of the deities on the altar," wrote Śrīla Prabhupāda, "the arrangement here in the Los Angeles temple is: Guru-Gauranga, Radha-Krishna, Jagannath. Gargamuni has taken some pictures of the temple room and I shall send a copy to you when they are printed. So make the altar very gorgeous according to your facilities there. That will be nice" (Letter, June 22, 1970).

Given his stated affirmation of the Deities as Rukmiṇī-Dvārakādhīśa—and also that these were "Radha-Krishna" Deities—it is clear that Prabhupāda saw no distinction between Rukmiṇī-Dvārakādhīśa and Rādhā-Krishna.

But should ordinary devotees be expected to see in the same way, without making a distinction between these various divinities? Should one merely imitate the vision of a pure devotee of the Lord? After all, Prabhupāda was by all accounts a fully enlightened Vaishnava, with the highest possible realization, and he was thus naturally able to see the supreme form of Krishna everywhere.

In point of fact, this is precisely what he was teaching his followers to do. While not neglecting the nuance of difference in the various forms of Krishna, which he clearly articulated, he wanted his followers to understand how Vrindavan-Krishna is present everywhere, not least in all of God's direct forms, whether Vishnu, Dvārakādhīśa, or otherwise.

Moreover, Prabhupāda taught that Deity worship, especially for those who are immature on the devotional path, *must* begin with awe and reverence—not just when worshipping Rukmiṇī-Dvārakādhīśa, but even when worshipping Deities that are ostensibly Rādhā-Krishna directly. All Deity worship begins like this, he tells us, and as one advances, one learns to see Vrindavan-Krishna in one's worshipful Lord, whatever the specific incarnation. As Prabhupāda says,

> Regarding your question about why we dress the deities in very opulent fashion and not as simple cowherds boy and girl, this is an intelligent question and the answer is that according to the regulative principles we cannot worship Radha-Krsna now. Radha-Krsna worship is meant for persons who have already developed spontaneous love of God. In the training period we are only worshiping Laksmi-Narayana. We worship Radha-Krsna because Laksmi-Narayana is there also, but actually we are not worshiping Radha-Krsna with our present deity ceremonies; we are worshiping Laksmi-Narayana. Narayana is there when Krsna is there, but actually we do not worship Radha-Krsna in Their original form. This is why we should worship Radha-Krsna in Their Laksmi-Narayana feature with all respect and reverence. If we deviate from this standard then we shall be *prakrta-sahajiya*, or a person who takes things very cheap. We worship Laksmi-Narayana and because Radha-Krsna includes Laksmi-Narayana there is no necessity of installing a Laksmi-Narayana deity. It is just like a king who is engaged in administering justice. Actually that business belongs to the justice department. But what is the justice department? It is all part of the king's energy, and the king also has the power to execute this function. (Letter, January 24, 1969)

"Rādhā-Kṛṣṇa," he further writes, "cannot be approached by the neophyte devotees; therefore temple worship according to regulative principles is offered to Lakṣmī-Nārāyaṇa. Although there may be a Rādhā-Kṛṣṇa *vigraha*, or form, the worship of the neophyte devotees is acceptable as Lakṣmī-Narayana worship."[14]

RESPONDING TO HIS DEVOTEES' DESIRE

"Kṛṣṇa is known as Bhakta-vatsala," writes Karuṇā Dhāriṇī. "That is, He enjoys taking the supporting role, if it pleases His devotees. Kṛṣṇa enjoys responding to the desire of His worshipers. The New Dwaraka disciples of Śrīla Prabhupāda felt inspired to worship the deities as their transcendental king and queen, and Kṛṣṇa helped them to do so. They designed the present temple room to look like a beautiful Dwaraka palace. They installed a nice marble floor and pillars, arched altar and front entry doors with brass plating of *maṇḍalas* and cows, velvet canopies, and elegant dioramas of various demigods looking down into the room. Beautiful golden-framed oil paintings of the *Kṛṣṇa* book pastimes were placed everywhere."[15]

In conclusion, and when contemplated in the present context, the words of both *Śrīmad-Bhāgavatam* and the *Caitanya-caritāmṛta* resound with deep meaning:

yad-yad-dhiyā ta urugāya vibhāvayanti

tat-tad-vapuḥ praṇayase sad-anugrahāya

"You are so merciful to Your devotees that You manifest Yourself in the particular eternal form of transcendence in which they always think of You" (*Śrīmad-bhāgavatam* 3.9.11).

yei yei rūpe jāne, sei tāhā kahe

sakala sambhave kṛṣṇe, kichu mithyā nahe

"In whatever form one knows the Lord, one speaks of Him in that way. In this there is no falsity, since everything is possible in Kṛṣṇa." (*Caitanya-caritāmṛta, Ādi* 5.132) As Prabhupāda writes in his purport: "If someone calls Lord Rāmacandra by the vibration Hare Rāma, understanding it to mean 'O Lord Rāmacandra!' he is quite right. Similarly, if one says that Hare Rāma means 'O Śrī Balarāma!' he is also right. Those who are aware of the *viṣṇu-tattva* do not fight over all these details."

FINAL REFLECTIONS

Wherever Krishna goes, he brings Vrindavan with him. Thus, Sanātana Gosvāmī's *Bṛhad-bhāgavatāmṛta* (1.7.7–8), for example, tells us that in Dwarka, there is a "Nava (New) Vrindavan," where Krishna can assuage his own intense separation from Vrindavan. The same Nava Vrindavan is mentioned in Rūpa Gosvāmī's play *Lalita Mādhava* (Act 6, Scene 1, texts 41–42). Essentially, Nava Vrindavan is a haven, complete with facsimiles of Krishna's family, friends, and favorite areas as found in the original Vrindavan. Viśvakarmā, the architect of the demigods, is said to have created it to lessen Krishna's intense pining for his village home. Similarly, New Dwaraka in Los Angeles, although opulent, has many of the same accoutrements as any other Krishna temple, with inescapable elements of the Vrindavan mood, like Krishna holding his flute. This is because it is an ISKCON temple and consequently partakes of Gauḍīya Vaiṣṇava standards and predilections.

When Krishna engages His Yogamāyā potency to recreate Vrindavan, even in an opulent environment like Dwarka, it takes on many of the characteristics of the original Vrindavan. Dwarka is thus non-different from Vrindavan even while retaining its kingly splendor. Also, while we know Vrindavan as a simple rural village, it is not lacking in grandeur. For example, Śrīla Viśvanātha Cakravartī Ṭhākura describes Krishna's home, Nanda Mahārāja's palace, in his *Vraja-rīti-cintāmaṇi* (16–18): "His palace is made of glistening sapphires, with coral pillars, gold and lapis lazuli roofs, crystal windows, and large gates made of rubies. His entire capitol is enclosed by a great wall built of sapphires." In other words, one sees transcendence according to the *bhāva*, or primary spiritual mood, in which one is absorbed.

Thus, opulence can be found in the simple village of Vrindavan, and simplicity can be found in the stately environment of Dwarka—each according to Krishna's desire and the mood of his loving devotee. Viśvanātha Cakravartī's disciple Baladeva Vidyābhūṣaṇa further develops these ideas in *Aiśvarya-kādambinī.* In the end, Vrindavan is inseparable from Krishna, and whether he manifests in his original form as a simple cowherd or as the king of Dwarka, Krishna is always Krishna, exhibiting both simple and opulent dimensions according to his transcendental, inexplicable, and sweet will.

NOTES

1. *Caitanya-caritāmṛta, Ādi* 3.16.

2. On *rasa* theology and the five dimensions of devotion, see David L. Haberman, trans. *The Bhaktirasāmṛtasindhu of Rūpa Gosvāmin* (New Delhi: Indira Gandhi National Centre for the Arts; Delhi: Motilal Banarsidass, 2003); Barbara A. Holdrege, *Bhakti and Embodiment* (New York: Routledge, 2015), 87–88; Neal Delmonico, "Sacred Rapture: A Study of the Religious Aesthetic of Rūpa Gosvāmin," PhD Dissertation, University of Chicago, 1990 and "Sacred Rapture: The Bhakti-Rasa Theory of Rūpa Goswāmin." in *Journal of Vaishnava Studies 6, no. 1 (Winter 1998): 75–98.*

For a practitioner perspective, see also Mathureśa Dāsa, "Counting the Ways," in *Back to Godhead* 21, no. 1 (January 1986): 8–11.

3. The illusion of such blessed souls is instigated by an energy called Yogamāyā. This exists in contradistinction to Mahāmāyā, the illusion of the material world: The former allows a living being to blissfully interact with God in the context of an "ordinary" relationship with him, as son, mother, lover, and so on, conveniently allowing a certain forgetfulness of his divinity (which in turn allows this relationship). The latter instigates a total forgetfulness of God, signaling our material predicament and our unfortunate series of reincarnations in the material world. For more on the various permutations of maya, see Gopal K. Gupta, *Māyā in the Bhāgavata Purāṇa: Human Suffering and Divine Play* (England: Oxford University Press, 2020).

4. See S. R. Rao, *Lost City of Dvaraka* (Delhi: Aditya Prakashan, 1999) and "The Ancient Dwaraka" (https://historicalindia.org/article/the-ancient-dwaraka). Also see http://mahabharata-research.com/about%20the%20epic/the%20lost%20city%20of%20dwarka.html.

5. See *Śrīmad-Bhāgavatam* (*Bhāgavata Purāṇa*), Canto 10: "The Summum Bonum," His Divine Grace. A. C. Bhaktivedanta Swami Prabhupāda, trans., Chapter 69, "Nārada Muni Visits Lord Kṛṣṇa's Palaces in Dvārakā."

6. This is explained by Śrīla Rūpa Gosvāmī in his *Lalita Mādhava*, Acts Five (Texts 18 and 51) and Six (Text 32).

7. Much of this history is derived from Karuṇā Dhārinī Devī Dāsī, "The Fiftieth Anniversary of New Dwaraka Dhama," in *Back to Godhead* 53, no. 4 (July/August 2019): 16–31.

8. See Satsvarūpa dāsa Goswāmī, *Śrīla Prabhupāda-līlāmṛta*/Volume One/Chapter 31 (Los Angeles: Bhaktivedanta Book Trust, 1980, https://editor.vedabase.com/jp/spl/1/31/).

9. See Karuṇā Dhārinī Devī Dāsī, "The Fiftieth Anniversary of New Dwaraka Dhama," op. cit. (http://btg.krishna.com/fiftieth-anniversary-new-dwaraka-dhama).

10. While most Krishna Deities are blackish, replicating the Lord's complexion as it exists in the spiritual world, Dvārakādhīśa's color is not unlike Rādhārāṇī's, which is very light, almost white. Some say that the reason for this is as follows: Krishna is so enthralled by Śrī Rādhā's beauty that, in a mood of separation, he turns a lovesick white, or even golden. Indeed, the contemporary *sādhu*, Śrīla Bhakti Prajñan Keshava Goswami, Śrīla Prabhupāda's *sannyāsa* guru, writes in his *Rādhā-vinoda-bihārī Tattvāṣṭakam* as follows: (1) "I worship the lotus feet of a particular form of Śrī Krishna: Due to being thoroughly immersed in separation from Śrīmatī Rādhikā, His own dark complexion vanishes and He assumes a complexion similar to Hers, with a bright, golden luster" (*rādhā-cintā niveśena yasya kāntir-vilopitā śrī kṛṣṇa-caraṇaṁ vande rādhāliṅgita vigraham*). Thus, many Deities of Krishna appear with a whitish complexion.

11. Ibid.

12. See *Caitanya-caritāmṛta,* Madhya 8.91, purport.

13. See https://www.vaniquotes.org/wiki/Dvarakadhisa.

14. See *Śrīmad Bhāgavatam* 4.24.45–46, Purport.
15. See Karuṇā Dhārinī Devī Dāsī, "The Fiftieth Anniversary of New Dwaraka Dhama," op. cit.

Chapter Eight

Śrī Nāthjī, Mādhavendra Purī, and the Dawn of Love

The Deity known as Śrī Nāthjī, worshipped today in the town of Nathdwara (literally, "Gateway to Nāthjī"), in the Aravalli Hills of Rajasthan, was founded by sage Mādhavendra Purī in the fifteenth century.[1] While this Rajasthani shrine is more than 350 miles from the rustic area of Govardhan, where the Deity was discovered, it has become non-different from Vrindavan-Govardhan, largely due to the presence of the Deity.

Śrī Nāthjī is Krishna as an adorable seven-year-old child, beckoning his devotees to come back to him, to reunite in pastimes of love. His nearly life-sized visage is distinctive, composed of black stone and stylized features, with his charmingly positioned left arm upraised, suggesting his pastime of lifting Mount Govardhan, and his right resting gently on his waist.[2] He is one of the most beloved forms of Krishna in the history of Vaishnavism.

In particular, devotees of both the Vallabha Sampradāya (Puṣṭimārga) and the Chaitanya Sampradāya (Gauḍīya Vaishnavism) have a special relationship with this Deity, since his worship arose in Vrindavan, ensconced as it is in Braj-bhakti, the central form of devotion for both lineages. As we will see, the Deity was moved from Braj to Rajasthan in the seventeenth century to protect him from invading adversaries.

Interestingly, there is an inextricable link between the story of Śrī Nāthjī and that of Mādhavendra Purī, the spiritual exemplar who discovered him. This is intriguing, for the Deity is commonly associated with the Vallabha Sampradāya, whereas Mādhavendra Purīpāda is primarily revered amongst the Gauḍīyas.

Still, their interrelation—and thus the "sharing" of both Deity and founder—speaks to the harmony that can exist between advanced Vaishnavas of all lineages.[3] Indeed, for both groups, the narrative of Śrī Nāthjī inevitably begins with Mādhavendra Purī, and so before discussing the Deity, we will explore the story of Śrī Mādhavendra and the Deity's origins.

WHO IS MĀDHAVENDRA PURĪ?

Śrī Mādhavendra's identity is unique. The great souls of various lineages are said to have intimate and confidential ontological identities that underlie their temporal bodily existence, identities that reveal them to be exceptional paradigmatic souls of the spiritual world. Although all great teachers in the history of Vaishnavism are said to be eternal associates of the Lord, with personal relationships ranging from friendship, the parental mood, conjugal love, and others, Mādhavendra Purī has the distinctive position of being a "wish-fulfilling tree" (*kalpa-vṛkṣasyāvatāro*),[4] indicating the fullness of his overarching devotion and his special place in the genesis of Śrī Chaitanya's movement.

Historically, Mādhavendra Purī is remembered as the guru who virtually defined Gauḍīya *siddhānta*—he was the teacher of Mahāprabhu's teacher, and thus the original seed that would sprout into the tree of Chaitanyite *bhakti*. As Śrīla Bhaktisiddhānta Sarasvatī Goswāmī so eloquently expressed it: "Mādhavendra Purī was the first shoot of the desire tree of divine love, which came out of the Madhva lineage. Prior to his appearance, there was no sign of the conjugal mood of devotion in the Madhva line."[5]

To be sure, the Brahma-Madhva lineage had always promoted love of Krishna. However, it was often focused on Krishna's more majestic feature, or even Vishnu, his plenary portion. The Gauḍīya contribution is the more intimate love of Rādhā and Krishna, confidential and Supreme, and it is this—in its most esoteric form—that Mādhavendra Purī contributed to Vaishnava thought. And this would be later developed, of course, by the Six Gosvāmīs of Vrindavan and their followers.

As far as the mood of Mādhavendra Purī, which can be found throughout the Gosvāmī literature, we must look to the more esoteric aspect of Vaishnava thought, most fully embodied in his teaching of divine "separation" (*viraha, vipralambha*), as a form of enhancing one's love of God. In fact, this became the seed that distinguished Gauḍīya Vaishnavism from other Vaishnava denominations, sharpening the intensity of the adherents' meditation and allowing it to grow into a formidable tree of *bhakti*—to a degree that would have been impossible without it.

Śrī Mādhavendra's key verse in this regard—deceptively simple in its construction and content—runs as follows:

> *ayi dīna-dayārdra nātha he/ mathurā-nātha kadāvalokyase// hṛdayaṁ tvad-aloka-kātaraṁ/ dayita bhrāmyati kiṁ karomy aham//*

"O My Lord! O most merciful master! O master of Mathurā! When shall I see you again? Because of my not seeing you, my agitated heart has become unsteady. O most beloved one, what shall I do now?" (*Caitanya-caritāmṛta*, Madhya 4.197, Antya 8.34)[6]

The super-excellence of this rich utterance is well documented: Chaitanya Mahāprabhu himself recited it with the highest praise. The *Caitanya-caritāmṛta* tells us that the verse itself is just like the moon, spreading illumination throughout the world. "As the Kaustubha-maṇi is considered the most precious of valuable stones," the text continues, "this verse is similarly considered the best of poems dealing with the rapture of devotional service. In fact, it was spoken by Śrīmatī Rādhārāṇī herself, and by her mercy only was it manifest in the words of Mādhavendra Purī. Only Śrī Caitanya Mahāprabhu has tasted the poetry of this verse. No fourth person is capable of understanding it." (That is to say, Śrīmatī Rādhikā, Mādhavendra Purī, and Śrī Chaitanya are the only entities that are fully able to understand this verse, so deep is its import.)

Prabhupada's commentary on these verses (Madhya 4.197, Antya 8.34) makes clear its singular value:

> When Śrī Kṛṣṇa left Vṛndāvana and accepted the kingdom of Mathurā, Śrīmatī Rādhārāṇī, out of ecstatic feelings of separation, expressed how Kṛṣṇa can be loved in separation. Thus devotional service in separation is central to this verse. Worship in separation is considered by the Gauḍīya-Mādhva sampradāya to be the topmost level of devotional service. According to this conception, the devotee thinks of himself as very poor and neglected by the Lord. Thus he addresses the Lord as *dīna-dayārdra nātha*, as did Mādhavendra Purī. Such an ecstatic feeling is the highest form of devotional service. Because Kṛṣṇa had gone to Mathurā, Śrīmatī Rādhārāṇī was very much affected, and She expressed herself thus: "My dear Lord, because of Your separation My mind has become overly agitated. Now tell me, what can I do? I am very poor and You are very merciful, so kindly have compassion upon me and let me know when I shall see You." Śrī Caitanya Mahāprabhu was always expressing the ecstatic emotions of Śrīmatī Rādhārāṇī that She exhibited when She saw Uddhava at Vṛndāvana. Similar feelings, experienced by Mādhavendra Purī, are expressed in this verse. Therefore, Vaiṣṇavas in the Gauḍīya-Mādhva sampradāya say that the ecstatic feelings experienced by Śrī Caitanya Mahāprabhu during His appearance came from Śrī Mādhavendra Purī through Īśvara Purī. All the devotees in the line of the Gauḍīya-Mādhva sampradāya accept these principles of devotional service.

These feelings of separation are summed up in Mahāprabhu's own stanza: *yugāyitaṁ nimeṣeṇa, cakṣuṣā prāvṛṣāyitam/ śūnyāyitaṁ jagat sarvaṁ, govinda-viraheṇa me//* ("My Lord Govinda, because of separation from you, I consider even a moment to be a great millennium. Tears flow from my eyes like torrents of rain, and I see the entire world as void in your absence."). Thus, the Gauḍīya mood asserts the necessity of incessant longing (*govinda-viraheṇa me*), which, perhaps counterintuitively, serves to intensify union. This, in turn, makes love for Krishna immeasurably sweeter than previously imaginable.

Consequently, the tradition supports the virtues of being separated—for this leads to an even greater union: In Rūpa Goswāmī's *Padyāvali* (240), for example, he has Rādhikā saying, "I prefer separation from Krishna to union, because in union I see Krishna only in one place, whereas in separation, I see him everywhere." Commenting on Rūpa's *Ujjvala-nīlamaṇi* (1.20), Jīva Goswāmī says that "the power of an elephant can only be seen when it is chained and using all its strength to break free; similarly, the power of Rādhā's love for Krishna can only be fully seen in her separation from him." In this way, separation is lauded throughout the Gauḍīya tradition.

"As the *gopīs* were thinking of Krishna in separation twenty-four hours a day," Prabhupāda writes in *Kṛṣṇa Book*, 46, "so Kṛṣṇa was also always thinking of the *gopīs*, mother Yaśodā, Nanda Mahārāja and the other residents of Vrindavan." Their exchange of love is thus complete and fully reciprocal. "The *gopīs* saw their beloved Kṛṣṇa at Kurukṣetra after a long separation," says *Śrīmad Bhāgavatam* 10.82.39. "They secured and embraced him in their hearts through their eyes, and they attained a joy so intense that not even perfect *yogīs* can attain it."

MĀDHAVENDRA LOCATES ŚRĪ NĀTHJĪ

The story of unearthing Śrī Nāthjī, which happened in the fifteenth century, is recounted in the *Caitanya-caritāmṛta* (Madhya 4): In his travels, Śrī Caitanya Mahāprabhu reached the border of Orissa, where He rested for some time in the celebrated village of Remuṇā. There, he narrated the story of Mādhavendra Purī, as he had heard it from his own spiritual master, Īśvara Purī.

Mādhavendra Purī, we are told, sat beneath a tree in the Govardhan area when an unnamed cowherd boy—whose identity is eventually revealed as Krishna himself—approached him with a pot of milk, placing it before him with the following words: "O Mādhavendra, please drink this milk. You have been fasting and you need some nourishment." When Mādhavendra saw the beauty of that cowherd before him, he began to know an inner satisfaction, forgetting all hunger and thirst. The milk before him became incidental. He asked the boy, "Who are you? Where do you live?" The response came quickly, "I am just a simple cowherd boy, and I reside in this village. I must go very soon to milk the cows, but I shall return to retrieve this milk pot from you."

Just then, the boy left as quickly as he had appeared. Mādhavendra's was astonished: "Who is this all-attractive boy?" After drinking the milk, he washed the pot and placed it aside. That evening, he chanted the holy name with great enthusiasm, as was his custom. He thought about the young cowherd, too, until he gradually fell asleep.

Then, in a dream, he saw that very same boy once more, who took his hand and led him to a bush in the jungle. "I reside in this bush," said the young cowherd, "and because of this I suffer from severe cold, rain showers, harsh winds, and scorching heat. Please bring the local villagers and, with them, rescue me from this outdoor climate. I am cold. Once I am free, please have them situate me nicely on top of the hill, where I can enjoy the sunshine."

Actually, in fact, it is said that the boy asked him to construct a temple on top of Govardhan, installing him as the temple's Deity. He said that after being so installed, he should be washed with large quantities of cold water so that his body may be cleansed from all that time in the bush.

"My name is Gopāla," said the boy. "I am the lifter of Govardhan Hill. I was originally installed by Vajra, but when foreigners attacked, the priest who was serving me hid me in this bush in the jungle. Then he ran away out of fear, never to return. Since the priest went away, I have been staying in this bush. It is very good that you have come at this time. Now just remove me with care."

After saying this, the boy disappeared, and Mādhavendra awakened from his sleep. He then started his day and began to consider all that had just happened, causing him to cry due to ecstatic love—he realized that Krishna himself had appeared before him, and in his dream as well. He then focused his mind on executing the order of Gopāla-Krishna.

Mādhavendra entered the village and assembled all the local people, as Gopāla had asked. Then he spoke as follows. "The proprietor of this village, Govardhana-dhārī (Krishna), is lying in the bushes. Let us go there and rescue him at once." This they did, with great effort, and when all was said and done they all celebrated by having a massive festival.

In this way, the now-famous Annakūṭa ceremony was performed, and Mādhavendra Purī personally made sure that everything was done as an offering to Gopāla.

Eventually, two *brāhmaṇas* arrived from Bengal, and Mādhavendra initiated them into the path of *bhakti*. He then entrusted them with the daily service of the Deity, which they enacted with great care. Thus, Mādhavendra Purī was pleased, and the worship of Gopāla—who would soon become known as Śrī Nāthjī—began at the holy site of Govardhan.

This continued uninterrupted for two years. Then one day Mādhavendra had a dream wherein Gopāla said, "Please bring sandalwood from the Malaya province and Purī and smear the pulp over my body to cool me.

Kindly go quickly. Since no one else can do it with the requisite love, you must go personally." After having this dream, Mādhavendra Purī started east toward Bengal.

Before leaving, of course, he made all arrangements for regular Deity worship, and he engaged different people in various duties. Then, taking up the order of Gopāla, he started on his journey. In fact, he was never seen in that area again, but his devotional adventures elsewhere in India have become legendary. Without ever returning to Govardhan, his service to Gopāla was thoroughly consummated.[7]

The *Caitanya-caritāmṛta* is silent about how the Bengali priests lost their service to the Deity, and how that service was eventually bequeathed to the followers of Vallabhāchārya, who founded the branch of Vaishnavism that came to be known as Puṣṭimārga. In Narahari Chakravartī's *Bhakti-ratnākara*, however, we are afforded a summary of what eventually transpired.[8] It was in the generation after Mahāprabhu and his immediate associates, during the time of Narottama Dāsa Ṭhākura, Śrīnivāsa Āchārya, and Śyāmānanda and toward the end of the sixteenth century, that Viṭṭhalanāth (c. 1516–1588), Vallabhāchārya's son, took charge of Gopāla's worship. Apparently, after the initial Bengali priests had passed away, the esteemed Raghunāth Dāsa Gosvāmī, one of the Six Gosvāmīs of Vrindavan, decided that Viṭṭhalanāth's love for Gopāla was incomparable, and that the service of the Deity should consequently go to him.[9]

PUṢṬIMĀRGA SOURCES

The Vallabha Sampradāya offers a slightly differing narrative regarding the earliest days of the Gopāla Deity, with added details. Braj historian David Haberman refers to the version found in the *Śrī Nāthjī kī prākatya vārtā* of Harirāya, the great-great-grandson of Vallabhāchārya. "This account," writes Haberman, "relates that in the year 1409 the left arm of Śrī Nāthjī suddenly appeared out of the ground. Around this time a resident of Braj climbed Govardhana Mountain in search of a cow and discovered the arm.

"For sixteen days," Haberman relates to us, "he told no one, but then realizing that he had never before seen anything like this, he called several local people and showed the arm to them. They were all astonished and concluded that it must be a god. An elder among them identified the raised arm as belonging to Krishna, the supporter of Mount Govardhana, who was now standing in a cave within the mountain. The elder urged the villagers not to uncover the rest of Śrī Nāthjī, but let him emerge when ready. In the meantime the villagers bathed the arm with milk, worshipped it with grains of rice, flowers, sandalwood paste, and Tulasi, and offered it fruit and yogurt. The arm was worshipped in this manner until 1478; in that year the lotus-face of Śrī Nāthjī appeared above ground. This occurred at precisely the same moment that Vallabhāchārya was born in Madhya Pradesh." Haberman continues:

> In the year 1492, Śrī Nāthjī appeared to Vallabha and announced: "I am the essential form that supports Mount Govardhana and am now residing in a cave there. You know that the residents of Braj have seen me. I have decided to reveal myself completely, but I am waiting for you. Come here quickly and perform my worship." Vallabha immediately set out for Braj, stopping first in Mathurā and bathing in the Yamunā River at Viśrama Ghaṭa. Then he proceeded to Govardhana. As he climbed the mountain, Śrī Nāthjī suddenly appeared before him and embraced him. Now fully manifest, Śrī Nāthjī commanded Vallabha to install him in a temple and establish his worship.
>
> . . .
>
> The arrangement set up by Vallabha lasted for some fourteen years, but soon after his death in 1530 tensions began to surface between the Bengali priests and the temple manager Krishnadasa. The *Śrī Nāthjī kī prākatya vārtā* . . . claims that the Bengali [priests] . . . were expelled from the temple three years after Vallabha died. The temple manager Krishnadāsa, who even barred Vallabha's son Viṭṭhalnātha from entering the temple for a short period, was a key figure in this change of priestly appointments.[10]

VRINDAVAN COMES TO NATHDWARA

By the late seventeenth century, imperial attacks by Muslim soldiers disrupted Vaishnava worship in Braj. With the destruction of Mathurā's Keshavadeva temple, many devotees fled the Vrindavan area, trying to protect their respective Deities. In 1669, under the threat of attack by Muslim troops, Śrī Nāthjī was moved as well.

Like many other important Braj Deities, he was moved to Rajasthan, but while the others were transferred to Jaipur and neighboring villages, he was moved to Nathdwara, some twenty-five miles north of the palace city of Udaipur. "The area," says David Haberman, "is now identified with Braj: the Banas River which flows by Nathdwara is the Yamunā; a nearby mountain is Mount Govardhana; and gardens are maintained as the love-bowers of Vrindaban."

Although the Vallabha tradition, like the other Vaishnava traditions, reveres many forms of Krishna in many temples, the shrine at Nathdwara has become the very emblem of Deity worship in the Sampradāya, and Śrī Nāthjī remains their preeminent Deity. As Professor Fred Smith writes:

> The Śrīnāthjī image is the characteristic or definitive image in the Puṣṭimārga, and the most important deity for public worship in the Puṣṭimārga, with many of its features, including the downcast eyes, appearing on all Puṣṭimārga *svarūps* or images. This temple has singular importance in the Puṣṭimārga because the deity, Srināthjī, was transported there on a bullock cart in the late seventeenth century from Mount Govardhan in Braj on a slow and wild ride, often miraculously escaping Muslims who tried to capture or destroy it, or so the story goes. The Śrīnāthjī temple is not only the most revered in the Puṣṭimārga, but is the only Puṣṭimārga temple with national recognition beyond the *sampradāya* itself. Virtually all Puṣṭimārgīs maintain a lifelong desire to visit Nathdvara and the Śrīnāthjī temple.[11]

The temple is exceptional in terms of Vaishnava worship, with an altar and a standard of dedication that are exemplary. Its various *āratī* ceremonies are known as *jhāṅkī,* which refers to a "quick vision," or a glimpse (*darśana*) that one must embrace while the opportunity presents itself. These various viewings are carefully constructed to reflect the mood, the time of day, and the season—correlating melodies, articles of worship, and meditations thus accompany the various *jhāṅkīs*.

Like most traditions originating in Braj, the Deities are worshipped according to the schema known as *aṣṭa-kālīya-līlā,* "the eight divisions of Krishna's day." The concept is illuminated in Vaishnava wisdom texts, such as the *Padma Purāṇa* (Patala khaṇḍa, Chapter 52) and the *Sanat-kumāra-saṁhitā* (Chapter 36), where Krishna's typical day in celestial Braj is divided into distinct time periods for meditative purposes.

These texts offer a sampling of the Lord's average day in the spiritual world, allowing accomplished devotees the facility to further focus on his intimate pastimes, and, through the process of *rāgānuga-sādhana*, enter into them. Several spiritual masters in the tradition, such as Krishnadāsa Kavirāja Goswāmī and Viśvanātha Chakravartī, have written commentaries to guide devotees in this practice, albeit with the repeated caution that it is only meant for advanced students. (See chapter on Radha Raman for more details).

In terms of the temple *āratī* ceremony and how it corresponds to *aṣṭa-kāliya-līlā*, the priests in Nathdwara incorporate certain procedures—using the traditional Maṅgala-āratī, Śṛṅgāra-āratī, Rāja-bhoga-āratī, Sandhyā-āratī, and so on—to illuminate remembrance of Krishna's day (*yāmas*) in Braj. According to an individual worshipper's *bhāva*, or emotion, they enter into the various time periods and see themselves as taking part in it, all while viewing Krishna as a child, as per Śrī Nāthjī's youthful age, or as a lover of the *gopīs*, and so on. This is done under the guidance of senior priests.

"The complex style of worship performed for Sri Nathaji," writes David Haberman, "has produced a wealth of artistic traditions, cultivating the creative development of an impressive array of special perfumes, clothing, jewelry, flower garlands, food arrangements, ritual instruments, and intricate decorations." Haberman elaborates on these artistic traditions:

> Viṭṭhalnātha was greatly influenced by the arts of his time; evidence that this influence still continues can easily be gained by roaming the colorful bazaars of present-day Nathdwara. Large numbers of artisans inhabit this town, and many are employed by the temple itself, producing their crafts in the various workshops that fill the temple compound. Perhaps the most important form of visual art to come out of the temple activities in Nathdwara is a style of painting known as Picchvai. These are large cloth paintings that are hung behind Śrī Nāthjī to convey and enhance the mood of a particular season or festival being celebrated. Picchvai paintings portray dramatic scenery, such as forests and spring flowers, and dramatic events, such as Krishna's love-dance with the *gopīs*.[12]

ŚRĪ NĀTHJĪ IN ISKCON

In 1978, ISKCON New York was already in its "skyscraper temple," as Prabhupāda called it, on West 55th Street in Manhattan. At the time, the Life Membership program, mainly comprised of practitioners from within the Indian community, was growing exponentially, and several Gujarati members, familiar with Śrī Nāthjī from their youth, expressed a desire to see a Western manifestation of the Deity. After all, they noted, Śrī Nāthjī is Krishna himself, and since ISKCON is a nonsectarian movement, open to all legitimate forms of God, why neglect this particular manifestation of Krishna?

It was then that Vedavyāsa-priyā Mahārāja, originally from Gujarat himself, stepped forward and championed the idea of bringing Śrī Nāthjī into Prabhupāda's movement. "I proposed that we should install Nāthjī to encourage our Gujarati congregation's spiritual lives, and the GBC approved the plan," he says. "So our craftsman and carpenter Maheshvara Dasa constructed a Deity of Śrī Nāthjī based on a traditional picture, with the help of a generous donation from life member Kirtikant Shah." The rest, as they say, is history.

NOTES

1. Mādhavendra Purī is usually said to have lived in the fourteenth century. However, in all likelihood, it was the fifteenth, given that he is the guru of several of Śrī Chaitanya's albeit elder contemporaries, who flourished in the latter part of the 1400s. Friedhelm Hardy confirms this in his classic article, "Mādhavendra Purī: A Link between Bengal Vaiṣṇavism and South Indian 'Bhakti'" in *Journal of the Royal*

Asiatic Society of Great Britain and Ireland, No. 1 (1974): 23–41. See p. 31, where the probable dates are given as c. 1420 to 1490.

As for the Deity of Śrī Nāthjī, it is said that Vajranābha, Lord Krishna's great-grandson, originally carved and installed him some five thousand years ago, along with seven other Deities: in Mathurā, Dīrgha-Vishnu (Keśava); in Vrindavan, Govindadeva; in Govardhana, Harideva; and in Gokula, Baladeva. These were the first four. Additionally he carved two "Nāthas"—Śrī Nāthjī, as mentioned, and Śrī Gopīnātha, now in Jaipur. Add to this the two "Gopālas" known as Śrī Madana Gopāla, renamed Śrī Madana-mohana, now in Karauli, Rajasthan, and Sākṣi Gopāla, now in Orissa, near Purī, and that constitutes the eight. It is said that Vajra also commissioned the carving of four Śiva Deities and four of the goddess, Śiva's consort, totaling sixteen. It was some four thousand years later that Mādhavendra discovered "Śrī Nāthjī" (though not yet known by that name) in the Govardhan area of Braj.

2. There is an esoteric reading on Śrī Nāthjī's upraised arm: The late American Vallabhite scholar/practitioner Shyamdas told me in personal correspondence (December 13, 2011) that there is a *mādhurya* interpretation emphasized by Vallabha practitioners in the know: "Pushti marg is an ocean of Sringara-rasa (*madhurya*). . . . The *bhava* of Sri Nathji is well known in the *sampradaya*—he is calling his *bhaktas* towards him and keeping the *rasa* of devotion in his lower left hand. The holder of the Govardhan Hill in the Pusthi marg is Lord Gokulnath [not Sri Nathaji]." This is cautiously confirmed by David Haberman in his article, "Sri Nathji: The itinerant Lord of Mount Govardhan" in *Journal of Vaishnava Studies* 3, no. 3 (Summer 1995). As the title suggests, Haberman primarily identifies Śrī Nāthjī as the lifter of Mount Govardhan, mainly citing as his source the *Śrī Nāthjī kī prākatya vārtā*, a famous Puṣṭimārga text. However, on page 12 of his article, he mentions the alternate tradition of Śrī Nāthjī as lover of the *gopīs*, saying that his raised hand is his gesture of calling his *bhaktas* toward him in a mood of love (as opposed to that of lifting Govardhan Hill).

3. Says Professor David Haberman in personal correspondence (October 18, 2020): "I actually see Shri Govardhan Nathji as a deity shared by both 'sampradayas' at a time when sampradaik boundaries were not so clearly established. This did change later when lines became more clearly defined. . . . The court case recorded in much literature seems to mark the time when the temple came under the control of the Pushti Marg [Vallabha lineage], but prior to that it was a temple shared by more than one group. In all accounts, Madhavendra Puri was a key figure."

4. See Kavi Karṇapūra's *Gaura-gaṇoddeśa-dīpikā* 22: *tasya śiṣyo mādhavendro yad dharmo 'yaṁ pravartitaḥ | kalpa-vṛkṣasyāvatāro vraja-dhāmani tiṣṭhitaḥ | prīta-preyo vatsalatojjvalākhya phala-dhāriṇaḥ* ("Lakṣmīpati's disciple was Mādhavendra Purī, who preached *bhakti*. He was the *avatāra* of a *kalpavṛkṣa* in Vraja, and held the fruits of *dāsya, sakhya, vatsālya* and *mādhurya rasas*.") Also see Viśvanātha Chakravartī's *Gaura-gaṇa-svarūpa-tattva-candrikā* 26, 27: *purā vrndāvane hy āsīd ayaiṁ kalpa-tarur hareḥ/ tasya śisya īśvarākhyaḥ purī yo vraja-maṇḍale// gargo munir nāma cakre śrī-rāma-krishna-candrayoḥ/ gaura-candraḥ svīkrtavāñ śisyatvaṁ yasya gauravāt//* ("Mādhavendra Purī was previously Lord Hari's desire tree in Vrindavan. His disciple was named Īśvara Purī, who in Vraja had been Garga Muni and had given the names to Krishna and Balarāma. Lord Gauracandra respectfully became his disciple").

5. Bhaktisiddhānta Sarasvatī, *Caitanya-bhāgavata*, Ādi-khaṇḍa 9.170, commentary.

6. There are two cousin verses that are similarly lauded as unparalleled in the Gauḍīya tradition. The first was a mysterious verse uttered by Śrī Chaitanya at Ratha-yātrā: *yaḥ kaumāra-haraḥ sa eva hi varas tā eva caitra-kṣapās/ te conmīlita-mālatī-surabhayaḥ prauḍhāḥ kadambānilāḥ// sā caivāsmi tathāpi tatra surata-vyāpāra-līlā-vidhau/ revā-rodhasi vetasī-taru-tale cetaḥ samutkaṇṭhate//* ("That very personality who stole my youth is now again my master. These are the same moonlit nights of the month of Caitra. The same fragrance of *mālatī* flowers is there, and the same sweet breezes are blowing from the *kadamba* forest. In our intimate relationship, I am also the same lover, yet still my mind is not happy here. I am eager to go back to that place on the bank of the Revā under the Vetasī tree. That is my desire").

The inner import of this verse was understood by Śrīla Rupa Gosvāmī, who wrote his own verse to make its esoteric meaning more overt: *priyaḥ so 'yaṁ kṛṣṇaḥ saha-cari kuru-kṣetra-militas/ tathāhaṁ sā rādhā tad idam ubhayoḥ saṅgama-sukham// tathāpy antaḥ-khelan-madhura-muralī-pañcama-juṣe/ mano me kālindī-pulina-vipināya spṛhayati//* ("My dear friend, now I have met My very old and dear friend Krishna on this field of Kurukṣetra. I am the same Rādhārāṇī, and now We are meeting together. It is very pleasant, but I would still like to go to the bank of the Kālindī River beneath the trees of the forest there. I wish to hear the vibration of His sweet flute playing the fifth note within that forest of Vrindavan").

These verses, like Mādhavendra's, are originally uttered by Śrī Rādhā, or express her mood of devotion, and they are said to embody the esoteric and highest truths of love in separation.

As such, Rūpa Gosvāmī's verse refers to the Divine Couple *meeting* at Kurukṣetra, whereas Śrī Mādhavendra's is about their *separation* as a result of Krishna leaving for Mathurā. Thus, Rūpa Gosvāmī's verse is technically an instance of *samṛddhimat-sambhoga* (a prosperous meeting) that takes place after residing in a distant place, with additional *bhāvī-viraha*, the anticipation of impending separation—for Krishna will return to Dvārakā and Rādhā to Vrindavan. That is Kurukṣetra. Mādhavendra's verse, by contrast, evokes *buddhi-pūrvakaḥ sudūra pravāsa*—intentional separation at a long distance, with Śrī Rādhikā being the *proṣita-bhartṛkā nāyikā*, i.e., the heroine whose beloved resides in a distant place. These are variations on the pain and bliss of divine separation, with Madhavendra's verse being a more literal instance of separation proper.

A related point for further emphasis: The verse "*ayi dīna-dayārdra nātha he . . .* ," composed by Mādhavendra, appears in Rūpa Goswāmī's *Padyāvali*, v. 334, in the section (of about 20 verses) called Śrī Rādhāyā vilāpaḥ ("Śrīmatī Rādhārāṇī's Lament"). The verses beginning with "*yaḥ kaumāra-haraḥ . . .* " and "*priyaḥ so 'yam . . .* " (Rūpa Goswāmī), however, which are also found in the *Padyāvali* (v. 386, 387), are in the section called Tatraiva sakhīṁ prati śrī-rādhā-vacanam ("Śrīmatī Rādhārāṇī's Words to a Gopī-friend at Kurukṣetra"). Thus, the latter verses are not traditionally considered instances of "*viraha*" (since the lovers are in proximity), even if nuances of separation are suggested.

7. There is an important teaching in Mādhavendra's journey, in which he sets out to bring sandalwood back to Govardhan: During his travels, he was ordered to apply

this sandalwood to another Deity of Krishna, Gopīnātha, showing that when love for Krishna is in the heart of the worshipper, all forms of Krishna become equal, and that it is the intent of the devotee that Krishna actually sees: While away collecting the necessary items for Gopāla, Mādhavendra again had a dream in which Gopāla came before him and said, "O Mādhavendra Purī, I have already received all the sandalwood and camphor. Now just grind all the sandalwood together with the camphor and then smear the pulp on the body of Gopīnātha daily [in Remuna, where you find yourself currently] until it is finished. There is no difference between my body and Gopīnātha's body. They are one and the same. Therefore, if you smear the sandalwood pulp on the body of Gopīnātha, you will naturally also be smearing it on my body. Thus, the temperature of my body will be reduced, as desired" (*Caitanya-caritāmṛta,* Madhya 4, text 158–60).

8. Quoted in David Haberman, "Sri Nathji: The Itinerant Lord of Mount Govardhan," in *Journal of Vaishnava Studies*, 3, no. 3 (Summer 1995): 21. See Narahari Cakravartin, *Bhaktiratnākara,* ed. Navinkrishna Paravidyalankar (Calcutta: Gaudiya Math, 1940), 142. This text was written in the late seventeenth or early eighteenth century.

9. Ibid.

10. Ibid. Interestingly, the Vallabhite version of Gopāla's origins has parallels with the Gauḍīya narrative of Rūpa Goswāmī's Govinda Dev Deity. Both Gopāla and Govinda Dev are given milk by a cow while buried beneath the earth, and the Deities only selectively or gradually reveal their divine bodies in due course. A comparative study of the two Deities would be a worthwhile endeavor.

11. See Frederick M. Smith, "Varieties of Puṣṭimārga Pilgrimage" in *Journal of Vaishnava Studies* 17, no. 1 (Fall 2018): 46–47.

12. David Haberman, op. cit., 19–20.

Chapter Nine

Hawaii Five-O

The Pañca Tattva in the Aloha State

When I was a kid in New York in the 1960s, I watched an array of popular TV shows, many of which were simple police dramas. American television was rife with them: *Adam-12*, *The Mod Squad*, *Hawaii Five-O*. The year was 1968, and like many of my peers I was a bona fide TV junkie. I particularly remember the show *Hawaii Five-O*, and even then I thought the title was peculiar. What did it mean? "*Hawaii Five-O*"? I soon realized that it referred to Hawaii's status as America's fiftieth state; additionally, the Five-O squad was made up of three to five members, which would be small for any actual police unit. But something else was rearing its head in 1968—something I would later relate to the title of that very TV show—though at the time such thoughts were further away than Hawaii itself. I will return to *Hawaii Five-O* at the end of this chapter.

It was in 1968 that His Divine Grace A. C. Bhaktivedanta Swami Prabhupāda began his mission in Hawaii, an extension of his worldwide effort then underway for some two years. In the case of Hawaii, he worked through his early disciples Govinda Dāsī and her husband Gaursundara. "In early August of 1968," writes Govinda Dāsī, "Srila Prabhupada began to encourage my husband, Gaursundara, and I, to go out and open temples. We had been traveling all over the United States with His Divine Grace for nearly a year, and were then staying in Montreal, Canada, near the newly opened Montreal ISKCON temple. At that time, there was only a handful of small storefronts that we called 'temples'—one in San Francisco, one in Los Angeles, one in Boston, one in New York, one in Seattle, one in Santa Fe, and of course the one in Montreal, that was a renovated bowling alley. . . . Srila Prabhupada wanted us to go somewhere that had a warm climate, since my health suffered so much in cold climates. He suggested Florida or Hawaii."[1] She continues:

> Gaursundara chose Hawaii, more as a stepping stone to Japan, since Srila Prabhupada wanted him to open a temple in Japan as well. . . . So in early September of 1968, shortly after we arrived in San Francisco, Gaursundara left for Hawaii. He went ahead to pave the way, leaving me alone to manage Srila Prabhupada's travel and household arrangements on the mainland. Soon thereafter, Srila Prabhupada left for Santa Fe for a brief visit, then Seattle for a month, and then Los Angeles. . . . When we arrived in Los Angeles, the former storefront had closed, and there was no temple at that time, so the Deities—Lord Jagannath, Kartamashayi, and Srila Prabhupada's small Radha Krishna Deities—were kept in one room of our apartment. Soon after, the old church building on La Cienega was secured, and it became the main ISKCON Hare Krishna Temple in Los Angeles. . . . Shortly thereafter, I left for Hawaii on January 4, 1969, right after Gaursundara secured an old beach house in Kaaawa, on the windward side of Oahu, a 45 minute drive from Honolulu. It was a large old Hawaiian style house perched on the side of a cliff, overlooking the vast expanse of the Pacific Ocean.[2]

Govinda Dāsī had a distinct Krishna Deity that she worshipped even at that time, as mentioned. Prabhupāda named him Kārtamīśa (which devotees at the time roughly translated as "the boss"), alternatively rendered Kartamaśāyī, Kartā Mahāśaya, and Kārtamaśī. He was a small, piercing-blue figurine of Krishna, his left hand placed gently on his hip, unlike most other forms of Krishna meant for formal worship. While early ISKCON devotees became quite fond of him, he was never installed according to traditional Vaishnava practice, though he was briefly placed on the altar in San Francisco, even before Jagannāth arrived.[3] Kārtamīśa would have a marked influence in ISKCON Hawaii.

The first couple of years in the Aloha State witnessed usual ISKCON development, with book and magazine distribution, congregational chanting, and "Sunday Love Feasts."

By 1970, however, Govinda Dāsī was again with Śrīla Prabhupāda in Los Angeles, and because she was artistically inclined, and had rendered various art services for him in her recent past, he asked her to make Gaura-Nitāi Deities for his still new temple in Hawaii. "Gaura-Nitāi" refers to Chaitanya and Nityānanda, the manifestations of Krishna and his brother Balarāma responsible for the origins of Gauḍīya Vaishnavism in Bengal. Thus, upon returning to Hawaii, Govinda Dāsī made her way to the university library and studied books on sculpture, materials, molds, and so on, hoping to fulfill her teacher's divine request. Although she was at a loss in terms of making Deities—she had never done this before—it was Prabhupāda's desire, and as a dutiful disciple, she was determined to render her prescribed service.

"Since Kartamashayi, my Child Krishna Deity . . . was made of paper mache," she writes, I considered this may be the best [way to approach it]. Paper mache is a very durable, moldable, wood product, and is used in India for making even fine bowls and vases, as well as *murtis*. So I decided to explore that route."[4] In pursuit of this vision, Gaursundara, her husband, constructed a metal armature that he then secured to a wooden base, and she purchased clay from a local pottery-making supply store. In addition, they accumulated an abundance of newspapers from supporters of the temple. With these materials as her kernel, Govinda Dāsī assembled full-blown papier-mâché images, sculpting the two Deities according to details that Śrīla Prabhupāda had given to her.

Traditionalists may find papier-mâché an interesting choice, and an unlikely medium for the making of authorized Deities. But Prabhupāda approved it. According to *Śrīmad Bhāgavatam* 11.27.12, the Deity can appear in any of eight substances—stone, wood, metal, earth, paint, sand, jewels, or the mind (*śailī dāru-mayī lauhī, lepyā lekhyā ca saikatī, mano-mayī maṇi-mayī, pratimāṣṭa-vidhā smṛtā*). In this case, though somewhat unorthodox, the metal base would correspond to *lauhī*, which was then augmented by *lepyā*—clay, sandalwood and similar substances—and *dāru-mayī*, or wood, could be extended to mean paper. Thus, the papier-mâché Deities did not abrogate scriptural specifications. Moreover, in the Vaishnava tradition, the main ingredient when it comes to Krishna is love, or *bhakti*. If this is used in the making and worshipping of Deities, then all is as it should be.

Govinda Dāsī worked with Kusha, then a newcomer to the movement, along with Lewis (soon to be initiated as Brishni Das), and the sculpting began. Other devotees pitched in as needed, and before long Govinda Dāsī was adding the finishing touches—painting of the forms through use of a watercolor sponge to create fuzzy, soft edges, especially on their cheeks and hands. Pictures were then sent to Śrīla Prabhupāda.

Interestingly, though satisfied with what she and the other devotees had accomplished, he immediately asked for more: "Oh, very nice. So now you have done Lord Chaitanya and Lord Nityānanda. . . . Now you should also do Pañca Tattva!"[5] Prabhupāda was creating historical precedent by establishing the worship of Mahāprabhu and his associates—the Pañca Tattva—in the Western world.[6]

WHO ARE THE PAÑCA TATTVA?

Before delving into Prabhupada's specific instructions for the Pañca Tattva Deities in Hawaii, it would be worthwhile to explain these Deities theologically, since this gets to the heart of Gauḍīya Vaishnava thought.

Pañca Tattva is Sanskrit for "Five Truths." In ordinary Hindu parlance, it can also mean "Five Elements," generally referring to earth, water, fire, air, and ether. The term is understood variously in Tantric and Buddhist traditions as well, but it has a unique application in Gauḍīya Vaishnavism, where it refers to Śrī Chaitanya and his intimate four associates: Nityānanda, Advaita, Gadādhara, and Śrīvāsa—all of whom had become part of our Earthly landscape in sixteenth-century India.[7] In essence, the Pañca Tattva speaks of one God in five features, which, conceptually, is similar to the Christian Trinity of one God in three features. The Indic version is briefly delineated as follows.

As a manifestation of Rādhā and Krishna in one form, Chaitanya Mahāprabhu is the original Godhead in his most confidential and intimate feature. As the prime member of the Pañca Tattva, he is accompanied by his plenary expansion (Nityānanda Prabhu), his incarnation (Advaita Prabhu), his internal potency (Gadādhara), and his marginal energy (Śrīvāsa). The first three—Chaitanya, Nityānanda, and Advaita—are considered aspects of Vishnu Tattva, or God proper; Gadādhara is Śakti Tattva, or the energy of the Lord; and Śrīvāsa is Jīva Tattva, the devotee, part and parcel of God.

Of these five truths, only Śrī Chaitanya is called Mahāprabhu ("the Great Master"), because even among manifestations of God, he is considered primary. He appears in this world in a vibrant golden form, much like that of Śrī Rādhā, whose essence he is said to epitomize. According to the tradition, he brings to the world the congregational chanting of the Hare Krishna Mahā-mantra, far beyond ritualistic forms of religion that offer ordinary salvation, and he brings, too, the inner core of spiritual love—the highest achievement in devotional religiosity: Prema-bhakti.

As the *Caitanya-caritāmṛta* makes clear, Chaitanya Mahāprabhu cannot be understood or approached without the special mercy of Nityānanda Prabhu, who is considered the cardinal guru of the universe and who serves as an intermediary between Chaitanya and the devotee—he is thus the paradigmatic spiritual master, who, in his closeness to Chaitanya, serves as a model for all gurus who follow. As Balarāma, Krishna's elder brother, is described as Krishna's "second body," so too is Nityānanda the second body of Śrī Chaitanya. He is the Lord's "active principle," so to speak, functioning as such in both material creation and in spiritual *līlā*, or the playful sport of God.

This indicates that Krishna in his original form is simply engaged in "play," for the pleasure of his devotees, while "serious business" is handled by his first expansion, Balarāma, and his various Vishnu manifestations, who are in charge of the material world's maintenance. In kingly terms, a monarch is merely interested in enjoying his well-deserved delights, while his immediate associates tend to his various services and obligatory necessities. This is similar to how the "servitor" forms of Godhead—whether as Balarāma or Nityānanda—function in relation to Lord Krishna (or Chaitanya).

Both Mahāvishnu and Sadāśiva aspects of the Lord, who evoke awe and reverence in their devotees, descend in Chaitanya's *līlā* as Advaita Ācārya.

Because he is identical to Vishnu, the all-pervading Lord, he is called *Advaita*, meaning "non-different."

The *Caitanya-caritāmṛta* teaches that Advaita Ācārya is the entity who brought Chaitanya to this world, as one cause among several: Chaitanya himself confirms that it was Advaita's prayers that instigated his pastimes on Earth.[8] Sadāśiva is the intermediary between the spiritual world and the material world; it is therefore fitting, say the great teachers of the Gauḍīya tradition, that Advaita was the one who brought Chaitanya to our planet—for he is Sadāśiva in a more contemporary form.

Advaita Ācārya, the senior Vaishnava of Navadvīpa, was middle-aged when Chaitanya was born, and an old man toward the end of Chaitanya's Earthly pastimes. Accordingly, Advaita is usually depicted with white hair and beard.[9] His clothes are as white as his facial hair, and sometimes their whiteness is compared to that of the moon or the jasmine flower. Devotees in the tradition meditate on him as the root of transcendental joy.

Gadādhara Paṇḍita is understood to be Krishna's *śakti*, or internal energy, and is described both as a direct incarnation of Rādhārāṇī and as an incarnation of Śrī Rādhā's effulgence. Chaitanya is often called "the life and soul of Gadādhara Paṇḍita." The relationship between them is intimate, but also perplexing. For example, since Śrī Chaitanya is both Rādhā and Krishna, and Gadādhara is in fact Rādhā as well, the overlapping of spiritual identities might seem untenable.

But mundane limitations should not be foisted upon divine personalities, say Gauḍīya Vaishnava texts.

In fact, a closer look reveals that while Chaitanya and Gadādhara are both Rādhā, they exhibit different moods, and in the spiritual realm, diverse moods manifest as distinct personalities. Śrī Chaitanya is Rādhā *in the mood of separation from Krishna*. In such a state, one is besieged by determination and unrelenting effort due to spiritual eagerness, and this takes precedence over all else.[10] In the intimacy of her love, Rādhā is inexcusably demanding of Krishna, and uncompromising in her service to him. Gadādhara, on the other hand, is Rādhā *in the mood of Rukmiṇī,* one of Krishna's prominent queens in Dvārakā, or even Candrāvalī, one of Rādhā's chief competitors for Krishna's affections.[11] In their particular brand of undeviating devotion, Rukmiṇī and Candrāvalī exhibit a mood that is conciliatory and accommodating, which is very different from Rādhārāṇī's. Of course, these nuances point to esoteric dimensions of love that are difficult to understand without spiritual accomplishment and its attendant realization.

Additionally, Chaitanya's position is articulated in various ways. Sometimes, he is not seen as Rādhā per se, but rather as Krishna himself *in the mood of Rādhā*.[12]

At least this much can be understood: Gadādhara is a perfect manifestation of Krishna's *hlādinī* potency, whose personification is seen in none other than Śrī Rādhā. The *hlādinī* potency is the power by which God enjoys pleasure. It is also the potency by which his servants enjoy pleasure, so that they might interact with him in simple exchanges of love. The essence of love of God is *bhāva,* or intense spiritual emotions, the ultimate development of which is called *mahābāva,* the ultimate spiritual emotion felt in the heart of Śrī Rādhā. As it is said, Lord Krishna enchants the entire world, but Śrī Rādhā enchants him. Therefore, she is the supreme goddess, above all others, eclipsing even Krishna in terms of her spiritual power. She is the *pūrṇa-śakti,* the full potency, and she manifests in Chaitanya *līlā* as Gadādhara Paṇḍita.

Finally, Śrīvāsa Ṭhākura is said to be an incarnation of Nārada Muni, one of the twelve great authorities acknowledged throughout the tradition.[13] Nārada, in particular, is unique, for, according to Puranic texts, he was blessed with a spiritual body. This allows him to travel the cosmos while awakening seekers to higher reality, especially through the chanting of mantras. In fact, Nārada is depicted as a musician, playing his *vīṇā* in his intergalactic mission of melodically spreading the chanting of Krishna's holy name.

As an incarnation of Nārada, Śrīvāsa Ṭhākura also emphasized chanting, and the unparalleled *kīrtanas* that took place in his courtyard are now legendary, with numerous stories of the confidential ecstasies experienced by devotees who chanted there. His house became a virtual "parent church" in the universal Saṅkīrtana mission of Śrī Chaitanya, and a facsimile of his house exists today in Māyāpur, known as Śrīvāsa Aṅgam. Śrīvāsa is considered an elder among Śrī Chaitanya's devotees, and is honored as such.

The above is merely a brief outline, but the truth of the Pañca Tattva is deep and cherished by Gauḍīya Vaishnavas worldwide. Conceptually, it goes back to the beginnings of the Gauḍīya tradition, with practitioners claiming it to be an eternal principle. In terms of textual evidence, it can at least be traced to Kavi Karṇapūra's work, the *Gaura-gaṇoddeśa-dīpikā,* which was composed in 1576—the earliest days of the Gauḍīya tradition. Interestingly, Karṇapūra does not refer to it as a new concept, even at that time, nor as something that he conceived on his own. In fact, he says that Svarūpa Dāmodara Gosvāmī, one of Mahāprabhu's earliest and most intimate associates, was the first to articulate it as such.[14] Thus, it is an integral part of the Gauḍīya tradition.

It is so integral, in fact, that within the Gauḍīya tradition to this day the glorification of the Pañca Tattva is standardized with a famous mantra that is sung or chanted prior to chanting the Hare Krishna Mahā-mantra, without which it is deemed impossible to reach spiritual perfection. This Pañca Tattva mantra is composed of the names of each of the five: *Jaya Śrī Krishna Chaitanya, Prabhu Nityānanda, Śrī Advaita, Gadādhara, Śrīvāsādi-gaura-bhakta-vṛnda* ("All glories to Śrī Krishna Chaitanya and to his personal expansion [Prabhu Nityānanda], his incarnation [Śrī Advaita], his energy [Śrī Gadādhara], his devotee [Śrī Śrīvāsa], and to all who follow in his wake.") It is no wonder that Prabhupāda wanted Deities of these important manifestations in all of his temples.

BACK TO HAWAII

Prabhupāda wrote to Govinda Dāsi explaining how each of the other Deities should look, since she had already constructed the forms of Chaitanya and Nityānanda. He noted that Advaita should have white hair and beard; Gadādhara should resemble Chaitanya but without a crown; and Śrīvāsa should be depicted with shaven head and knotted *śikhā* (the tuft of hair in the back of the head, worn by all Vaishnavas who adopt monastic life), since he was to indicate the ideal devotee. Prabhupāda gave her further instructions as well, so that his disciple could reproduce them as they appeared in Bengal some years earlier.

"More blending paper mache, pressing molds, drying, sanding and painting soon followed," she writes. "FINALLY, after months of work, our Pancha Tattva Deities were complete! . . . Srila Prabhupada received the Pancha Tattva photos, and he let us know he was pleased. He began making plans to come to Hawaii to install our Pancha Tattva Deities as he had promised. We began decorating the temple room, designing and creating a beautiful Vyas Asana [sic], and preening the rose and Tulasi gardens that graced the front of our Manoa temple."[15]

"By the end of 1971," remembers Kusha, "we were close to finishing everything the Lord required for installation. The boys began constructing an altar large enough to accommodate Panca Tattva. Govinda Dasi met someone who was going to India and arranged that they would send us two crowns; one for Lord Chaitanya and one for Lord Nityananda only, as per Srila Prabhupada's instructions. We were so excited when the crowns arrived from India. Somehow the crowns seemed to bring the whole project nearer to reality. They were a very nice symmetrical design, made of gold colored metal and multi-colored rhinestones. To this day I have never seen any other crowns like those, even after all my own years in India. Govinda Dasi wrote to Srila Prabhupada and a date for the installation of Panca Tattva was set for early May [1972] when Prabhupada's travel schedule brought him through Hawaii."[16]

And so it happened on May 7, 1972, when Śrīla Prabhupāda stepped foot into the temple room, turning Hawaii into the spiritual realm. Kusha remembers the installation day:

> When the curtains concealing Their Lordships were opened for the first time, it was for most of the temple devotees, the first sight of Them. The anticipation was tremendous. . . . there was a roaring *kirtan* . . . there was *prasadam* . . . I remember the energy in the temple room bursting with transcendental happiness. Srila Prabhupada stood in front of Their Lordships and made a speech of how much it meant to him that this installation of the first ever appearance of Panca Tattva in the Western world, was completed by the sincere determination of Govinda Dasi. He gave her his blessings and with that he exited the temple room, into his car, accompanied by Gaursundara and Govinda Dasi, and went to his temporary residence in Waimanalo to rest. Their Lordships were also put to rest, as is customary after the noon offering. The devotees celebrated with *prasadam* downstairs and then they went out on street Harinama in Waikiki.[17]

For some five years the devotees happily worshipped these Deities, until it was noticed that their Lordships started "leaning" and the devotees' fears were soon realized: The Deities had to be replaced, much as wooden Jagannāth images in India are often replaced when the "matter" from which they are constructed begins to show signs of decay.[18] The Pañca Tattva Deities did not have sufficiently reinforced steel ankles and consequently softened in the hot afternoon sun.

Thus, in 1977, just before Prabhupāda left this world, he encouraged the devotees to have new Pañca Tattva Deities made with more durable substances.[19] And within months, the Hawaiian ISKCON temple soon received replica Deities that were supplied by F.A.T.E.—Prabhupāda's "First American Theistic Exhibition," which was essentially an artistic enterprise meant to create "diorama" museums that would depict Krishna-conscious themes throughout the world. By 1978, the original papier-mâché Deities were no longer, having been replaced by more durable forms made of artificial stone/fiberglass resin, with a more solid foundation. Indeed, the replacements were replaced yet again in 1987, using a still more sophisticated method, Deities that last to this day.

CONCLUSION: WHY *HAWAII FIVE-O*?

The notion of the Pañca Tattva is deceptively simple. But if one has background in the Gauḍīya tradition, and in Indic philosophy in general, one sees how the idea of God in five features flies in the face of pervasive Māyāvādī notions of tepid universal oneness and the depersonalization of God, so common in India.

Clarity emerges when we seek a complete understanding of the Absolute. Is God five or zero? Or both?

As Professor Sanyal, one of Prabhupāda's early colleagues, wrote, "If God were really a zero we could be saved the trouble of attempting to describe His nature. If God is not zero, He should logically be both everything and no particular thing, at one and the same time. Everything is in Radha-Krishna; but Radha-Krishna is not identical with anything except Themselves. In other words, Radha-Krishna has a specific individual existence of Their own, simultaneously with Their external all-pervasive existence."[20]

Prabhupāda offers another insight: "Everything is zero without the Lord, who is the digit that transforms zero into ten, two zeros into one hundred, three zeros into one thousand, and so on. Thus a 'zero man' cannot become happy without the association of the Lord, the supreme '1.'"[21]

Vaishnava theology asserts that God is all-inclusive and all encompassing by definition, incorporating both the notion of zero and the notion of one—of nothing and everything, all at once. In other words, he is both zero *and* five.

Such truths are suggested by the phrase *achintya-bhedābheda,* meaning "the inconceivable oneness and difference between God and the living being." This is the technical nomenclature for Mahāprabhu's distinct philosophical position in contradistinction to other Indic schools of thought.[22] *Achintya-bhedābheda* wonderfully encompasses the essential truths of Advaita Vedānta, or the impersonal school of thought, wherein God might be envisioned as an ultimate zero, i.e., the part of the *Hawaii Five-O* title that represents transcendental nothingness. But the same system of philosophy also includes a sense of "difference," or "otherness," or "distinctness," beautifully represented by the five entities of the Pañca Tattva.

Of course, none of this really has anything to do with the American TV show. But years later, learning about Vaishnavism and how it both incorporates and refutes impersonalism, I couldn't help but think of the title of *Hawaii Five-O*, and how the Deities in Hawaii, manifesting the Absolute as five personalities, inadvertently speaks to this dance between the zero and the many.

Here we see the idea of the "unity of opposites" in its most developed form. Mature religious understanding, Śrī Chaitanya argues, is a constant dialogue between one and zero, form and formlessness, positive and negative, feasting and fasting, yes and no—seeing harmony in the obvious differences of diametrically opposed phenomena. Indeed, "harmony" presupposes an interaction of different elements working together. This is the paradox of the One and the Many—a paradox that has been resolved by monists or impersonalistis in one way, and by Vaishnavas in quite another.

To describe the Absolute as *merely* impersonal, or without quality and attributes, is to render him imperfect by reducing him to a nonentity. Gauḍīya Vaishnavism would not stand for this. Rather, it specifically points to divinity as a person—or as five persons—through which relationship (*rasa*) is possible, and love can become a reality. Once the absolute, complete, and perfect nature of divine personality is thus recognized, the philosophy of impersonalism necessarily takes a backseat. It is, no doubt, part of the overarching truth, but it can no longer be central. Love and relationship reign supreme.

Ultimately, of course, the Absolute is both personal and impersonal—both dimensions must exist for God to be totally and perfectly complete. But—and the Chaitanya tradition makes careful record of this—the Absolute is primarily personal, because only in a personal Absolute, possessing infinite and inconceivable characteristics and potencies, can the manifold forms of Godhead, like the Pañca Tattva, including the impersonal Brahman, make any sense, rising to the fore and assuming its rightful place as ultimate reality, and only in such an environment can love exist in all its fullness.

NOTES

1. See Govinda Dāsī's website: http://www.govindadasi.com/hare-krishna-hawaii-blog.

2. Ibid.

3. Personal correspondence with Nara Narayan Vishwakarma dasa, April 25, 2022: "Govinda dasi saw this deity in San Francisco, and asked me if I could make plaster castings. She was in love with Him! Srila Prabhupada agreed that she could, and I drove to San Francisco and more or less kidnapped the original Kartamasayi and brought him to our temple in LA on La Cienega Ave. (This was a year before New Dwarka on Watseka). So, I made a latex mold, and I found out that the original was made from papier-mâché. So I made seventeen Hydrostone castings of Kartamasayi (until the mold began to warp). This equaled one for each temple that we now had around the USA. So I cast them, and Govinda dasi painted them, and they were exquisite! (She sponged reddish pink on his bright blue cheeks!) When I finished the mold, I returned the original to San Francisco. . . . they were so relieved and happy to get him back!"

4. See Govinda Dāsī's website: http://www.govindadasi.com/hare-krishna-hawaii-blog.

5. See Govinda Dāsī's website: http://www.govindadasi.com/hare-krishna-hawaii-blog/gour-nitai-makes-their-appearance.

6. Although the Pañca Tattva Deities in Hawaii were the first in the Western world, it is said that Prabhupāda wanted them in all of his temples, as per the memory of one of his sculptor disciples, Ādideva Dāsa (in personal correspondence, June 9, 2022). After Hawaii, Pañca Tattva Deities would indeed become ubiquitous in the movement, gracing ISKCON altars in Laguna Beach, California; Newcastle upon Tyne, UK; Almvik, Sweden; Dublin, Ireland; Belfast, Northern Ireland; Swansea, Wales; Ljubljana, Slovenia, and elsewhere. Of course, in India, Pañca Tattva Deities were established long ago at Mahāprabhu's birthplace, and, along similar lines, though

quite distinct, one finds the oversized and one-of-a-kind Deities worshiped on the altar in ISKCON Māyāpura.

7. For a thorough analysis of the Pañca Tattva individually and as a group, see A. C. Bhaktivedanta Swami Prabhupada, *Lord Caitanya in Five Features: Chapter 7, Ādī-Līlā Of Kṛṣṇadāsa Kavirāja Gosvāmī's Srī-Caitanya-caritāmṛta* (Los Angeles: Bhaktivedanta Book Trust, 1973). This was an excerpted volume from Prabhupāda's larger seventeen-volume *Caitanya-caritāmṛta,* translation and commentary. His choice of excerpting this portion of his major life's work is significant, speaking to the importance of the Pañca Tattva in general. See also Steven J. Rosen, *Śrī Pañca Tattva: The Five Features of God* (New York: Folk Books, 1994). The following description of Vaishnavism's "five truths" is based on these two works.

8. See *Caitanya-caritāmṛta,* Ādi 13.70–71.

9. The tradition is beleaguered by some controversy on this score: The famous Deities of the Pañca Tattva at Śrī Chaitanya's birth site, commissioned by Śrīla Bhaktisiddhānta Sarasvatī, Prabhupāda's guru, depicts Advaita with no beard and in the prime of youth. The same is true for Advaita Deities in Śrīvāsa Aṅgam and in Śantipura. Similarly, the traditional Gosvāmī-parivāras insist that he should not be depicted with a beard, and the famous *Advaitāṣṭakam* says he should be rendered as eternally youthful as well. Finally, Bhaktisiddhānta's commentary on the *Caitanya-bhāgavata* Madhya 16.99 says clearly that Advaita should be clean-shaven.

Conversely, Prabhupāda often said that Advaita should be depicted with a beard: See his lecture on the *Caitanya-caritāmṛta* Madhya 20.66–96 on November 21, 1966 and at Brandeis University, April 29, 1969. He also wrote by letter, "Advaita Prabhu has a full white beard. He was an old man. He was practically older than the father of Lord Caitanya. He was an elder gentleman in the town of Navadvipa, elder of the *brahmana* community" (Letter to Govinda Dasi, November 20, 1971). This letter was specifically written in reference to the Deities in Hawaii, but he had written the same thing in numerous other letters to various disciples. The Pañca Tattva Deities in Māyāpura at the famous Temple of the Vedic Planetarium also has Advaita with a beard. Needless to say, in one sense, the controversy is moot: Advaita is not a static individual—he could have had a beard at times and no beard at other times.

10. See *Caitanya-caritāmṛta* Antya 14.14, purport.

11. See Swami B. V. Tripurari, Gadadhara Pandita—Radharani, June 13, 2015 (https://www.radha.name/news/philosophy/gadadhara-pandita-radharani).

12. See *Caitanya-caritāmṛta* Ādi 4.99–100: "To spread the teachings of *prema-bhakti* [devotional love], Krishna appeared as Śrī Krishna Caitanya with the mood and complexion of Śrī Rādhā" (*prema-bhakti śikhāite āpane avatari, rādhā-bhāva-kānti dui aṅgīkāra kari,' śrī-kṛṣṇa-caitanya-rūpe kaila avatāra, ei ta' pañcama ślokera artha paracāra*).

13. The word *mahājana* is translated as "great authorities," referring to twelve specific individuals lauded throughout India's wisdom texts. This is based on *Śrīmad-Bhāgavatam* 6.3.20–21, which cites the authoritative personalities as Brahmā, Nārada, Śiva (Śrīvāsa, in the current context), the four Kumāras, Kapila (the son of Devahūti), Svāyambhuva Manu, Prahlāda Mahārāja, Janaka Mahārāja, Grandfather Bhīṣma, Bali Mahārāja, Yamarāja, and Śukadeva Gosvāmī.

14. Kavi Karṇapūra's *Gaura-gaṇoddeśa-dīpikā* offers evidence that the notion of the Pañca Tattva is traceable to Svarūpa Dāmodara: *ataḥ svarūpa-caraṇair uktaṁ tattva-nirūpaṇe* | *upādhi-bhedāt pañcatvaṁ tattvasyeha pradarśyate* ||9|| *pañcatattvātmakaṁ kṛṣṇaṁ bhakta-rūpa-svarūpakam* | *bhaktāvatāraṁ bhaktyākhyaṁ namāmi bhakti-śaktikam* ||10|| After these two verses, Karṇapūra offers several more to explain the concept theologically.

Another early source for the Pañca Tattva comes from Dhyānachandra Goswāmī's *Śrī Gaura-govindārcana-smaraṇa-paddhati* (https://www.scribd.com/document/88069163/Gaura-Govindarcana-Smarana-Paddhatih-by-Dhyanacandra-Gosvami). In verses 42–44 and 71, we learn how to meditate on each of the Pañca Tattva for personal edification.

As to exactly where one might find Svarūpa Dāmodara's original verse, some say it was originally from his diary (Brzezinski), whereas others opine that it was likely from his book, *Gaura-tattva-nirūpaṇa* (De), neither of which are currently extant (and may have in fact been the same book). For the former theory, see Jagadananda Dasa, "Keeping Faith with Kheturi, Part III," August 21, 2015 (http://jagadanandadas.blogspot.com/2015/08/keeping-faith-with-kheturi-part-iii.html); for the latter, see S. K. De, *Early History of the* Vaiṣṇava *Faith and Movement in Bengal* (Calcutta: Firma K. L. Mukhopadhyay, 1961), 32, 39–41.

15. See Govinda Dāsī's website (http://www.govindadasi.com/hare-krishna-hawaii-blog/sri-sri-panchatattva-appears-finally).

16. Kusha Devi Dasi, personal correspondence, May 12, 2022.

17. Ibid.

18. In India, there is a ritual in which Lord Jagannāth's external form, made from sacred wood, is replaced to sustain his worship over the centuries. The ceremony itself is called "Nava-kalevara" (or, in the local dialect, Nabakalebara), which literally means "new body." Approximately every twelve to nineteen years, the transcendental bodies of the Lord and his associates (Balarāma and Subhadrā) are changed: New trees are brought in and the Deities are made afresh. For more, see our chapter on Lord Jagannāth.

Similarly, the early Jagannāth Deities in Hawaii had become termite-ridden and needed to be replaced. At one point, however, devotees in Hawaii had their renewed Jagannāth sculpted from koa wood (*Acacia koa*), native to the islands and termite resistant. Interestingly, it is said that the Koa tree does not naturally grow outside Hawaii. This indigenous wood has an honored heritage and is revered as sacred, much like the trees in Puri that are used for the rejuvenation of Jagannāth in Orissa. The beautiful grain of the koa wood is renowned for its deep, rich colors and varied patterns. Koa is a hard wood and has high crush resistance and shock absorbance. It is often compared to walnut, but weighs considerably more, making it durable, and its interlocking grain makes for an exceptionally beautiful image. Its thin, light-colored sapwood that surrounds its inner hardwood have been described as tantamount to a unique lustrous, swirled marble, just right for Deity construction.

19. Prabhupāda wrote to his disciple Baradraj, who was the founder and chief artist of F.A.T.E., on April 8, 1977: "The Pañca Tattva Deities in Hawaii are now many years old and they are beyond being repaired. Please therefore immediately make new

Deities of the same size as the ones that are now installed. They should be made in the same process as you are now doing for Fiji."

20. See Nisikanta Sanyal, *Sree Krishna Chaitanya* (Madras: Sree Gaudiya Math, 1933), 90.

21. See A. C. Bhaktivedanta Swami Prabhupāda, trans., *Mukunda-Mālā-Stotra: The Prayers of King Kulaśekhara*, mantra 1, Purport (Los Angeles: Bhaktivedanta Book Trust, 1992, reprint), 4.

22. Soon after Mahāprabhu's time, Jīva Gosvāṃī, one of the Six Gosvāṃīs of Vrindāvan, gave the Lord's philosophical school its formal title, "Acintya-bhedābheda." This is passed down to us through his masterwork, *Sarva Saṁvādinī*, specifically where he comments on his own *Paramātmā Sandarbha* (Anuccheda 77, 78). The context is revealing: He analyzes the various traditions of "difference" (*bheda*) in the history of Indic literature, but then he singles out the specific variant he inherited through Śrī Chaitanya. He writes, *sva-mate tu acintya-bhedābhedaḥ* ("but my view is specifically 'Acintya-bhedābheda'").

Chapter Ten

Śrī-Śrī Rādhā-Gopīnāth

The Apogee of Krishna Consciousness

People conceive of God in various ways, depending on the particular religion they adhere to: Some see him as (1) an impersonal force, or an abstract principle that underlies the universe; others see him as (2) a more localized being, mystically pervading and sustaining all existence. Still others view him as (3) the Supreme Personality, existing in his own transcendental abode while engaging in loving relationship with everything and everyone else, for he is their source.

In Vedic parlance, these varying concepts are called Brahman, Paramātmā, and Bhagavān. Rather than choosing between them, the Vaishnava tradition of India accepts all three, and while they are viewed as but various expressions of the same one supreme Lord, they are far from identical.

That is to say, while God's formless aspect (Brahman), his manifestation as the Oversoul of the universe (Paramātmā), and his original form, playfully sporting in a world beyond time (Bhagavān), are all expressions of his essential nature, the former two arise from the latter. Bhagavān is the original Godhead, from whom all other manifestations draw their substance. He is thus the most complete and pristine form of Divinity.

But even in terms of Bhagavān, there is variance in his many incarnations and manifestations, as outlined in the Purāṇas. He exists in gradations, as it were. Some of his forms exhibit the full expression of his divine identity, while others only partially reveal his Godhood.

Among all such forms of God, Krishna is said to be supreme—he is the original *manifestor* from whom all other manifestations arise. This is confirmed by the great Vaishnava teachers throughout history, particularly in the Gauḍīya tradition, as well as in both the *Bhāgavata Purāṇa* and the *Gīta-govinda*.[1]

Still, even within the category of Krishna himself, there are innumerable gradations. Overall, the tradition teaches that he is supreme in Dvārakā, more supreme in Mathurā, and most supreme in Vrindavan. This refers to his historical sojourn in the material world, where he manifested some five thousand years ago in these three regions of India. Although these spiritual hamlets exist in the subcontinent, even today, they have their original counterparts in the spiritual realm—diverse transcendental regions in the kingdom of God, where Krishna in his original form is primary.

"In the world of three dimensions," writes Śrīla Prabhupāda, "Krishna's pastimes at Vrindavan were finished by the end of his fifteenth year, after which he traveled to Mathurā and Dvārakā, where all his other pastimes took place. . . . Krishna's pastimes in [these secondary places] are displayed by his Vāsudeva portion, his immediate expansion, yet there is no difference between the Vāsudeva portion manifested in Mathurā and Dvārakā and the original manifestation of Krishna in Vrindavan."[2]

In other words, Krishna's primeval form is in Vrindavan, and then he expands into a secondary form to enter Mathurā—and he expands yet further to enter Dvārakā. All these manifestations are the selfsame Supreme Lord, but he exhibits his essence in all its fullness in Vrindavan. This fullness is special. It is in this fullness that he engages in the deepest pastimes of love with his intimate associates, especially the *gopīs*, the spiritual cowherd maidens of Vraja, whose love for him is considered the ultimate in spiritual accomplishment. Prabhupāda continues:

> When Krishna appears, all His incarnations, plenary portions and portions of the plenary portions come with Him. Thus some of His different pastimes are manifested not by the original Krishna Himself but by His expansions. . . . When Krishna left the *gopīs* [in Vrindavan] and went to Mathurā, the *gopīs* cried for Him the rest of their lives, feeling intense separation from Him. . . . Nonetheless, they cannot forget Him. This means that in one sense they were never actually separated from Krishna. There is no difference between thinking of Krishna and associating with Him. Rather, *vipralambha-sevā*, thinking of Him in separation . . . is far better than serving Him directly. Thus, of all the devotees who have developed unalloyed devotional love for Krishna, the *gopīs* are most exalted, and out of all these exalted *gopīs*, Śrīmatī Rādhārāṇī is the highest. No one can excel the devotional service of Śrīmatī Rādhārāṇī. Indeed, even Krishna cannot understand the attitude of Śrīmatī Rādhārāṇī; therefore He took Her position and appeared as Śrī Caitanya Mahāprabhu, just to understand Her transcendental feelings.[3]

It is this unequalled standard of otherworldly love that is evoked in Vrindavan, and particularly by the personality of Gopīnāth, who is Krishna in his highest feature, as the paramour of the Braj cowherd girls. By contemplating the truth of Gopīnāth, one gradually becomes privy to the highest dimensions of divine love. The level of Gopīnāth realization—which may be seen as the summit of

Bhagavān realization—exists in a realm of divine separation (*vipralambha*), a mystical level of spiritual accomplishment that is rarely attained in this world, and as we briefly discussed in our chapter on Śrī Nāthjī.

Normally, separation is considered distasteful. No one wants to be separated from loved ones. Spiritual separation, however, is the exact opposite: It is deeply desirable, even if this may seem counterintuitive. It is desirable because it embodies a form of divine hankering that is at first maddening and even heartrending, but that ultimately transforms into spiritual union (*sambhoga*). Indeed, the topmost union with God is only achieved through such separation, bringing us, in the end, into divine presence more than ever before.[4] This allows entrance into blissful relationship with the Lord. Once in that state of consciousness, one finds that it is in fact more fulfilling than anything else, material or spiritual. This is Gopīnāth consciousness.

A VERY SPECIAL NAME

The name Gopīnāth encapsulates the specific esoteric level of love indicated above. Generally, the name is simply understood as a reference to Krishna, indicating that he is the Lord (*nātha*) of the *gopīs*.[5] But the Gauḍīya conception offers a more confidential reading of the name, wherein the truth is inverted to express the summit of spiritual realization: Krishna is in fact controlled by the love of his devotees, and not the other way around.[6]

From a superficial point of view, this latter reading may seem problematic. Linguistically, *nātha* is masculine, and the *gopīs* are not. Gopī-nāth as a name for Krishna is a *tat-puruṣa* compound meaning *gopīnām nāthaḥ*, the Lord (or protector) of the *gopīs*. If this word were to refer to the *gopīs* instead of Krishna, it would be a *karma-dhāraya* compound, and would require a feminine ending (singular: *gopī-nāthā*; plural, *gopī-nāthāḥ*). And this is not how the word is commonly understood.

However, in Sanskrit, there is a grammatical device called a *bahu-vrīhi* (an exocentric compound), which allows for a gender indeterminate reading of words such as "*gopīnāth*." An English illustration would be "white collar" to designate a certain class of people, not a particular collar as such nor the color, white. So, from this perspective, the word *gopīnāth* could mean, "having the *gopīs* as masters," with neither the *gopīs* nor the *nātha* referring to Krishna, but to the compound as a whole.

This works as a legitimate reading for the name Gopīnāth, and has in fact been used this way to bring out a more sophisticated and theologically elaborate understanding of Krishna and the love of his most intimate servitors. In the end, then, Gopīnāth refers to "Krishna whose masters are the *gopīs*."

In fact, such a reading suggests a certain transcendental irony in the word Gopīnāth, much loved by devotees in the Gauḍīya tradition. This is because "*nātha,*" again, could never technically refer to a female, and yet, in the word Gopīnāth, it reaches its highest meaning precisely when referencing the *gopīs*. Thus, the mystery and richness of the name Gopīnāth is as follows: Krishna is ostensibly the Lord of the cowherd maidens, but in fact they overpower him with their perfect and undying love.

SAMBANDHA, ABHIDHEYA, AND PRAYOJANA

Krishna in the form of Gopīnāth is eternal, but he has revealed himself in the course of history as one of the primary Deities of Vrindavan. In the *Garga Saṁhitā* (*Aśvamedha-khaṇḍa*, 62.26–30) and in Prabhupāda's book *Kṛṣṇa* (chapter 90), we read about Krishna's son Pradyumna, who had a son named Aniruddha, who in turn had a son named Vajranābha (Vajra). This was Krishna's great-grandson. He was the king of Mathurā and, wanting to "immortalize" his great-grandfather, commissioned the first Krishna Deities that were crafted soon after the Lord's departure from this world.

According to tradition, Vajra had never seen Krishna when he walked the earth, so he depended on the descriptions given by Uttarā (the mother of Mahārāja Parīkṣit) and the great devotee Uddhava, who knew Krishna well. With their guidance he began with three different images, but none of them, tradition relates, perfectly represented what Krishna actually looked like: Govindajī's face captured the Lord's facial features; Madan-mohan appeared like Krishna from the navel down to the lotus feet; and Gopīnāth perfectly replicated the torso of the Lord, from the navel to the neck. Upon seeing all three, one's life becomes sublime.

These three Deities reveal the entire truth of Gauḍīya Vaishnavism—*sambandha* (the relationship), *abhidheya* (the path), and *prayojana* (the goal). The *Caitanya-caritāmṛta* (*Ādi* 1.19) says, "These three deities [Madan-mohan, Govinda, and Gopīnātha] have absorbed the heart and soul of the Gauḍīya Vaishnavas. I worship Their lotus feet, for They are the Lords of my heart." Śrīla Prabhupāda writes in his purport to this verse, echoing his teacher, Śrīla Bhaktisiddhānta Sarasvatī Ṭhākura:

> Worship of Madana-mohana is on the platform of reestablishing our forgotten relationship with the Supreme Lord. In the material world we are presently in utter ignorance of our eternal relationship with the Supreme Lord. *Paṅgoḥ* refers to one who cannot move independently by his own strength, and *manda-mateḥ* is one who is less intelligent because he is too absorbed in materialistic activities. It is best for such persons not to aspire for success in fruitive activities or

> mental speculation but instead simply to surrender to the Supreme Personality of Godhead. The perfection of life is simply to surrender to the Supreme. In the beginning of our spiritual life we must therefore worship Madana-mohana so that He may attract us and nullify our attachment for material sense gratification. This relationship with Madana-mohana is necessary for neophyte devotees. When one wishes to render service to the Lord with strong attachment, one worships Govinda on the platform of transcendental service. Govinda is the reservoir of all pleasures. When by the grace of Kṛṣṇa and the devotees one reaches perfection in devotional service, he can appreciate Kṛṣṇa as Gopījana-vallabha [Gopīnāth], the pleasure Deity of the damsels of Vraja. . . . According to the Vedic principles, there are three stages of spiritual advancement, namely, *sambandha-jñāna, abhidheya* and *prayojana*. *Sambandha-jñāna* refers to establishing one's original relationship with the Supreme Personality of Godhead, *abhidheya* refers to acting according to that constitutional relationship, and *prayojana* is the ultimate goal of life, which is to develop love of Godhead.[7]

The same truths are reflected in one of the sacred Vaishnava Gāyatrī mantras chanted three times a day by Gauḍīya *brāhmaṇas* worldwide: Madan-mohan, Govinda, and Gopīnāth are referred to in this mantra, though in slightly veiled form. Traditionally, the word *kṛṣṇāya* ("unto Kṛṣṇa") in the mantra is taken to refer to Madan-mohan, *govindāya* to Govindadeva, and *gopījana vallabhāya* to Gopīnāth. These three Deities, according to the Gauḍīya *sampradāya*, represent the full embodiment of the Absolute Truth. After generations of worship, these Deities were lost until, some five hundred years ago, they were again unearthed by the Gosvāmīs of Vrindavan.

VAṀŚĪ-VAṬA

Although the Deity of Gopīnāth was originally crafted by Vajra, he was rediscovered in the time of the Gosvāmīs, some five hundred years ago. The place of discovery was Vaṁśī-vaṭa, where he lay buried in the ground near a famous banyan tree.

The word *vaṁśī* means "flute" and *vaṭa* means "banyan tree." The tradition tells us that the area of Vaṁśī-vaṭa is where Gopīnāth initiated the famous Rāsa dance, interacting with his beloved *gopīs* in a mood of incomparable celebration. The banyan tree is famous because it marks the exact spot: It was under this tree that Krishna engaged his fabled woodwind, beckoning the *gopīs* to join him in Vrindavan's forest of love. This love, it should be underlined, is entirely spiritual—an interaction between God and his foremost devotees. Any apparent similarity to prurient interest is because the latter is a perverted reflection of the former. In other words, Krishna's love for the *gopīs*, and theirs for him, is pure and untainted by any material quality.[8]

Upon hearing the enchanting flute music emanating from Krishna's lips, the *gopīs* left all other activities aside, running to Vaṁśī-vaṭa for Krishna's pleasure. After reaching their desired destination, Krishna and the *gopīs* spent the entire night enjoying the highest form of spiritual love, dancing and playing in the various groves of Vrindavan forest. Although the dance lasted one evening in terms of earthly years, the texts tell us that in fact it cannot be measured by material time.[9]

The *Bhakti-ratnākara* (Fifth Wave) says. "Please see the wonderfully beautiful Vaṁśī-vaṭa on the bank of the Yamunā, the shade of the Vaṁśī-vaṭa tree removes the distress of the world. Lord Gopīnāth eternally enjoys His pastimes here. His attractive dress enchants the world and His movements are flawless as the sound of His flute attracts the *gopīs*." In the *Caitanya-caritāmṛta* (1.1.7 and 17), it is said: "Śrī Gopīnāth, who originated the transcendental mellow of the Rāsa dance, stands on the shore at Vaṁśī-vaṭa and attracts the attention of the cowherd damsels with the sound of His celebrated flute. May they all confer upon us their benediction." Even today, at Vaṁśī-vaṭa, one can see the offshoot of the original banyan tree, commemorating the Rāsa dance of Lord Krishna.

When considering Gopīnāth's supreme position in terms of Krishna's various manifestations, the exalted place given to the Rāsa dance is significant. Let it be clear: In the *Caitanya-caritāmṛta* (2.21.44), Krishnadāsa Kavirāja Gosvāmī glorifies the dance as "the quintessence of all divine pastimes" (*rāsādi-līlā-sāra*), and, when commenting on the first verse of the Rāsa-līlā, the highly regarded Viśvanātha Chakravartī calls it "the crown jewel of all God's activities" (*sarva-līlā-cūḍa-maṇi*). Indeed, that Krishna in the form of Gopīnāth is associated with the Rāsa dance speaks volumes about Gopīnāth's culminating dimension in terms of Krishna Tattva.[10]

As a sidenote, perhaps, the Rāsa-līlā has numerous manifestations and is even associated with Mahāprabhu's chanting party—and in all chanting parties that glorify Krishna purely, with heart and soul.[11] Thus, in the summer of 1966, for example, Prabhupāda began taking the first Western devotees to Tompkins Square Park, where they would chant and dance in ecstasy. His disciples and their followers continue this to the present day.

But even in the earliest days of Prabhupāda's movement, he often mentioned this chanting process as enabling one to enter into the Rāsa-līlā: "Oh, he has attained the highest perfection, to go back to Krishna, *mad-yaji-no 'pi mam*, 'one who comes to Me.' So this is the greatest benediction to human society, to train them to go back to Krishna and dance there with Krishna in Rāsa-līlā."[12] There are many such statements: "The whole process is to enliven the sleeping conditioned souls to the real life of spiritual consciousness so that they may thus become as perfect as the ever-liberated souls in the Vaikuṇṭhalokas [the spiritual realm]. Since the Lord is *sac-cid-ānanda-vigraha*, He likes every part and parcel of His different potencies to take part in the blissful *rasa* because participation with the Lord in His eternal Rāsa-līlā is the highest living condition, perfect in spiritual bliss and eternal knowledge."[13]

The great spiritual master Bhaktivinoda Ṭhākura sums up in his *Hari-nāma-chintāmaṇi* (1.19): "In Vraja [it is called] Rāsa-līlā. In Navadvīpa [it is] Saṅkīrtana. These are the forms of Lord Krishna's wonderful pastimes." (*vraje rāsa-līlā navadvīpe saṅkīrtana/ ei rūpa kṛṣṇa līlā vichitra gaṇana*). To state it more directly: singing and dancing in glorification of Krishna, when brought to perfection, is non-different from engaging in Lord Krishna's Rāsa dance. Such engagement stands at the summit of Gopīnāth realization.

MADHU PAṆḌITA

Madhu Paṇḍita Gosvāmī—a prominent disciple of Gadādhara Paṇḍita, Mahāprabhu's intimate associate—came to Vrindavan looking for the Gopīnāth Deity. But his initial efforts bore no fruit, leaving him bewildered. "Where is my Lord?" he wondered, searching desperately throughout the Braj region. He was certain that his beloved Gopīnāth would be at Vaṁśī-vaṭa, where the Rāsa dance had taken place. But the Deity was nowhere to be found. Feeling bereft, alone, and without recourse, Madhu Paṇḍita succumbed to depression, abandoning food and drink. All he could do was weep, for days on end, bemoaning his pitiful plight of separation. With great remorse, he sat at Vaṁśī-vaṭa, praying for a miracle.

Soon, the river Yamunā played her part, and as her forceful waves crashed against her bank, the incomparable Deity of Gopīnāth emerged from the sand, making the sacred region of Vaṁśī-vaṭa even more sacred. It was not Madhu Paṇḍita, however, who was the first to see the Deity: That honor goes to Paramānanda Bhaṭṭācārya, another disciple of Gadādhara Paṇḍita, who, on that very morning, happened to be bathing in the Yamunā, at that exact spot. It was he who found the gorgeous Deity. Nonetheless, due to the deep love he saw in his godbrother, Madhu Paṇḍita, he entrusted Gopīnāth's service to him, and Paṇḍita would be identified with the Deity's worship forevermore. "Thus did Madhu Paṇḍita, the object of Śrī Paramānanda Bhaṭṭācārya's affection, achieve the privilege of Śrī Gopīnāthjīu's service."[14] In fact, Madhu Paṇḍita built the famous Gopīnāth temple in the Deity's honor.

The Vaishnava community honors them both with special *praṇām-mantras*: "I offer my respectful obeisance to the great Madhu Paṇḍita. His strong loving affection for the Lord is as sweet as honey as he takes part in the transcendental pastimes of the Rāsa dance in the spiritual realm of Śrī Vṛndāvana-dhāma (*madhu-sneha-samāyuktaṁ/ premāsaktaṁ mahāśayam// vṛndāvane rāsa-ratam/ vande śrī-madhu-paṇḍitam//*). And for Paramānanda Bhaṭṭācārya: "I offer my respectful obeisances to Śrī Paramānanda Bhaṭṭācārya who is engrossed in the transcendental moods of pure devotional service, bestowing upon his followers the shelter of the lotus feet of Śrī Gadādhara Paṇḍita, Śrī Gaurāṅga and Śrī Śrī Rādhā-Govinda" (*vande śrī-paramānandaṁ/ bhaṭṭācāryaṁ rasa-priyam// rādhā-govinda-gaurāṅga-gadādhara-pada-pradam//*).[15]

It may seem curious that Śrī Śrī Rādhā-Govinda are mentioned in this latter verse, since Madhu Paṇḍita and Paramānanda Bhaṭṭācārya were both known as loving servants of Śrī Śrī Rādhā-Gopīnāth. The explanation lies in historical context: Rūpa Gosvāmī was the leading *mahānta* of the Gauḍīya *sampradāya* at the time, and his Deities, Rādhā-Govinda, were at the center of Braj, with all the assembled devotees lending a hand in their worship. This included Gopāl Bhaṭṭa Gosvāmī, Gadādhara Paṇḍita and Raghunātha Bhaṭṭa Gosvāmī. Although many Deities were eventually established—and some, such as Rādhā-ramaṇa and Rādhā-Gopīnāth, would soon become prominent—Rūpa Gosvāmī's Deity maintained a special place throughout.

Still, Madhu Paṇḍita and his Gopīnāth temple quickly became the pride of Vrindavan. According to *Bhakti-ratnākara* (Seventh Wave), Madhu Paṇḍita blessed Śrīnivāsa Ācārya with Gopīnāth's garland before the famous triumvirate, Śrīnivāsa, Narottama, and Śyāmānanda, embarked on their famous book distribution tour to Bengal and Orissa. This indicates how highly the temple was regarded: The garland could have come from Śrī Rūpa or Śrī Jīva Gosvāmī's temple or other major centers of Krishna worship at the time. But Gopīnāth's temple was unanimously chosen to bless this most important out-reach effort.

In the spiritual world, Madhu Paṇḍita serves as the female assistant known as Maṇḍalī in the group of Campakalatā-sakhī, one of Śrī Rādhā's most intimate girlfriends.[16] His *samādhi*, or burial place, is in the Rādhā-Gopīnāth Temple in Vrindavan, just as one enters on the right. It is also said that he placed special emphasis on the worship of Tulasī-devī, Lord Krishna's favorite plant, and that he wore a jacket and cap made completely of *tulasī* wood—both are preserved at the Rādhā-Gopīnāth temple in Jaipur. But before exploring the temple in Jaipur, we should more thoroughly mention the original temple in Vrindavan.

THE RĀDHĀ-GOPĪNĀTH TEMPLE

The temple of Rādhā-Gopīnāth is nestled between many of the most famous temples of Vrindavan, a brief walk from the renowned Rādhā-ramaṇa and

Rādhā-Gokulānanda Mandirs. It is said that Lord Gopīnāth was worshipped for nearly four decades before a red sandstone temple was finally built in his honor. Madhu Paṇḍita simply saw no need for a formal structure, happily worshipping his Lord in the natural environment of Braj.

Eventually, however, he decided to engage the king of Khandela, Raisal Darbari (r. 1584–1614), one of emperor Akbar's chief advisers, in construction work, to expand the worship of his loving Lord, and, considering just who the Deity is, chose an obvious place to build the temple: near Nidhivan in the area of the Rāsa dance. Nidhivan, of course, is today most identified with the Deities of Bāṅke Bihārī, but it is also adjacent to Vaṁśī-vaṭa, where Rādhā-Gopīnāth currently reside.

Much of the original temple is now merely ruins, destroyed during the Mughal Era as a result of Muslim-Hindu hostilities. The central dome of the temple was completely dismantled and the gateway adjoining the main entrance was all but destroyed. Islamic art now decorates a certain portion of the decaying edifice, an obvious attempt to usurp the structure for Muslim purposes.

Nonetheless, Deities of Lord Jagannāth and Vaṁśīdhārī Mahāprabhu, sometimes called Muralīdhara Mahāprabhu (Śrī Chaitanya playing Krishna's flute) were placed in the temple, and pilgrims still come to see these holy forms.[17]

On the northern side of this structure, however, there now stands a new Rādhā-Gopīnāth temple, reinstating Gopīnāth's singularly divine presence for all sincere worshippers. The new building was constructed in 1819 by a Bengali militant named Shri Nand Kumar Basu.

Glorious in their demeanor and ambiance, Śrī Rādhikā and Lord Gopīnāth grace the new altar with a spiritual glow, even if the original Rādhā-Gopīnāth Deities were long since moved to Jaipur for their own protection against violent Muslim incursions. That is to say, substitute Deities were placed in Vrindavan's new Rādhā-Gopīnāth Temple.[18] The details of the original Deities' subsequent temple in Jaipur will be outlined below.

But there is more to say about their manifestation in Vrindavan, where they were worshiped alongside a Jāhnavā Ṭhākurāṇī Deity, Lord Nityānanda's transcendental consort. In Krishna's *līlā,* She is Anaṅga Mañjarī, Rādhikā's younger sister. This is significant in terms of Gopīnāth's unique position as most esoteric of all Krishna Deities.[19] Her appearance in such a temple is unusual altogether, again underlining Gopīnāth's superlative position—Jāhnavā Ṭhākurāṇī and her alter ego Anaṅga Mañjarī are considered the very emblem of *mādhurya-rasa*, or the quintessence of conjugal love.[20]

Śrī Jāhnavā Ṭhākurāṇī herself supervised the placement of this Deity in this temple, specifying exactly where each form should be positioned on the altar: Gopīnāth stands with her (Anaṅga Mañjarī) to his left, and Rādhikā to his right. The famous *gopīs* Lalitā and Viśākhā are there as well, flanking them as loving servants.[21] Pilgrims also visit the temple to see the burial place of Madhu Paṇḍita, which lies to the east side of the new temple.

But Rādhā-Gopīnāth were never destined to stay in Vrindavan, or, rather, they would soon bring Vrindavan to other lands. The pretext, at this time, was Aurangzeb's reign, in 1669, when it became clear that the Deities should be moved and could stay in Vrindavan no longer. They ostensibly needed protection from the violent hands of Muslim aggressors. But the Deities could never really be hurt, and their faithful servants knew that. Rather, the tradition teaches, Their Lordships wanted to spread their mercy to sincere souls everywhere.

Thus, Madan Mohan, Govindajī, Gopīnāth, and several other prominent Deities, were "protected" by their devotees through an exodus that took them through much of Uttar Pradesh and beyond. Gopīnāth went first to Rādhā-kuṇḍa and Kāmyavan, where he stayed for nearly ten years, and then to Jaipur in 1775, where he was worshiped at a temporary shrine. After seventeen years, he was brought to his eternal home: "Thereafter," temple records tell us, "in the year 1792, the then Deewan of Jaipur, Shri Khushali Ram Bohra, consecrated the holy images of Lord Radha-Gopinathji in his Haveli at Purani Basti Jaipur converting and dedicating the same to the Temple Shri Gopinathji Maharaj (the present temple premises)."[22]

CONCLUSION

One may question the implications of Rādhā-Gopīnāth leaving Vrindavan (Braj). Does the apparent absence of the Deities somehow leave Vrindavan bereft? Does their potency dissipate when they travel to a foreign land, like Jaipur? Gauḍīya Vaishnava theology asserts that where Krishna is—there too is Vrindavan, and vice versa. The Lord and Vrindavan are inseparable. Additionally, Gopīnāthjī's presence as the *pratibhū* Deity of Vrindavan, as mentioned, allows him to be fully present in that holiest of holy lands, even if he leaves it, for a *pratibhū* Deity, by definition, is not different from the original.

Still, the sense of "separation" evinced by Krishna leaving Braj only makes devotees pine for him more. That is also built into the theology, as already explained. In common parlance, absence (read: separation) makes the heart grow fonder, and when it comes to Krishna, it makes one love him even more intensely. This is the principle of Viraha-bhakti, love in separation, wherein the deepest level of loving affection arises in one's heart, and this is especially so when it comes to Gopīnāth.

But there was a second question: Does Krishna diminish when he goes to foreign lands? The answer is "no": Krishna is always Krishna. He is absolute and unchanging. Moreover, he transforms whatever land in which he appears—he makes it Vrindavan proper, merely by his presence, for, again, Vrindavan and Krishna are forever linked. As long as he is truly present, worshiped with divine love by his pure devotees, he agrees to make himself available, no matter what the locale. As Hinduism scholar Amy Joy Hirschtick, who specializes in the Deities of Jaipur, writes:

> Their [the Deities] relocation to Rajasthan created not a breach with Vraj, but an expansion of it. *Radha Damodar Darpaṇ* explains, "The Pink City is not only pure (*pāvan*) like Vrindavan, it truly is Vrindavan because of the revered figures of Govinddev, Gopīnāth, Radha-Dāmodar, and Radha-Vinod." Sacred landscape migrated with the Gauḍīya Krishnas. Govinddev, Gopīnāth, Radha Dāmodar, and Vinodilāl reign in Jaipur as they reigned in Vrindavan. Govinddev and the other Krishna figures brought from Vraj took root in Jaipur and thereby created a center to Krishna devotion in a young city. In the words of Śrīvatsa Goswāmī, "If Bhakti dances in Vrindavan, it is victorious in Jaipur."[23]

And Krishna has gone elsewhere as well, even in the form of Lord Gopīnāth. By the grace of Śrīla Prabhupāda and his International Society for Krishna Consciousness (ISKCON), he is even in the Western world: There are Rādhā-Gopīnāth temples in Sydney; Belgium; Longdenville, Trinidad and Tobago; Bali, Indonesia; Toronto, Canada; and elsewhere. Truly, the mood and intensity of Rādhā-Gopīnāth worship is universal, and it is awaiting each and every devotee who wants the most precious gift of Krishna Consciousness.

ADDENDUM

There is an important subject that is not directly related to the Gopīnāth Deity but is nonetheless integral to the same level of love that Gopīnāth represents—*payojana*—and so it should be briefly explored here.

While Madan Mohan is served by Śrīla Sanātana Gosvāmī, the teacher of Sambandha-jñāna; Govinda is served by Śrīla Rūpa Gosvāmī, the teacher of Abhidheya-jñāna; and Gopīnāth is served by Śrī Madhu Paṇḍita, a great devotee from the Braj region, only the first two teachers are representative of the same *tattvas*, or truths, for which their Deities are known. That is to say, it is Śrīla Raghunātha Dāsa Gosvāmī (1495–1571), not Madhu Paṇḍita, who is considered the representative teacher of Payojana-jñāna, the perfection of love of God.

This is because Raghunātha Dāsa Gosvāmī, the *prayojana-ācārya*, teaches Rādhā-dāsyam, the service of Śrī Rādhā, as the pinnacle of Krishna Consciousness, both in his written works and through his personal example. He is therefore considered the archetype of this highest level of love, associated with Lord Gopīnāth and the *gopīs*.

"One who has not worshiped the dust of Śrīmatī Rādhārānī's lotus feet," writes Raghunātha Dāsa Gosvāmī, "has not taken shelter of Śrī Vrindavan that is decorated with Her footprints, and has not conversed with the great devotees who are deeply immersed in Her service. How will such a person ever relish the most mysterious fathomless ocean of love that is Śrī Krishna?" (*Stavavali*). He further writes: "O Rādhikā, to become a servant of Your lotus feet is the highest position; leaving this I do not desire anything else (such as the position of Your direct *gopī* lovers). I pay obeisance to Your *gopīs* eternally. However, please let me always remain rooted in the position of Your maidservant, merely assisting the *gopīs*—this is my request" (*Vilāpa Kusumañjali*). Such statements are not uncommon in his writing.

In fact, Raghunātha Dāsa Gosvāmī's three major works—*Stava-mālā* (or *Stavāvalī*),[24] *Dāna-carita*, and *Muktā-carita*—offer the world the highest nectar in the form of Rādha-dāsyam, explicating the mood of the *gopīs* in no uncertain terms.

Svarūpa Dāmodara Gosvāmī, one of Śrī Chaitanya's most intimate associates, taught Dāsa Gosvāmī the internal method of performing *rasamayī-upāsana*, or love-infused worship. At Purī's temple of Ṭoṭā Gopīnāth, for example, Svarūpa Dāmodara invited Raghunātha to hear the *Bhāgavatam* directly from Gadādhara Paṇḍita—a more cherishable and purifying engagement is hardly imaginable.

Through Svarūpa Dāmodara, Raghunātha Dāsa learned and noted down all the transcendental activities of Śrī Chaitanya Mahāprabhu, explicating each major pastime of the Lord. These pastimes are briefly described in Dāsa Gosvāmī's *Śrī Gaurāṅga-stava-kalpavṛkṣa*, and were used by Krishnadāsa Kavirāja Gosvāmī in writing his *Śrī Caitanya-caritāmṛta*. Dāsa Gosvāmī became famous for living near Rādhā-kuṇḍa and showering its inhabitants with all of these stories and the highest level of divine love.

In the spiritual land of Braj, he is Rati Mañjarī, who is under the shelter and guidance of Lalitā-devī, one of Śrī Rādhā's primary *gopīs*, and is fully trained by her in all the arts and loving moods of devotional service. This is revealed in several important Gauḍīya texts: "Raghunātha Dāsa is ascribed three different names from his previous identity as a *mañjarī* in Krishna-līlā: Rasa Mañjarī,[25] Rati Mañjarī, and Bhanumati (*Gaura-gaṇoddeśa-dīpikā* 186). According to Dhyānachandra Gosvāmī's *Gaura-govindārcana-smaraṇa-paddhati* (304), Rati Mañjarī is part of Indulekhā's group, and her *kuñja* is in Indulekhā's garden at Rādhā-kuṇḍa. This qualifies her for service to Lord Gopīnāth.

Raghunātha Dāsa Gosvāmī's eternal resting place (*samādhi*) is in the Rādhā-Gopīnāth compound of Rādhā-kuṇḍa, where worship in the mood of Gopīnāth reigns supreme.

NOTES

1. *Bhāgavata Purāṇa* 1.3.28: "All of the above-mentioned incarnations are either plenary portions or portions of the plenary portions of the Lord, but Lord Śrī Krishna is the original Personality of Godhead. All of them appear on planets whenever there is a disturbance created by the atheists. The Lord incarnates to protect the theists." (*ete cāṁśa-kalāḥ puṁsaḥ/kṛṣṇas tu bhagavān svayam//indrāri-vyākulaṁ lokaṁ/mṛḍayanti yuge yuge//*) Jayadeva Goswami, too, avers that Krishna is the source of all forms of Godhead. See *Gīta-govinda* 1.15, 16: "I salute Krishna, from whom the ten incarnations emerge" (*daśākṛtikṛte krishnāya tubhyaṁ namaḥ*).

2. His Divine Grace A. C. Bhaktivedanta Swami Prabhupada, *The Nectar of Devotion* (New York: ISKCON Press,1970), chapter 26 (https://prabhupadabooks.com/nod/26?d=1).

3. See Prabhupada's *Kṛṣṇa* (Los Angeles: Bhaktivedanta Book Trust, 1970), Chapter 90; his *Teachings of Lord Chaitanya*, (New York: ISKCON Press, 1968), chapter 9; and *Nectar of Instruction* 10, purport (https://prabhupadabooks.com/noi/texts/noi_10).

4. To help us understand the idea of love in separation and why it is so special, several quotes from the Vaishnava *ācāryas* might be helpful, as I have mentioned elsewhere: In Rūpa Goswāmī's *Padyāvali* (240), for example, he expresses Rādhikā's mood, "I prefer separation from Krishna to union, because in union I see Krishna only in one place, whereas in separation, I see him everywhere." Commenting on Rūpa's *Ujjvala-nīlamaṇi* (1.20), Jīva Goswāmī says that "the power of an elephant can only be seen when it is chained and using all its strength to break free; similarly, the power of Rādhā's love for Krishna can only be fully seen in her separation from him."

5. Although in common usage, *nātha* refers to "Lord," as in the name Jagannāth, "Lord of the Universe," in fact it doesn't merely mean "Lord" or "controller" at all. It is more nuanced than that. It more properly means "protector," as in one who has loving stewardship over someone else.

6. In the Gauḍīya conception, Krishna feels indebted to Rādhā and the *gopīs* for their deep and abiding love. In this tradition, they clearly have the upper hand. Those in the line of Rūpa Gosvāmī prefer to see Krishna controlled by the *gopīs* than the other way around. This truth is part of *prayojana tattva* and thus indicative of everything the name Gopīnāth stands for. In the *Gīta-govinda*'s Eighth Canto, for instance, Krishna begs Rādhā's forgiveness for appearing to have other interests (8.1). His supplication, in which he beseeches her mercy, shows the extent to which he cannot live without her, indicating her superior position. Further, he exhibits the ultimate sign of

submission by asking her to place her feet on his head (*dehi pada pallavam udaram*, 10.8), signaling, once and for all, her superiority. This notion of Rādhā's preeminent status has led to lineages such as the Rādhāvallabha and Nimbārka Sampradāyas, where Rādhā reigns supreme—and it is found, no less, in the Gauḍīya Sampradāya. But even with all of this being said, one might argue that, in the end, it is neither Rādhā nor Krishna who take the preeminent role in Vaishnava thought, but rather love (*prema*) itself, and that, ultimately, is the truth of Gopīnāth. Rādhā's superiority to Krishna is also evident toward the end of the Rāsa-līlā's fourth chapter, where Krishna admits his inability to reciprocate with her and her *gopī* companions for their selfless love (4.22). Their only reward, he tells them, will have to be their own purity of heart, which—as a message to all of us—is the greatest reward of all.

7. It should be noted that while these verses identify the three major Deities of Vrindavan, it does not specifically align them with *sambandha, abhidheya*, and *prayojana*. Rather, that connection was initially revealed by Bhaktisiddhānta Sarasvatī in his commentary to the *Caitanya-caritāmṛta* (*Anubhāṣya*), which was then paraphrased by Śrīla Prabhupāda. He further relates these three Deities to the three names in the Gopāla-mantra (Krishna, Govinda, and Gopījanavallabha), aligning them, too, with *sambandha, abhidheya*, and *prayojana*. In his commentary to *Caitanya-caritāmṛta,* 2.8.138, Sarasvatī Ṭhākura also links these three Deities to the Kāma-gāyatrī. He explains: "The initiating spiritual master, represented by Sanātana Gosvāmī, brings us to Madana-mohan's lotus feet. To those who are unable to tread the path of Braj, the souls who have forgotten the Lord, he gives the awareness that the Lord's lotus feet are all in all. The *śikṣā-guru*, represented by Śrīla Rūpa Gosvāmī, bestows the qualifications to serve (*sevādhikāra*) the lotus feet of Śrī Govinda and his dear devotees . . . " (*Anubhāṣya* 1.47). And Śrīla Prabhupāda elaborated: "Śrīla Sanātana Gosvāmī is the ideal spiritual master, for he delivers one the shelter of the lotus feet of Madana-mohana. Even though one may be unable to travel on the field of Vṛndāvana due to forgetfulness of his relationship with the Supreme Personality of Godhead, he can get an adequate opportunity to stay in Vṛndāvana and derive all spiritual benefits by the mercy of Sanātana Gosvāmī. Śrī Govindajī acts exactly like the *śikṣā-guru* (instructing spiritual master) by teaching Arjuna the *Bhagavad-gītā*. He is the original preceptor, for He gives us instructions and an opportunity to serve Him. The initiating spiritual master is a personal manifestation of Śrīla Madana-mohana *vigraha*, whereas the instructing spiritual master is a personal representative of Śrīla Govindadeva *vigraha*. Both of these Deities are worshiped at Vṛndāvana. Śrīla Gopīnātha is the ultimate attraction in spiritual realization" (See Ādi 1.47 and 7.73).

8. Prabhupāda explains the traditional commentaries as follows: "Some may take it for granted that Krishna was very lusty among young girls, but Parikshit Maharaja said that this was not possible. He could not be lusty. First of all, from the material calculation He was only eight years old [when this occurred]. At that age a boy cannot be lusty. [Additionally] *apta-kama* means that the Supreme Personality of Godhead is self-satisfied. . . . Another important point is that none of the *gopis* who danced with Krishna were in their material bodies. They danced with Krishna in their spiritual bodies. All their husbands thought that their wives were sleeping by their sides. The so-called husbands of the *gopis* were already enamored with the influence of the

external energy of Krishna; so, by dint of this very energy they could not understand that their wives had gone to dance with Krishna. What then is the basis of accusing Krishna of dancing with others' wives? . . . Krishna is the supreme person, the whole spirit, and He danced with the spiritual bodies of the *gopis*. There is therefore no reason to accuse Krishna in any way." See Prabhupāda, *Śrīmad Bhāgavatam* 10.33, concluding purport.

9. "According to [*Bhāgavatam* commentator] Viśvanātha Chakravartī, the Rāsa dance was performed during the long period of Brahmā's night, but the *gopīs* could not understand that. . . . In one night, therefore, they enjoyed the company of Krishna as their beloved husband, but that night was not an ordinary night. It was a night of Brahmā, and lasted millions and millions of years. Everything is possible for Krishna, for He is the supreme controller." See Prabhupāda, *Śrīmad Bhāgavatam* 10.33, concluding purport.

10. In addition to signifying Krishna's ultimate love dance, the word *rāsa,* with its strengthened first-syllable vowel (i.e., *a* becomes *ā*), is taken by preeminent Vaishnava commentators to mean the ultimate *rasa* among the five primary *rasas* [the others are *śānta* (peaceful), *dāsya* (servitude), *sakhya* (friendly), and *vātsalya* (nurturing)]. Commentator Viśvanātha Chakravartī, for example, defines "*rāsa*" as the essence of *śṛṅgāra or mādhurya rasa*, i.e., the *rasa* of conjugal love, which is the most intimate and the most intense of all *rasas*. See Graham M. Schweig, "Rāsa: The *Bhāgavata*'s eternal Dance of Divine love," in *Journal of Vaishnava Studies* 27, no. 2 (Spring 2019): 6.

11. Even traditionally, there are various forms of Rāsa-līlā, which gives additional emphasis to the notion that the dance itself can be extended to Harināma, congregational chanting, and even as an ultimate destination for practitioners who reach perfection. Along these lines, it should be noted that the Rāsa-līlā as depicted in the *Bhāgavata Purāṇa* takes place in the fall (*śarada*), while Jayadeva's version takes place in the spring (*vasanta*). The autumn dance is performed eternally in Vrindavan, under the shade of the Vaṁśī-vaṭa tree, and all grades of *gopīs* participate in it—those who are just entering the liberated state and those who are eternal associates of the Lord. The spring dance takes place in Govardhana (in the village of Parsauli), near Lake Chandra Sarovara, and only the higher echelon *gopīs* are allowed to participate. Moreover, in this vernal celebration, Lord Krishna openly demonstrates the prominence and superiority of Rādhikā, whereas in the fall, her identity is concealed. (See Srila Narayana Maharaja, "Vasanta-Panchami and Sri Radha's Glories" https://bhaktabandhav.org/vasanta-panchami-sri-radhas-glories/).

12. Prabhupāda (Room Conversation with John Lennon, Yoko Ono, and George Harrison) And further: "Therefore the intelligence is that we should again go back to home, go back to Krishna, and dance with Him in His Rāsa dance" (Lecture, *Śrīmad Bhāgavatam* 3.26.19).

13. *Śrīmad Bhāgavatam* 3.25.4, purport.

14. *Bhakti-ratnākara* 2.94.

15. Yadunandana Dāsa's *Śākhā-nirṇaya*, a book often quoted by Bhaktisiddhānta Sarasvatī, mentions these *praṇama-mantras* for Madhu Paṇḍita and Paramānanda Bhaṭṭācārya. These same mantras are quoted in the *Gauḍīya Vaishnava Abhidhāna*.

16. See Dhyānachandra Goswāmī's *Śrī Gaura-govindārcana-smaraṇa-paddhati,* Verse 256 (https://www.scribd.com/document/88069163/Gaura-Govindarcana-Smarana-Paddhatih-by-Dhyanacandra-Gosvami).

17. The idea of a Mahāprabhu Deity at the old Rādhā-Gopīnāth temple—Śrī Chaitanya with Krishna's flute—is suggestive, leading to the notion that Mahāprabhu and Krishna in his most intense feature are actually one and the same. The *Caitanya-caritāmṛta* opens with glorification of three Deities, as noted: Madan Mohan, Govinda, and Gopīnāth. This occurs early in Ādi-līlā, and, as the *Caitanya-caritāmṛta* comes to a close, we see a hint of their glorification yet again. But in the ending text, it can be argued that a special secret is revealed: While the first two Deities are mentioned, the final one, representing *prayojana,* is not referred to as Gopīnāth but as Śrī Caitanya, indicating, in an indirect way, that Mahāprabhu is the selfsame Gopīnāth, the highest manifestation of Krishna: "Since this book, *Caitanya-caritāmṛta,* is now complete, having been written for the satisfaction of the most opulent Deities Madana-mohanajī and Govindajī, let it be offered at the lotus feet of Śrī Krishna Caitanyadeva." (Antya 20.155) This poetic reference takes on even greater meaning when we consider the tradition that Śrī Chaitanya, to complete his Earthly pastimes, entered into the Ṭoṭā-Gopīnāth Deity in Purī, who, granted, is not the Gopīnāth Deity in Vrindavan but is considered non-different from him (see https://kripa.tv/tag/gopis/page/2). Regarding Mahāprabhu being Gopīnāth, we can extrapolate that since he is Rādhā-Krishna, and Krishna's form with Rādhā is Gopījanavallabha, Mahāprabhu is also the *prayojana* Deity Gopīnāth, giving the highest goal of *mādhurya-prema.*

18. The Deity currently in Vrindavan is known as a *pratibhū* (substitute) image of Krishna, since the original Gopīnāth was moved too Jaipur. Monier Williams defines *pratibhū* as follows: "to be equal to or on a par with." A variation is *pratimā,* "an image, likeness"—a synonym for "a Deity." See Monier-Monier Williams, *A Complete Sanskrit-English Dictionary* (Oxford: The Clarendon Press, 2002), 668. Traditionally, a *pratibhū* Deity is considered non-different from the original. Teachers of the tradition often quote the *Bhāgavatam*'s Rāsa-līlā (10.33.19) to give a sense of just how identical the *pratibhū* is to the original: "Expanding Himself as many times as there were cowherd women to associate with, the Supreme Lord, though self-satisfied, playfully enjoyed their company" (*kṛtvā tāvantam ātmānaṁ/ yāvatīr gopa-yoṣitaḥ// reme sa bhagavāṁs tābhir/ ātmārāmo 'pi līlayā*). In other words, Krishna himself, in numerous identical forms, was inconceivably dancing with each cowherd woman, individually, at the same time.

19. The highly esoteric position of Jāhnavā/Anaṅga Mañjarī should not be underestimated. She is a particularly sublime incarnation of Servitor Godhead, but specifically in the mood of conjugal love. *Anaṅga-mañjarī-sampuṭikā* 1.12 indicates that Nityānanda Prabhu himself appears as Anaṅga-mañjarī—the source (Nityānanda) and the energy (Jāhnavā) are both forms of Śrī Rādhikā's younger sister, inconceivably. Moreover, just as Rādhā is Krishna's potency, says the *Anaṅga-mañjarī-sampuṭikā,* Anaṅga Mañjarī is considered the potency of Balarāma (1.14). All of these personalities are mystically interrelated in ways that transcend ordinary logic.

Bhaktivinoda Ṭhākura's *siddha-praṇālī-dīkṣā* line begins with Jāhnavā Ma, whom he, too, identifies as Anaṅga-mañjarī (who serves in Lalitā's group of *gopīs*), and so all those in the Bhaktivinoda-parivāra naturally give her pride of place. She is seen as the very emblem of Guru Tattva and the dissemination of divine love. Incidentally, *Anaṅga-mañjarī-samputikā* is a sixteenth-century text by Ramai Gosai, republished by both Bhaktivinoda Ṭhākura and, later, by Bhaktisiddhānta Swarasvatī. Ramachandra Goswami (Ramai Gosai), the author, was born some time in 1533 or 1534, the year of Śrī Chaitanya's disappearance, and was the grandson of the Lord's intimate associate Vaṁśīvadana Ṭhākura. Ramai was adopted by Nityānanda Prabhu's wife Jāhnavā and initiated by her as well. He traveled with her to Braj and spent many years there. According to *Muralī-vilāsa*, Jāhnavā Devī herself admitted that she was an incarnation of Anaṅga Mañjarī.

20. Parts of the above paragraphs were adapted from http://www.brajdarshan.in/radha-gopinath/.

21. There is an alternate version of this story explaining that the Jāhnavā/Anaṅga Mañjarī Deity arrived after Jāhnavā's departure from this world. Jāhnavā Ṭhākurāṇī, it seems, had visited Vrindavan and fell deeply in love with the Deity of Gopīnāth. (She traveled there twice, once before the demise of Rūpa and Sanātana and once thereafter.) Some time after her second visit, one of her followers, ostensibly at her behest, came to Vrindavan from Bengal carrying a Jāhnavā Deity to be placed at Lord Gopīnāth's side. That very night, it is said, Gopīnāth appeared to the temple *pūjārī* in a dream, revealing that Jāhnavā is non-different from Anaṅga Mañjarī, further saying that the Rādhā Deity should be moved to the right of Gopīnāth, and that the Jāhnavā Deity be placed on the left. This is the tradition's rationale for the unusual placement of the Deities at the new Gopīnāth Mandir in Vrindavan.

Still another version of the story involves the size of the Deity that originally accompanied Lord Gopīnāth: "When Lord Nityananda's wife, Jahnava Mata, visited Vrindavana on pilgrimage in the year 1582, she felt that the Deity of Radharani being worshipped in the temple was far too small, and when she returned to Bengal she asked one of her disciples to carve a new Deity of Radharani for the Gopinath temple. This new Deity was then sent to Vrindavana and immediately installed next to Sri Gopinath. When all the devotees in Vrindavana saw the new Deity of Radharani, they felt that it looked just like Jahnava Mata" (See https://sthalapurana108.wordpress.com/2014/08/03/radha-gopinath-temple/).

22. Interestingly, although all three of the mentioned Deities—Madan Mohan, Govindajī, Gopīnāth, and others—passed through Kāmyavan on their way to Jaipur (with Madan Mohan attaining final residence in Karoli, i.e., Karauli, Rajasthan), Śrī Gopīnāthjī, for some unknown reason, is considered the principal Deity of Kāmyavan, literally "the forest where all one's desires are fulfilled." The tradition of Gopīnāth's special place in Kāmyavan goes back to the *Bṛhan-nāradīya Purāṇa* as quoted by Nārāyaṇa Bhaṭṭa, the great historian of Vrindavan. He writes in his *Vraja-bhakti-vilāsa*: "Gopīnāth is the sovereign Lord of Kāmyavan." Much of the history summarized in these paragraphs has been adapted from the official temple's website in Jaipur: http://gopinathji.net/History.htm.

23. See Amy Joy Hirschtick, "The Krishnas of Jaipur," PhD thesis, Indiana University, June 2017, 53. For the Shrivatsa Goswami quote, see "Sri Sri Radhadamodarau Jayatah," in *Shri Radha-Damodar and The Sacred Shri Giriraj Shila* (Jaipur: Print-O-Print, n.d.), 2. See also Sugata Ray, "In the Name of Krishna: The Cultural Landscape of a North Indian Pilgrimage Town," PhD Thesis, University of Minnesota, April 2012.

24. *Stavāvalī* is composed of twenty-nine shorter works, including *Vilāpa-kusumāñjalī*, *Vraja-vilāsa-stava*, and *Manaḥ Śikṣā*, which are perhaps his most popular books.

25. The name Rasa Mañjarī is usually attributed to Raghunātha Bhaṭṭa Gosvāmī, as opposed to Dāsa Gosvāmī. However, sometimes the latter is also known by this name. In the *Gaura-gaṇoddeśa-dīpikā*, verse 185, it is said that Raghunātha Bhaṭṭa Gosvāmī was formerly the *gopī* named Rāga Mañjarī.

Bibliography

Addams, Sara M. "From Narasiṁha to Jagannātha." *Journal of Vaishnava Studies* 17, no. 1 (Fall 2008): 5–28.

Barry, Ellen. "Sashimani Devi, Last of India's Jagannath Temple Dancers, Dies at 92." the *New York Times* (March 23, 2015).

Beck, Guy L. *Sonic Theology: Hinduism and Sacred Sound* (Columbia: University of South Carolina Press, 1993).

———. "An Introduction to the Poetry of Narottam Dās." *Journal of Vaishnava Studies* 4, no. 4 (Fall 1996): 17–52.

———. "The Devotional Music of Śrīla Prabhupāda." *Journal of Vaishnava Studies* 6, no. 2 (Spring 1998): 125–40.

———. *Alternative Krishnas: Regional and Vernacular Variations on a Hindu Deity* (Albany: State University of New York Press, 2005).

———. "Kīrtan and Bhajan." In *Brill's Encyclopedia of Hinduism,* vol. II, ed. Knut A. Jacobsen (Leiden: Brill Academic Publishers, 2010), 585–98.

Bhatia, Varuni. "Devotional Traditions and National Culture: Recovering Gauḍīya Vaishnavism in Colonial Bengal" (PhD thesis, Columbia University, 2009).

Brahmachari, Mahanamabrata. *Vaiṣṇava Vedānta*: *The Philosophy of Śrī Jīva Gosvāmī* (Calcutta: Das Gupta and Co., 1974).

Broo, M. *As Good as God: The Guru in Gauḍīya Vaiṣṇavism* (Åbo: Åbo Akademi University Press, 2003).

———. "The Vrindavan Goswāmins on *Kīrtana*," *Journal of Vaishnava Studies* 17, no. 2 (Spring 2009): 57–71.

Brooks, Charles R. "Hare Krishna, Radhe Shyam: The Cross-Cultural Dynamics of Mystical Emotions in Brindaban." In *Divine Passions: The Social Construction of Emotion in India*, ed. Owen M. Lynch (Berkeley: University of California Press, 1990).

———. "The Blind Man Meets the Lame Man: ISKCON's Place in the Bengal Vaishnava Tradition of Caitanya Mahāprabhu." *Journal of Vaishnava Studies* 6, no. 2 (March–April 1998): 5–30.

Bryant, Edwin F. "The Date and Provenance of the *Bhāgavata Purāṇa*." *Journal of Vaishnava Studies* 11, no. 1 (Fall 2002): 51–80.

———. *Krishna: The Beautiful Legend of God—Śrīmad Bhāgavata Purāṇa Book X* (New York: Penguin Books, 2003).
———. ed., *Krishna: A Source Book* (New York: Oxford University Press 2007).
———. *Bhakti Yoga: Tales and Teachings from the Bhāgavata Purāṇa* (New York: North Point Press, 2017).
Bryant, Edwin, and Maria Ekstrand, eds. *The Hare Krishna Movement: The Post-Charismatic Fate of a Religious Transplant* (New York: Columbia University Press, 2004).
Brzezinski, Jan K. "Jīva Gosvāmin's *Gopāla-campū*," PhD thesis, School of Oriental and African Studies, University of London, 1992.
————. "Prabodhānanda Sarasvatī: From Benares to Braj." *Bulletin of the School of Oriental and African Studies* 55, no. 1 (1992): 52–75.
————. "Prabodhānanda, Hita Harivaṃśa and the '*Rādhārasasudhānidhi.*'" *Bulletin of the School of Oriental and African Studies* 55, no. 3 (1992): 472–97.
————. "Women Saints in Gauḍīya Vaiṣṇavism." In *Vaiṣṇavī: Women and the Worship of Kṛṣṇa,* ed. Steven J. Rosen (Delhi: Motilal Banarsidass, 1996).
————. "The Parampara Institution in Gaudiya Vaishnavism." *Journal of Vaishnava Studies* 5, no. 1 (Winter 1996–1997): 151–82.
————. "Does Kṛṣṇa Marry the Gopīs in the End? The *Svakīya-vāda* of Jīva Gosvāmin." *Journal of Vaishnava Studies* 5, no. 4 (Fall 1997), 49–110.
Buchta, David. "Pedagogical Poetry: Didactics and Devotion in Rupa Gosvāmin's *Stavamālā*," PhD thesis (University of Pennsylvania, 2014).
Cakravartin, Narahari. *Bhaktiratnākara*, ed., Navinkrishna Paravidyalankar, in Bengali (Calcutta: Gaudiya Math, 1940).
Carney, Gerald T. "The Erotic Mysticism of Caitanya." *Journal of Dharma* 4, no 2 (1979): 169–77.
————. "The Theology of Kavikarṇapūra's *Caitanyacandrodaya*, Act II," PhD Thesis (Fordham University, 1979).
Case, Margaret. "Sevā at Rādhāramaṇa Temple, Vrindavan." *Journal of Vaishnava Studies* 3, no. 3 (Summer 1995): 45–46.
————. *Govindadeva: A Dialogue in Stone* (New Delhi: Indira Gandhi National Centre for Arts, 1996).
————. *Seeing Krishna: The Religious World of a Brahman Family in Vrindaban* (New York: Oxford University Press, 2000).
Chakravarti, Sudhindra Chandra. *Philosophical Foundations of Bengal Vaiṣṇavism* (Calcutta: Academic Publishers, 1969).
————. "Bengal Vaiṣṇavism." In K. R. Sundararanjan and Bithika Mukerji, eds. *Hindu Spirituality: Postclassical and Modern* (New York: The Crossroad Publishing Company, 1997), 47–62.
Chandan Goswami, Vaisnavacharya, trans. *Shri Radharaman Prakatya* (self-published: Anupam Goswami: 2018).
————. *Śrī Rādhāramaṇ Gītā: Nitya Līlā* (Vrindavan: Anupam Goswāmi, 2019).
Clough, Bradley S. "Buddha as Avatāra in Vaiṣṇava Theology: Historical and Interpretive Issues." *Journal of Vaishnava Studies* 26, no. 1 (Fall 2017): 161–88.

Clooney, Frank X., and Tony K. Stewart. "Vaiṣṇava." In S. Mittal and G. Thursby, eds., *The Hindu World* (Abingdon: Routledge, 2004), 162–184.

Cummins, Joan, ed. *Vishnu: Hinduism's Blue-Skinned Savior* (Ahmedabad, India: Mapin Publishing, in association with Frist Center for the Visual Arts, 2011).

Das, Madhavananda. "The Life Force of Lord Jagannātha." *Sri Krishna Kathamrita Magazine* no. 4 (Odisha, India: Gopal Jiu Publications, 1997).

———. "Nava-Kalevara: Lord Jagannātha's 'Change of Body' Pastime." *Sri Krishna Kathamrita Magazine*no. 4 (Odisha, India: Gopal Jiu Publications, 1997).

———. "Regaining a Lost Kingdom: Excerpts from the Life of Maharaja Chodagangadev." *Sri Krishna Kathamrita Bindu* no 6: 17 (Bhubaneswar, Odisha: Gopal Jiu Publications, June 2001).

———. "Jagannath Puri Dham: Two Opposites in One Container." *Journal of Vaishnava Studies* 27, no. 1 (Fall 2018): 123–56.

Das, Raghava Chaitanya. *The Divine Name* (Bombay: the author, 1954).

Das, Rahul Peter. *Essays on Vaiṣṇavism in Bengal* (Calcutta: Firma KLM, 1997).

Dāsa, Dhruva Mahārāja. *Jaya Jagannātha: The Culture and Worship of Lord Jagannātha East and West* (Los Angeles: Bhaktivedanta Book Trust, 2007).

Dasa, Gopīparāṇadhana, trans. *Śrī Bṛhad Bhāgavatāmṛta of Śrīla Sanātana Gosvāmī*, 3 vols. (Los Angeles: Bhaktivedanta Book Trust, 2002–2003).

————. *Śrī Tattva-sandarbha of Śrīla Jīva Gosvāmī* (Vrindavan: Girirāja Publishing, 2014).

Dāsa, Haridāsa. *Gauḍīya Vaiṣṇava Abhidhāna*, 4 parts in 2 vols., in Bengali (Navadvīpa: Haribola Kutīra, 471 GA. [1957]).

Dāsa, Jayaśacīnandana, trans., and dāsa, Jayatīrtha, ed. *The Process of Deity Worship (Arcana-Paddhati)*. Los Angeles, CA: Bhaktivedanta Book Trust, 1978.

Dāsa, Kuśakratha, trans. *Śrīla Vrndāvana Dāsa Ṭhākura's Śrī Caitanya-bhāgavata*, Complete in One Volume (Alachua, Florida: The Kṛṣṇa Institute, 1994).

Dasa, Narada Rishi. "Why Krishna Appears as Jagannatha" in *Back to Godhead 41, no. 4* (September/October 2007) (http://btg.krishna.com/why-krishna-appears-jagannatha).

Dasa, Nitai. "The Appearance of Lord Jagannatha." *Back to Godhead 10, no. 7* (July 1975) (http://www.krishna.com/appearance-lord-jagannatha).

Dāsa, Ravīndra Svarūpa [William H. Deadwyler III]. "With Kṛṣṇa in the Peaceable Kingdom." *Back to Godhead* 17, no. 8 (August 1982): 29.

————. *Encounter With the Lord of the Universe: Collected Essays, 1978–1983.* (Washington, DC: Gita-nagari Press, 1983).

————. "The Devotee and the Deity: Living a Personalistic Theology." In *Gods of Flesh Gods of Stone: The Embodiment of Divinity in India,* ed. Joanne Punzo Waghorne and Norman Cutler (New York: Columbia University Press, 1985), 69–87.

————. "The Scholarly Tradition in Caitanyaite Vaiṣṇavism." *ISKCON Review* 1, no. 1 (Spring 1985): 15–23.

————. "Rādhā, Kṛṣṇa, Caitanya: The Inner Dialectic of the Divine Relativity." *Journal of Vaiṣṇava Studies*10, no. 1 (Spring 2001): 5–26.

———. “Lord Chaitanya at Ratha-yātrā.” *Journal of Vaishnava Studies* 17, no. 1 (Fall 2008): 43–56.

Dasa, Rupa Vilasa. *A Ray of Vishnu* (Washington, MS: New Jaipur Press, 1988).

Dasa, Satyanarayana, trans. *Śrī Bhagavata Sandarbha* (Vrindavan, UP: Jiva Institute of Vaishnava Studies, 2014).

Dāsa, Satyarāja. “Madan Mohan: Mesmerizer of Mesmerizers.” *Back to Godhead* 56, no. 4 (July/August 2022).

———. “Kṛṣṇa’s Long Journey from Braj to Brooklyn.” *Back to Godhead* 52, no. 5 (September/October 2018).

Dasa, Shukavak N. *Hindu Encounter with Modernity: Kedarnath Datta Bhaktivinoda, Vaishnava Theologian* (Los Angeles: Sanskrit Religions Institute, 1999).

———. “Bhaktivinoda and Scriptural Literalism.” In *The Hare Krishna Movement: The Post-charismatic Fate of a Religious Transplant*, eds. Edwin F. Bryant and Maria L. Ekstrand (New York: Colombia University Press, 2004), 97–111.

Dāsa, Vṛndāvana, *Caitanya-bhāgavata*, ed. Nitāikaruṇākallolinī ṭīkā by Rādhāgovinda Nātha, in Bengali, 6 vols. (Kalikātā: Sādhanā Prakāśanī, 1964).

Dasa Adhikari, Vaiyasaki. *Śrī-Śrī Rādhā-Dāmodara Vilāsa (The Inner life of Vishnujana Swami & Jayānanda Prabhu)*: Volume One 1967–1972 (Vrindavan: Ras Bihari Lal and Sons; 2009, reprint; original printing, 1999).

Dash, Kailash Chandra. *Legend, History and Culture of India* (Calcutta: Punthi-Pustak, 1997).

De, Sushil Kumar, ed. *The Padyāvalī: An Anthology of Vaiṣṇava Verses in Sanskrit Compiled by Rūpa Gosvāmin, a Disciple of Śrī-Kṛṣṇa-Caitanya of Bengal* (Dacca University Oriental Publications Series, No. 3. Dacca: The University of Dacca, 1934).

———. “Caitanya as an Author.” *Indian Historical Quarterly* 10 (1934): 301–20.

Dehejia, Vidya, *Antal and Her Path of Love: Poems of a Woman Saint from South India* (Albany: State University of New York Press, 1990).

Delmonico, Neal. “Sacred Rapture: A Study of the Religious Aesthetic of Rūpa Gosvāmin.” PhD dissertation, University of Chicago, 1990.

———. “Sacred Rapture: The Bhakti-Rasa Theory of Rūpa Goswāmin.” *Journal of Vaishnava Studies* 6, no. 1 (Winter 1998): 75–98.

Desai, Ankur Vijay. “Visions of Grace: Svarūpa Imagery and Veneration in the Puṣṭimārga Sampradāya,” MA thesis (The Ohio State University, 2011).

Devi, Parama Karuna, and Rahul Acharya. *Puri: The Home of Lord Jagannatha* (Chandanpur, Orissa: Jagannatha Vallabha Research Center, 2009).

Dimock, Edward C., Jr., trans., and Tony K. Stewart, ed. *Caitanya Caritāmṛta of Kṛṣṇadāsa Kavirāja: A Translation and Commentary.* Harvard Oriental Series, vol. 56 (Cambridge, MA.: The Department of Sanskrit and Indian Studies, Harvard University, 1999).

Eaton, Richard. “Temple Desecration and Indo-Muslim States.” *Journal of Islamic Studies* 11, no. 3 (2000): 283–319.

Eck, Diana L. “Krishna Consciousness in Historical Perspective.” *Back to Godhead* 14, no. 10 (1979): 26–29.

————. *Darśan: Seeing the Divine Image in India* (Chambersburg, PA: Anima Books, 1985).

Eidlitz, Walther. *Kṛṣṇa-Caitanya, The Hidden Treasure of India: His Life and His Teachings* (English translation by Mario Windisch, Bengt Lundborg, Kid Samuelsson, and Katrin Stamm, 2014).

Elkman, Mark Stuart. *Jīva Gosvāmī's Tattvasandarbha: A Study on the Philosophical and Sectarian Development of the Gauḍīya Vaiṣṇava Movement* (Delhi: Motilal Banarsidass, 1986).

Entwistle, Alan W. *Braj: Centre of Krishna Pilgrimage* (Groningen: Egbert Forsten, 1987).

Eschmann, Anncharlott, Hermann Kulke, and Gaya Charan Tripathi, eds. *The Cult of Jagannāth and the Regional Tradition of Orissa* (South Asia Institute, Heidelberg University, South Asian Studies, no. 8. New Delhi: Manohar, 1978).

Ghosh, Abhishek. "Vaishnavism in Bengal." In *Contemporary Hinduism,* ed. P. Pratap Kumar (London: Routledge, 2013), 178–89.

————. "Vaiṣṇavism and the West: A Study of Kedarnath Datta Bhaktivinod's Encounter and Response, 1869–1909," PhD thesis, (University of Chicago, 2014).

Ghosh, Pika. *Temple to Love: Architecture and Devotion in Seventeenth-Century Bengal* (Bloomington: Indiana University Press, 2005).

Goldman, Robert P., and Sally Sutherland. *Devavāṇīpraveśikā: An Introduction to the Sanskrit Language*, 4th Edition (Berkeley, CA: Institute for South Asia Studies, 2019).

González-Reimann, Luis A. *The Mahābhārata and the Yugas: India's Great Epic Poem and the Hindu System of World Ages* (New York: Peter Lang Inc., 2002).

Gosvāmin, Rūpa. *Bhaktiṛasāmtasindhu,* translated with introduction and notes by David L. Haberman (New Delhi: Indira Gandhi National Centre for the Arts and Motilal Banarsidass Publishers, 2003).

Goswāmī, Dhyānachandra. *Śrī Gaura-govindārcana-smaraṇa-paddhati* (https://www.scribd.com/document/88069163/Gaura-Govindarcana-Smarana-Paddhatih-by-Dhyanacandra-Gosvami)

Goswāmī, Jīva. *Bhagavata Sandarbha,* translated by Bhanu Swami (Chennai: Sri Vaikuntha Enterprises, 2013).

Goswami, Mukunda. *Miracle on Second Avenue* (Badger, CA: Torchlight Publishing, 2011).

Goswami, Padmanābha, Śālagrāma-śilā (Vrindavana: Radharamana Temple, 1993).

Goswami, Shrivatsa. "Man and God Bound in Love: A *Vaiṣṇava* Approach." In *In Search of the Divine: Some Unexpected Consequences of Interfaith Dialogue,* ed. Larry D. Shinn (New York: Paragon House Publishers, 1987), 3–17.

————. "Acintya-bhedābheda." In *Vaiṣṇavism: Contemporary Scholars Discuss the Gauḍīya Tradition,* ed. Steven J. Rosen (New York: Folk Books, 1992. Reprinted, Delhi: Motilal Banarsidass, 1998), 249–59.

Goswami, Tamal Krishna. *Jagannātha-Priya Nāṭakam: The Drama of Lord Jagannātha* (Los Angeles: Bhaktivedanta Institute of Religion and Culture; 1st edition, 1985).

Goswami, Tamal Krishna, with Graham Schweig. *A Living Theology of Krishna Bhakti: Essential Teachings of A. C. Bhaktivedanta Swami Prabhupāda* (New York: Oxford University Press, 2012).

Graheli, Alessandro. "Narration and Comprehension of Paradox in Gauḍīya Literature." *Rivista di Studi Sudasiatici 2 (*2007): 181–208.

Goyal, Ayush. "The *Dasavatara-Stotra* of Sri Jayadeva's *Gita-Govinda*: A Vaishnava Perspective." *Journal of Vaishnava Studies* 22, no. 1 (Fall 2013): 55–68.

Haberman, David L. *Acting as a Way of Salvation: A Study of Rāgānugā Bhakti Sādhana* (New York: Oxford University Press, 1988).

————. "Shrines of the Mind: A Meditative Shrine Worshiped in Mañjarī Sādhana." *Journal of Vaishnava Studies* 1, no. 3 (Fall 1993): 18–35.

————. "On Trial: The Love of Sixteen Thousand Gopees." *History of Religions* 33, no. 1 (1993): 44–70.

————. *Journey through the Twelve Forests: An Encounter with Krishna* (New York and Oxford: Oxford University Press, 1994).

————. "Sri Nathji: The Itinerant Lord of Mount Govardhan." *Journal of Vaishnava Studies* 3, no. 3 (Summer 1995).

Hardy, Friedhelm. "Mādhavendra Purī: A Link between Bengal Vaiṣṇavism and South Indian *Bhakti*" *Journal of the Royal Asiatic Society of Great Britain and Ireland* 106, no. 1 (1974): 23–41.

————. *Viraha-Bhakti: The Early History of Kṛṣṇa Devotion in South India* (Delhi: Oxford University Press, 1983).

Harināmāmṛta-vyākaraṇam of Jīva Gosvāmī: The Grammar with the Nectar of Hari's Names, Volumes One and Two, trans. Matsya Avatāra Dāsa (Vrindavan, UP: Rasbihari Lal & Sons, 2016).

Hawley, John S. "How Do the Gauḍīyas Belong? Kavikarṇapūra, Jaisingh II, and the Question of Sampradāya." *Journal of Hindu Studies* 6, no. 2 (2013): 114–30.

————. *A Storm of Songs: India and the Idea of the Bhakti Movement* (Cambridge: Harvard University Press, 2015).

Hegewald, Julia A. B., and Subrata K. Mitra. "Jagannatha Compared: The Politics of Appropriation, Re-Use and Regional Traditions in India" (https://archiv.ub.uni-heidelberg.de/volltextserver/8015/).

Hein, Norvin. "Caitanya's Ecstasies and the Theology of the Name." In *Hinduism: New Essays in the History of Religions* (Leiden: E.J. Brill, 1976).

Hirschtick, Amy Joy. "The Krishnas of Jaipur" PhD thesis, Department of Religious Studies, Indiana University (June 2017).

Holdrege, Barbara A. "From Nāma-Avatāra to Nāma-Saṅkīrtana: Gauḍīya Perspectives on the Name." *Journal of Vaishnava Studies* 17, no. 2 (Spring 2009): 3–36.

————. "Meditation as Devotional Practice in Jīva Gosvāmin's Philosophy of Education." *ISKCON Studies Journal* 2 (2014): 45–70.

————. *Bhakti and Embodiment: Fashioning Divine Bodies and Devotional Bodies in Kṛṣṇa Bhakti* (Abingdon: Routledge, 2015).

Hopkins, Thomas J. "The Social and Religious Background for Transmission of Gaudiya Vaisnavism to the West." In *Krishna Consciousness in the West*, eds. D. G. Bromley and L. D. Shinn (Lewisburg, PA: Bucknell University Press, 1989).

Horstmann, Monika. *In Favour of Govindadeva: Historical Documents Relating to a Deity of Vrindaban and Eastern Rajasthan* (New Delhi: Indira Gandhi National Centre for the Arts, 1999).

Hudson, Dennis. *Krishna's Mandala: Bhagavata Religion and Beyond* (New York: Oxford University Press, 2010).

Jain, Meenakshi. *Flight of Deities and Rebirth of Temples: Episodes from Indian History* (Delhi: Aryan Books International, 2019).

Jānā, Nareśacandra. In Bengali, *Vṛndāvanera chaya gosvāmī* (Calcutta: Calcutta University Press, 1970).

Kapoor, O. B. L. *The Philosophy and Religion of Śrī Caitanya* (New Delhi: Munshiram Manoharlal, 1977).

———. "Bhakti, the Perfect Science." *Back to Godhead* 1, no. 53 (March 1, 1973).

———. "Vṛndāvana: The Highest Paradise." *Journal of Vaiṣṇava Studies* 1, no. 1 (Fall 1992): 42–49.

Karṇapūra, Kavi. *Gaura-gaṇoddeśa-dīpikā*, Bengali trans. by Ram Narayan Vidyaratna, ed., Ramdev Miśra, 4th edition (Berhampore: Radharaman Press, 1922).

Keśava Gosvāmī Mahārāja, Śrīla Bhakti Prajnāna. "Introduction: The Deity and Deity Worship." In *The Process of Deity Worship (Arcana-paddhati)*, translated by Jai Sacīnandana Dāsa (Los Angeles: Bhaktivedanta Book Trust, 1978).

Kinsley, David. "Without Kṛṣṇa, There is no Song." *History of Religions* 12, no. 2 (November 1972), 149–80.

Klostermaier, Klaus K. *Hindu and Christian in Vrindaban* (London: SCM Press, 1969).

———. "Hṛdayavidyā: A Sketch of a Hindu-Christian Theology of Love." *Journal of Ecumenical Studies 9, no.* 4 (Fall 1972), 750–75.

———. "The *Bhaktirasāmṛtasindhubindu* of Viśvanātha Cakravartin." *Journal of the American Oriental Society* 94, no. 1 (1974): 96–107.

Kramrisch, Stella. *The Hindu Temple*, 2 vols. (1946, reprint, Delhi: Motilal Banarsidass, 1976).

Kulke, Hermann, and Dietmar Rothermund. *A History of India*, Third Edition (London: Routledge, 2002).

Kumar, Panda Saroj. *The Kitchen of Srimandir: Biggest in the World* (Bhubaneswar: Department of Information and Public Relations, Government of Odisha, 2006).

Kumarappa, Bharatan. *The Hindu Conception of the Deity as Culminating in Ramanuja* (London: Luzac & Co., 1934).

Lipner, Julius J. *Hindu Images and Their Worship with Special Reference to Vaiṣṇavism: A Philosophical-Theological Inquiry* (London: Routledge, 2017).

Mahārāja, Śrī Śrīmad Gour Govinda Swami. *The Confidential Meaning of Ratha-Yātrā* (Bhubaneswar, India: Tattva Vicara Publications, 1994).

———. *The Embankment of Separation* (Bhubaneswar, Orissa, Gopal Jiu Publications, 1996).

———. *Mathura Meets Vrindavan* (Bhubaneswar, Orissa, Gopal Jiu Publications, 2003).

————. *Three Logs of Wood*, excerpted from *The Embankment of Separation* (Bhubaneswar, Orissa: Gopal Jiu Publications, 2004).

Mahārāja, Śrī Śrīmad Bhaktivedānta Nārāyaṇa Gosvāmī, translation and commentary, Viśvanātha Chakravartī Ṭhākura. *Śrī Bhakti-rasāmṛta-sindhu-bindu: A Drop of the Nectarine Ocean of Bhakti-rasa* (Mathura: Gaudiya Vedanta Publications, 1996).

————. *Viśvanātha Chakravartī Ṭhākura's Rāga Vartma Chandrikā: A Moonbeam to Illuminate the Path of Spontaneous Devotion* (Mathura: Gaudiya Vedanta Publications, 2001).

————. *Jaiva Dharma, Our Eternal Nature* (Vrindavan: Gaudiya Vedanta Publications, 2001).

————. *Śrī Rāya Rāmānanda Samvāda* (Vrindavan: Gaudiya Vedanta Publications, 2009).

Majumdar, A. K. *Caitanya: His Life and Doctrine* (Bombay: Bharatiya Vidya Bhavan, 1969).

Majumdar, Biman Bihari. *Kṛṣṇa in History and Legend* (Calcutta: University of Calcutta, 1969).

Marglin, Frederique. "The Famous Ratha Jātrā Festival of Puri." *Journal of Vaiṣṇava Studies* 7 no. 2 (Spring 1999): 131–74.

Matchett, Freda. *Kṛṣṇa: Lord or Avatāra? The Relationship Between Kṛṣṇa and Viṣṇu* (London: Curzon, 2001).

McDaniel, June. *The Madness of Saints: Ecstatic Religion in Bengal* (Chicago: University of Chicago Press, 1989).

Michell, George. *The Hindu Temple: An Introduction to Its Meaning and Forms* (New York: Harper & Row, 1977).

Miller, Barbara Stoler, trans. *Love Song of the Dark Lord: Jayadeva's Gītagovinda* (New York: Columbia University Press, 1977).

Misra, Bijoy M. "Shri Krishna Jagannatha: The Mushali-parva from Sarala's *Maha-bharata.*" In Edwin F. Bryant,ed., *Krishna: A Sourcebook* (New York: Oxford University Press, 2007).

Mukherjee, Prabhat. *History of the Jagannath Temple in the 19th Century* (Columbia, Missouri: South Asia Books, 1977).

————. *History of the Chaitanya Faith in Orissa* (South Asian Institute, Heidelberg University, South Asian Studies, no. 10. New Delhi: Manohar, 1979).

————. *The History of Medieval Vaishnavism in Orissa* (Delhi: Asian Educational Services, 1981).

Narasingha Maharaja, B. G., ed. *Śrī Dāmodara Kathā* (Vrindavan: Gosai Publishers, 2008).

Nārāyaṇa Goswāmī Mahārāja, Śrī Śrīmad Bhaktivedānta. *Dāmodara-Līlā-Mādhuri*, Volume One (Singapore & Kuala Lumpur: Sri Caitanya-Mudrani Publications, 1999).

————. *Acrana-dīpikā: The Light That Illuminates the Process of Deity Worship* (New Delhi: Gaudiya Vedanta Publications,1999).

————. *Śrī Braja Maṇḍala Parikramā* (Delhi: Gaudiya Vedanta Publications, 2001, reprint).

———. *The Origin of Ratha-Yātrā* (Vrndavana: Gaudiya Vedanta Publications, 2003, 1st Edition edition).

Narayanan, Vasudha. "Arcāvatāra: On Earth as He Is in Heaven." In *Gods of Flesh, Gods of Stone,* eds. Joanne Punzo Waghorne and Norman Cutler (New York: Columbia University Press, 1996).

———. "Śrīvaishnavism." In *Brill's Encyclopedia of Hinduism*, ed. Knut A. Jacobsen, Vol. III (Leiden: Brill, 2011).

———. "A Note on the Buddha and Buddhism from a Vaiṣṇava Perspective." *Journal of Vaishnava Studies* 28, no. 1 (Fall 2019): 183–96.

———. "The Distinctive Features of the Śrīvaiṣṇava Sampradāya." *Journal of Vaishnava Studies* 29, no. 2 (Spring 2021).

Packert, Cynthia. *The Art of Loving Krishna: Ornamentation and Devotion* (Bloomington: Indiana University Press, 2010).

———. "An Absent Presence in Vrindavana." In *Radha: From Gopi to Goddess*, ed. Harsha V. Dehejia (New Delhi: Niyogi Books, 2014), 50–57.

Patra, Avinash. *Origin & Antiquity of the Cult of Lord Jagannath* (Oxford University Press, 2011).

Pauwels, Heidi. "A Tale of Two Temples: Mathurā's Keśavadeva and Orcchā's Caturbhujadeva." *South Asian History and Culture* 2, no. 2 (April 2011): 278–99.

Prabhupāda, His Divine Grace A. C. Bhaktivedanta Swami. *Teaching of Lord Chaitanya* (Boston: ISKCON Press, 1968). Reprinted as *Teachings of Lord Caitanya, the Golden Avatar* (Los Angeles: Bhaktivedanta Book Trust, 1988).

———., translation and commentary, *Śrīmad Bhāgavatam*, 12 vols (Los Angeles: Bhaktivednata Book Trust, 1972).

———., translation and commentary. *Bhagavad-gītā As It Is* (Los Angeles, California, 1989, reprint).

———. translation and commentary, *Śrī Īśopaniṣad* (Los Angeles, California, 1995, reprint).

———., translation and commentary, Krishnadāsa Kavirāja Goswāmī's *Śrī Caitanya-caritāmṛta*, 9-volume set (Los Angeles, California, 1996, reprint).

Preciado-Solis, Benjamin. *The Kṛṣṇa Cycle in the Purāṇas: Themes and Motifs in a Heroic Saga* (Delhi: Motilal Banarsidass, 1984).

Prentiss, Karen Pechilis. *The Embodiment of Bhakti* (New York: Oxford University Press, 1999).

Ramnarace, Vijay. "Rādhā-Kṛṣṇa's Vedāntic Debut: Chronology & Rationalisation in the Nimbārka Sampradāya," PhD dissertation (The University of Edinburgh, 2014).

Roberts, Michelle Voss. *Dualities: A Theology of Difference* (Louisville: Westminster John Knox Press, 2010).

———. *Tastes of the Divine: Hindu and Christian Theologies of Emotion* (New York: Fordham University Press, 2014).

Rosen, Steven J. *India's Spiritual Renaissance: The Life and Times of Lord Chaitanya* (New York: Folk Books, 1989).

———. *The Six Gosvamis of Vrindavan* (New York: Folk Books, 1991).

————. *The Lives of the Vaishnava Saints: Shrinivas Acharya, Narottam Das Thakur, Shyamananda Pandit* (New York: Folk Books, 1991).
. *Śrī Pañca Tattva: The Five Features of God* (New York: Folk Books, 1994).
———. *The Hidden Glory of India* (Sweden: Bhaktivedanta Book Trust, 2002).
———. Essential Hinduism (Westport, Connecticut: Greenwood Publishing Group/ ABC-CLIO, 2006; Lanham, MD.: Rowman & Littlefield, paperback edition, 2008).
———. *The Yoga of Kirtan: Conversations on the Sacred Art of Chanting* (New York: Folk Books, 2008).
———. *Śrī Chaitanya's Life and Teachings: The Golden Avatāra of Divine Love* (Lanham, MD: Lexington Books, 2017).

————. "Who Is Shri Chaitanya Mahaprabhu." In *The Hare Krishna Movement: The Postcharismatic Fate of a Religious Transplant*, eds. Edwin F. Bryant and Maria Ekstrand (New York: Columbia University Press, 2004), 63–72.
————. "The Reincarnation(s) of Jaya and Vijaya: A Journey through the Yugas." *Religions* 8, no. 9 (2017): 178.
Rosen, Steven J., ed. *Vaiṣṇavism: Contemporary Scholars Discuss the Gauḍīya Tradition* (Delhi: Motilal Banarsidass, 1994).
Roy, Asim Kumar. *History of the Jaipur City* (Delhi: Manohar, 1978).
————. *Vṛndāban theke Jaipur* ("From Vrindāvan to Jaipur"), Bengali edition, ed., Kiran Candra Rāi (Calcutta: Jijnasa, 1985).
Ruppel, A. M. *The Cambridge Introduction to Sanskrit* (New York: Cambridge University Press, 2017).
Sarasvatī, Gosvāmī, Bhaktisiddhānta, trans. *Śrī Brahma-saṁhitā*, with commentary by Śrīla Jīva Gosvāmī, Sri Gaudiya Math 1932; Los Angeles, Bhaktivedanta Book Trust, 1985, reprint.
Sarasvatī, Prabodhānanda. *Śrī Śrī Rādhā Rasa Sudhā Nidhi: The Nectar Ocean of Sri Rādhā's Flavours* (Transliterated Text, Word-to-Word Meaning, Translation and Detailed Commentaries), trans., Śrīla Bhaktivedānta Nārāyaṇa Gosvāmī Mahārāja (Vrindavan: Bhaktabandhav, 2016).
Satyanand, Joseph. *Nimbarka: A Pre-Sankara Vedantin and His Philosophy* (New Delhi: Munshiram Manoharlal, 1997).
Schelling, Andrew, ed. *The Oxford Anthology of Bhakti Literature* (New Delhi: Oxford University Press, 2011).
Schweig, Graham M. *Dance of Divine Love: the Rāsa Līlā of Krishna from the Bhāgavata Purāṇa, India' s Classic Sacred Love Story* (Princeton, NJ: Princeton University Press, 2005).
————. *Bhagavad Gita: The Beloved Lord's Secret Love Song* (San Francisco: Harper San Francisco, 2007).
———. "An Analysis of the Structure of Polarities in the Caitanya Vaishnava Tradition." Unpublished paper, Harvard Divinity School, December 1984.
———. "Synthesis and Divinity: Śrī Chaitanya's Philosophy of Acintya Bhedābheda Tattva." In *Synthesis of Science and Religion: Critical Essays and Dialogues*, ed. T. D. Singh (Bombay: The Bhaktivedanta Institute, 1988): 420–29.

———. "Universal and Confidential Love of God: Two Essential Themes in Prabhupāda's Theology of *Bhakti*." *Journal of Vaishnava Studies* 6, no. 2 (Spring 1998): 93–123.

———. "The *Upadeśāmṛtam* of Rūpa Gosvāmī: A Concise Teaching on Essential Practices of Kṛṣṇa *Bhakti*." In *Caitanya Vaiṣṇava Philosophy: Tradition, Reason and Devotion,* ed. Ravi M Gupta (Farnham: Ashgate, 2014).

Sen, Dinesh Chandra. *History of Bengali Language and Literature* (Calcutta: Calcutta University Press, 1911).

. *The Vaiṣṇava Literature of Mediaeval Bengal* (Calcutta: Calcutta University Press, 1917).

———. *Chaitanya and His Companions* (Calcutta: Calcutta University Press, 1917).

———. *Chaitanya and His Age* (Calcutta: Calcutta University Press, 1922).

Sharma, B. N. K. *History of the Dvaita School of Vedānta and Its Literature: From the Earliest Beginnings to Our Own Times* (Delhi: Motilal Banarsidass, 2000, reprint).

Shapiro, Allan Aaron. "The Birth-celebration of Śrī Rādhāramaṇ in Vrindaban," MA thesis (Columbia University, 1979).

———. "Śalagrāmaśilā: A Study of Śalagrāma Stones with Text and Translation of Śālagrāma-parīkṣā," PhD thesis (Columbia University, 1987).

Sharma, Krishna. *Bhakti and the Bhakti Movement: A New Perspective* (New Delhi: Munshiram Manoharlal, 1987).

Sherbow, Paul. "A. C. Bhaktivedanta's Preaching in the Context of Gaudiya Vaishnavism." In *The Hare Krishna Movement: The Post-charismatic Fate of a Religious Transplant* (New York: Colombia University Press, 2004), 129–46.

Sheridan, Daniel P. *Advaitic Theism of the Bhāgavata Purāna* (Delhi: Motilal Banarsidass, 1986).

———. *Loving God: Kṛṣ ṇa and Christ: A Christian Commentary on the Nārada Sūtras* (Leuven, Belgium: W.P. Eerdmans, 2007).

Shibasundar, Pattanaik. "Sudarsan of Lord Jagannath." *Orissa Review* (July 2002): 58–60.

Smith, Frederick M. "Varieties of Puṣṭimārga Pilgrimage." *Journal of Vaishnava Studies* 17, no. 1 (Fall 2018): 46–47.

Śrīdhara, Swami B. R. *The Search for Sri Krishna: Reality the Beautiful* (San Jose, CA: Guardian of Devotion Press, 1986).

———. *The Golden Volcano of Divine Love* (Nadiya, West Bengal: Sri Chaitanya Saraswat Math, 1996, reprint).

———. *Śrī Guru and His Grace* (Nabadvip: Sri Chaitanya Sāraswat Matha, 1999).

Śrī Gopāla-campū of Śrīla Jīva Gosvāmī, (Pūrva 1.3), trans., Bhanu Swami (Madras: Tattva Cintāmaṇi Publishing, 2017).

Śrīla Gurudeva, Bhaktivedānta Nārāyaṇa Gosvāmī Mahārāja Bhaktabāndhav. *Rāgātmikā Vrajavāsī & Prayojana-tattva Ācārya Śrīla Gopāla Bhaṭṭa Gosvāmī* (Vrindavan: Bhaktabandhav, 2018).

Śrīmad Bhāgavatam: A Symphony of Commentaries on the Tenth Canto Volume Two Chapters 4–11, trans. Charles A. Filion (Vindavan, UP: Rasbihari Lal & Sons, 2018)

Stewart, Tony K. *The Final Word: The Caitanya Caritāmṛta and the Grammar of Religious Tradition* (New York and London: Oxford University Press, 2010).

———. "The Biographical Images of Kṛṣṇa-Caitanya: A Study in the Perception of Divinity," PhD thesis (Department of South Asian Languages and Civilizations, The University of Chicago, 1985).

————. "On Changing the Perception of Caitanya's Divinity." in *Bengal Vaiṣṇavism, Orientalism, Society and the Arts*, ed. by Joseph T. O'Connell, South Asia Occasional Paper no. 35 (East Lansing, MI: Asian Studies Center, Michigan State University, 1985), 37–45.

————. "When Biographical Narratives Disagree: The Death of Kṛṣṇa Caitanya." *Numen* 38, no. 2 (1991): 231–60.

————. "The Biographies of Śrī Caitanya and the Literature of the Gauḍīya Vaiṣṇavas." *Vaiṣṇavism: Contemporary Scholars Discuss the Gauḍīya Tradition*, ed. Steven J. Rosen, foreword by Edward C. Dimock Jr. (New York: Folk Books, 1992; reprint, Motilal Banarsidass, 1994), 101–25.

————. "When Rāhu Devours the Moon: The Myth of the Birth of Kṛṣṇa Caitanya." *International Journal of Hindu Studies* 1, no. 2 (August 1997): 21–64.

————. "Reading for Kṛṣṇa's Pleasure: Gauḍīya Vaiṣṇava Meditation, Literary Interiority, and the Phenomenology of Repetition." *Journal of Vaiṣṇava Studies* 14, no. 1 (Fall 2005): 243–80.

————. "Religion in the Subjunctive: Vaiṣṇava Narrative, Sufi Counter-Narrative in Early Modern Bengal," *The Journal of Hindu Studies*, vol. 6 (2013).

————. "Caitanya," Oxford Bibliographies Online (New York: Oxford University Press, 2013): http://oxfordbibliographiesonline.com/.

Stewart, Tony K., translator. "The Exemplary Devotion of the 'Servant of Hari.'" In *The Religions of South Asia in Practice*, ed. Donald S. Lopez, Jr. (Princeton: Princeton University Press, 1995), 564–77.

Stietencron, Heinrich von. "Orthodox Attitudes Towards Temple Service and Image Worship in Ancient India." *Central Asiatic Journal* 21, no. 2 (1977): 126–38.

Swami, Bhakti Vikasa. *Śri Bhaktisiddhānta Vaibhava*, three volumes (Surat, India: Bhakti Vikas Trust, 2010).

Swami, Hayagriva. *Vrindaban Days: Memories of an Indian Holy Town* (West Virginia: Palace Publishing, 1988).

Swāmī, Śivarāma. *Śrī Dāmodara Jananī*, Kṛṣṇa in Vṛndāvana series, Vol. 4 (Budapest: Lāl Publishing, 2016).

Ṭhākura, Bhaktivinoda. "The Temple of Jagannātha at Purī." *Tājpore*, September 15, 1871.

————. *Shri Chaitanya Mahaprabhu, His Life and Precepts*, originally published in 1896 (Nabadwip: Shri Goudiya Vedanta Samiti, 1981, reprint).

————. *The Bhagavat, Its Philosophy, Ethics and Theology*, ed. Bhaktivilas Tirtha, 2nd edition (Madras: Madras Gaudiya Math, 1959, reprint).

————. *Shri Chaitanya Shikshamritam*, Bijoy Krishna Rarhi, translation (Madras: Sri Gaudiya Math, 1983, reprint).

———. *Gaurāṅga-līlā-smaraṇa-maṅgala-stotra—Auspicious Meditations on Lord Gaurāṅga,* Kuśakratha dāsa, translation (Los Angeles: Kṛṣṇa Institute, 1988, reprint).

———. *Śrī Krishna-saṁhitā*, trans., Bhumipati Dasa (New Delhi: Vrajraj Press, 1998, reprint).

———. *Jaiva Dharma*, *Our Eternal Nature*, Bhaktivedānta Nārāyaṇa Mahārāja, Araṇya Mahārāja, et al., translation (Mathura: Gauḍīya Vedānta Publications, 2002, reprint).

Thompson, Richard L. *Maya: The World as Virtual Reality* (Alachua, FL: Govardhan Hill Publishing, 2003).

Tripurāri, Swami B. V. *Aesthetic Vedanta: The Sacred Path of Passionate Love* (San Rafael, CA: Mandala Publishing, 1998).

———. *Form of Beauty: The Krishna Art of B. G. Sharma* (Eugene: Mandala Publishing Group, 1998).

Truschke, Audrey. *Aurangzeb: The Life and Legacy of India's Most Controversial King* (Stanford: Stanford University Press 2017).

Valpey, Kenneth R. *Attending Kṛṣṇa's Image: Caitanya Vaiṣṇava Mūrti-sevā as Devotional Truth* (Abingdon: Routledge, 2006).

———. "Kṛṣṇa-sevā: Theology of Image Worship in Gauḍīya-Vaiṣṇavism," MA dissertation, Graduate Theological Union, Berkeley, 1998.

———.

———. "Gauḍīya Vaiṣṇavism." In *Brill's Encyclopedia of Hinduism, vol.* 3, ed. Knut A. Jacobsen (Leiden: Brill, 2011), 312–28.

Vidyāvinoda, Śrīpāda Sundarānanda. *Śrī Kṣetra: Vaikuṇṭha on Earth*, produced and published by Īśvara dāsa, translated by Bhumipati dāsa (Kolkata: Touchstone Media, 2017).

Vilas, Shubha. *Two Fingers Short* (Mumbai: Tulsi Books, 2015).

Williams, Monier-Monier. *A Complete Sanskrit-English Dictionary* (Oxford: The Clarendon Press, 2002).

Wong, Lucian. "Negotiating History in Colonial Bengal: Bhaktivinod's *Kṛṣṇa-saṁhitā*." *Journal of Hindu Studies* 7, no. 3 (2014): 341–70.

———. "Gauḍīya Vaiṣṇava Studies: Mapping the Field." *Religions of South Asia* 9, no. 3 (2015): 305–31.

Wulff, Donna M. *Drama as a Mode of Religious Realization: The Vidagdhamādhava of Rūpa Gosvāmī*, American Academy of Religion, Academy Series (Chico, CA: Scholars Press, 1984).

———. "Radha: Consort and Conqueror of Krishna." In *Devi: Goddesses of India*, ed. John Hawley and Donna Wulff (Berkeley: University of California Press, 1998).

Zaidman-Dvir, Nurit. "When the Deities Are Asleep: Processes of Change in the Hare Krishna Temple," PhD dissertation (Temple University, 1994).

Index

Abhigamana, 98
Adam-12, 207
Advaita, 211; sacred precincts of, 84; meaning of, 210; Mahāvishnu aspects, 210; Sadāśiva aspects, 210; deity, appearance of, 213
Advaita Vedānta, 215
Aiśvarya, 167; Krishna, moods of, 13, 165; Lord Vishnu, mood of, 83, 181, 182
Ajmer (Rajasthan), 38
Akbar: Jīva Gosvāmī, *darshan* of, 58; Mahārāja Man Singh of Amber, 59; Govinda Deva, 60; Madana Mohan temple, 60; Raisal Darbari, 229
Alexander Cunningham, 38
Āḻvārs, 49
Ananga Bhima Deva, 136
Ananta Śeṣa, 81
Anantavarman Chodaganga: founder of Jagannāth temple, 132; construction of Jagannāth temple, 136
Aniruddha: manifestations of, 6; shrines of, 181; son of, 224
Añjana, 35
Anncharlott Eschmann, 138
Appalachian Mountains: New Vrindaban, 12, 171–73; Radha-Vrindaban Chandra, 166, 172
Aravalli Hills, 195
Archaeological Survey of India, 179
Arjuna: Subhadrā, marriage to, 180
Arjuna trees: Dāmodara Līlā, 51, 68
Atlantis, 179
Aurangzeb: Vrindavan, 61; Rādhā-Dāmodara, 62; shift of deities, 230
Aurobindo Ghose, 40
Avantipura (Ujjain), 129
Ayodhyā, 35
Ayush Goyal: Daśāvatāra representations, 38

Badrinath, 179
Bahulavana (Bahulaban): New Vrindaban, replication in, 171–73; arms of Krishna, 170; farmhouse in New Vrindaban, 172; transfer of deities, 173
Baladeva: Śrī Raṅgam, 84; appearance of, 130; divine love, 141; installation at Los Angeles, 182
Baladeva Vidyābhūṣaṇa, 191
Balarāma, 131, 132, 134–35; Krishna Avatāra, 35–36, 38; Baladeva, 130; transcendental body of, 133; colors of, 136, 147; Sudarśana, 137; Ratha-yātrā, 139, 140; ISKCON Deities, 144, 146; marriage of, 180; shrines

About the Author

Steven J. Rosen (Satyaraja Dasa) is a biographer, scholar, and author in the fields of philosophy, Indic religion, and comparative spirituality. He is the founding editor of the *Journal of Vaishnava Studies* and associate editor of *Back to Godhead* magazine. His thirty-plus books include *Essential Hinduism* (Rowman & Littlefield); *Yoga of Kirtan: Conversations on the Sacred Art of Chanting* (FOLK Books); *Krishna's Other Song: A New Look at the Uddhava Gita* (Praeger-Greenwood); and *Sri Chaitanya's Life and Teachings: The Golden Avatara of Divine Love* (Lexington Books).